W9-ACQ-091

The
Communications
Revolution

A TAXONOMY OF
CONCEPTS IN COMMUNICATION
by Reed H. Blake and Edwin O. Haroldsen

COMMUNICATIONS AND MEDIA
Constructing a Cross Discipline
by George N. Gordon

ETHICS AND THE PRESS
Readings in Mass Media Morality
Edited by John C. Merrill and Ralph D. Barney

DRAMA IN LIFE
The Uses of Communication in Society
Edited by James E. Combs and Michael W. Mansfield

INTERNATIONAL AND INTERCULTURAL COMMUNICATION
Edited by Heinz-Dietrich Fischer and John C. Merrill

EXISTENTIAL JOURNALISM
by John C. Merrill

THE COMMUNICATIONS REVOLUTION
A History of Mass Media in the United States
by George N. Gordon

Humanistic Studies in the Communication Arts

The Communications Revolution:

A History of Mass Media in the United States

by GEORGE N. GORDON

COMMUNICATION ARTS BOOKS
Hastings House, Publishers · New York 10016

For Eric

P
92
U5
G6

Copyright © 1977 by George N. Gordon

Library of Congress Cataloging in Publication Data

Gordon, George N
    The communications revolution.

    (Communication arts books)
    Bibliography: p.   Includes index.
    1. Mass media—United States—History. 2. Mass media—Social aspects—United States. I. Title.
P92.U5G6   301.16'1'0973   77-3037
ISBN 0-8038-1218-3
ISBN 0-8038-1219-1 pbk.

Published simultaneously in Canada by
Saunders of Toronto, Ltd., Don Mills, Ontario

Printed in the United States of America

Contents

Introduction

ONE DAY A LEARNED PSYCHOLOGIST will publish a thesis, I hope, on the reasons that most non-fiction authors write *Introductions* to their books after they have finished writing the text rather than before they start.

The answer, I suspect, has to do with a number of evils, not the least of which is a desire to dispel most writers' inevitable feelings of despair and depression that extensive exercises in English composition generate in all but neophyte authors. Another reason centers, I imagine, on the writer's desire to try to explain away what he did *not* accomplish in his book and to diminish his guilt feelings for not having created the sort of volume he should have and could have, he thinks, if everything had gone right. (It never does!) He also, I think, is convinced that his potential readers will be either cretins or vultures, and therefore attempts to explain his or her version of what a short perusal of the work *should* reveal even to cretins or vultures: what he has accomplished and what he has not accomplished.

In sum: by the time a non-fiction author gets to his *Introduction,* he is attempting to cheer a heavy but twitchy heart by pleading "not guilty" to various charges he thinks to level at himself. He is, in truth, hedging his bet by admitting those ineptitudes and intellectual crimes that he thinks (or knows) he has already committed.

I speak only for myself in the conjectures above. Okay, *mea culpa!* The reader will therefore understand the motives behind these few observations I feel it necessary to make about this volume, before he or she turns blithely to Chapter 1.

The original impetus for *The Communications Revolution* was what dime-store psychoanalysts call these days a "felt need." Having been a teacher and student of subjects having to do with mass communications for many years, I cannot help but notice an extraordinary imbalance in the types of books published yearly on the subject I have grown both to love and hate.

My bookshelves boast a glut of volumes about the role of broadcasting, movies and the press in the modern world—too many, I think—a matter to which I shall refer in the pages to come. Also extant and in press are a number of excellent press histories, including such a monumental work as Frank Luther Mott's *A History of American Magazines* (in five volumes) and my favorite journalism book (now revised by Emery alone), *The Press and America* by Edwin Emery and Henry Ladd Smith. Following the lead of Paul Rotha's classic work, *The Film Till Now* (first published in 1930 and revised in a number of editions since then), the last 10 or 15 years have seen no shortage of film or cinema histories of many kinds: general histories, movie chronologies, technological histories, critical histories, *genre* books and so forth—almost beyond imagining. Pickings are somewhat slimmer in regard to the history of broadcasting, particularly in its non-technological phases, but a number are also available. They begin with Gleason L. Archer's *History of Radio* (to 1926) and end, for all practical purposes, with Erik Barnouw's well known and overpraised trilogy telling the story of American broadcasting from the beginning until the early 1970s.

But where, I some time ago asked myself, may I find a *single* volume, treating in concise fashion, and more or less fairly, the entire history of mass communications from the invention of print to film to video? I held high hopes for my ex-colleague (and friend) John Tebbel's book, *The Media in America,* until I discovered that it was simply and properly an excellent press history salted with considerable media criticism, social history and some passing references to broadcasting but containing almost no material about the movies.

My first inclination, therefore, was to attempt to outline a hefty three-part omnibus, containing detailed histories of journalism, the motion pictures, radio and television, considerations of their allied arts and technologies around the world, from the fifteenth century to the present. I suppose I came up with a good idea, but I am, at the moment, extremely glad that I immediately discarded it. Neither have I enough left of this lifetime to research and construct such an opus, nor have I sufficient active protoplasm remaining between my ears, to say nothing of sheer patience.

This book is therefore a second thought. But it is also, as far as I know, the first one of its kind. I hope it will not be the last, nor will my original intention be overlooked by some younger, more intelligent writer.

Put simply, I have in these pages attempted to tell, in general terms, the story of The Communications Revolution, with emphasis upon its growth and development in the United States of America. After much indecision concerning the organization of the material, I decided to follow Lewis Carroll's brilliant advice to begin at the beginning, go on until the end, and then stop. In other words, I decided that a chronological record of biographies, inventions and events, not a series of media histories, might turn out to be the most rewarding way to solve my problem. As obvious as this solution seems to me now, I puzzled and puttered about a good deal before reaching it, mostly because I wondered why nobody had ever seemed to have tried it.

The result inevitably produced, I grant, an uneven book, although I both think and hope that my method makes historical sense. Print being the oldest of the media of mass communications, I found myself in some measure wrestling with Professor Tebbel's apparent problem in *The Media in America*. For more than 400 years, the major—in fact only—instrument of mass communication remained one or another version of the old printing press. Many events of historical importance occur in 400 years! Motion pictures are a phenomenon dependent, as we shall see, upon much nineteenth century technological invention and cannot conceivably be called "mass media" until roughly 1905, if then. Radio broadcasting is a post-World War I cultural innovation, followed by television after World War II.

For these reasons, the narrative that follows moves quite quickly—possibly too quickly—as we make our way from the fifteenth to twentieth centuries. I hope I have paced neither too fast nor too slowly the first half dozen chapters in an attempt to set the stage for the, at first, double- and then triple-pronged inquiry into the history of all three major media that follows, not only as each developed alone, but also as one affected the other in a number of ways: social, cultural, financial, political, economical and technological.

In this respect, I am immodest enough to stake a claim for what I hope is the unique aspect of my efforts as well as, I hope, a notable contribution this book may bring to a field that has lately gathered about it too much literature, much of it redundant and of transient interest. Most of the best of the media histories I have read, and I think I have read most of the best of them, have, of necessity, been forced to assume a monolithic or cyclopian view of a particular medium, be it film, print or broadcasting, in delineating its role in the culture at large. The best have accomplished this cleverly. Movies, for instance, did not evolve in a social and artistic vacuum but responded to all manner of external pressures as they developed around the world, and a good film historian adeptly exploits and analyzes this fact as he writes. A bad one does not.

One advantage of the approach employed in the pages to follow, I think, centers upon the breadth of my concerns about just such pressures and their consequences.

Let me explain. Both personally and professionally, I am certainly not what youngsters today call a journalism, movie, radio or television "freak." As noted above, I both love and hate all the mass media in their past and present manifestations equally, both respecting the many ways in which they have, each in their own ways, civilized much of the world, and at the same time despising the many times that *all* of the media have often barbarized it, simply for fun and profit or both. If I am a "freak" of any kind, I am a "culture freak" (with a small "c") whose peculiar enthusiasms are mass phenomena of all kinds, particularly those related to recent technologies. The main bias of my freakishness is directed toward attempts to consider fairly and carefully the ways that man's various institutions have directed the use and functions of mass media. I find most interesting the ways each has refracted, one to the other and back again, so many similar qualities. Last and most important, I am deeply concerned with how the media have, over the years, influenced what environmentalists call so glibly "the quality of life."

The Communications Revolution, therefore, does not either favor or disdain the social and cultural contributions to civilization of print, film, broadcasting or any other ancillary instruments that are part and parcel of the Communications Revolution. Let me quickly add, however, that I certainly believe that, at any moment in history (including the present one), different media seem to perform different cultural tasks in different ways and produce different sorts of effects upon both young and old. One is therefore entitled to make certain judgments, or hazard guesses, about their social role at any time. Woodward and Bernstein, for instance, in their contemporary roles as gentlemen of the newspaper press, were certainly in a position *today* to unmake a president (and all of his men), whereas Walter Cronkite, for all his skill and eminence as a television anchor man, was not. The reason, of course, is largely a matter of current values or, if you wish, social history.

I hold—and shall hold—that so-called "cross-media differences" have little or nothing to do with McLuhan's mysticisms or so-called "peculiar powers" of sound, pictures and print about which much is written and argued. I do not believe in voodoo, but I do believe in history. If the various media seem vastly different aesthetically, psychologically and even spiritually, one from the other, I think that the main reasons are discovered in the history of one when it is held up to the history of another.

This assumption, I believe, has been reasonably upheld in this volume by means of considerable good evidence. I have, of course, proven nothing in a scientific sense. I believe, however, that the gods of common sense are better served by simple scrutiny of the ways that the past has become the present than by recourse to Dr. McLuhan's revealed truths and charming but foolish gnostic land of demiurges. I also believe that my methodologies are a good deal more "hip," exciting, modern and provocative than McLuhan's now generally discredited witchcraft.

Whether I have succeeded in what I have tried to do is another matter entirely. This I must let the reader judge. Even if I have failed, I nevertheless maintain that the key to "understanding media" is hidden in the development of their technologies, the growth and social assimilation of each medium, the cultural climate in which each evolved, and an empathetic understanding of why people expect what they expect from their books, movies, newspapers, television receivers, radios, recordings and other gadgetry.

As I say, there is nothing complicated about what I have attempted to achieve. While this approach may be a simple one, let me assure the reader that the many historical vectors that have influenced the history of the mass media of communications in the United States have been anything *but* uncomplicated.

Nor may their story be told in a simplistic way. For this reason, I have had to assume that the reader of this volume is reasonably familiar with most important aspects of American history.

(He or she should be! For reasons I cannot understand, in the United States, we teach the history of our country *three* times to most of our students who survive a college education, repeating this instruction on each level of schooling, presumably correcting the errors we made each time before. In my career as a pedagogue, I have had the dubious pleasure of teaching American history on all three levels. I remain bewildered, nevertheless, by the ignorance in this respect of so many supposedly liberally educated people I meet, including university teachers, who appear to remember so little about a subject they have studied so often.)

I think I have said enough about this book at this point to vindicate my initial hypothesis concerning the reasons that authors write *Introductions* to their scribbles as an ultimate act of contrition to their readers. My only unfinished business remains in the department of personal gratitude.

So many people aided me one way or another with the preparation of the manuscript that I cannot list them all. Harriet Griffith, Elsa Spector and Ann Cudlipp did much of the dirty work of preparing the manuscript. Dorothy MacLennan helped me obtain and organize certain materials. Russell Neale of Hastings House remained his usual patient self, as I missed deadlines and shuffled him a series of lame excuses. Many of my students have also served me well by writing good term papers on a number of the topics treated in this volume and by asking good questions in class that illuminated for me many notable areas of my own ignorance.

I am not, nor have I ever been, a professional historian, and I am certain that this book is guilty of numerous sins of professional omission and commission. To specialists in the history of each communications medium, I am also certain that I have demonstrated unforgiveable naiveté and provided incomplete, biased, opinionated and unfair coverage of certain holy topics and saints in the pantheons of journalism, films and broadcasting. So be it. These inevitable criticisms will be, I think, for the most part reasonable. But they are also inevitable consequences of the particular purview I have attempted and of the objectives I have set for myself, most of which are spelled out above.

Let me assume all blame for what I have written that is wrong and/or stupid, just as long as I also receive some credit for what is honest and right about *The Communications Revolution*.

GEORGE N. GORDON
Forest Hills, N.Y.

1

Cultural Keystones

REGARDLESS OF HOW HARD one searches, he or she will rarely discover the origin of any major aspect of cultural life in one event, one discovery, in one era of history or even within one civilization.

Simplifiers of the study of communication enjoy talking about mankind's movement from oral traditions to written traditions to print traditions, as if they occurred like fast dissolves on movie film, and as if one so-called "tradition" sedately dies while another rises healthy from its ashes. This is certainly not the case in any phase of The Communications Revolution, as we shall see; nor does it fairly describe the way man has used any of the techniques or technologies he has invented in his various cultures.

Every history must, however, start somewhere and at some moment, if only for convenience sake—and this one is no exception. The reader has a number of choices, however.

The Word Machine

The art of printing is usually singled out as the first step in the development of *mass* communications—that is, human interaction involving a few people speaking somehow to many others in different times and different places. But printing is not an art that was discovered in a single moment and embraced by a waiting world, simply because few things are.

The origins of the printing press are indeed ambiguous, and therefore remain the reader's choices. Considerable evidence exists that methods of printing similar to those later discovered in Europe were known in the Orient in the first century A.D. during the Han dynasty. We are certain that books were printed on hand-carved wood blocks in Japan during the eighth century A.D. and that by the ninth the first known printed book, *The Diamond Sutra*, appeared in China. In the tenth century, Fong Tao, a Chinese minister was responsible for the publication of a series of classical works containing 130 volumes. By the eleventh century, Pi Sheng, an alchemist, invented a system of movable typefaces years before similar instruments were rediscovered in Europe. Such an innovation was all the more incredible because of the enormous number of pictographic letters (actually segments of words) in Oriental languages. In the early part of the fourteenth century, a jurist, Wang Chen, appears to have manufactured a printing device of this kind employing more than 60,000 discrete characters in order to publish an historical treatise. Similar instrumentation was developed during the next century in Korea, where the number of different bronze type characters used in printing exceeded 100,000. This is one choice.

How much of this Eastern technology—if any—found its way to the Western world directly or indirectly, we cannot be certain. Both war and commerce brought printed materials to Europe in many ways during the late Middle Ages and into the early Renaissance. But before a technology is imitated by a society, that culture must manifest some use for it. Otherwise, imported samples of it are simply curiosities, or possibly works of art. Were the religious books and school books—most notably Aelius Donatus' famous Latin grammar text—imitations of Chinese books, because they were hand carved from wood blocks the way Orientals had done centuries before? Or were they spontaneous inventions of clever late fourteenth and early fifteenth century craftsmen in an age soon to be dominated by the perfection of *many* new arts and crafts? We cannot ascertain their motives now, and so we shall never know.

The Page

Another choice: Critical to possible uses of the printing press was the invention of paper and, once again, we find the origins of this technology in the Orient. Since antiquity, records had been kept on clay tablets, stones, papyrus (made from dried reeds) and the membranes of animals, still known (and used) as parchment and vellum. Paper making, however, required grinding and mixing of some sorts of vegetable fibers into a mulch that could be spread in a film-like layer, dried to yield a clear, consistent, light flexible surface upon which clear and discrete marks could be made.

The Chinese were apparently producing paper more than a thousand years before Europeans, having invented a technique shortly after the birth of Christ in the West. This secret remained in the Orient for 750 years, however, until Arab soldiers met Chinese as the Moslem faith moved east to the famed city of Samarkand, after which paper making became an Arab secret—and so remained until about 1200 A.D. As Moslems moved onto the European continent in their invasions of Sicily and Spain, their culture traveled with them and spread quickly to those countries nearest to European points of contact with the Moslem culture: that is, Spain, Italy and France.

Some scholars claim that northern Europeans, particularly Germans, more or less rediscovered the Arabic-Oriental invention of paper making without having first discovered the earlier secrets of its fabrication. At any rate, the use of water power to grind up linen and other fibers was indeed a north European innovation. Paper production was a profitable industry on much of the continent by 1350.

From Pen to Print

Another choice (a side issue of the fact that printing was not invented until it was needed): The reproduction of written material was quite satisfactorily handled for those who required it during the Middle Ages by copyists, some of whom achieved high degrees of skill in this art. While they worked slowly, there was no shortage of them. Most were monks who labored in large cloistered factories side by side and devoted their lives to little but copying manuscripts, thus demonstrating their devotion to God. From about the second century A.D. until the fifteenth century, these "scriptoria," as they were known, provided most of the books and illustrations circulated throughout Europe. The Benedictine Order was particularly impressed with the virtues of literary scholarship, but other monastic orders were also convinced of the necessity of preserving and copying ancient documents, many of them Judeo-Christian but some of them also pagan classics of antiquity.

Among the monasteries, methods were worked out for the circulation of books, both religious and secular. These volumes were, of course, also used by the various universities founded in the late Middle Ages. Hebrew Talmudists also copied their own religious documents by hand, including medieval commentaries upon the Old Testament and evolving Jewish law, circulating their precious volumes among one another, especially to their "rabbis," who were simply teachers who sometimes copied out, or commented upon, various other books or religious lore. Among Hebrew males, literacy (or, at least, the ability to read) was a prized and not uncommon accomplishment.

Hand-copied "illuminated" manuscripts from monasteries obviously proliferated enormously over the centuries. Until the beginning of the Reformation, Europe suffered from no shortage of generally circulated written materials or from a lack of books.

With the beginning of the fifteenth century, however, new needs began to develop for more written matter by more people. Even for this phenomenon, we are able to discover no *single* cause. The population of Europe was rising as the ravages caused by the Crusades and great plagues were diminishing. Certainly, literacy (or the ability to read) was also increasing, and schooling now became more widespread than it had during the so-called "Dark Ages." Science, or the scientific method, was in the process of being discovered. New technologies were invented. The material standard of living of the population was rising. Most important, the Reformation and the spreading heresy of Protestantism was both secularizing and nationalizing much of the continent. To read and write one's *own* language (instead of church Latin) became a symbol of this revolt, and the proclivity of many Protestants to publish their anti-Roman ideas outstripped the capacity—and certainly the inclinations—of the careful copyists in the scriptoria of old to preserve knowledge by patient hand-written methods.

More than this, Europe was discovering a new secular life in the remarkable fifteenth century. With the influence of the Renaissance felt nearly everywhere on the continent, more people apparently had more things to write about and to *want* to *know* about than in the preceding millenium and a half. We think often of the Renaissance as an Italian phenomenon devoted mostly to the rediscovery of the genius of the pre-Christian era, but it was obviously much more than this. Its boundaries spread far beyond the Italian peninsula to Scandinavia, England and East Europe. The glorious arts and technologies invented and "rediscovered," although devoted to the glory of the Roman church and clergy in main thrust, ramified into almost every aspect of culture on the continent. In the end, they provided an instrument that helped to sever the near universal influence that the Church (not yet Catholic) held upon the lives and the intellects of people living in what eventually took shape as the *nations* of Europe.

Effects were felt most deeply in the ambitious and turbulent cultures of middle Europe that we loosely call today "Germany," including Austria, portions of modern France, parts of many nations to the east and Switzerland and North Italy. Combined with the impetus of modern commerce and the growth of cities, a large reading class of merchantmen—in addition to clergymen, lawyers and teachers—discovered that they needed to read charts, books on navigation or technology and, of course, business contracts. Lancelot Hogben, in his delightful history of communications technology, also reminds us that the invention—or wide use—of clear glass for windows in houses and shops facilitated the art of reading by lighting interior spaces, as did the crude prisms that the elderly perched on their noses with the development of the first eyeglasses. All of these developments, minor and major, stirred the inventive talents of middle Europeans to discover a quick and relatively easy way of taking the monopoly on book production away from the scriptoria (and the Church), secularizing it and giving it to the man in the street.

The First Presses

A good deal of printing was accomplished reasonably well during the half century before the famous work of Johannes Gutenberg,* and was ac-

---

* Gutenberg's name is frequently spelled with two "t"'s—that is, "Guttenberg." I have followed S. H. Steinberg's spelling in his definitive history of printing. (See Bibliography.)

complished not far from the places where he worked. Two methods were used, and each had its advantages and drawbacks. As we have seen, nothing was (or is) essentially wrong with large wood blocks as printing devices, except that the whittling of letters in each block is painstaking work and difficult to accomplish well. Magnificent playing cards and illustrations, many hand colored, were printed in central Europe well before Gutenberg, and words in print or script are found on many of them that survive to this day.

We also possess records that indicate that metallographic printing by means of a sophisticated process related to the skills of silversmiths and metal workers was also developed between 1430 and 1440 in France, Holland and on the very territory where Gutenberg was to work some ten or so years later. While this process did not require the patience of wood block printing, it depended upon the use of engraved metal letters in the form of dies (similar to those later "invented" by Gutenberg) pressed one by one into clay from which a lead plate was cast into a single block, similar to the wood block. Properly inked, it produced copies of the uniform letters. As advanced as the idea was, it apparently produced shoddy manuscripts, the problem being to press each die individually into the clay in such a way as to create legible words in a straight line.

Gutenberg

Of Johannes Gutenberg himself, we know all too little. In fact, we are not even certain that he *did* indeed invent the printing press himself, or, if he did, exactly when, where and how. Gutenberg was a fifteenth century silversmith, one of many involved in the inchoate art of printing at the time. At Mainz, Germany, in association with a lawyer, Johannes Fust, and working with the latter's future son-in-law, Peter Schöffer, he seems to have produced a number of books, most of them religious—in particular the 42-line Bible of 1455 for which he is best known. Gutenberg personally is credited with printing this document largely because there exists today records of a lawsuit his partners waged against him that describe the kind of books that were being produced at his Mainz studio, and because it is likely that Gutenberg—not Furst or Schöffer—would possess the special skills and technical ingenuity to develop the first moveable type printing press. Schöffer's son, Johannes, denied vehemently in public, some years after his father's death, that Gutenberg had anything to do with the invention, although he had also publicly accredited Gutenberg with the invention but a few years before.

Apparently Gutenberg was an eccentric tinkerer and a miserable businessman, inclined to a high temper and irascible nature. Only five years after the publication of his most beautiful Bible, he went blind. He died in 1465 at the age of about 70; the record is unclear. His work, his methods and his ideas remain with us, however, along with his name that does not, incidentally, appear in any of his printed work. Most important, he left for others the memory of his workshop, so that the technological devices he had worked upon could be copied by them. And copied they were, with remarkable speed.

Gutenberg's achievement consisted largely of bringing currently available technologies together to work out a process for printing letters (and pictures) far more efficiently and effectively than anyone had before him. Nothing that he did was *new*, but the way he achieved his ends and the use he made of the crafts available to him were indeed revolutionary, considering the excellence of the books today credited to his hand.

Eschewing wood blocks, his type pieces were cast from and in metal, and multiple dies of single letters were kept in type cases so that they might be set in straight individual lines. He arranged a matrix, or form, into which these metal pieces might be aligned along a "stick" and in which the dies might be "justified," so that lines were about equal and pages were uniform, by placing little pieces of lead between individual lines. He appears, also, to have discovered—or borrowed—just the right type of ink to provide clear impressions as well as a workable system of inking the matrix by means of a leather pad. From the wine makers of his period, he borrowed the all-important notion of the *press* to provide the proper pressure of type upon paper, and the worm screw vise that held the entire affair together. This type of screw was modified after Gutenberg's death into a multiple thread device to allow for more precise control than his earlier version.

Printing was not an easy art or craft after Gutenberg, but it was a practical and precise—if exhausting—one. Without his two major inventions, it would probably have remained the hit-or-miss affair it had been for the previous century. First, the casting of type and the possibility of re-using type faces after a number of pages had been printed insured uniformity of the final product. Only *one* letter needed to be designed for capitals, lower case letters and marks of punctuation; multiple reverse dies could be made easily by replica casting. Second, Gutenberg's use of ink was apparently unique, a mixture of contemporary inks and other chemicals that was both uniform and remained consistent during the entire operation of printing a book, which might take considerable time. Credit for the invention of the press itself we must give the wine producers, although it remained the integral instrument in hand printing until the nineteenth century. As change did come, however, it was the substitution of metal for wooden parts that was first and most notable in the modification and further perfection of Gutenberg's early instrument.

Certain technical inventions spread their influence rapidly, while others take centuries to affect culture in a noticeable way. Printing spread quickly—or rather, Gutenberg's innovations were freely noted and borrowed with amazing speed, so great was the need at the time for literary material in Europe. We have records of printing presses—probably offsprings of Gutenberg's—in Basel in 1466, Rome in 1467, Venice in 1469, Paris, Nuremberg and Utrecht in 1470, Milan, Naples and Florence in 1471, Cologne in 1472, Lyons, Valencia and Budapest in 1473, Cracow and Bruges in 1474, Lubech and Breslau in 1475, London in 1480, Antwerp and Leipzig in 1481, Odense in 1482 and

Stockholm in 1483! No wonder that by the turn of the century Schöffer the younger was trying to steal credit for this phenomenon from Gutenberg and place it into the hands of his father and grandfather by marriage! The invention was hardly a secret. Although none of Gutengerg's inventions were—or could be—patented, credit rather than cash was what Schöffer seemed to be after.

William Caxton

Our tradition now leads us to follow briefly the career of an Englishman, William Caxton, a man of letters and writer, who, at about the age of 20 expatriated himself to western Europe, where he steeped himself in continental culture and translated and wrote copiously. In Cologne, between 1470 and 1472, he learned the craft of printing. Taking his knowledge to Bruges, he printed his own translation of the *Recuyell of the Historyes of Troye* (otherwise known as *The Iliad*) in English and exported it to his mother country. Caxton's *Recuyell* may probably be considered the first book printed in English, followed by another Caxton import, a translation of a contemporary French volume.

Returning to England, Caxton set up a printing shop in London's Westminster in 1476, probably in the Abbey, where he set to work producing a prodigious number of variegated volumes, ranging from Chaucer's *Canterbury Tales* to Malory's *Morte d'Arthur*—in fact, most of the classics of his era—until his death in 1491. More than 100 titles emerged from his presses. Caxton was apparently a successful businessman who single-handedly introduced printed literature to England. Despite severe conflicts between the royal houses of Lancaster and York, he worked in a period of comparative freedom for the distribution of secular literature. He lived, however, to see Henry VII, the first of the Tudors, establish a ruling house with an iron hand upon the nation that would, by 1529, require that all printers be officially licensed and that all books distributed in Britain bear the imprimatur of the King. This state of affairs, as we shall see, continued almost into the eighteenth century, with varying degrees of severity and force.

With Caxton, the printing trade had been established in England. Throughout the rest of Europe, the so-called "print revolution" was about over, or just beginning, depending upon how you judge revolutions. Not only were the ancient monasteries feeling the thrust of the Reformation, the old scriptoria simply died away for the most part, taking with them the marvelous illustrated manuscripts on parchment of the Middle Ages. To some degree—for Jews, Christians, Moslems (and pagans) also—the mysticism that the hand-printed, and much coveted, book had gathered about itself over the past thousands of years was also dying. What men produce with ease, they consume and destroy with ease, and the antithesis of everything pre-printed books once had stood for was now also about to be invented: the newspaper or journal of events that, unlike the books of old, did not serve to pass on the heritage of the past but centered rather upon the illumination and glorification of the present moment.

Spreading The News

More than 150 years separated the death of Caxton and his printed classics from the English ancestors of the modern mass press and today's daily journal. This was a period of cultural foment and change in European history, and probably most of the claims made today concerning the role of print in these indelible changes are true, to one degree or another. The circulation of books encouraged literacy and education. Education inspired independent thought. Such thinking was one fundament of the Reformation. Growing feelings of nationalism and patriotism were moving across the continent. While the spread of relatively expensive, limited circulation books was hardly a ''mass'' phenomenon in modern terms, populations in cities (the centers of culture) grew, and literacy spread as never before in history among the new, emerging middle classes. Universities mushroomed, as students and teachers discussed (and printed) their ideas, poetry and narrative fiction (soon to become the modern ''novel''). More important, many so-called ''average'' men and women began to take notice of new social forces around them and to recognize that they had the *power* to do something about what they did not like. In this simple manner, then, did the revolution of print spark numerous other revolutions: political, social, religious and cultural—or, at least, it facilitated their progress across the continent from east Europe to Ireland.

The daily newspaper itself was not an idea born in the seventeenth century, although seventeenth century technology was a necessity for its birth in modern form. Once again, one discovers roots in China, still visible in some Oriental communities—even American Chinatowns today—on billboards posted in towns and cities, reporting current events for those literate enough to read their pictograms. Records exist of such methods of spreading news during the Tung dynasty in the tenth century, but these *Pao* or reports are probably far older than this.

In fairness to our own tradition, one may well count the Roman *Acta Diurna* as the ''original'' newspaper, a daily hand-written document posted in various public places in this great city as early as 59 B.C. Whatever it was that town criers were later to cry, the *Acta* also briefly announced: deaths, births, entertainments, hangings, new laws and the like. They were posted adjacent to the *Acta Senatus,* a report that recorded the more austere and formal actions of the Roman governing body. It is difficult to trace the fate of these *Actae,* because they were swallowed by history, probably in the first few centuries after Christ, when Rome turned, as Juvenal lamented, into a polyglot city of ''foreigners,'' Greeks and Hebrews among others. Latin was now spoken only by the aristocracy. Illiteracy spread, and nobody read posters any longer, not out of indifference but rather because most people were no longer capable of doing so.

Gossips and town criers carried the news, or as much news as they could carry, through the Middle Ages, until the record finally shows the emergence of hand-written newsletters circulating among the financial communities of the larger central European cities. The idea seemed particularly attractive to the population of Renaissance Venice, the great seaport, not only to help in the exchange of goods but of ideas and news as well. This Adriatic city became, for all intents and purposes, the birthplace of the *Fogli d' Avvisi,* a written newsletter of events from afar, read aloud by a learned man to a privileged group of Venetians who paid one *gazeta,* or less than a penny, to attend the hearing. This custom continued well after its origins in 1563 and into the era of printed "gazettes" that followed them, because, printed or written, most Venetians simply could not read. The first known printed *gazeta* was issued, incidently, by the Venetian government and dealt with news from the front of Venice's war with Turkey.

War news was also the topic of a printed pamphlet of four pages issued by Richard Fowkes in 1513 in England entitled *The Treu Encountre,* delineating the downfall of James IV, the Scottish king who had invaded England and died on Flodden Field in a dramatic and disastrous battle. A one-time, one-issue newspaper, it was the model for what was to come: pamphlets on various current events of public interest written, printed and apparently *not* read aloud (much) in central Europe, Switzerland and in England during the rest of the sixteenth century. In the latter part of the century, some unremembered genius also conceived the notion of publishing these documents more or less regularly—yearly, monthly or even weekly—in the manner of modern periodicals. The *Mercurius Gallo Bellicus,* printed in England but written in Latin and published yearly from 1594 to 1639, was probably the one first reguarly printed news documents in the style of our modern "almanac."

Of pamphleteers in England during the late sixteenth century, there was no shortage. But most of them published regularly for only short periods, due to the activities of the King's Star Chamber which then acted as prior censor of all printed material. Puritan zealots, most notably Robert Waldgrave, produced dozens of irregularly printed tracts against the national church. Waldgrave was merely exiled, but Catholic pamphleteer William Carter was executed for his publications in 1584. Despite the number and the courage of the men who wrote and printed them, these pamphlets were hardly newspapers in today's sense, although in tone and intent they were not unlike some documents distributed by the modern underground press.

"Corantos"

In the more permissive climate of Holland (an eventual stopping place for many British dissidents including the Puritans), the modern newspapers was actually born in a style and manner similar to the journals that we might recognize as newspapers today. Inspired by Belgian commercial journals like the *Niewe Tighidenghen* of Antwerp and the *Courante Bladen,* which appeared in the first decade of the seventeenth century as well as various German commercial news reports, Dutch printers began publishing *corantos* or "currents of news'' about 1618. They were widely imitated in France and other European countries. Most of these corantos were primarily trade journals (in all probability), but they contained foreign news of many kinds gleaned from port cities and, also possibly, a modest quantum of local happenings—and even advertisements of sorts.

The first British coranto was printed in London in 1621 by Thomas Archer without official approval. For his arrogance, Archer landed in prison, although the offending document was probably just an English translation of a Dutch journal. Nathaniel Butter, apparently at one time Archer's partner, then sought and received a license for his coranto. Thus the first British newspaper of record, *Corante, or News from Italy, Germany, Hungarie, Spain and France* of 1621, was printed and circulated under Butter's aegis. For the next 20 years, Butter continued printing his corantos, often with Archer's help and in collaboration with the prominent book editor, Nicholas Bourne. The latter used his prestige to obtain a license and "publish with authority" a "news book," as it was then called, entitled the *Weekly Newes*—and later *The Continuation of our Weekly Newes*.

This journal was far from weekly or, for that matter, regularly published. News awaited the arrival of ships from foreign ports (and some published corantos from Holland). The triumverate ran into periodic problems with the Privy Council regarding licenses and fees. They also had difficulties with circulation, solved for a while by Butter who employed street-roving newsgirls to sell his paper—later replaced by newsboys for reasons best left to the imagination.

First Newspapers

As the British weekly corantos died, a new type of journal replaced them: the daily newspaper, which was able, because of its timeliness, to devote itself to matters other than foreign and commercial news, particularly political issues, and often conveniently to "scoop" word-of-mouth gossip concerning the ongoing battle between the King and Parliament.

In a period marked by a somewhat relaxed climate of freedom, the *Diurnal Occurrences,* edited and probably written by John Thomas, appeared in the winter of 1641 in London. Licensing was temporarily abolished and, accordingly, so were many restirctions upon the British press including the infamous Star Chamber. Shortly thereafter, the poet John Milton and editor William Walwyn published their impressive defenses of freedom of speech that were to doom press licensing in England to permanent oblivion by the end of the century. Milton's *Areopagitica* is regarded to this day as a stunning defense of liberty, although Walwyn, Henry Robinson, Richard Overton and John Lilburne, among others forgotten by history, argued almost as persusively at the time for the end of press censorship by government.

Freedom—and the new diurnals—had a difficult time during the 16 years between the executed Charles I and the Restoration of Charles II to the British throne. Britain's "popular" dictator, Oliver Cromwell, was, in some ways, more oppresive to British printers than the monarchy from which he had temporarily liberated them. His own newspapers replaced the independent ones in the form of such supportive propaganda journals as the *Mercurius Politicus, A Perfect Diurnal* and the *Publick Intelligencer,* all of them speaking for his regime.

After the Restoration of Charles II in 1660, there was little dramatic change in the growth of the British newspaper. Henry Muddiman continued to publish the *Mercurius* and the *Intelligencer* as he had under Cromwell. A Licensing Act was passed in 1662, and Roger L'Estrange (a not-so-curious name for a favorite of the restored king who brought to Britain much that was "foreign" from his exile in France), himself a publisher, was appointed "surveyor of the press," meaning the few loyal newspapers that were irregularly printed by royal consent and, apparently, an infinite number of unofficial, hand-copied corantos beyond the control of the new but now dying press control legislation.

Henry Muddiman takes a significant place in the history of the mass media, because he is responsible for the founding of the *Oxford Gazette* in 1665. Printed twice a week, on Tuesdays and Fridays, the Gazette started its life in the university town while a plague ravaged London, but it moved to the big city the following year. Its name was changed to the *London Gazette* and, as of the prsent writing, it is still being published—although it now contains official lists of public appointments and announcements. It functions as an official organ of Her Majesty's court. In better and younger days, it also served an an organ of news, albeit also an official one, of wider and more parochial interest.

A Free Press

Between the Restoration of Charles II and the Revolution of 1688, the Crown attempted to maintain its old controls on the British presses. But the scent of new freedom was in the wind and, legislation notwithstanding, it was difficult to control the various maverick printers and editors who were eager to test the law. With the ascension to the Crown of William and Mary, licensing died with the seventeenth century. New papers sprang up in the provinces, in Scotland and, of course, in London.

In 1702, Elizabeth Mallet founded the *Daily Courant,* a newspaper that had a noble, notable 33-year life. Succeeding Mallet after its first, disastrous few days, Samuel Buckley eventually contrived to publish a daily journal of a single sheet's length that employed or originated many of the modern conventions of journalistic writing and format.

The *Courant* was a newspaper, not a journal of opinion or shipping list. Although Buckley was an ardent Whig, his reportage did not reflect his personal politics, except when so labeled. He was scrupulous in his use of datelines, identifying the date and location of each news story and declined to print rumors or unfounded gossip. The reverse side of his paper was usually devoted to advertising, except when there was a glut of news. Advertisements were clearly labeled as such, although they were written in much the same literary style as the rest of the paper. In its earliest days, the *Courant* ran translations of articles in continental newspapers, although, as Buckley prospered in revenues from circulation and advertising, he was able to afford his own exclusive foreign news sources.

The start of the eighteenth century marks a signal change in British journalism, the birth of the "essay papers" or editorial journals that were eventually to be the butt of Richard Brinsley Sheridan's satire in his minor (but often performed) play, *The Critic,* written in the latter part of the century.

Daniel Defoe, novelist and social satirist, edited *Mist's Journal* from 1717 to 1720. Jonathan Swift edited and wrote for a number of others. But it was Sir Richard Steele and Joseph Addison who are most closely associated with this *genre,* the forefathers of today's British *Punch* and the American *New Yorker.* The team achieved recognition as editors and publishers of, first, Steele's *Tatler* from 1709 to 1711, and then Addison and Steele's *Spectator* from 1711 to 1712. The former was issued three times a week, the latter daily, and the *Spectator* was revived for a time in 1714. Circulation claimed for the latter reached 3,000, and it was said that its readership reached 60,000 people, probably both inflated figures. Unlike the newspapers that followed in the style and manner of *The Courant,* these satirical journals were different matters, not only conduits of opinion but of humor and irony and, in the case of masters like Defoe and Swift, superb satire, frequently taken seriously, Their function was to inform, amuse and—sometimes—to anger.

First Colonial Newspapers

At about this place in history, the American press severs from British history in the person of one Benjamin Harris, a nervy English publisher who had been convicted in England of producing a journal in defiance of the King's licensing laws in 1686. He set sail for the American colonies via Bristol after two years in a British prison, unable to pay his fine at home. In 1690, we find him in Boston publishing a newspaper, *Publick Occurences, Both Foreign and Domestick.* Not only was Harris a maverick printer in England, upon his arrival in Massachusetts he had achieved a criminal record as an anti-Catholic ally of the infamous British demagogue, Titus Oates, and was an apparently active conspirator against enemies of Charles II, among other things.

Setting up a coffee house and book shop in Boston upon his arrival in the colonies, Harris cultivated the intelligentsia of the busy city as friends and customers. He seemed to prosper. When, in 1689, the American colonists (in delayed response to the British Revolution of 1688) sent the British governor Sir Edmund Andros, loyal servant of Charles II, back to Britain to be tried in court for attempting to extend his authority beyond the domains of New York into New England, Harris felt that his time had come. Coffee and books were all well and good, but he used this opportunity to cash in on people's interest in public affairs by hiring a printer to produce his four-page *Publick Occurrences* on September 25, 1690.

For the same reason that unlicensed newspapers could not survive in England, however, Harris' journal died in the colonies—after one issue. It was not licensed and was published without royal consent, in addition to which it promised, even in a single, maiden issue, to reflect the candor and revolutionary fervor of its editor, as well as his love of gossip, including a purported sex scandal concerning the King of France and the wife of a prince.

Harris' time had not come. It never would. *Publick Occurrences* was discontinued by decree of the Governor and Council of the colony for its presumptions, both literary and legal. Harris eventually returned to London. He lost his money there operating still another newspaper, ending his life as a salesman of patent medicines and fake cure-alls.

Fourteen years later, in the same city of Boston, a more sophisticated man than Harris, John Campbell, the local postmaster, arranged with Bartholomew Green, a printer, to start the *Boston News-Letter,* a weekly journal that may properly be called the first *continuing* newspaper in the New World. In spite of two suspensions by local authorities, it continued publication under Campbell until 1723, and thereafter by others until it became a Royalist casualty of the American Revolution.

Campbell was no rebel like Harris. As postmaster, he and his brother Duncan both had been copying local news from the port of Boston for transmission to the other colonies in longhand since 1700. The idea of a newspaper seemed a natural next step to the conservative Scotsman. Having duly licensed his document with the authorities to avoid repetition of Harris' problems, he published the first issue of the *News-Letter* on April 24, 1704.

In style, it was somewhat imitative of the official *London Gazette,* being largely a journal of record containing foreign news, particularly from England, local events, maritime news and a few short advertisements. Also, like most foreign newspapers of the period (including Harris' ill-fated journal), it often included blank pages, or parts of them, on one of its two printed sides for the reader to fill in his own news before he passed it along for others to read. In its long history under Campbell's aegis, also, the *News-Letter* ran a constant battle with the erratic and uncertain ocean travel arriving from overseas. Sometimes Campbell found himself apologizing for his inability to handle it all, printing extra pages or delaying some until the next edition—with regrets.

The circulation of the *News-Letter* was not large, a few hundred at most, although its cost was apparently small: two pence an issue. Despite its advertising revenues and Campbell's Scotch origins, the paper was continually in debt, suspending publication occasionally because of lack of funds. Because it was an approved and semi-official journal that included public notices, it sometimes received financial subsidies from the government. Eventually, it passed from Campbell's hands to those of Green, the printer, to the latter's son-in-law John

Draper—a respected and reasonably accurate newspaper, considering its time and place.

For 15 years the *News-Letter* was Boston's only paper, but, when Campbell left his postmastership in 1719, he took the *News-Letter* with him. William Brooker, his successor, accordingly started the *Boston Gazette* in that year, printed at first by one James Franklin, elder brother of the famous Ben, whose own exploits in the field of journalism were later to be considerable. The *Gazette,* however, was the postmaster's infant, and five successive men who filled this post continued it until it merged with one of its rivals, the *New England Weekly Journal.*

The Franklins

James Franklin, however, was the first American publisher after Harris to have ciruclating in his veins at least a modicum of rebel blood. When Brooker's successor at the postoffice took the *Gazette's* printing business away from his shop, Franklin (with the encouragement of various other anti-establishment types) began to print his own paper, *The New England Courant,* a weekly which first appeared on August 7, 1721.

Particularly in its earliest years, the *Courant* was markedly different from its competitors, which were growing numerous, not only in Boston but in other American cities as well. Franklin attempted to emulate and print extracts from London literary journals like the *Spectator* and *Guardian,* as well as the satirical writings of literary figures like Daniel Defoe. He published human interest stories, light pieces that made fun of local stuffed-shirts and attempted to use his newspapers to crusade for political and social ideas in which he believed. In fact, under the by-line "Silence Dogood," younger brother Ben wrote satirical essays and other material imitating the great Addison and Steele.

Most important, James Franklin printed his paper without an official license, thereby bringing to the colonies the same current of, or desire for, press freedom that was, at the time, blowing through the literary community in the mother country, England. Franklin indeed spent his time in jail for his outspokenness—particularly his attacks upon the Puritan clergymen Increase Mather and his son Cotton—giving young Ben a chance to print the paper himself for a month. James continued publication until 1726 or 1727, when he left the Massachusetts colony for the freer climes of Rhode Island.

Brother Ben found his way to Philadelphia via New York. The latter city saw its first newspaper, *The New York Gazette,* started in 1725 by William Bradford, an ex-Philadelphia printer, who had, in 1693, set up the first printing press on Manhattan island and returned to New York when he was over 60 years old to start its first notable newspaper. Bradford's son, Andrew, had launched the *American Weekly Mercury* in Philadelphia on December 22, 1719. Both father and son were outspoken journalists in the mold of the Franklin brothers. They began a tradition that continued in the Bradford family well into the revolutionary period as brave and committed spokesmen for liberty and against British authority.

Benjamin Franklin himself became manager of the *Pennsylvania Gazette,* founded by an eccentric exponent of scientific deism, Samuel Keimer, in 1728. It was Keimer's idea to publish an entire encyclopedia in tandem with the paper. In fact, Keimer called the newspaper *The Universal Instructor in All the Arts and Sciences: and Pennsylvania Gazette,* appropiately shortened by Franklin the next year when he bought it. Competing with Bradford's *Mercury,* Franklin, then in his early twenties and with his experience and skill, could easily establish the *Gazette* as the most literate, accurate and highest circulating paper in the region. It accordingly commanded formidable advertising rates. Before he retired from publishing at the age of 42, Ben's business acumen had served him well in establishing the first newspaper chain in the New World and permitted him to amass a fortune from his publishing exploits, along with a reputation as a respectable journalist and man among men—and women— among his other and more famous interests.

The Colonial Press

As immigration increased and the colonies grew in size, so the newspaper press thrived as well. By the latter third of the eighteenth century, 37 newspapers were being printed in the colonies, all of them printed by hand, their type set in a manner not unlike that used by Gutenberg. Printing was at the heart of the newspaper business, and print shops produced not only newspapers but books, Bibles, handbills and public notices, as well as official documents for general distribution. Obviously, editors had both to cooperate and compete with one another: cooperating by passing "intelligence" among themselves, but competing both for readership and advertisers. Most important to the future of the press, it was clear that journalism could be a profitable profession in the new, largely agrarian colonial, capitalist society of the American colonies, and that its basic function constituted a public service in providing the literate population with news from afar, as well as spreading political ideas and taking an editorial stance on issues that affected newspaper readers.

The Communications Revolution that had started 300 years before in the center of European continent was now to provide impetus for a political revolution on a virgin continent thousands of miles away, where a shot would soon be fired that would reverberate around the world for another 200 years, at least. The moving finger of history was soon to begin to write ever more rapidly, as the printing presses of the West were to multiply, speed up and finally explode into a world where they would function as vanguards of social and political change during the years just ahead.

2

The Press of Freedom

CIVIL LIBERTARIANS, communications scholars, journalists and American history teachers are nearly unanimous in their celebration of the famous libel trial of Peter Zenger in July of 1735. Zenger was imprisoned for printing in his *New York Weekly Journal* severe criticisms of Governor William Cosby. Two years before, Zenger had charged the newly appointed, British-born Cosby with a number of indiscretions (or possible illegalities), including the specific item that Cosby had allowed French military vessels to search out defensive position in New York bay, and far more general ones satirically written (probably by hot-blooded anti-British lawyer, James Alexander) that Cosby was replacing his enemies in the Colonial administration and courts with personal toadies to the somewhat egocentric, choleric governor.

The Zenger Trial

The *Journal,* which first appeared in November of 1733, was probably, in fact, begun by strong anti-Cosby partisans in New York. At least they encouraged Zenger to print his vitriol, correct or incorrect, and the German-born editor of the *Journal* complied. Just a year later, Zenger was arrested by the Crown's officers and slapped into jail awaiting grand jury charges of "raising sedition." Zenger's personal role in the attacks on Cosby by editing the newspaper may be induced from the curious fact that the *Journal* continued to be printed with little change in style during the considerable period when Zenger was imprisoned, probably by Alexander and William Smith and other irate victims of Cosby's apparent arrogance.

In the face of chronic inaction from the grand jury, Zenger was eventually arrested for "seditious libels" against Cosby and his administration and, a year and one-half after his first detainment, at last faced judge and jury. His plight had become well known among the northern colonies, and various insurgents and rebels who were later to spearhead the revolution (including "The Sons of Liberty") hired the aging libertarian attorney, Philadelphian Andrew Hamilton, to come to New York to plead Zenger's cause in court.

In fact, of course, Hamilton was not pleading Zenger's cause as much as he was using a well provoked and publicized incident to wear down the absolute authority of the British Crown in the colonies, one of the first of many abrasions that eventually sparked the American Revolution some 40 years later. In *this* sense, as a symbol and a brave beginning to a noble end, is the Zenger trial important to American history. In the light of the years that have passed, its legal value—or interest—is open to question, as well as the trial's effect on journalism in the colonies. Its political significance, however, is beyond doubt.

Hamilton's defense of Zenger and the *Journal* is magnificent rhetoric, often quoted. It achieved its immediate end: Zenger's acquittal. Hamilton argued for *truth* as the test of any libel and for the "cause of liberty," in his words. It is an emotional argument and a stirring one, but open to many qualifications. First, establishing either the truth or falsehood of Zenger's satire was difficult to do, as is the case with similar invective today. Cosby was an unpopular governor, and Zenger exploited that unpopularity. But Cosby was also an agent of the *British* Crown. Had he been guilty of irregularities in using *that* authority—as it was claimed he was—the colonists had recourse by legal means to, at least, air their grievances in open court. Second, an appeal to truth (even a truth difficult to establish) is always emotionally stirring; but Hamilton apparently had few, if any, legal grounds at the time to cite truth as a test of libel. Truth was not then a criterion of libel under British law, and was not permanently recognized as such in American courts until 1804.

There being few precedents for a case of this kind, Justice Delancey, usually portrayed in the re-telling as a Tory bigot, could have overruled Hamilton early in his defense of freedom and possibly reversed the verdict. The jury may even have acted improperly by freeing Zenger, in that their charge was *not* to decide whether libel had been done (in the absence of laws to this effect and evidence other than the Governor's word), but rather *whether or not Zenger had printed the issues of the Journal in question.* The sentiments of the jury apparently reflected public opinion, not the issue at hand. And it was upon this psychological factor that shrewd old Hamilton pounced. Legally or illegally, Zenger was freed.

The Zenger trial was a curious affair. The Justices—and Governor Cosby himself—were the first high British officials in the colonies forced to bow before the growing insurgency of the anti-Loyalists in an official arena. Had the legal precedent of the Zenger trial been eventually followed in our new nation—as it might have been—no one can calculate the results. The new government was to be suitably constrained by law, not by public pressure as in the

Zenger trial. To say, as many do, that the Zenger trial, however, set the precedent for freedom of the press in the United States seems also something of an exaggeration, conducted, as the trial was, in a fairly small, highly charged, emotional community whose main opinion leaders had closed ranks against one man: William Cosby.

If the Zenger trial provides us with a heritage, it is a much more subtle one, centering upon the right of newspapers to criticize public officials responsibly without fear of reprisal—*if* their charges are reasonable and responsible. It also limned a rough code of behavior for civil authorities who *believe* they have been libeled by the press: that is, it warned them (and still warns them) not to use their punitive powers directly against the press even if they have *really* been libeled, but to find recourse in our judicial system, which is exactly what Cosby eventually did.

The Press and Revolution

The burgeoning colonial press appears to have emerged from the Zenger incident neither better nor worse off than it was before. As new newspapers and magazines—Andrew Bradford's *American Magazine* and Ben Franklin's *General Magazine* were launched within a week of one another in 1741—sprang up like crabgrass, they allied themselves more and more with the major political issue of the century in the colonies: They were either for or against the British, with a number in the middle. The safest road was obviously the center one, appeasing the authorities as well as an ever increasing roster of insurgents among the literate population. A surprising number of newspapers, however, espoused their polar positions with unbridled vigor.

Most important, American newspapers were establishing themselves as indispensable organs of home-grown *political* opinions, ideas, programs and prejudices, although they continued to function also as European newsletters, mercantile trade journals and instruments of advertising. It was, as we shall see, this ever-increasing tendency of the colonial press to *politicize* itself that provided the foundations for the legal guarantees American newspapers were eventually to receive regarding their freedom to print whatever their editors and publishers decided was newsworthy. To this end, the temper of the times, not the trial of a Peter Zenger, played a critical role.

One cannot assume, however, that the American press, both newspapers and magazines, ignited the specific series of events that led to the Revolution. Circulations were too small, illiteracy rates too high, and too many other factors were involved in the increasing discontents of the colonists. In addition, a great proportion of those able to read and who could afford newspapers were themselves members of the ruling class: Tories, loyalists or what you will. Many of the papers, however, gave form and substance to the revolutionary currents in the air, and, no doubt, encouragement as well. The press, as it has always been, was both reflective and directive of the social action swirling around it, but, in this instance, usually more reflective.

In response, for instance, to the famous Stamp Act of 1765, some papers were published without the hated tax stamp on them, claiming that they were not taxable publications simply by dropping their mastheads or by merely printing a notice that they had been prevented from buying stamps because of mob actions against the stamp vendors. Others, like the *Pennsylvania Journal and Weekly Advertiser,* lamented the new taxes by printing funeral margins on their columns, and still others, like the *Boston Gazette* and *Maryland Gazette,* put skulls and crossbones on their front pages the day the taxes were enacted. There is also evidence that plans for the wild and nervy "Boston Tea Party" of 1773 were hatched in the offices of the *Boston Gazette,* an anti-Tory newspaper that numbered among them its contributors such revolutionaries as Samuel Adams (in some respects the most effective propagandist for the Revolution in the colonies), John Adams and John Hancock, all of them writing under so many pseudonyms that it is difficult to identify today who wrote what.

Early Magazines

Just exactly what differentiated newspapers from magazines—and other kinds of periodicals—in this period and up to the nineteenth century is also a subject about which it is difficult to be precise. The term "magazine" appears to have been born in London as late as 1731, when it was applied to the first English language periodical of its kind, the *Gentlemen's Magazine,* a document vaguely similar in some respects (except the most obvious ones) to today's *Playboy.* "Magazine," as the word was originally used in Britain and America, was more or less synonymous with word "storehouse", which clearly illustrates its early function without providing the slightest notion of *what* was to be stored in it. Frank Luther Mott has called the magazine a "bound pamphlet issued more or less regularly and containing a variety of reading matter. . . . that has a strong connotation of entertainment," which was pretty much what the first magazines of Bradford and Franklin were. The term, as Mott uses it, differentiates clearly, in this "strong connotation," magazines from newspapers, journals, professional periodicals, other reviews and similar publications, although this is obviously not a harsh or exclusive difference.

Almost from the first, some magazines published illustrations, primarily woodcuts, and poetry and literature—although American magazines of the eighteenth century were also heavily larded with the same political flavor as newspapers, their polemics and tracts often written by the same writers. One noted magazine, *The Pennsylvania Magazine; or American Monthly Museum,* was edited, for most of its short life from 1775 to 1776, by Thomas Paine who, of course, published some of his most famous revolutionary tracts in its pages. By the end of the eighteenth century, about 100 (possibly more) magazines had, for the most part, come and gone in the major cities of the colonies. Few were long-lived, despite the continual claim of the recently defunct *Saturday Evening Post* that it was founded by Ben Franklin in 1728, more a downright lie than an exaggeration. (Samuel Keimer started the *Pennsylvania Gazette* in 1728. Franklin bought it the next year. The *Post* was begun in the same city by Samuel Atkinson and Charles Alexander a mere 93 years later!)

Political Functions

If ever a public was thoroughly politicized, it was the adult, male property-owning and more or less literate population of the Thirteen Colonies, the same minority who were later to constitute the corpus of enfranchised voters in the United States after the Revolution. Politics, as much as trade, agriculture and religion, was among the major topics of common discourse, especially in the cities. The press reflects clearly the obsessive concern of the colonists with issues of government that increased rapidly as the American Revolution germinated. True enough, there were many settlers and farmers removed from the pro- and anti-British ferment. Slaves and others, particularly the entirely uneducated, were probably indifferent. Women played a marginal role in political life, despite myths later spun about the Betsy Rosses, Martha Washingtons and others. But in the lives of the people who counted—and were soon to *be* counted—questions concerning British rule and similar issues made up the major debates of this era, from the New England states to South Carolina.

One important newspaper was the *Massachusetts Spy*, founded by Isaiah Thomas and Zechariah Fowle in 1770. The *Spy* shortly became the property of Thomas while still in his twenties. He endeavored, editorially at any rate, to steer clear of politics and attempted to follow a middle course between Whigs and Tories. This, of course, was impossible, although Thomas apparently tried to keep his pages "Open To All Parties—But Influenced By None." Despite the success of this policy, and a circulation second only to James Riverton's pro-British *New York Gazetteer* (whose influence was felt far beyond the New York community), Thomas, bit by bit, took up the revolutionist cudgels in Boston until his columns were well laced with "anonymous" articles by many of that city's notable insurgents.

Possibly Thomas' greatest moment as a newsman was provided by the story he printed in the *Spy* on May 3, 1775, reporting at first hand and as an eye witness, the start of the American Revolution at the British militia raid upon Concord and Lexington, thus re-telling as an eyewitness the events involved in "the shot heard round the world"—with accuracy if not total objectivity. Moving to Worcester to avoid pro-British ire in Boston, Thomas eventually expanded his printing operation into a publishing house of books and magazines. The *Spy* was to continue publication until 1904.

Their news functions aside, the American newspapers and magazines of the period were among the main conduits for the revolutionary pamphleteers, among them Thomas Paine, who spread their doctrines throughout the colonies. In addition, Whig newspapers paraphrased the issues and ideas of revolutionary rhetoric and thereby gained public support for them. The Declaration of Independence, for instance, appeared in print in colonial newspapers before it was issued as a manifesto or reprinted elsewhere. It was included in its entirety in the *Pennsylvania Evening Post* on July 6, 1776, just two days after its acceptance by the Continental Congress and was copied in full by most of the other Whig newspapers as soon as possible. Reliable estimates tell us that about 40,000 homes received revolutionary newspapers. Their readership was probably far greater, and those who listened to others read or summarize the news and opinions they carried naturally spread their influence further still.

Not only was this pre-revolutionary press highly politicized, it was obviously polarized by the war itself into newspapers that were clearly pro-British, as opposed to those that supported the rebels. In their way—like nearly all newspapers published in societies in turmoil—they became part of the war itself. Objectivity and nonpartisanship were impossible. At war's end, therefore, most of those papers which had supported the Tories soon died. Of the approximately 35 newspapers published in the colonies when the Revolution began, 20 survived the war, and a great number of new ones subsequently sprang up to take the place of those that had expired.

The Post-Revolutionary Press

Both the politicization and polarity of newspapers continued after the war, however, but now along different lines and in a way that served as a model for the two-party press that survives to this day in the U.S.A. One development was the rise of the *daily* newspaper, the origins of which begin 1783 with the publication of Benjamin Towne's *Pennsylvania Evening Post* (started in 1775) which made a transition from an irregular monthly to semi-weekly, and finally to a daily newspaper that lasted all of a month. By 1785 the *Morning Post,* in New York City, had begun daily publications, as well as John Dunlap and David C. Claypool's *Pennsylvania Packet, and Daily Advertiser* and Francis Child's *New York Daily Advertiser.* Although dailies had long been circulated in Europe, they had not been feasible in America until the birth of the new nation, largely for economic reasons. With the need for mercantile news now running high in America's large cities, however, and the number of notable, newsworthy items of interest to the population of the vigorous, young nation expanding, they multiplied almost like rabbits.

Political these post-revolutionary papers certainly were, but they remained commercially oriented as well. Thus their importance to the new nation increased with their numbers. While the old Whig-Tory alignment had been settled by the Revolutionary War, political polarities among the American population had not. Although political views were not always articulated in terms of black and white, matters of doctrine that centered upon two members of Washington's Cabinet drew support from the early newspapers. They aligned themselves behind Alexander Hamilton or Thomas Jefferson, each of whom was closely identified with Federalists and anti-Federalists respectively. The Federalists, led by Hamilton, espoused the cause of a strong, responsible national government with considerable power to guide or direct state governments; the anti-Federalists (eventually called Republicans) were anxious that the federal government maintain the widest measure of freedom so that the states might direct their own destinies.

The press reflected this schism, and outstanding among the partisan newspapers were John Fenno's *Gazette of the United States,* a semi-weekly published in New York, that spoke clearly and loudly for Hamilton and the Federalists from its first issue on April 15, 1789. Jefferson's cudgels were taken up by poet Philip Freneau who traveled to the capital in Philadelphia in 1791 to begin his own anti-Federalist semi-weekly, the *National Gazette.* Other newspapers, dailies and weeklies, of course followed these more or less official "spokesmen" for political causes. Among them was the avid, Jeffersonian *Aurora* of Philadelphia, edited at first by Benjamin Franklin Bache and later by William Duane. The *Aurora* was a journal noted for its vitriolic hatred of President George Washington and his Federalist inclinations.

Whatever their sentiments, the newspapers were fully caught up in the political life of the new nation. They were, in fact, major forums for the expression of ideas and policies in the air. From a stylistic perspective, there was little fair-minded or dispassionate about these journals. Whatever distinction they had (or have), it did not stem from the accuracy of their news but from the intensity and fervor of their opinions, expressed even in news columns, often with considerable poetic latitude. Nor were they written for the common or semi-literate man. The vocabulary they employed was comparatively large. Their rhetoric was literary and their graphic formats conservative. They were clearly written for the literate elite of the new nation, men (and women) whose deepest interests were either political or commercial and who could afford them—their price, in general, calculated to preclude from readership all but people of means.

The Bill of Rights

Their vital role as political instruments was just as obvious to the citizens of the new nation as it is to us. As early as the drafting of the State of Virginia's own Bill of Rights in 1776, ideas about press freedom (previously included in the Declaration of Rights by John Dickinson at the first Continental Congress of 1774) were adopted variantly by the individual states as the early years of the new Republic passed.

In essence, they affirmed the necessity of a *free* press, independent of government controls of any kind, as a prerequisite to the functions of a Republic where citizens elected their own representatives and governors. The press was a mediator of political ideas, and it was also the *one* instrument in society that might spread them widely, as well as familiarize the public with candidates who ran for various offices. Newspapers were thus indispensible for effective democratic government, at least as long as the government itself was restrained from interfering with them.

The United States Constitution, ratified by the various states between December, 1787 and May, 1790, contained no such guarantee of press freedom, however, nor did it mention the press' role in democratic government. This was apparently the result of Federalist pressure. Hamilton argued persuasively that a stated imposition against denying freedom of speech by the federal government was, first, unnecessary because it was, in effect, a pre-condition for the function of the Constitution itself and, second, already affirmed by most of the states within their own constitutions. One can easily understand why the Federalists, particularly, would oppose any legislation that they thought might, one day, critically limit the powers of the federal government to restrain the states or prevent some serious national sedition in the future.

The first ten Amendments to the Constitution, or the Bill of Rights, were, on face, concessions eventually granted by the Federalists to the philosophy of government for which the Constitution stood. In all probability, James Madison was largely responsible for obtaining these concessions as one condition for the prior ratification of the document by all of the 13 states. At the first session of the United States Congress, the Bill of Rights became an important issue. And freedom of the press, of all the guarantees therein, was obviously a matter of priority.

The First Amendment is most explicit: "Congress shall make *no law* respecting an establishment of religion, or prohibiting the free enterprise thereof, or abridging the freedom of speech, *or the press;* or the right of the people peaceably to assemble, and to petition the Government for a redress of grievances." Now that it stood firm in cold print, ratified by Congress in 1791, the concept, it appeared, was irrefutably the law of the land!

The Alien and Sedition Laws

It was not. The pendulum of liberty had swung in one direction. But seven years later, it was swinging in another. French refugees from the revolution at home, as well as English and Irish emigres, influenced growing public sentiment—or fear—that the United States might have to face, either with France (primarily) or the British, a counter-revolution of some sort.

Thus, Alien and Sedition Acts were passed by Congress in 1798, both of which ran directly against both the spirit and the letter of the First Amendment. The Alien Act gave the President wide powers to deny citizenship to non-citizens and to deport them. The Sedition Act made it a crime to write or print anything abusive of the United States Government or the Congress that might be considered "false, scandalous or malicious." Penalties included fines and imprisonment. A number of editors and publishers, who naturally opposed the Acts, were punished for such frivolities as printing insults to the President, to the army and similar indiscretions—as well as attacking directly the legality of the Acts themselves.

Most historians today agree that the passage of the Alien and Sedition laws, particularly the latter, was a political scheme on the part of the Federalists to maintain their control of the federal government and to silence critics among the press, as well as other anti-Federalists, many of whom, like Jefferson, were not only politicians but persuasive writers. That a climate of opinion existed in which such legislation was accepted by the public is more difficult to understand, except that it underscores how uncertain at the time many citizens were of the ability of the United States to survive political arguments within and/or hostilities from without. Both Acts were clearly unconstitutional. But the matter could not be tested as such, because the Supreme Court's power to act on legislative matters was not established procedurally until 1803.

The major question posed by the laws referred back fundamentally to the unrestrictive nature of the First Amendment and the *absolute* freedom granted the press from government, as well as by implication, any other controls. The Federalists particularly, but others as well, were acutely aware of how sharp an instrument newspapers might become in times of crises, and how effectively they might be used to topple governments. Did the First Amendment mean what is said, and if it did *not,* exactly where was Congress (or the states) to draw the line regarding free speech and a free press? Sedition? Libel? Falsehood? Mischief? Blasphemy?

Even Alexander Hamilton himself objected to these laws, as did ex-President George Washington and incumbent John Adams. But there was little they could do to stop the groundswell of Federalist extremism. It was Thomas Jefferson, however, writing anonymously as Vice President, and James Madison, the adroit compromiser, who were largely responsible for the Virginia and Kentucky resolutions that threatened nullification (that is, state repudiation of federal laws) of the hated Acts.

In hindsight, the nation would indeed have been fortunate if all of the issues surrounding the Alien and Sedition laws of 1798 had been entirely cleared up at the time—including the principle of nullification. Unfortunately, they were not. The Virginia and Kentucky resolutions, it turned out, were not particularly popular with the press, whether because of the Federalist leanings of many of the editors or because the resolutions did not clearly enough affirm the general principle of the First Amendment, it is difficult to determine. Instead, the abuses to which the Alien and Sedition Acts were put led directly to their demise: the idiocy of jailing editors, publishers and writers who criticized President Adams or who, like British citizen William Cobbett ("Peter Porcupine" of Philadelphia's *Porcupine Gazette*), wrote pro-British, anti-Federalist prose of extraordinary venom. The American press from 1798 to 1801 was most definitely *not* free, and this unhappy, self-evident fact caused considerable soul searching among Federalists who had good cause to wonder whether the present growing tyranny of government to which they were a party was not precisely one of the main reasons they had participated so recently in a war against Great Britain.

With these second thoughts hovering over them, the Alien and Sedition Acts simply expired as the century turned. And, for a time at least, the First

Amendment shone all the more brilliantly for the test it had undergone. Many Federalists had lost their zeal for the Acts when it was apparent that the Republic was, in fact, more secure than they had imagined, that little threat of open hostilities with France or England obtained and, even if it did, advocates for it would not gain wide public or newspaper support. They also appeared to recognize that repression was a double-edged blade: silencing anit-Federalists today might mean (*did* mean in some cases) repression of Federalists tomorrow.

Calculating the dangers on all sides, most responsible public opinion eventually came to agree with Jefferson for non-partisan reasons that a free press was more important to a free people than a strong government or, if the choice had to be made, possibly than any government at all. But the question of whether the First Amendment meant what it said under *all* conditions had yet to be tested. When more difficult and realistic issues later arose, the answer (up to the present moment) was to be a qualified, hesitant *"No."*

The Press in the New Nation

The election of 1800 saw the Republicans victorious. With Jefferson as President, the spirit of freedom had a strong ally. During the first two decades of the century, then, the American press had an opportunity to use its constitutional advantages during the first burst of growth by the young nation. In many ways, the foundations of modern journalism were invented during this period, both for newspapers and magazines.

American editors had a notable model to follow in the birth of *The Times* of London in 1788 and *The Observer,* both English newspapers of quality in typographical layout style and news coverage. True, Jefferson as President—and later in retirement—had his second thoughts about absolute press liberty, his commitment to freedom clearly counter-balanced by what all presidents have since discovered in the U.S.A.—that they and their office frequently receive unfair and antagonistic criticism at the hands of editors and reporters who are not held accountable for most of what they write and print.

In the first two or so decades of the century, the number of newspapers in the United States increased many times. Dailies are difficult to sever in the record from weeklies, but about 200 newspapers of either kind were being printed in 1800; by 1810, there were nearly 400; by 1828, the year Jackson was elected President, the number rose to 900; by 1833, about 1200 papers were printed in the country, only about 500 less than the number published today. While the hand-operated printing press was a fairly complicated instrument, it was also reasonably portable and efficient and could operate almost anywhere. Small towns and villages often boasted their own newspapers, if they could afford them. And many could.

Most newspapers were, by now, almost entirely political journals, and their individual histories are closely entwined with politics. At the turn of the century, for instance, Harry Croswell, publisher of *The Wasp* in Hudson, New

York published a libel of Jefferson. In his arguments for a retrial of Croswell, none other than Alexander Hamilton, in 1804, delivered a brilliant defense of press liberty. Croswell did not get away with his lies, but Hamilton, in a personal blast at his arch-enemy Jefferson, established (or re-established) a number of important legal principles regarding American libel laws and affirmed Croswell's right to a trial that would determine whether he had told the truth or not.

The problem in this instance was that Croswell had lied. But the principle that neither the high, mighty or (even) the virtuous were immune from responsible criticism in print was the real point at issue. When Jefferson was the victim of such an attack, Hamilton was only too ready to defend the rights given newspapers by the Constitution of the United States to defame his enemy. In a way, the trial merely re-affirmed the substance of the Zenger case, this time in reference to a law of the Republic as written now in the First Amendment.

Other Publications

The story of the American press during the early years of the new Republic is not told entirely by or in newspapers. Technology, particularly the iron press that replaced the wooden one about 1800, made printing easier and more uniform, if not faster than it had been. And the literary appetite for all forms of print was rapidly growing in every western nation, particularly in the United States. Despite the growth of a good-sized publishing industry, only slightly more than one-third of the books sold in America were printed there. The rest were imported, mostly from England. Between 1810 and 1825 the number of American publishers increased 300 per cent—and the number of titles of volumes of American origin in circulation by that time was formidable. An exact count is difficult, but the number of newspapers, magazines *and* books of American origin in print well exceeded 50,000 discrete titles.

To a great degree, publishers in the U.S.A. imitated British publishers like John Bell who published more than 100 volumes of collected English poetry before 1800. In the early part of the century, American books, like their British counterparts, were expensive. Large collections were reserved for the aristocracy. It is significant that Thomas Jefferson's own magnificent collection of volumes, covering nearly all extant subjects, was purchased in 1815 by the government itself to form the nucleus of the Library of Congress, a government agency that continues to the present day.

These years also saw the birth of many publishing houses, the names of which still appear on new books; J. B. Lippincott founded his printing firm in 1792; John Wiley and Sons traces its history to 1807; and the Harper Brothers (now Harper and Row)—over the years, a publisher of many types of periodicals and books—began operating in 1817. It was, incidentally, a not uncommon practice for American publishers to plagiarize (or ''reprint'') British volumes almost as soon as the ships carrying them docked in the United States. The original authors and publishers received no royalties from them, a somewhat unethical matter in its own day but hardly an illegal one, because international copyright laws did not then exist. A certain free and easy attitude towards the work of American authors also obtained among printers and publishers. It was usually understood that, once an author or playwright had been paid for his work, he did not possess a claim to any profits subsequently derived from it. Much the same principle applied to books and magazines: that having purchased a single copy, one had also purchased the right to republish it, if he desired. The idea of the copyright protection of printed material goes back in American law to 1790, but it took some years for these laws to be gathered and implemented and enforced by Congressional action.

Readership

The American press, including weekly and monthly magazines, grew substantially in the early nineteenth century. The country's output, by the middle 1820's, outstripped in circulation that of Great Britain, and American newspaper readership was larger than any country's in the world. But both the circulation of printed materials and the ability to read them were circumscribed by two factors. First, subscriptions to newspapers or magazines might cost from $5 to $10 a year—more if bought individually. Given the economy of the period, keeping oneself well read either required a fat pocketbook or a good deal of ingenuity. Second, until the age of Jackson, reading skills were not a mass phenomenon. Among those who *did* read, newspapers were likely to be among the most common printed materials available, second only to the Bible. The first of these factors was shortly to be affected by technological change, of which more later in this chapter. The second was rapidly responding to a slow social change that was gaining impetus during the first quarter of the nineteenth century.

On one hand, our Constitution makes no reference to the *need* for education by the electorate. But men like Jefferson and others recognized that schooling—at least literacy—was a necessity in order to justify the basic assumptions of representative government. Not only must a citizen be able to think for himself, his thoughts must be fired by education and the ability to grapple with the major issues of his time. More and more people from the middle (and even lower) classes were joining the literate elite in this democratic objective as the years passed. Fifty colleges dotted the various states in the first quarter of the nineteenth century, and encouraged by the Supreme Court's prohibitions against state acquisition of existing private universities, a good number of private elementary or "grammar" schools were to be found in the major cities of the nation. Some, like the still-functioning Boston Latin School and New York's Columbia Grammar (now "Preparatory") School, provided early education for numerous middle class youngsters before the notion of "free public education" had spread across the new nation.

On the other hand, the United States was beginning to develop its own scholarly traditions, manifest mostly in literary publications and books. As it grew, it also provided enormous impetus for citizens who wanted to read American writers speaking of their own nation in terms the readers understood. Here we discover the America of Washington Irving, playwright and story-teller; the frontier adventures of James Fenimore Cooper; and the start of a tradition that was to flower in the writings of Nathaniel Hawthorne, William Cullen Bryant and eventually Ralph Waldo Emerson. As these and other writers were to be honored in their native land, Europeans would eventually appreciate them as well.

The growth of an American theatre also meant the development of American writers. American poets and playwrights soon found themselves figures of celebrity, their words and works achieving prestige similar to political and commercial discourse in newspapers and magazines, as well as occupying honored places heretofore given only to European writers.

The Spread of Printing

More readers naturally meant more publications, the bulk of them catering to populations in the commercial and urban centers of the East. But many also moved west with the opening of the frontier and the development of new technologies. In 1800, *daily* papers thrived only in big—or relatively big—cities. Six were being printed in Philadelphia, five in New York, three in Baltimore and two in Charleston. Boston apparently depended upon the gossip in coffee houses, popular at the time, as well as weekly and semi-weekly journals and newspapers sent by mail to the city. As people moved west by land or along the waterways, so did the journeyman printer and his portable printing press: into Kentucky, Ohio, Indiana, Michigan. New states were added to the Union. Schoolhouses and even universities followed the printer's path with remarkable rapidity, creating new readers wherever frontier settlements sprang up.

The rapid and dramatic growth of the American West fired the imagination of the new nation. One of the causes of the War of 1812, and a number of its battles, centered on the protection of the frontier territories. The American general who was responsible for the United States' only notable victory during the conflict, the Battle of New Orleans (fought two weeks after the war was officially over), was eventually to sweep into the White House. He was a symbol of the new frontier spirit and energy, followed closely by his ghost-writer Amos Kendall, one-time editor of the *Argus of Western America,* published in Frankfort, Kentucky. Jackson's very person was symbolic of a new spirit of "grassroots democracy" that was to flavor so distinctively American life and history for the next half century, as well as its printed media of communication.

The Alien and Sedition Acts had indeed died. But anti-American sentiment was still feared by many and expressed itself in numerous ways during the War of 1812. The anti-war newspaper, the *Federal Republican* of Baltimore, was physically attacked and its printing plant wrecked, the editor sent into hiding. Most of those who opposed the war were Federalists. Opposition to them was demonstrated in a more personal way and more directly, for the most part, than mob action by means of such civilized devices as printed protests and editorials against President Madison. During the entire period, however, the American press remained markedly independent and free, possibly more open and critical of the current administration than during any wartime period up to the 1960's.

During these years, also, newspapers like Samuel Harrison Smith's *The National Intelligencer* began to work out methods for reporting and covering the activities of the legislative branch of government, in the absence of a formal Congressional Record, which was not actually begun until 1839. In fact, the *Intelligencer* served the press of the nation as the source of much of the news that came from Washington, the new capital, and from the Houses of Congress. It served as a semi-official publication of record, frequently printing verbatim quotes of debates and speeches, transcribed in the recently invented method of shorthand writing.

In addition, the years before 1820 saw the establishment and growth of a number of significant magazines that were to serve as prototypes for many others that followed: Robert Aitken's *Pennsylvania Magazine, The Farmers Weekly Museum* (which attempted to exploit a whole new class of readers in urban America); the *American Museum,* that was to become the forerunner of the later serious general magazine, giving full and extended coverage to important issues as well as suitable illustrations; the anti-British *North American Review,* a scholarly journal eventually associated with Harvard University; as well as Hezekiah Niles' modestly titled *Niles' Weekly Register* of Baltimore, which set the pattern for later, more or less objective news-magazines that covered controversial issues by printing a number of arguments germane to all sides of various issues.

Print Technology

In the first half of the nineteenth century, however, technological progress of the press may well be more noteworthy than these literary or journalistic developments. Instrumentation was developed during this period that permits us at last to fairly use the word "mass" as an adjective to describe print communication (without qualifying what we mean) for the first time in history. These developments did not emerge all at once, nor did they find their ways into printing plants on a single day or in a single year. But they were, after 1814 in England and the early 1830's in the U.S.A., to influence critically both the nature of printed materials, particularly newspapers, and the audiences to which they might profitably be spread.

In all sorts of publishing ventures, various jobs once accomplished by hand were slowly ceded to the machine. Book binding in cheap cloth, rather than fine leather, was one. The notion of covering a bed of type with plaster or a soft metal to make a matrix—or number of matrices—of the set type was an old one. The idea was to use this inverse impression to make as many *new* type beds as needed from *one* hand-set page. Lord Stanhope, in 1805, perfected a process of "plaster stereotyping," as the invention was called, for England's Clarendon Press. It was not until 25 years later, however, that printers were to discover that simple *papier maché* could make better impressions than plaster or molten metal for casting new beds of type, and accomplish the job more easily. It took still another 25 years for inventors to devise a simple method of *bending* the paper stereotypes in order to cast a circular model of the type-face, mount it on a wheel and, in effect, substitute a fast rotary printing surface for the much slower flat bed. The rotary press was to become an eminently practical technological development that mid-nineteenth century printers thought was entirely new. In fact, it had been proposed by Leonardo da Vinci nearly 300 years before stereotyping began in England, but the secret lay locked in Leonardo's unpublished, unread notebooks.

During this period of innovation, as we have noted, iron replaced wood as the material of which printing presses were built, and the metal's stability allowed the lever principle to be applied to the actual process of stamping paper with ink. Richard Hoe and Company was the foremost manufacturer of presses in the United States; and a lever operated hand press was constructed by one Peter Smith in 1822. In 1827, Samuel Rust invented the Washington Hand Press, an ingenious gadget and sturdy instrument that provided adequate service, with some modifications, for printing certain materials fairly rapidly for more than a century. It operated at about the rate of 250 impressions per hour.

The true father of the *mass* communications revolution is a little known German printer named Friedrich Koenig (or König) who was born in 1774 and died in 1833. He was co-founder of the firm of Koenig and Baur, manufacturers of printing presses. As early as 1803, it had occurred to Koenig—and probably to others elsewhere as well—that it might be possible somehow to take the essential instrument of the Industrial Revolution, the steam engine, and mate it with the iron printing press. Perfecting the idea, however, took many years. But apparently Koenig and Baur produced the first steam-operated printing press in 1811. Three years later the *London Times* installed one of these instruments in its offices. It was capable of printing an astounding 1,100 single-sided sheets in one hour, the inking accomplished by the same two cylinders that pressed the paper against the type. By 1818, Koenig and Baur had so redesigned the machine that it was able to print both sides of a sheet of paper more or less simultaneously, and production speed was increased apace.

Koenig's invention seemed to spread—and be copied—rapidly in Europe. It was not immediately exported to and used in the United States for the best of reasons: it probably was not needed. Three-hundred impressions per hour from the highly reliable lever and hand presses, operated by a slave or apprentice, was simply fast enough to produce the requisite number of the kinds of American newspapers, magazines and books we have been discussing in this chapter. Labor was cheap, and America industrialized her handcraft trades at her own rate through the first part of the nineteenth century.

Koenig and the *London Times* notwithstanding, the Americans were apparently independently bent on inventing their *own* steam press. To this end, Daniel Treadwell invented his own version in 1822, and, in the same city of Boston where Treadwell worked, Isaac Adams perfected *his* own successful steam press in 1830. Meanwhile, in England, one David Napier in the same year modified Koenig's original invention in such a way that its printing speed was tripled. In the same year, also, Hoe and Company in America began manufacturing their own version of Napier's instrument, a press capable of producing 4,000 sheets per hour, printed on both sides of the page. (Hoe also pioneered the rotary press, mentioned above, in 1844, upon which the type itself was mounted on a rolling cylinder. In 1849, Hoe developed a rotary press that finally employed stereotyped castings on the cylinder. These instruments were able to print upwards of *8,000 pages per hour.*)

Feeding and using the new printing techniques required other inventions that followed closely: such innovations as the mass production of paper, particularly newsprint, and the development of new types of inks, and clever ways to speed up the setting of type—still accomplished entirely by hand. Novel methods of newspaper and magazine distribution naturally followed new methods of production. Various developments in transportation systems during the nineteenth century were accordingly rapidly drawn into the communications revolution.

Technological change appears to occur in spurts. For instance, Gutenberg's old printing press had satisfied the needs of Western society for hundreds of years. As that society changed, so did his invention to the degree that he would hardly have recognized it by 1830—a change that occurred within a period of roughly 25 years. Upon second thought, Koenig was hardly a technological genius like Gutenberg, nor was he similar to others we shall meet in the pages to come, whose gifts led them to create novelties undreamed of by societies in their time. The steam press was a triumphant combination of *well known* techniques that had already been, for the most part, perfected. This explains why the instrument was apparently invented in a number of places at about the same time, although Koenig beat his competitors in the game by producing the first instrument of its kind that really worked.

At any rate, the world seemed to be waiting for his invention, or, at least, the new masses of literate citizens in the United States and Europe were. Ever since the invention and wide use of the steam printing press, the West has not been quite the same, both for better *and* for worse, as we shall observe in the unfolding story of mass communications that is not only told in the wake of this puffing, noisy, dirty but incredibly efficient machine. The steam press was tailor-made for the kind of new popular democratic government being invented and perfected in the United States, and it was also to influence, in one way or another, and for similar reasons, almost every other nation on the globe during the next century and a half.

3

Populists and Pennies

IN OUR OWN ERA when instruments of modern communications—radio, television, books, magazines, movies and newspapers—are so pressing and present in daily life, it may be difficult for us to conceive of the idea of *mass* media (or a *mass* medium) as a philosophic idea. But philosophic it is, and its first apostle was a man who discovered its main principle for entirely practical, non-philosophical reasons. He probably had no inkling of the way in which his thinking would change the intellectual climate of the entire world in one century.

Benjamin H. Day's bones are probably revolving in his grave at the suggestion that he was, in any sense, a philosopher, but if ideas that change the thinking of millions are the fuel of philosophy, Day qualifies for a place among the community of history's great thinkers. Of course, Day's contribution to culture—the *mass* circulating instrument of communication, available to the common man, talking his language and satisfying his needs at a price he could afford—was not only an idea but a pragmatic result of times and circumstances as well.

Day's "Penny" Paper

The time was the 1830s, a period in the history of the United States when notions of popular democracy and the participation of the so-called "common man" in all manner of public affairs were riding high. Jacksonian populist democracy and the frontier spirit had wrought America's second political revolution. Thus began a period of widening political and social participation among the masses rather than the elite governing and decision-making classes. Immigration, too, was rapidly expanding the American middle class. So was increasing industrialization, prosperity and the new nation's genius for business, meaning the production and spread of wealth. Cities were growing more populous, literacy rates were rising, and coins were jingling in peoples' pockets.

Day, of course, did not create his idea out of thin air. Like others, he noted the absence of a "popular" newspaper in the big cities of the United States. He was perfectly aware, good businessman that he was, that the new steam presses were able to mass produce many copies of a single issue of a newspaper fast, thereby cutting the cost per copy to the degree that a paper could be sold cheaply, particularly if large readerships attracted many and/or affluent advertisers. A cheap newspaper for the common man was not only a good idea, it was a money making one! *But* obviously, there must be more to the trick than simply reproducing multiple copies of the same kind of newspaper that had served a wealthier literary elite. Day's problem, then, was the same one that has faced all good commercial ideas before and since: exactly how to go about putting it into action.

Others also tried. In London, the *Times* was employing new printing technologies to good advantage. But newspaper prices remained fairly high, and the appeal of the British press remained directed towards the well-to-do, even as the *Time's* readership rose from 5,000 in 1815 to 50,000 in 1850. The *London Morning Herald* attempted to bolster its readership by printing lively reports of daily activity at the Bow Street court, but, taken alone, police reporting seemed to have only limited appeal.

American newspapers were deeply immersed in party politics, and numerous attempts were made, some successful, to embroil them also in political party games. President Jackson was said to have had some 60 journalists on the federal payrolls during his administration, including Amos Kendall, Jackson's alter-ego, then of the *Washington Globe,* which, along with the *United States Telegraph,* were sounding-boards for "Old Hickory."

In their time, these were important newspapers, but only for the minority of people actually involved with the federal government and the games politicians play. Cheaper newspapers, like the *Boston Transcript* and others, some journals in Philadelphia and Horace Greeley's first newspaper, the *New York Morning Post,* all attempted to devise the right combination of ingredients that would produce a "popular" newspaper in the fullest sense of the word. *All* failed in this objective.

Ben Day had the advantage of learning from all of these mistakes. By the time he launched the first successful "penny" newspaper on September 3, 1833 (the birthday, I suppose, of the *mass* communications revolution), he was already a seasoned journalist at the age of 22. Day had moved to New York in 1831, having learned the newsman's craft in Massachusetts, where he had been an apprentice on the *Springfield Republican.* In the big city, he ran a printing shop that fell financial victim to the yellow fever plague which emptied the city in 1832. Apparently broke but with good credit, and in spite of warnings from old-time journalists that he was certain to fail, Day founded the *Sun,* with an American eagle on its masthead and, most important, the words "Price: one penny" on its dateline. Four pages in length, it was to open a whole new world of possibilities for the information industries that followed it!

After six months, the circulation of the *Sun* was double that of its closest rival, its circulation having risen from 2,000 after two months to 5,000 in four months to about 8,000 in six months. It was to reach about 30,000 in 1837, more than the combined circulation of all New York newspapers four years before! A strong factor in this phenomenal success was naturally its inexpensive unit price, about $3 a year—pay as you go for most at the rate of six cents a week. Most other newspapers of substance in the country were sold by subscription, $6 to $10, payable in full in advance. Both the price and manner of payment were attractive to workingmen, small businessmen and school teachers. The steam press was technically competent to meet their demand. And so was the army of newsboys who sold the *Sun.*

The Mass Formula

Price and technology were not only responsible for the notable success of the *Sun.* With a new readership, Day recognized that the interests of his customers would be considerably different from those to whom newspapers had previously been directed. At the end of its first week, Day hired George Wisner, a man familiar with British attempts at police-station reporting and the already harshly criticized coverage of crime presently printed in papers like New York's *Enquirer* and *Courier.* Day gave Wisner a fee hand to exploit whatever sensational news he could find at police stations and in courtrooms. Wisner was a master at the art of covering the seamier side of life in the big city, to this day the most attractive staple of large mass circulating newspapers in the U.S.A. Stories about drunks, toughs and rascals were Wisner's specialty for the first two years of the *Sun*'s life, after which he quarreled with Day and left the paper. But Day, and many another reporter to follow, had learned the lessons Wisner taught.

Although crime reporting was the *Sun*'s forte, it also differed from the other newspapers in other ways. Short feature stories and items bordering on fiction were given new prominence in a daily paper. *Some* of it *was* fiction. Wisner's successor, the well-known journalist at the time, Richard Adams Locke, even concocted a story, printed in 1835, about the discovery of life on the moon: plants, animals and even a population of bat-like men. Other papers copied the story, and the "moon hoax" is today remembered as one of many in a historic series of egregious journalistic public confidence schemes, differing from most others in that it was motivated by mischief—and possibly a desire to sell newspapers. However, the *Sun*'s readers seemed to enjoy the canard, and circulation continued to rise. Other New York newspapers took Day to task for his (or Locke's) joke, probably all the more angry that the *Sun*'s following did not desert the paper to their camps as a result.

As coverage of popular news expanded, and the breadth of the *Sun*'s concern with human interest increased, so did its coverage of political matters decrease, a new but soon to be general trend in much of the American press. In its way, this also reflected the personal orientation of the *Sun*'s readers: less interested in the power struggles of the high and mighty than in the doings of their next door neighbors and gossip current in the community that closely effected their daily lives. A tension therefore developed in the first half of the nineteenth century between serious news coverage (that was important to the mass audience despite their indifference to it) and the mass appetite for trivia (that amused or excited it). This antagonism followed the history of all the mass media, including print, to the present day, a tension that has over the years been resolved by tradition, treaty and sometimes law.

Ben Day, like the imitators who followed him, was acutely sensitive to what the public *wanted*. And he gave it to them. He also knew what they *needed:* to be alert and sentient citizens, and he gave such news to them—in limited quantities and in a way as not to interfere with the *Sun*'s popularity. Mott reports, for instance, that the *Sun* printed President Jackson's message to Congress in 1833 in full. Jackson, however, was a popular hero. By and large, the *Sun* digested and treated lightly what most other papers regarded as the most important news. It was certainly not a ponderous newspaper. The turgid style of writing, large vocabularies and literary flavor of most previous American journals was discarded in favor of a simpler, direct and breezy manner of writing, more suitable to its contents and the reading levels of its subscribers.

Mass Communication

Day combined almost all of the various elements that eventually resulted in the development of what we call today "mass communication": first, mass production of information; second, new methods of mass distribution; third, low costs *per unit* by means of modern technology; fourth, the development of formats for content that have wide appeal to the average man and woman; fifth, formulas for exploiting those formats by speaking to the mass audience in a language it understands and appreciates; and, sixth, a viable financial base, dependent upon large circulation and small profits *per unit,* as well as auxiliary profits from advertising, in the case of newspapers, magazines and later radio and television broadcasting.

Ben Day's methods would later be modified and further developed by others, but, in merely four years, he demonstrated that *mass* communication was both feasible and profitable. Others, it turned out, had greater faith in his discoveries than he did. In 1837, frightened by a financial panic and temporary red ink on his balance sheets, Day sold the *Sun*. Other penny papers, mostly his imitators, were also failing financially. Day had also lost a suit for libel, and his mood of despair is understandable, but his panic turned out to be unwise.

Although comfortably off, Day's subsequent attempts at publishing were less than spectacular. He fared better as a patriarch of a notable family than a publisher by the time he died in 1889. One son, Benjamin, Jr., invented the famous Ben Day (spelled today "benday") process—for printing shaded illustrations, the basic concept of which is still used today. His grandson, the writer, Clarence Shepard Day, Jr. (who died in 1935), achieved distinction as the author of a charming book, *Life With Father,* dramatized in turn on stage, film and television, the main character of which, Clarence Sr., was the brother of Benjamin Jr.

The *Sun* itself fell into the hands of Day's son-in-law, Moses Y. Beach, whose own two sons, Moses S. and Alfred E., eventually ran the paper with considerable success, although Alfred E. quit the journal in 1852 to found *The Scientific American*. The *Sun* was once again to rise to its old stature under Charles A. Dana during the Civil War. It continued as an independent New York newspaper until 1950, when it merged with the *World-Telegram* which, in its turn, eventually expired, the word *"Sun"* still aboard its masthead, in 1966.

The New Mass Press

The change wrought by Day was almost immediately felt by most of the American press, or at least that part of it which was published in large cities. It also influenced journalism abroad, particularly in England, where, in 1843, the *News of the World* began imitating the human interest orientation of the *Sun*. And other types of journalists adapted their techniques to the new technologies and social conditions of the times.

A highly popular general monthly magazine, the *Knickerbocker,* began successful publication in 1833. It published the works of America's best writers. In its class as a popular literary journal, it remained almost alone until the founding of Philadelphia's *Graham Magazine* in 1841, with no less a figure than Edgar Allan Poe as its literary editor. The immensely popular Godey's *Lady Book* was begun in the latter city in 1830 and was published until the end of the century. It perished in 1898. Louis A. Godey's *Lady Book,* later called *Godey's Lady Book and Ladies Magazine,* the first of six modifications of its original title, followed guidelines set by the *Sun* in appealing (in a more genteel manner) to little *except* human interest, or, at any rate, concentrating upon sentimental articles and stories that appealed to women of the middle class throughout the United States. Other magazines, like *Peterson's* (founded in 1842) followed the same formulas and attempted to reach the same readership. These magazines, and others we shall discuss subsequently, were all part of an expanding appetite for printed materials during this period.

The Popular Theatre

Nor should we forget entirely the American theatre during these years of revolution in mass communication. As noted above, theatrical coverage was one vital ingredient of the new newspaper, mostly because the drama was an art that was now increasing in popularity with the masses. New York City was the theatrical center of the country during the 1830s, but both professional and amateur theatrical companies were found in small towns. And touring companies took the theatre even to the frontier.

At first, the new nation's playhouses had concentrated upon English dramas and classics of Elizabethan and Restoration fame. Next, American writers like Royall Tyler began, in the eighteenth century, to treat American themes in poetic dramas that imitated Shakesperian language and style. By the 1840's, a popular American drama, geared less for the intelligensia and aristocrat than for the man in the street, was developing. Centering for the most part upon American themes, serious and comic, poetic authors like John Howard Payne, Robert M. Bird, John Augustus Stone and comic writers like James Nelson Barker and Anna Cora Mowatt Richie (and others) had produced a repertoire of American plays that were no worse than those of the British or European theatre of the time, and displayed the virtue, at least, of being popular.

So were the actors who played in them, especially the great Edwin Forrest whose fame precipitated the chauvinistic Astor Place riot of 1849, when William C. Macready, a British actor, dared to woo the loyal Forrest audience by playing *Macbeth* in New York. Other performers had equally ardent followers by the thousands. The theatre, without benefit of steam technology, certainly played a role in the growth of mass communications by providing for the United States a great and widespread medium for mass public satisfaction during the first part of the nineteenth century.

Urban Growth

New York, however, was not unique during this period. It was merely the hub of a new, expanding and vital nation, increasing in population and industrialization in cities and expanding also into the seemingly limitless frontier territories. In the world of literature, the arts, theatre and the press, however, New York had rapidly taken the lead as a city of pace-setters. Although many of America's best writers came from New England, old Boston still cossetted its conservative, Puritan heritage. Philadelphia, the cradle of the Republic, remained a freer, vital city but lacked the fine harbor that brought ships from Europe to New York. Washington was (and is) a place where government is the main business and pleasure of its inhabitants; and Baltimore and Charleston were both thriving communities, dependent in great measure upon southern agriculture. New York, however, became the mecca for cultural life in the nation.

Other cities followed rather than led in the innovations, like the penny press and growth of the publishing industry that developed there.

We remember Ben Day as a remarkable innovator, but his career as a newspaper publisher was remarkably short—although profitable. With cash in his pockets from the sale of the *Sun,* his days of innovation were over. But the idea of the penny press, and the communications and social revolution it was to fuse, were just sparking to life. One did not need to be a genius to see the possibilities that the mass press held out for profit and power, once it was clear that the scheme worked. Advertisers particularly were enthusiastic about reaching new and large publics affluent enough to purchase their goods and services. They, of course, stimulated publication revenues and commerce in general, thereby increasing the number of newspaper readers, a number of whom might, at such a low cost, buy more than one newspaper. Like many of the innovations that were to follow in the world of mass media, the penny press achieved success apparently by lifting itself up by its own bootstraps—that is, creating the very conditions which were responsible for its own success.

What the revolution of the popular press required was an apostle, a person who might exploit its possibilities to the utmost and develop more fully the changes that Day had made in the world of journalism. In years to come, the world of newspapers and magazines found not one but many such apostles, all exploiting different possibilities in different ways.

James Gordon Bennett

Few were as colorful as James Gordon Bennett or as ingenious in exploiting both the press and the public for his own ends. Hardly a modest soul, Bennett at one or another point in his career compared himself to Shakespeare, Milton and Lord Byron. And, in some ways, the comparisons were not so far-fetched.

Bennett was born in Scotland in 1795 and found his way to the U.S.A. via Nova Scotia in 1819. After some experience on a Charleston paper, he became Washington correspondent for the *New York Enquirer* and was involved with the merger of that newspaper with the *Courier* in 1829. Angry and disillusioned when his editor stopped supporting President Jackson, he attempted to start strictly political newspapers in New York and Philadelphia, but the coverage of politics was apparently not his talent. These failures taught him merely how to use politics to sell newspapers, a talent that he was shortly to exploit.

Hoping to join forces with Day on the *Sun,* he was rebuffed by Day. After attempting (but failing) to interest Horace Greeley in the project, he started his own newspaper, the *New York Morning Herald* in 1835. He was forty years old at the time, and legend reports that the *Herald* was begun on a capital investment of $500, all Bennett's. The paper was an open imitation of the *Sun,* but infused with Bennett's personal enthusiasm and flair. In its early days, it had to be, because it was a one-man operation. As a court and police reporter, Bennett excelled, and so did the *Herald*. Vivid writing and sensational news turned the trick, and, by 1836, Bennett could raise his price to two pennies without endangering his rising circulation, explaining to his readers that they were getting *twice* as much in the *Herald* as from any other paper. In terms of color, humor and excitement, they probably were. Despite a fire that destroyed his plant during its first year, the *Herald* grew fast in readership, breadth of content and influence.

Exposés of corruption in government, armchair detective work, an expertly executed financial section and aggressive methods of news coverage were all characteristics of the early *Herald*—or of Bennett—that sold his newspaper. They also, naturally, made enemies as well, both in the journalistic and cultural community of New York City. Occasionally, Bennett would bend to them. Accused of printing blasphemy, he swallowed his agnostic's pride and began reporting church and religious news. Circulation rose even further. With 20,000 readers and $1,000 in profits per week, Bennett could write of his two-year old brainchild in 1836, "With this sum, I shall be enabled to make the *Herald* the best and most profitable paper that ever appeared in this country." And, depending upon one's perspective, his boast was fulfilled.

As his ego inflated, so did Bennett's circulation. In 1840, he announced his own impending marriage in terms that might best be reserved for royalty. "Association, night and day," he wrote, "in sickness and in health, in war and peace, with a woman of this highest order of excellence, must produce some curious results in my heart and feelings, and these results the future will develop in due time in the columns of the *Herald*." In short, Bennett was the first of many publishers of newspapers, magazines and books to follow who not only sold their wares to the public but also sold *themselves*. As the circulation of the *Herald* climbed (reaching 30,000 per day by 1850), so did Bennett's personal wealth, the result in great part of the excellent advertising medium he had created. But much of the *Herald's* profits was invested in the paper: its staff, office building, printing plant and facilities for gathering news and for filling, by mid-century, five of its eight pages with hard-hitting news and editorial matter and three pages with lucrative advertising every day.

Other Imitators

Nor was the *Herald* the only newspaper to follow the path of the *Sun*. William M. Swain and Arunah S. Abell, friends of Ben Day who had declined his offer of partnership in founding the *New York Sun*, jumped on the bandwagon in 1836 with the *Philadelphia Public Ledger*. Abell was also responsible for founding the *Baltimore Sun* in 1837. With an early attempt at syndicated reporting, he sometimes shared news stories with Bennett's *Herald* in New York. Other penny papers, including the *Boston Daily Times*, popped up elsewhere. But the penny press innovation seemed to remain most attractive in its native city.

Cash investments necessary to begin new publishing ventures were not too large in this era. Between 1830 and 1840, accordingly, about 35 different one-penny newspapers appeared in New York City. All but the *Sun* failed. (The *Herald* had technically disqualified itself from competition by doubling its price.) What entrepreneurs were discovering was simply that mass communication was indeed a deep and bountiful well, but it operated within a spectrum that limited possible saturation of the public with its products, first, economically, and second, by the amount of time and attention the public was willing to give to any mass publication. The well, in other words, had a bottom, and the bucket could only be worked at a certain speed.

Horace Greeley

Among the failures of the penny newspapers during this decade was one published by a man who was destined to play a later and singular role in the history of mass communications: Horace Greeley. He was the awkward, homely, prodigious father of today's journalistic idealism who is best remembered by the public for his sage advice to "Go West, young man." Greeley was born in 1811 in New Hampshire, something of a child prodigy, whose printing experience began when he was fifteen years old. Five years later, in 1831, after a series of jobs with various printers in upstate New York, he found himself in the big metropolis of New York with $10 in his pocket and the clothes he was wearing, ready to take on the challenge of newspaper publishing. He was, unfortunately, not ready enough!

Greeley had trouble finding his first job in New York largely because of his strange looks and even stranger homespun, small-town clothing. He finally managed to get some freelance work, a job on the *Evening Post*. Then he printed a weekly newspaper that published, mostly, lottery advertisements. In 1833, Greeley and a partner, Francis Story, joined forces with a dentist named Dr. H. D. Shepard. Shepard claimed to have money and claimed experience in publishing medical journals. Greeley, no doubt thinking much like Ben Day, set about printing a newspaper to be sold on the streets, the partners had hoped, for one cent per copy.

The idea was a good one, naturally. But it did not work for Greeley. First, the paper had to be priced at two cents in order to have a chance to make a profit—which it never did. Second, the newspaper, the *New York Morning Post,* first saw daylight on January 1, 1833, the morning after a long and deep snowfall had covered the city, followed by a frost. Third, Dr. Shepard turned out to be more eccentric and less skilled as an editor than Greeley and Story had expected. It turned out that he was considerably less solvent as well. The *Post* lasted for a little more than two weeks and then folded. Greeley and Story turned to printing lottery tickets until Story's death a few months later.

For the next eight years, Horace Greeley was to continue his efforts to publish and edit a newspaper, one which would deal with politics, his greatest interest that was to color—and finally finish—his career. Greeley's rise to fame now moved rapidly. In 1834, he started the *New Yorker,* a literary journal that was well written and professionally edited. At the same time, his interest in politics led him to writing political articles and editorials for the *Daily Whig.* In a short time, Greeley was running a political newspaper for the Whig Party in Albany, and, during the presidential campaign of 1840, he edited a campaign newspaper for the Whigs called *The Log Cabin.*

By 1841, he was ready to try another penny paper in New Yory City.On April 10, the first issue of the *New York Tribune,* a daily paper, appeared. A short while afterwards the *Weekly Tribune* followed, and, in time, became immensely popular not only in New York but in rural areas and small towns across the nation. Using special subscription inducements and premiums, Greeley built his paper, his weekly and himself into national institutions. He saw to it that his daily paper emerged at exactly the right time of year as well. There were no snowstorms in April, and the Whigs, for whom Greeley had labored hard in Albany, had just won a presidential victory.

The young Greeley had made many of the right friends in political circles, and his paper arrived on the New York scene just at the time when moral yelps were being heard from many sensitive souls about the sensationalism and pandering to public tastes by Bennett in the *Herald.* The more conservative *Tribune* seemed to be the answer to them, and, while its circulation never reached that of the *Herald* or the *Sun* during the period of the penny press, the *Tribune* bespoke the political reformism of the idealistic Horace Greeley and reflected his faith in popular democracy. We shall examine both Greeley and his great antagonist Bennett and their ideas of how to run a newspaper (and a nation) in some detail subsequently.

Progress in Transportation and Technology

We have discussed some of the changes for which the penny press and the beginnings of the communications revolution were responsible during the fervent years between 1830 and 1840. There were many others as well, less the result of the communications revolution alone than the way in which the industrial revolution itself was changing the manner in which men lived, and, possibly more important, the way they *traveled.*

At the beginning of the 1830s, for instance, news took four weeks to get from England to America by clipper sailing ship. By the end of the next decade, steamers had cut the time in half. Enterprising newspaper editors figured out schemes with carrier pigeons dispatched fom the ships to shore to speed the news even faster along its way. Horses were the quickest means of getting news across land, even after the invention of the early locomotive. But eventually the steam engine halted the special express riders who brought news daily between Washington to Boston, Philadelphia and New York.

Of course, the telegraph was faster than any of these devices. But the first working models were not in operation until the middle 1840s, when telegraphy then rapidly expanded across the nation. The first telegraphic dispatch to a newspaper occurred in Baltimore on May 25, 1844, The *Baltimore Patriot* printed the results of a House of Representatives' motion in distant Washington, some 39 miles away. By 1847, however, the nation was literally strung with telegraphic wire from Portland, Maine to St. Louis to Charleston, and on to Chicago and Milwaukee. This meant that nearly every city within the frontier boundaries could now communicate with every other city.

None of these changes were *caused* by the mass communications revolution, but the demand for news from far away places, delivered as fast and accurately as possible, was intimately related to their rapid spread and use.

As long as newspapers in different cities were not competing with one another, there was also no reason why news stories could not be shared, or sent from city to city. We have already seen that a few cooperating papers in the 1830s formed a mini-press service. In 1835, however, Charles Havas founded the European news agency that still bears his name. Havas had purchased the *Correspondence Courier,* a French translating agency, and reorganized it into a bureau which gathered and translated extracts from European journals for French newspapers. Before very long, Havas was in the business of sending carrier pigeons bearing news between London, Brussels and Paris. The first news service was born! The idea was transported to the United States, and, as we shall see, dissatisfaction with the kind of cooperation newsmen were experiencing in the sharing of news between newspapers in America led to the organization of the Associated Press in 1848.

The Changing Newspaper

A careful comparison of the major newspapers in the U.S.A. in 1830 with those in 1840 demonstrates how the communications revolution, in but a few years, influenced the world in which it grew. The country itself had changed as the result of remarkably rapid expansion and growth, not only in technology but in an increasing population and in deepening interest by more and more people in social and political matters. Newspapers in 1830 were more like papers printed a generation before than a decade after that date as far as their content was concerned, although the old formats remained quite similar. By the same yardstick, newspapers in 1840 were more like those to follow them at the end of the next generation than those printed in 1830.

In the first place, we have already seen how mass-produced papers were (and had to be) popularized and simplified to meet the needs of their tens of thousands of readers. Second, newspaper editors discovered that news was, or could be, found almost anywhere—if reporters were sent out to discover it. Up to this time, editors, for the most part, had waited for news to come to them. Now, reporters sent out to cover police beats, legislative bodies and political clubhouses soon discovered that enough news occurred on their rounds to more than fill their daily quotas. Third, speed in transportation gave coverage of distant news a new urgency. The world of the local newspaper spilled far beyond the borders of a local community, especially in the United States to Washington, D.C., a city that literally dripped correspondents for local newspapers by mid-century.

Most important, probably, was the new sense of power that newspapermen were beginning to feel, not as mere passive recorders of events occurring in an outside environment, but active agents capable of influencing that environment for better or worse. Neither Greeley nor Bennett were the first "crusading journalists." Political pamphlets and revolutionary journals were no strangers to American shores as early as 1770. But most editors of this decade some sixty years later were not exponents of militant revolution. They saw themselves in a new role, one that they were to play with increasing vigor during the years to come: that of social reformers and defenders of the rights of common men.

They began to recognize that newspaper editors and reporters not only possessed those rights and privileges granted to them by the United States Constitution, but they also had obligations to their readers as well: the price of these rights and privileges. Thus did they begin to investigate and expose civil and criminal corruption wherever they found it—in politics, in the church, in the financial community or among law enforcement officials. In addition, they began to espouse old-style polemic, partisan, political arguments less and less, and programs of social reform and change more. The black-and-white adversary nature of the old political party press of pre- and postcolonial days was turning now to various shades of gray. Policies and programs were often more important than parties and politicians, particularly insofar as those policies and programs might affect the daily lives of newspaper readers.

It was, these editors and publishers discovered, simply good business to look after the social and financial welfare of their patrons. They came to realize, in fact, that if they, as newspaper editors and publishers, did not, the established politicians—local, state and national—probably would *not* either. To the degree, therefore, that the public began to trust their newspapers more than many of their office holders and seekers, a number of these editors gained considerable power in influencing the policies and platforms of politicians.

While the decade ended seeing newspapers as relatively modest enterprises compared to many other expanding businesses in the new nation, the direction that the industrial side of the American press was to take in the future was clear as well. Newspapers and magazines were soon to become big businesses. Mass circulation became increasingly lucrative, as the costs of building and maintaining a newspaper operation increased. The early pioneers of the penny press might have started their papers on an investment of a few thousand dollars, their own or borrowed. A decade later, such an investment would hardly rent a printing plant for one day's "press run" of a newspaper, or pay the costs of editing and setting in type a good-sized magazine. Large operating costs and large profits went hand in hand. So did ever increasing advertising revenues from American mass industry, which was itself growing by leaps and bounds.

Papers got longer and thicker, and much of the length and thickness resulted from advertising copy, which, in turn, lubricated the wheels of commerce and added to the general prosperity upon which the newspapers ultimately and naturally depended for their own financial viability.

The Role of Telegraphy

We have already mentioned the ways in which developments in transportation and communication affected news gathering, but their relationship to all of commerce and the role journalism played in it is worthy of special emphasis again, especially the one previously mentioned technological device that stands out as the first electrical instrument of telecommunication—that is, point-to-point instantaneous communication over a great distance. The instrument was, of course, the telegraph that was developed and perfected, like most inventions, exactly when it was needed most: during the era of the expanding popular penny press. The contribution of this remarkable gadget was not simply a matter of stringing wires from one place to another. The telegraph also marks the start of the use of the one-time parlor novelty of electricity for a practical purpose—in this case communication, but later including nearly all aspects of human endeavor.

The idea of telegraphy is naturally quite simple. Its prototype was any one of a number of ancient instruments that were, through the eighteenth and into the nineteenth century, perfected to a relatively high degree of sophistication without employing electricity. They functioned optically, of course, and optical telegraphs, like the present day semaphore, displayed—and still maintain—certain advantages over the electrical instruments that followed them. Anything you could *see*—smoke signals or light from a box with shutters—might transmit a message with a comparatively wide variation of jots (or letters) depending upon speed, size, diameter or other cues, including colors, as far as the horizon. The main disadvantage, naturally, of optical telegraphs was the limited distance of their effective operation and atmospheric interference.

During the eighteenth century in Europe, however, systems of optical telegraphs, sending signals from horizon to horizon, connected many of the main cities of the continent. They were also used in the U.S.A., from New York to Philadelphia, for instance, until the 1850s. Versions of optical telegraphy are still employed between ships at sea, and similar optical communication instruments may be found today on our nation's towers and rooftops that provide signals of various kinds to aircraft pilots as back-up devices for their more complicated electronic instrumentation.

That electricity could somehow be employed for telecommunications was obvious to many inventors in the eighteenth century. But it also seemed to present numerous insoluble problems, the main one being the maintenance of a current along a wire or in a liquid and a method of translating electrical impulses into letters of the alphabet. In fact, one of the first practical electrical telegraphs conceived and built by the Ignace Chappe in France in 1816 was able to transmit impulses that printed out letters rather like the now obsolete stock tickers that once consumed "ticker-tape" by the mile. A few years later, a six-wire instrument, employing electrical impulses that used both a code and six needles which pointed to various letters on a dial, was developed by William Cooke and Charles Wheatstone in England and was to provide considerable competition abroad for the American telegraph that later replaced it.

The particular telegraph credited to the American painter, Samuel F. B. Morse (and his partner Alfred Vail), possessed two advantages over its multiple-wire electric predecessors. In the first place, Morse's instrument depended upon electromagnetism for its operation and, second, it eschewed (after various attempts to produce ten different marks on paper) a complex system of signals for simple dots and dashes that could be recorded on a strip of paper and were audible at the same time. In fact, the sounder, or audible aspect of Morse's telegraph, eventually became more important than the embossers and inkers for greater speed in transmission.

Morse's greatest contribution to telegraphy was possibly the development of his famous code, a new language at which operators might become remarkably proficient in "reading" the dots and dashes resulting from the opening and closing of magnetic fields as fast as the human hand could manage. Skilled telegraphers could—and can—handle 25 words a minute—some as many as 35. A single wire was also necessary, and the essential simplicity of the instrument made it a standard, with many modifications, for long distance communications, until it was adapted for use with a typewriter late in the nineteenth century, and until the invention of the wireless shortly thereafter.

The first demonstrations of Morse's remarkable instrument were given in Morristown, New Jersey, at New York University, and in Philadelphia and Washington in 1838. Morse did not receive a government grant for his famous Washington-Baltimore line until 1843, however. A year later the famous words "What hath God wrought?" went clicking along that wire and, in effect, began an age of electric telecommunications that will probably not end while man inhabits the earth. Used first and mostly in conjunction with railroad transportation (the first telegraphers often being station masters), the telegraph eventually developed a life of its own, as it freed itself from the railroad tracks along which its wires were usually strung.

The Role of Correspondents

Of equal importance in the development of this first medium of electric telecommunications was a rising sense of professionalization among journalists concerning the ways in which news was covered. In addition to local reporters who covered "beats," uncovering facts of interest to the public, and special correspondents located in places like Washington where news was in the air, the concept of "breaking news"—that is, a story which might originate anywhere and require rapid reporting—was evolving. An earthquake or discovery of gold was indeed breaking news. But how could it be reported in a distant newspaper in less than, say, a month, if reporters were not on the spot to cover the event, and if methods to communicate their news to newspapers were not available to them? The first special techniques for the covering of breaking news with rapidity and conciseness evolved, naturally enough, from environments where news stories were certain to break: the battle fields.

George W. Kendall, a veteran Washington reporter and veteran of Greeley's *New Yorker* does *not* deserve the distinction of being called America's first eye-witness war correspondent. (Isaiah Thomas holds that honor!) Kendall, however, was co-founder of the *New Orleans Picayune* in 1837. He was something of an adventurous character who had advocated war with Mexico over California territories. At the outbreak of the Mexican War in 1846, he therefore managed to join forces with General Zachary Taylor's army. In this capacity, Kendall became America's first *full-time* war correspondent, covering the Battle of Buena Vista, the collapse of Monterey and Vera Cruz and General Scott's march into Mexico City. Unlike many war correspondents to follow, Kendall was not only an observer of the action but apparently a soldier as well, taking part in the hostilities while reporting on them. Neither was he the only reporter in the field during that particular war, but he was, according to Frank Mott, the first one officially recognized as a "war correspondent," and probably also "the first outstanding regular reporter of military movements and action."

News from reporters like Kendall and from newspapers close to the scenes of action during the Mexican War, like the *New Orleans Picayune,* was communicated as rapidly as possible by whatever means were available to distant papers along a route that covered the nation, to papers like the *Charleston Courier* to the *New York Sun*—or the *Baltimore Sun* to the *Philadelphia Public Ledger* to the *New York Herald.* Copy was sent by train, telegraph, horseback rider or whatever means were available. As far as I can gather, the fastest and most reliable means of carrying news from remote places during the middle 1840s's remained a good rider on horseback. But travel the news did, even permitting the *Baltimore Sun* in April of 1847 to "break" the news to the East that Vera Cruz had fallen, according to some authorities, the first important "scoop" in newspaper history. This story was printed a mere 12 days after the event, having traveled by steamship, pony express and shank's mare. It seems to have been a record for its time!

Possibly the role of the newspaper in engaging the populace in breaking news is best exemplified in an old print reproduced in many history books. The drawing illustrates a group of "city slickers" crowding the front porch of a hotel (in what could have been Baltimore) listening, mouths agape, to one of their number (wearing a beaver hat in shirt sleeves) reading the latest news from Mexico to his astounded audience—all male except a black child standing next to his (or her) father, who is also attending the reader. Costumes and details aside, the drawing is probably both typical and distinctive of its period, not because it shows a group of people interested in events that have occurred at a distance but because they seem so involved in what the reader says and in such a *hurry* to hear the news.

Both the pace and tempo of culture were speeding up, and the newspaper was the first cultural institution in the Western world to respond to this new sense of urgency and engagement. Common men and women everywhere were beginning to feel that the always significant, and sometimes trivial, events happening in remote places were almost invariably more interesting than what was going on at home. No, newspapers were not *causing* this change, although to some observers they may have seemed to be doing just that. They were responding rather to a vibrant period of rapid conquest, industrial expansion, broadening democracy and continued inventiveness. The revolution in mass communications through which these people were living was a powerful educational instrument that integrated news from everywhere and gave it meaning to their individual lives.

4

An Era
of Giants

NEWSPAPERS WERE TO THE nineteenth century what films, radio and television are to the twentieth: daily mediators of the outside world for the masses—painters of the image of the society in which people believe they live. In their way, and performing a multitude of functions, mass communication by means of print became a necessary adjunct of democracy, along with increased literacy and a public awareness of an expanding culture and the growing political structures of the New World.

All of this meant, of course, that the press of America (and Canada and Western Europe) was becoming increasingly powerful. To the degree that the Bennetts and Greeleys and others could sway the will of the masses, they were also, as we have noted, men of power—political power and economic power— and therefore both loved and hated for the influence they apparently held over the minds of others. Unlike elected representatives, however, their particular referendum was held daily by the public who bought or rejected their newspapers, and, accordingly, bitter rivalries often developed between them.

New York was, of course, not America. As we shall see, great and powerful men ran newspapers in cities like Chicago and Washington. But New York, favored by her location, harbor and tradition was indeed the center of newspaper power in the United States for the greatest part of the nineteenth century. This was largely because the rapidly growing population of this city permitted the rise of mammoth circulations of different newspapers that competed with one another for their shares of the city's affluence and large advertising revenues.

The Success of the *Herald*

We have already met the most flamboyant—and possibly colorful—man of middle eighteenth century American journalism: James Gordon Bennett of the *Herald.* (The *"Morning"* in its title was dropped from its masthead early in its life.) Bennett was, among other things, a profound egotist. The *Herald,* in some respects, served as a reflection of his own colorful character, which, in turn, influenced the most successful of American newspapers of the nineteenth century. Between 1850 and 1860, Bennett had probably brought the circulation of his newspaper to a figure well over 77,000 copies per day, making it the largest circulating daily paper in the United States. The figure is equivocal: we have to take Bennett's word or it. But the immense popularity of the *Herald* is not. It was an instrument of *mass* communication with enormous power, the alter ego of James Gordon Bennett and, in time, that of Bennett's son.

Of what was the Herald's success compounded? It is difficult to say positively—comparing it to other papers of its time. Bennett was a mature journalist before he started the paper. He combined a shrewd business sense (he had been a teacher of economics) with a newsman's nose for the sensational and unusual, as well as an apparently native sense of showmanship. News in the *Herald* was, for the most part, reasonably accurate, and Bennett, as we have seen, spared neither expense nor ingenuity in getting it to the public as quickly as possible. Bennett also hired men of the highest journalistic calibre to edit his paper, professionals, for instance, like Frederic Hudson who stayed with the *Herald* from 1836 to 1866.

The political stance of the *Herald* in no way seemed to relate directly to its popularity, except in its earliest years when it tried to remain apolitical and run a middle road between liberality and conservatism. As the Civil War approached, however, Bennett's sympathies for the South were unmistakable in the *Herald*'s pages, but they did not seem to influence its rising circulation and/or Bennett's growing personal prestige. Respectability finally caught up with Bennett, however. Not only did he live down the sensational nature of his newspaper in its earliest days, but, as the years passed, he modified his position regarding the Southern states, bringing it into line with popular pro-Northern opinion in New York. An antagonist of President Lincoln early in his career, the *Herald* roundly supported the North during the war between the states, although Bennett's admiration for Lincoln was never more than dilatory and unenthusiastic, supportive of anti-Lincoln anti-abolitionists for most of the period. During the Civil War, the *Herald,* however, dispatched 63 correspondents into its battlefields, assuring both timely and accurate coverage for its readers.

Bennett died in 1872. One of his most formidable contributions to American journalism may well have been the start of the dynastic tradition that has kept the ownership and operation of newspapers in the United States frequently within single families, as we shall see. His son, James Gordon Bennett, Jr. was, naturally, *not* a self-made man and devoted less of his time and intelligence to the day-by-day operation of the *Herald* than his father had. He was, however, a man of power by birth, and he knew it.

In some ways, one may even credit the younger Bennett with perfecting the art of *making* news where none exited, and often *big* news at that. For instance, Bennett dispatched a reporter named Henry M. Stanley (born John Rowlands) in 1869 to find a "lost" missionary named Dr. David Livingstone who had seemingly disappeared into the African wilds. Livingstone, unfortunately, had no idea that he was lost and was in fact capable of leaving Africa anytime he wanted, but anxious to continue his explorations and religious duties. Stanley's story of the meeting of the two men was newsworthy, and so were Stanley's subsequent dispatches to the *Herald,* as he personally continued Livingstone's trail-blazing through the dark continent after the latter's death, achieving a place in history not primarily as a reporter for the *Herald* but as an explorer.

Bennett Jr. was far from the dedicated newspaperman his father had been. He piloted the *Herald,* mostly from an absentee domain in Paris, through a series of hoaxes and circulation-gaining "stunts," in the words of Frank Luther Mott. He also founded the Paris edition of the *Herald* that survives to this day as the English language *Paris Herald Tribune.* James Gordon Bennett, Jr. lived and died (in 1918) a rich and powerful man, presiding over his newspapers (both the *Herald* and the *Evening Telegram*) from his self-imposed exile with an iron hand, hiring and firing reporters and editors at will.

Despite the success of his newspapers and the $30 million he supposedly made from them, competition from other empire builders became too great in the latter years of his life, and the *Herald* finally merged with Greeley's *Tribune*—long after Greeley had died, of course. The younger Bennett was as daring as his father, but he was neither as clever nor hard-working. The *Herald* had risen to greatness under Bennett Sr., even though it did not, very often, reflect popular political philosophies of its day. It achieved success by virtue of its excellent news coverage, good, clear writing and experimentation with new printing methods and methods of reproducing illustrations.

The *New York Tribune*

The *Herald's* main competition in New York City was the *Tribune.* And this paper was piloted by a man whose colorful personality was the mirror image of that of James Gordon Bennett Sr.

In his own manner, the *Tribune's* Greeley was also an egotist, but a far less flamboyant one and much more intellectually and academically inclined than Bennett. He was also as poor a businessman as Bennett was a good one. Greeley was fortunate to have a Thomas McElrath at his elbow, not only to keep his eye on the *Tribune's* ledgers but upon the modest earnings Greeley himself took from his newspaper. Two other newspaper giants we shall meet in this chapter, Charles A. Dana and Henry J. Raymond, received early training at the *Tribune* under Greeley, whose perfectionism rubbed off on them both.

Greeley's circulation always trailed behind the *Herald,* although this state of affairs apparently satisfied Greeley most of the time. Rarely did he attempt to pull off the circulation stunts for which Bennett and his son were famous. Nor did he cover even the most sensational news in a particularly sordid manner. In fact, the *Tribune* was not above castigating the *Herald* for its sensationalism and pandering. Throughout his career, Greeley took a public position of moral stature and dignity, although he might occasionally and temporarily compromise with some of these principles in the heat of competition with the *Herald.*

In this respect, Greeley was sometimes accused of being a hypocrite, decrying lurid reports of criminal trials in other papers while printing them himself, condemning the abuses of the very advertisers whose copy his paper carried daily, and inveighing against the corruptions of both theatrical folk and their audiences while publishing advertisements and notices of stage performances. Greeley's personal and professional character was enigmatic and complex. He was apparently able to justify these anachronisms in his own mind and to others. It was, in fact, Greeley himself, rather than the *Tribune,* who eventually developed a weighty reputation for integrity, morality and consistency— one of the first journalists in America after Ben Franklin to be so regarded by countless people.

Horace Greeley is probably also the first American to have achieved public stature as a national figure almost entirely because of a role in the world of mass communications, blazing a trail later filled by colorful figures as different, one from the other, as Bernarr Macfadden from Bennett Cerf. Frank Mott calls Greeley, in his time, "influential"—not necessarily "revolutionary" or "trail-blazing"—but a man whose opinions, public and stated, were both listened to and often acted upon. Mostly, he was a genuinely respected celebrity, not only by other newspapermen and his readers, but by many politicians, academics and other people of "influence" like himself.

Greeley's career is, however, filled with a series of contradictions. In his day, he was considered by many a socialist, although he believed strangely in benevolent capitalism and espoused vigorously the gusto of America's economic expansionism. For most of his life, Greeley supported the Whig party which was, in general, opposed to popular rule, but he also supported all manner of social reforms that would provide the poor and laboring class with education and a greater measure of participation in directing their own destinies. Among the causes he championed were the Utopianism of the American Fourierists (communities like Brook Farm), a high tariff (to protect American labor rather than industry), unionism, women's rights (but not suffrage), the abolition of capital punishment and the total prohibition of alcoholic beverages, gambling and smoking.

As the Civil War loomed, Greeley's *Tribune* reflected the generally accepted liberal northern stance against the instiution of slavery, although his indignation lacked the vigor or power of serious journalistic abolitionists like William Lloyd Garrison. Greeley is best remembered for his advice, "Go west, young man," reflecting his general enthusiasm for the promise of homesteading beyond the frontier, agriculture and the migration of the masses towards the Pacific. Greeley, however, while hardly a "city-slicker" in any way, settled and stayed in New York City and reached, particularly by means of the *Weekly Tribune,* America's rural population from the comfortable urban editorial offices of his newspaper. A writer of considerable power, his actual handwriting was almost illegible (in those days before the invention of the typewriter), and Greeley himself was famous for his personal awkwardness and shyness.

Greeley also had a taste for active politics, but he showed little talent for the game. Nearly all of the presidential candidates supported by the *Tribune*— except Lincoln—were defeated at the polls. Although Greeley himself ran for office a number of times, including a try for the presidency, he was elected to nothing more than one term in Congress. In his early career, he supported New York's Whig political boss, Thurlow Weed (who had given Greeley his first newspaper position) and Governor William H. Seward, later Secretary of State under Lincoln.

In 1854, however, he finally broke with the Whigs to become a Republican, an alliance that continued until Greeley refused to support Lincoln for a second term. Thereafter, he showed inordinate (and un-Northern) sympathy for defeated Confederate President Jefferson Davis after the Civil War. Greeley finally formed his own faction of the Republican party. He ran for President of the United States, and was roundly defeated by ex-General Ulysses S. Grant in 1872. Despite the *Tribune's* popularity in its own native city, Greeley drew most of whatever political support he had from the hinterlands: New England and the mid-west, where he had consistently championed, in the *Weekly Tribune,* the rights of rural Americans to self-determination in the conduct of their own affairs. Paradoxically, he also supported a strong and benevolent federal government for most of his life.

The *Tribune* itself was not a journalistic masterpiece, nor was it responsible for any great or lasting innovations in mass communications. By and large, it was probably more reflective than directive of its readers' opinions and ideas. It also lacked the showmanship and glitter of the *Herald*. Probably its greatest asset—and notable characteristic—was its openness to a wide range of ideas and opinions, whether or not Greeley happened to agree with them. Greeley himself was forever mindful of the spirit of the First Amendment: that the American press was free, not to abuse its license in advocacy and distortion, but to use it to spread all manner of ideas, both popular and unpopular. Greeley's idealism was reflected in his newspaper, where he made good his belief in the essential intelligence and morality of the common man. While it did not achieve an enormous circulation in New York, its $2 a year weekly edition sold briskly in the hinterlands, particularly the mid-west, accounting for a good part of the *Tribune's* influence and reputation.

Greeley—like the *Tribune*—has come down to us over the years as a figure of controversy. Some historians have called him a "safe radical." Others have called him one of the most vigorous exponents of a genuine liberal philosophy in his time. The columns of the *Tribune* were invariably open to the wildest social reformers of the period. Among its writers and reporters was none other than Karl Marx himself, who served for about ten years as the *Tribune*'s London correspondent. Among his 200,000 or so daily or weekly readers, Greeley must certainly have angered many of them with his constant and sometimes inconsistent cries for economic and political reform. But they were also aware that Greeley had "socialized" the *Tribune* itself by distributing his shares in it among the people who wrote and printed the paper, and that he did not depend upon journalistic sensationalism or artifice either for his reputation or readership.

After Greeley's death in 1872, the *Tribune* was never to be the same again, although it maintained modest popularity until its ironic junction with the *Herald* about a generation later. Greeley had not sired a son, nor had he created a formula that could be carried on without him. Whatever the *Tribune* was, it fully reflected the faith and talent of the relatively unschooled New Englander who edited it for 31 years, keeping it, for most of the time, more politically engaged and controversial than any of its competitors in New York.

Raymond and the *Times*

A *Tribune* alumnus who was to create a newspaper—and a journalistic tradition that remains alive to this day—was Henry J. Raymond, a giant of his time despite certain personal and professional shortcomings—among them a character far less colorful and arresting than that of either Bennett or Greeley. Raymond, unlike Greeley, was a college graduate and a scholar, who had actually begun his newspaper career writing for the *Tribune* while attending the University of Vermont. After a stint on the *Tribune* in New York (Raymond did not get along with Greeley), the *Courier* and *Enquirer* and *Harper's New Monthly Magazine,* Raymond and two young associates, George Jones and Edward B. Wesley, raised the approximately $100,000 necessary to start *The New York Times.* Raymond's one-fifth interest in the venture was backed entirely by his editorial ability, not cash. On September 18, 1851 the first issue of the *Times* rolled from the presses. It sold for a penny a copy.

Raymond, like Greeley, also had a yen to jump into the political arena. He was fresh from a two-year term in the New York State Assembly when he started the *Times* with his associates, and, because he was willing to battle his former boss Greeley on the temperance issue, actually achieved a minor political office in the Whig party during its dying days. But, all in all, Raymond was no more adept at practical politics than Greeley, although he tried to be both journalist and politician for most of his career, severely hampering his performance as a great editor. Despite his later personal influence in the Republican party, however, Raymond started the *Times* itself off in a direction that it has (unevenly) followed ever since: that of reporting news as objectively and fairly as possible in order to maintain the record of daily events for historical purposes.

Unlike the sensational *Herald* or the doctrinaire *Tribune,* the *Times* was both "good" and "gray" from its earliest days. Raymond attempted to follow a middle path on hot issues and to report, as accurately as he could, cooler ones. By 1860, Raymond was the *Times'* sole owner and, following the *Tribune,* the *Times* was now among the four leading one-cent (later two-cent) newspapers in New York City. Unlike two of the other three, however, the *Times* did not depend on angles or gimmicks of any sort for its relative success. It was a large, lackluster publication that was edited intelligently, neither sensationally nor eccentrically. Nor was it the personal reflection of anybody's prejudices—including Raymond's. Neither was it a moral tract nor instrument of social reform but simply a newspaper, with an accent on "news," particularly serious items and "events from abroad," as balanced and fair in its coverage as possible and carefully edited. When and if it did advocate a particular position, its tone was gentlemanly, more like the *Times* of London than the *Sun, Herald* or *Tribune* of New York. It began life as a highly respected, moderately well circulating newspaper. Its main fault, if fault it was, was that many readers found it deadly dull, but apparently many read it anyway—a curiosity that has followed the *Times'* destiny from Raymond to the present, and one which none of its editors has felt compelled to do much about, at least in terms of basic journalistic strategy.

Raymond himself served the paper as a foreign correspondent in Italy in 1859. His reports apparently displayed his mettle not only as an editor but reporter as well. During the Civil War, he attempted to cover personally the battle of Bull Run, but was "scooped" by younger reporters after concluding too early that the northern troops had won and therefore required time to rewrite his original story. As a Whig turned Republican, Raymond at first opposed Lincoln in favor of Seward. But once the Civil War began, he supported the President, even chairing the National Republican Committee in 1864 and getting himself successfully elected to Congress at the same time.

During one short lapse of political objectivity while in Washington, Raymond threw the weight of the *Times* in favor of granting constitutional governments to the defeated southern states, an unpopular position among *Times* readers in the North. Having fought for the inclusion of this policy at the National Union Convention in Philadelphia in 1866, he was soon swamped by the "get tough" position of the Copperheads. Both he and the *Times* suffered public opprobrium, the latter losing both advertisers and readers as a result.

Three years later, Raymond was dead at the age of 49. He was a far less spectacular or revolutionary journalist than many of his peers, but he was also a highly respected one, whose newpaper had been, and was to become, a standard of quality by which others might measure their performance as civil instruments of mass communication.

Newspapers After Mid-Century

Other cities, of course, produced fine newspapers of various types before and during the Civil War era, but none of them infuenced American journalism in the years to come the way the giants of New York that we have discussed so far in this chapter did. Bennett, Greeley and Raymond, in fact, cut the general pattern for the three main types of mass newspapers that were to become financially and culturally successful in the century to come: the sensational journal, the crusading periodical, and the civilized document of the news of the day, week or month. Not only were most newspapers to follow these paths, but other instruments of mass communication dealing in current events and issues followed them as well: magazines at first, but later broadcast, film and television news organizations, as well as press and photographic services. The lineage of the giants was to continue long after their careers were over, and it was to extend far beyond New York City and print journalism.

Were this book more comprehensive, we would now follow in detail the careers of Thurlow Weed, best known as a New York State political boss, and his *Albany Evening Journal,* as well as Samuel Bowles II and his son Samuel Bowles III, founders and editors of the *Springfield Republican,* one of the great political newspapers of the period that, like the *Tribune,* published a weekly edition that extended its influence well beyond the borders of the state of Massachusetts. We would also examine a dozen or so other newspapers in the major cities of the nation, as well as some in smaller communities. While the price of starting to publish a large newspaper rose rapidly after the middle of the last century, it was still possible for journeymen printers to begin modest weeklies in frontier towns to serve smaller communities on more or less of a shoestring. The number of newspapers in the United States was, accordingly, rapidly increasing to such a degree that, after the Civil War, it would (in little more than a generation) reach an all-time high that has been slowly decreasing ever since.

Among the most significant newspapers to appear in this age of giants was the *Chicago Daily Tribune* founded originally in 1847 by John L. Scripps, whose great nephew later began a chain of newspapers that still carries his name. The paper floundered until 1855, when Joseph Medill (and some partners he subsequently bought out) took over, establishing another journalistic dynasty that continues to the present both in Chicago, where the *Tribune* still thrives, and much later in New York with the establishment of the astounding *Daily News,* a unique phenomenon of mass journalism, in the twentieth century.

New York, however, remained the focal point of a rapidly expanding American press for three reasons. First, New York newspapers boasted the largest circulations in the country, and, with their weekly editions, their infuence, excellence and superior coverage were well known across the nation. As a result, they were supported by a new breed of *national* (not necessarily New York based) advertisers. Second, the first formal press association, the New York Associated Press of 1860, began to create for itself a near-monopolistic organization for the transmission of news to member newspapers around the nation using the best journalistic talent in the country, much of it based in New York. Third, New York had long been the prime port where major ships from Europe had docked with their cargos—and news.

After the installation of the trans-Atlantic cable, New York was also its main terminus—for a time. Ever-spreading telegraph lines across the country diminished this advantage, of course. But, little by little, New York's influence on American life was nevertheless increasing with each new wave of immigration, as moguls of industry, culture and political power settled there and ran their tributaries of influence south and west to such cities as Washington and Chicago.

New York became the center, not only of the American newspaper world, but also the entire publishing industry as well. Possibly, the founding of *Harper's Monthly* in New York in 1850 was the first clear indication of what was to come. *Harper's* had been a successful book publisher. It subsequently began an enormously successful series of periodical publications, most of them illustrated: first a monthly and then a weekly magazine, the former reaching a circulation of 200,000 by the 1860s. Nor were foreign language newspapers uncommon in big cities, and the bigger the cities, the greater the variety of languages. And special interest newspapers like William Lloyd Garrison's Boston-based *Liberator,* the outspoken abolitionist journal of national reputation, was one of the best and most influential examples of a new kind of newspaper that fit the tempo of big city publishing during the last half of the century.

The War Between the States

The Civil War remains one of the most divisive experiences through which the United States has gone to date. (We received a modern taste of such divisiveness in the last years of the Vietnam conflict, which, in lesser ways, left our nation nearly as psychologically and culturally bewildered and divided as the Civil War. Both events resulted in political traumas in Washington: one, the assassination and near impeachment of a President, and the other, a resignation of a President and Vice President.)

By and large, the Union press naturally supported the war and the northern military effort. It had to, reflecting popular opinion—just as the southern papers backed the Confederacy. If antagonism on the Union side existed, it was directed largely against the person of Abraham Lincoln, whose love-hate relationship with the press barons—men like Bennett and Greeley—oscillated almost weekly, or sometimes daily. The war was not the issue; the proper conduct of it was, along with such other critical matters as slavery, inflation, the draft and the conduct of the Union's generals—as well as the President's own personal behavior and that of his wife and family. Cartoonists and editorialists treated Lincoln much as they have other wartime Presidents since: Wilson, Roosevelt, Johnson and Nixon. (Truman and Eisenhower during the Korean War are, for the most part, America's two exceptions.)

War brings out the best and worst in people. And in the North the emotion-laden conflict of the "war between the states" seemed to bring out both in the press also. James Gordon Bennett was an on-and-off critic of the President. Greeley was equally ambivalent, stubbornly enduring the stoning of the *Tri-*

bune offices when he supported the draft, but advocating an early peace with the South and showing considerable sympathy for Confederate President Jefferson Davis after the South's surrender. By and large, the Union press was, during the conflict, free to publish as it pleased. Incidents like the "Burnside Decrees" of 1864 were rare, when General Ambrose Burnside, a Union officer, took action against the *Chicago Times* for published insults to Lincoln and his policies simply by closing down the newspaper for three days. Lincoln himself suspended Burnside's order.

Possibly the cruelest blows to Lincoln himself were dealt by cartoonists, who could not resist caricaturing the President as everything from an ape to a devil, depending upon the editorial policies at the moment of the newspapers and magazines for which they worked. After the war, and with the assassination of the Great Emancipator, most publications attempted to make amends for their cruelties and printed many of the most moving political cartoons in newspaper history honoring Lincoln. While he was alive, however, Lincoln was subject to enormous editorial censure before, during and after the war, and the new art of political cartooning was directed with all its venom towards his physical awkwardness, habits of dress and grotesque features.

Military Censorship

Two other new journalistic phenomena resulted from the Civil War. Methods of communicating news had developed to such sophistications of accuracy and speed that the hostilities attracted literally an army of reporters representing newspapers in the United States and overseas. War news filled newspapers throughout the country as a result. Because reporters in both the North and South were given more or less free access to command posts and frequently to official communications, it was inevitable that sometimes their stories contained military intelligence of use to the enemy army. As a result, military censorship, particularly of stories sent to newspapers by telegraph, were censored. (Personal messages employing the telegraph were also subject to official scrutiny.)

While a number of agencies monitored dispatches at first in the North, eventually a workable system of censorship to maintain military security was instituted by Secretary of War Edwin M. Stanton in 1862. In time, accreditation of journalists as official "war correspondents" and methods of cooperating with the armed forces were evolved that provided a model for systems of coverage of hostilities by the press in many countries since the Civil War and to the present.

Matthew Brady

Second, pictorial coverage of warfare was not new but had largely been confined, until the American Civil War, to the drawings of artists that could be printed in magazines and newspapers, mostly in the form of wood cuts or engravings. It was impossible to print photographs, especially the early "daguerrotypes" (discussed in Chapter 5) which were printed on metal. Matthew Brady was a master of this primitive form of photography, both on metal and glass, an art he learned from Samuel F. B. Morse with whom he had, in 1839, actually visited the inventor of the process, Louis Daguerre, in France. Following the lead of Roger Fenton, who had photographed hostilities in the Crimea in 1855, Brady brought his own version of the Scottish "wet plate" photographic process, darkrooms and all, directly onto the battlefields of the Civil War to provide posterity with a remarkable record that, for the most part, still survives in the form of roughly 3500 photographs of the actual sights and scenes of the War Between the States.

Before the war, Brady was a well known and wealthy portrait photographer. Exactly why he wanted to record in such detail the battles of the Civil War is unclear. Methods of reproducing his pictures in printed form would not be invented until 1877, and it was some years before this invention was of practical use in journalism. Apparently, the government offered to purchase Brady's daguerrotypes at the war's end, and gave him freedom to travel where he pleased within combat areas. Despite the enormous personal investment he made in the project, Brady became, for years after the war, a victim of bureaucratic red tape. The original offer was forgotten, and Brady was finally paid a fraction of his costs ($25,000) for his enormous collection of original and duplicate photographs. By this time, however, Brady was both broke and broken. He had lost track or forgotten where he had stored most of his photos. Brady finally died in a charity hospital ward in Washington in 1896, a forgotten and abused pioneer of a new type of reporting: photojournalism.

Many, if not most, of the superb photographs credited to Matthew Brady were not, in fact, taken by him, but rather by one of the more than twenty assistants he assigned to cover the Union forces. But Brady himself was present at many notable battles, Bull Run, Antietam and Gettysburg among them. His assistants, particularly Alexander Gardner and Timothy H. O'Sullivan, were actually responsible for many of the "Brady photographs" we treasure today, while Brady himself supervised this remarkable project from his offices in the nation's capital. That he personally photographed Lincoln visiting Union troops and is responsible for the famous photograph of Robert E. Lee after his surrender at Appomatox is certain, but for one man to have been able to produce this prodigious output of pictures with the equipment of the day would have been impossible.

What this giant of pictorial reporting accomplished himself, however, must not be underestimated. Brady functioned during the war much like the editor of a newspaper, covering certain "stories" himself and assigning others to competent assistants. (Not the least of his troubles was the fact that various of his staff quit their posts in the midst of hostilites, including his best assistants, Gardner and O'Sullivan.) Although no system of distribution existed for his work, when Brady's stark and realistic photographs were eventually reproduced and circulated, they changed forever the popular image of warfare on the battlefield and of the people who actually fight there.

Nineteenth century painters like the French artist David, had romanticized war on canvas as a glorious adventure, and even the bitter etchings of the Spanish genius, Goya, had merely caricatured the horrors of war. But Brady's photographs were (and are) neither romantic nor caricatures. They reveal stark reality, silent and mute testimony to the brutality of warfare, shorn of glory and redolent of the filth of real battlefields. Because Brady's cameras could not stop scenes clearly involving motion, panoramas of dead bodies and silent battlefields *after* hostilities permitted his photographers to make time-exposures quite easily. It is these scenes that speak most eloquently about the consequences of war and destruction on the battlefield. Others show us portraits of lined and tired faces of men in combat, almost identical with so many other faces that war photographers have been recording on film since. Brady's multitude of pictures of the Civil War mark, in fact, both the invention of photojournalism and one of its greatest moments.

Charles A. Dana

The outstanding post-Civil War journalist in the United States was a man who had served for 15 years working for Horace Greeley on the *Tribune,* much of the time as managing editor. He was Charles A. Dana. A dispute with Greeley led to a wartime career that eventually employed Dana's talents as an Assistant Secretary of War, followed by a short peacetime stint as editor of a newspaper in Chicago. In 1868, Moses Beach offered to sell New York's *Sun* to Dana—lock, stock and barrel. Dana seized the opportunity by forming a stock company and eliciting the aid of a number of wealthy New York politicians and business leaders to grab the property.

His success was almost instantaneous in terms of circulation. In less than three years, the *Sun's* 43,000 circulation had risen to 102,870 (according to Dana's count), and, by 1876, it reached 131,000 per daily issue, selling at two cents a copy, as opposed to four cents for most other New York dailies at the time.

The secrets of Dana's success were relatively simple. A war-weary public was ready for the same type of simple, occasionally sensationally and generally well written news that had made Bennett's *Herald* such a success in its early days, and which still seemed to attract readers in difficult and complicated times. Many of Dana's writers had a sense of humor, and he encouraged them to use it. His exposés and coverage of the seamier side of life was usually accomplished lightly and in enjoyable, readable fashion. Under Dana's editor, John B. Bogart, reporters learned how to write little human interest features about common men and women containing a pathetic or amusing "twist" but lacking, by older standards, much (or any) hard news value. Bogart is the coiner of the famous chestnut about a man who bites a dog being news. In its trite way, it sums up Dana's philosophy. In serious, journalistic terms a man may *eat* an entire dog, and the event is not necessarily newsworthy. But it *is* interesting, curious and, to some, even attractive. It is certainly extraordinary. Out of such an approach to the events of the day was Ben Day's old *Sun* once again to shine on New York.

Dana wrote and commissioned editorials that were, for their time, equally clever. Politically and socially astute, yes, but short, often amusing and sometimes dealing with nothing more than fads and fancies of the period. Rather than speaking in a polemical voice, they were rapier thrusts, often studded with slogans and catch-phrases like, "Turn the rascals out!"—an epithet directed at Grant's presidential administration. In general, the *Sun* was a conservative paper, although it supported various liberal politicians, including Greeley when he ran for President, largely at Dana's whim, and sometimes echoed the publisher's often jaded youthful liberalism and was reflective of his years with the idealistic Greeley.

Dana likened his newspaper to a photograph that captured and froze the whole world's news in a light and lively way. His metaphor fit. The best newspapermen in New York regarded the *Sun* as the most professional paper in town, because it demanded from them the best writing, best reporting and best style journalists could produce and nothing less. Dana was undoubtedly a sly humorist as well as a shrewd journalist. The *Sun* was a newspaper that centered on *people,* not on issues, campaigns and causes or sensational events. This recipe appeared to work. Even the *Sun's* office cat found his way into the paper's editorials, starting with the day that a dispatch was lost and the cat was blamed—in print. Possibly the *Sun* was sometimes too frivolous, too light and too human, digesting complex political issues into simple slogans. It also followed Dana's personal bent towards conservatism in resisting all manner of social reforms and change, even advocating such wildly imperialistic schemes as the annexation of Canada to the United States. But whatever the *Sun* did, it did with style. In the year of Dana's death, 1897, the most famous editorial in Western newspaper history, an answer to a child named Virginia, whose question, "Is there a Santa Claus?" was printed in the *Sun.*

The *Sun* reached its circulation zenith in 1876 during the Tilden-Hayes election campaign. But sales ebbed during the next two decades in its ongoing competition with the *Herald,* first, and second and later, Joseph Pulitzer's *World.* The latter was, in many ways, a different kind of newspaper from the two others. It combined the novelty and adventurousness of Bennett's *Herald* with the political thrust of the *Tribune* and the humanism of the *Sun.*

Some of America's best newspaper editors and reporters earned their spurs on the *Sun,* because it was Dana's practice to hire the best and the brightest young men he could find and train them in the arts of journalism.

While it was editorially erratic, following Dana's on-and-off-again conservatism, the *Sun* achieved a literary status that made it unique for its time in America.

Other giants in the world of print publications during the latter part of the nineteenth century were not necessarily publishers or editors of daily newspapers. Edwin Lawrence Godkin, for instance, deserves a place in our history as the founder of the *Nation,* one of the first weekly opinion journals to achieve both national circulation and influence.

Edwin Lawrence Godkin

Godkin was a man of wide experience. He was born in Ireland and educated there and in England. He came to America as a young man before the Civil War to write articles on America for a British paper. Changing his plans and deciding to become an attorney, he studied for, and passed, his bar exams. Then he decided to form a corporation to print a weekly magazine along the lines of the old London *Spectator.* The result was the *Nation.* Its circulation was never large, particularly in its earliest days, but some of the best writers of the day were found in its pages, filling them with social commentary, literary criticism and political editorials of power, most of them conservative in flavor.

In 1881, Henry Villard, a railroad millionaire, brought together the successful *Nation* and the not-so-successful *Evening Post* of New York by purchasing them both. The *Post* had had a long, distinguished but somewhat colorless past, beginning in 1801, when it was founded. William Cullen Bryant, best remembered today as a poet and essayist, became its long-time editor in 1829, a job he held until 1870, when he went into semi-retirement to work on a translation of the epics of Homer. Bryant continued to call himself "editor-in-chief" of the *Post,* however, until 1878 when he died. Villard subsequently took over the *Post.* Historians of the press make little of the *Post's* longevity or Bryant's tenure, possibly because the *Post's* competition was so colorful, and the *Post* was so drab. At times, however, the *Post* was the only Democratic newspaper in New York. Bryant himself was a stern moralist and political liberal, as well as an outstanding champion of free speech and an editor of literate meticulousness.

After some slight power skirmishes, Godkin assumed editorial control of the *Post* as editor in 1881, and ran Villard's properties for him. Godkin was a political animal. The *Nation* had been the sounding board for his generally liberal views during the years that he edited it. He disapproved of more things and people than he approved of, and his unflattering "Voter's Dictionary" (published in the *Post*) featured short biographies of political candidates, most of them unflattering, that resulted in a series of libel suits.

By the 1880s, Godkin was New York's most notorious (or famous) editor because of his leadership in a newspaper war against the hold of Tammany Hall's political grafters upon New York's municipal government. As the *Times, Tribune, Herald* and *Sun* began to lose influence in New York, the *Post's* star rose by doing a little of what the other papers were doing and diving deep and full into the political life of the city. The *Nation,* meanwhile, went along its reformist, liberal way in a less strident manner—reaching but a fraction of the readership of the *Post* throughout the entire nation.

Godkin has been called a "mid-Victorian liberal," which means that, for his time, he believed that government had a right to intervene in social affairs to an extensive degree, although he usually drew the line at federal interference with economic matters. An opponent, for the most part, of workingmen's labor unions, he was a coldly intellectual thinker, whose British background was frequently construed as personal and professional snobbishness.

As an editor, it is generally agreed that Godkin handled the *Nation* better than the *Post,* despite the former's small (but influential) circulation. Godkin was less a "newspaperman," in today's construction of the term, than any of the other editorial giants we have met in this chapter, with the possible exception of Bryant. None of the journalistic techniques that, by this time, were necessary for the success of a really great paper—Raymond's accuracy, Bennett's "scoops," Greeley's political style and Dana's literary style—were of major interest to Godkin. Human interest stories meant little to him, and reports of crime, violence and other coverage that the masses were looking for in the daily press, he found distasteful. Retiring from the *Post* in 1899, Godkin died in 1902. It is interesting to note, however, that except for the *Times,* the *Post* is the only New York newspaper once edited by a major figure that survives to this day—and so does the weekly *Nation,* still small but influential.

The Press After the Civil War

Students of this period of American press history sometimes refer to the latter half of the former century as the "age of great editoralists." I prefer the word "giants" for two reasons. Not all of these highly creative men were masters of editorial writing or thinking. Greeley certainly was, and possibly Godkin. The rest, including the poet Bryant, were great editors and, at various times, also publishers who brought out the best, or influenced in specific ways, the output of other reporters and writers. Authors of the great American editorials, with the exception of the Colonial pamphleteers, were (and are) difficult to identify. American editorials are usually anonymous, sometimes written by an editor but more often by a specialist in this kind of writing.

At any rate, the men we have met in this chapter were far more than editorialists. In effect, they originated both forms and substance for all types of mass communication that followed them, first, by *identifying* the particular desires and needs of certain parts of an increasingly literate public and, second, in *exploiting* these needs by giving the public what it seemed to want—or was willing to pay for.

The older aristocratic "class" press directed at special interests, with its high price and small circulations, still existed during this era (as it exists today), but, like the *Nation* then and now, it did not exert a profound influence upon the masses of common men. Nor did the elite press, with certain exceptions, yield profits large enough to generate families of publishers or editors that might be called "dynastic." There has always been room in the Western world for numerous journals that cater to many sorts of special interests. They survive, however, as an auxiliary to the mass press. Time Incorporated, at present, provides a contemporary example. *Time* magazine, *Sports Illustrated* and possibly *People* (and hopefully *Money*) are mass publications. *Fortune* and *Architectural Forum* (also published by Time) are not. In all probability, the latter two could not exist in their present form on their own, that is, without the *Time* dynasty behind them to guarantee their survival.

Thomas Nast

Neither were the giants we have met all men of letters or writers, most notably a man like the ill-fated Matthew Brady. Another, and not dissimilar figure of the period, is the famous cartoonist, Thomas Nast, who is usually given cursory attention in histories of the press and in books on cartoons in America. True, Nast was hardly a journalist in contemporary textbook terms. The editorial views he reflected were largely those of his employers. He was also one of many talented illustrators of his period; some of them were possibly better draftsmen and more clever caricaturists: William Newman, Joseph Keppler and the Gilliam brothers, whose work appeared in such journals as *Puck* (the American version of the venerable British *Punch*) and *Frank Leslie's Illustrated Weekly*. The best cartoonists of the time worked for the weekly magazines during a fertile period from, roughly, 1860 until the end of the century. Most of their drawings were quite detailed and printed from wooden blocks, so, accordingly, none of them could keep up with the breaking news of a daily newspaper. But they did not have to.

Some artists, it is true, specialized in rapidly drawn naturalistic pictures of various sorts that newspapers, magazines and books printed until the halftone process for reproducing photographs was perfected. In time, the art of journalistic illustration became increasingly sophisticated, some of it deadly serious and some of it both serious and comic at the same time. Purely comic drawings, devoid of either news value or editorial statements, however, did not find their way into American newspapers (and most magazines) until *after* the photograph had rendered obsolete the news function of graphic art, both naturalistic and caricature. The editorial or political cartoon remains with us to the present day, while reportorial art is reserved only for occasions, like courtroom trials, from which photographers are legally barred.

Nast's competition was pretty tough. But he is remembered today indeed as a giant of his time, not only for his invention of the Democratic donkey, the Republican elephant and our bearded Santa Claus in ermine and velvet, as well as (and here opinions are divided) old Uncle Sam himself, but also because of the political influence of his work in his own day and the freshness that his drawings still offer the modern viewer.

Nast was born in Germany in 1840 and was brought by immigrant parents to New York at the age of six. Having displayed artistic talent as a youngster, he studied at the National Academy of Design, and, because of his prodigious and meticulous interest in graphic detail, he landed a job on *Leslie's Weekly* as a draftsman at the age of 15. Five years later, Nast traveled to Italy as a serious illustrator-reporter to cover Garibaldi's revolution for American journals and for *The Illustrated London News*. Upon his return, he began an alliance with *Harper's Weekly* that was to last for two decades, during which time he was to do his most outstanding work.

Like *Harper's,* Nast naturally supported the Republicans and Lincoln, for the most part, during the Civil War. He was even called by Lincoln, "our best recruiting sergeant." After the war, he joined other Republicans in portraying President Johnson as a traitor to the northern cause. An admirer of General Grant, he apparently could not bring himself to attack his hero's weak administration and instead turned his attention, like most of New York's journalists, to corrupt politics in New York City, most specifically Democratic politics.

The results were his best known cartoons for *Harper's,* his invention of the Tammany Hall "Tiger" and his merciless savaging of William ("Boss") Tweed, caricatures that are said to have caused the undoing of this powerful, corrupt civic politician by virtue of their vitriol. Nast's imagination was wild and colorful. Boss Tweed might appear as an oriental potentate or as a predatory eagle; the Tammany Tiger might be found in a Roman arena, chewing on the corpse of the body politic (female). The drawings were cruel and incisive. Tweed is supposed to have been toppled by them in a single year. Laughter, Nast knew, was a powerful weapon. And a picture, while not the equal of a thousand (or even 10,000) of the *right* words, might say things in merciless ways that words could not.

Turning his attention to Horace Greeley's abortive candidacy for the presidency, Nast's bile and artifice were now directed at a fellow journalist—and, he thought, a renegade Republican. Greeley was a natural for a cartoonist's pen, and possibly Nast's meanest drawing of him reproduces the masthead of the *Tribune* after the election and shows Greeley being carried out of his office dead, his pot belly and bewhiskered face protruding from a stretcher carried by henchmen. Legend has it that Greeley suffered severely from Nast's satire and that this particular drawing contributed to the stroke that ended his life shortly after it was printed. Possibly so; possibly not. Greeley was not a "Boss" Tweed, by any means. But Nast's pen did not know the difference.

Nast left *Harper's* in 1886 and began contributing to other journals, but less and less frequently as the years passed. He possessed both the talent and temperament for serious painting and is responsible for a number of excellent oils. The best of them reflect the lighter moods of his happier cartoons: portraits of comic actors in costume and similar works. Like Brady, however, Nast's destiny was not a happy one. Nast eventually lost all his savings in the failure of a brokerage house. He became destitute, finding it increasingly difficult to sell his drawings and impossible to make a living as a painter. Shortly after the turn of the century, friends procured for him a meaningless government post as Consul General in Guayaquil, Ecuador, where he died in 1902.

As one looks at Nast's works today, the bitterness and acid quality of most of them have been neutralized by time. What remains is Nast's talent and inventive genius in bringing an art well over a century old—that of political drawing—to a height of excellence in the United States that many believe it has not reached in quite the same way since then.

The Press as An Institution

Journalism during the nineteenth century in America—and in countries across the Atlantic as well—permitted the maverick talents of innovators like Bennett, Brady, Greeley and Nast to flourish. But this fertile period also witnessed an increasing institutionalization and bureaucratization of the press. Newspaper jobs became more and more specialized. Press services were relied upon increasingly to supply news to great numbers of papers, and competing papers themselves became interdependent, employing one another as training grounds for new talent and literally dividing up the mass market between themselves in the major American cities.

The American press, including the magazine and book publishing industry, began to take on all the configurations of big business and to join slowly but certainly the rest of the business community. In the first place, starting and printing a newspaper was no longer a penny-ante business. It was complex and expensive, demanding the specialized talents of many different sorts of people to write, print and distribute the product. Second, the American press—like it or not—was, with the exception of book publishing, becoming increasingly dependent upon advertising for the most important part of its financial revenue: that is, the difference between profit and loss. The kind of advertising that really paid the papers lucratively was no longer the short personal or commercial notice, but the eighth, quarter, half or even full-page illustrated ad, prepared by professionals, a part of the rising advertising agency business, and representing, in one way or another, interests of the growing community of ever-richer American big businessmen.

If one attempts today to predict the future of American journalism at the end of the nineteenth century *solely* by examining these old newspapers, the fate of American newspapers and magazines seems quite clear: a takeover eventually by the big business community. That our American newspapers have, on the contrary, remained relatively free of extraordinary pressures from American business (despite their dependence upon advertising to this day) is one of the major curiosities of American popular culture during the present century. Of course, there are good reasons, but one could not possibly have foreseen them in the late 1800s, because enormous counter-influences upon American life —new social, political, economic and technological forces just around the corner—were themselves impossible to predict. Let us now examine some of them, particularly those which resulted from America's peculiar genius for the perfection of new technologies that changed the lifestyle of a nation and the direction of the nineteenth century revolution of mass communications.

5

New Technologies: Print and Cinema

BECAUSE THE SOCIAL HISTORY with which we have so far been dealing has concerned mostly the spread of printed literature to the masses, the technological instrument upon which we have largely concentrated has been the printing press. True enough, we have also briefly discussed advances in transportation and wire communications because of the influence they played in the development of the mass press. In passing, we have noted men like Matthew Brady and Thomas Nast, both formidable figures by their own rights in the history of pictorial art, but primarily as men whose life's works related to the development of the journalistic traditions of their times.

Brady was a rare bird: a journalist without an outlet. His impulses were those of a reporter, and we shall never know what complex motives led him to engineer the project of producing a record of the Civil War in much the same way reporters had reported wars for a century—but by means of photographs. Possibly, Brady saw himself as a new type of gallery artist whose work would someday hang in museums, visited by people who wanted to experience the harsh realities of the War Between the States. There is little—if any—evidence that he ever tried to use the multitude of photographs he owned for this purpose during his lifetime, however.

Nast, on the other hand, was a journalist with an artist's pen and brush, also quite different from the average editor or reporter of his day and unintentionally closer in technique and spirit to many powerful mass communicators of motion pictures who followed him and blended the narrative and pictorial arts into new communications instruments than to the scribes whose prose was printed adjacent to his cartoons.

Technology and Science

In many places and in many ways, I have repeated Jacques Ellul's observation that changes in technology do not force societies—or individuals—to adopt these novelties. But once technology *has* changed any aspect of culture, there seems to be no turning back to undoing the impression that these new techniques, instruments or inventions have made upon culture. So important do I consider this observation, that I shall probably repeat it periodically until they summon the undertaker. Roughly speaking, the period between the last half of the eighteenth century and the end of World War I was, in my opinion, probably the most fertile time in the West up to the present moment for the introduction to culture of new and fantastic technologies, most of which rapidly followed one another.

One matter should be clear, however: It was *not* an equally vibrant period for the development of *scientific* theories and laws, particularly in the United States. Possibly one reason is that science deals mainly with ideas, and technology deals largely with material objects. The two do not usually exist very well side by side. Interest in one may distract from the other; but, as I say, this is merely a guess.

I grant that a certain few great advances in science were indeed also made during this time—mostly outside the United States—and that some of them also did, after a while, encourage the invention of technological instruments of consequence, some simple and some complex. Possibly, the most important were the theory of evolution, the laws of genetics, theories of electro-magnetism (like Hertzian waves), Einsteinian relativity ideas, Freud's construction of the unconscious, the germ theory, atomic theory, Marxian social economics and other concepts that entered the annals of intellect roughly during this same period, *none* which (with the possible exception of the laws of evolution) were to attract but a fraction of the general public's attention or money that the new, flashy technologies did.

Advances in Printing

Since we have already traced the evolution of printing to the rotary press, let us now look at some of the ways that new technologies of printing began to influence not only journalism but the masses who depended upon print for their images of the world about them. We have seen how the rotary press—and the idea of stereotyping—were feasible technical notions since the invention of the flat steam presses of the early nineteenth century. Demand for newspapers like the *Herald* was so great during the Civil War (135,000 *Heralds* were printed and sold on the weekend after the attack on Fort Sumter) that considerable pressure was put upon manufacturers like R. Hoe continually to improve the cylindrical printing press in order to speed up the process in whatever ways would work efficiently.

William Bullock, between 1863 and 1865, had produced a ''web perfecting'' press in prototype as well as a working model that actually printed on two sides of a piece of paper at the same time, the natural next challenge in the development of the rotary press. By this time, also, newsprint (paper) was produced from wood pulp in large rolls, similar to those in use today. Bullock incorporated into his device a continual feeding process that printed double impressions on an entire roll of paper. Inventive technologist that he was, Bullock also devised an instrument, operated automatically, that then cut the printed pages in precisely the right places (most of the time). After 1870, another instrument actually folded them as well. Bullock's printing presses, produced eventually as standard items by R. Hoe and Company, were capable of producing 12,000 complete newspapers (of about four pages length) in one hour. The potential production capacity of the printing press, therefore, seemed to be—and was—literally endless. Because numerous stereotypes of any page, or set of pages, could be quickly produced, multiple presses might all print identical copies of the same newspaper at the same instant.

As fast as machines could print material that was already set in type, however, certain stumbling blocks to efficiency and speed remained that constituted for editors and publishers an annoying delay in the time required to conceive of an idea (let us say), write it in English, set the copy in type and finally move it on to a rotary press. The first delay, writing the material, was partially solved in newspaper offices by dividing the actual labor of writing among specialists whose talents were speed and accuracy. Certain formats (column headlines, editorials, mastheads, etc.) could be preset, waiting for columns of type to fill in the gaps. Advertisements were simple to set at leisure, and so were certain feature stories. Breaking news was another matter, and division of labor in composition was usually the best answer. This technique was fine for newspapers—and still is—but the periodical press and the book publishing industry still suffer from the tyranny of the inordinate amount of time it takes one person to write printable copy.

As of the moment, no machine has solved this problem. Every writer grapples with it in his own peculiar way, some by dictating, these days, into tape recorders, some by pounding electric typewriters. Some, like me, prefer to write by pencil on lined pads, consigning the script to a typist who copies it. In all cases, corrections must, of course, be made on various drafts, less carefully on newspapers than for periodicals and books, for the most part. If a final and ''perfect'' copy is necessary, it must then be typed again.

Technology has influenced these labors little, and let me add, they entail a long, laborious, tiring and lonely process, unlike the technological time-savers that will eventually transmute an author's words into a newspaper, book or magazine article. Except for the financial rewards, which, considering the time required, are less extravagant than most non-authors believe, I shall never understand why so many people experience the apparently irrational compulsion to write for publication of any sort.

The Linotype

It was obvious for a long time, however, that the one part of the process that *might* be sped up was the actual hand-setting of type. If one has ever watched an old fashioned hand-typesetter at work, he knows that this skill (or art) may be mastered with amazing rapidity and accuracy. The fastest hand-typesetter, however, cannot operate as fast or efficiently as a fairly good typist working at an old fashioned Remington. As early as 1812, William Church in Boston had invented a cumbersome instrument employing a keyboard that automatically released new type fonts into a matrix while old ones were being cast, a step in the direction of speed.

During the next half century, literally hundreds of variations of Church's instrument were constructed. Some of them worked pretty well, filling up parallel channels in a matrix with type and also justifying the proper spaces between letters and words. They were used mostly by publishers of books and similar journals, because they required less skill at typesetting than hand work, and the results were often neater than books set by hand. Because none of these devices could set more than 5,000 pieces of type in an hour (about the same speed as a skilled hand-setter) they were, however, impractical for newspapers. Neatness and ease were not problems for the publishers of mass newspapers. Speed was.

German-born Ottmar Mergenthaler was the technological genius who solved this problem, at least the typesetting part of it. His typesetting and casting instrument, the Linotype, became the standard automatic instrument for the entire printing industry (except commercial printers who used hand-set types for items like billboards and tickets and printers of illustrated materials) until the present day.

The Linotype itself was perfected in the early 1880s, and in 1886 the first one was installed in the newspaper printing plant of the *New York Tribune*. It remained essentially the same instrument throughout its entire career. The Linotype looked like a cross between a dirty typewriter and pipe-organ. It operated by casting fresh full *lines* of type from matrices made up of individual molds of each letter (and spaces) slid into place as the appropriate letter was pressed manually on a keyboard. Full lines of hot lead type, properly notched (to indicate their correct positions) might then be justified quickly with wedges, poorly cast slugs re-made, and full columns of type set out in trays or galleys. A printed proof could then be taken of them manually to check the copy for corrections. The type was finally placed into the page matrix of the newspaper, ready for the production of stereotypes.

The Linotypist at work, in fact, carried out two operations, the latter pretty well automated even in the instrument's earliest days. He was, first, setting up molds of letters, numbers and spaces for each line of type, and, second, casting hot lead reproductions from the mold that subsequently fell into a tray at his side. Once the casting had been done, the individual letter molds would move back to their original position waiting to be used again. And once stereotypes of the pages were made, the type might be broken-up, the lead re-melted and re-used.

The advantage in terms of speed that the Linotype held over previous instruments was not very great. It increased typesetting rates to about 7,000 pieces (or characters) per hour, about 2,000 more than achieved by old fashioned hand-setters. It was, however, rugged, reliable and efficient. Competing machines like the Monotype, invented in 1885, cast single type pieces and eventually was operated by a perforated strip of paper that was easily prepared on a separate keyboard. Another instrument, the Intertype, permitted simple changes of type face, and the "Washington I. Ludlow" cast hand-set type for (mostly) advertisements. Each displayed certain and particular advantages over the simpler Linotype—and each was used for special purposes, along with other printing instruments. But, from 1890 to well beyond the middle of the twentieth century, Mergenthaler's miraculous Linotype was the workhorse of hot type printing, that is, printing which depended upon casting molds in lead. Eventually, rows of Linotypes in newspaper pressrooms and printing plants would permit printers to set mountains of type in a fairly short time.

Print and Pictures

When the problem of typesetting had been more or less solved by the Linotype, printers were free to turn their attention to other matters. Typefaces themselves were cleaned up and made more easily readable than they had been. The old Gothic type used by most of the nineteenth-century papers was slow in changing, but eventually it was redesigned. Headlines began appearing in clearer Italian-style type (like Bodoni), and italics and other distinctive typefaces were used for variety and emphasis. New fast drying inks were also perfected. And by 1896, steam as the energy source for printing opeations began to be replaced by electricity in large cities.

Nothing, of course, had ever prevented newspapers from being printed in color, at first by means of a "fudge box," a little blank space left on the front page of a paper where late hand-set news items might be separately printed in colored ink on a relatively small cylinder, saved for up-to-the-minute news. By the late 1890s, color presses using different colored inks, multiple cylinders and stereotype molds for each color were being used for special occasions. In a few years this method was used to print cartoons or comics, for which the colors might easily be separated, one from the other.

The Halftone and Gravure

Woodcuts that had been used for a long time to print drawings yielded, in the 1870s, to Zincographs, a process by which drawings were etched on zinc with acid. At first zinc etchings took days to produce. But, by 1884, a method had been evolved to prepare them in four hours. Zinc engraving led the way to photoengraving, an invention of Frederick E. Ives of Cornell University, an absent-minded professor who worked from 1876 for a decade in order to perfect this process—for which he forgot to take out a patent! Others accordingly grew rich from his invention: the halftone reproduction of photographs that is still in use today.

Employing Ives' invention on rotary presses, however, presented many problems, especially in the hurry-up world of newspaper publishing. Ives had solved the main problem involved in printing photographs: translating the various tones of gray and subtle variations and shading of line one sees even in primitive tintypes, deguerreotypes and similar early photographs to a metal surface, which, when inked, would reproduce faithfully the blacks, whites and grays of the original pictures.

Ives' solution, as anyone who ever ever examined a newspaper photograph with a magnifying glass knows, was quite simple. Accomplishing it, however, was testimony to his cleverness. The photograph was indeed engraved onto metal. But first it had been broken up into a multitude of dots or points, close together or dense in the dark parts of the picture and more sparse as black turned to gray to light gray. No dots, no image. When the dots were inked, the resulting impression produced a print in which each *single* dot was equally black, but their proximity, one to the other, produced the illusion of smooth tones of gray when observed at an ordinary reading distance, and, as the halftone process was improved, under close scrutiny by the naked eye.

As we have noted, the process worked well enough on a flat-bed printer, but how did one transfer Ives' photoengraved "cuts" to a rotary press and achieve anything but a blur of distorted dots? Novel stereotyping and inking methods perfected by Stephen H. Horgan permitted the *New York Tribune* to print its first halftone in 1897. (As early as 1874, however, the famous "ben-day" process had been employed, chiefly for drawings, to separate an image into distinctive components of light and dark sections and lines that might be mechanically and reliably transferred onto a metal plate and thereafter printed clearly on a flat bed.) Horgan used a galaxy of technological advances in photoengraving to move halftones to cylinders.

Critical to this complex process was the development of halftone *screens,* an early French idea commercially perfected by Max and Louis Levy in Philadelphia in 1890, that actually broke a photograph up into the requisite dots by diffusing its image through thin ruled lines on two glass plates held at right angles to one another. The light emerging through the screens took the form of dots which might be engraved by photosensitive acid onto metal, a process still generally used by photoengravers in preparing cuts for reproduction by the halftone process.

Halftones were not the only method of reproducing photographs in print at the time, nor are they today. One other method, the gravure process, is best known for the way it is easily used (in full pages) on rotary presses; hence, the term "rotogravure" which once described not only the process but special sections of newspapers printed by this method that appeared until about World War II in the U.S.A. (The technique has been memorialized by Irving Berlin's line in his song, "Easter Parade," with the promise to a beautiful girl, "You'll find that you're in the rotogravure.")

Gravure was a German invention of Karl Klietsch who, in 1878, dispensed with the idea of dots and screens entirely and engraved pictures by means of a photosensitive sheet of gelatin that permitted an entire copper plate to be chemically etched in varying degrees, according to the amount of light that passed through the gelatin. The plate might then easily be bent to fit a rotary press.

Because rotogravure was a process that worked best for full pages, it could not compete in flexibility and speed of preparation with the halftone "cut" that might be inserted into a page of type at any place. On the other hand, special sections of newspapers and individual pages of books and magazines took advantage of gravure's capacity for producing subtle reproductions on the printed page of gradations of gray (and later color) in photographs that were lost in the mass of halftone dots.

New Uses for Pictures

Photoengraving, of course, did not supersede or eliminate the reproduction of drawings in newspapers, magazines or books, although it did indeed cut down on their use for many purposes. It served eventually, also, to reproduce in print many types of drawings, paintings and other kinds of art work.

Printed photographs were responsible for the rise of a new form of reporting, one that Matthew Brady had foreseen a generation earlier: that of photojournalism. These techniques contributed to the development of printed photography as a journalistic art, usually for the purpose of illustrating a news column or prose selection, but eventually for telling stories entirely made up of pictures.

In fact, the technology of photography was to become one of two major inventions of the nineteenth century that was to influence critically and broaden the spread of human communications during the last part of the nineteenth and early twentieth century by means, not only of still pictures, but of pictures that moved—first on film, and somewhat later electronically on television screens. (The other invention was a method for the transmission of sounds by radio broadcasting over great distances to large audiences, discussed in the next chapter.) So we have gotten ahead of ourselves in this history, because, at the same time that printers and engravers were patiently learning to reproduce still pictures, other inventors were figuring out ingenious devices to achieve what seemed even less possible—methods for making still photographs appear to *move*.

The History of Photography

The development of photography during the nineteenth century was, of course, the birth of a miracle in its own day. We have covered some of its complex history in the preceding chapter. The story is long and colorful and worthy of the many books devoted to it.

Photography probably had its origins in France in 1826 when the French lithographer, Joseph Nicephore Niépce, evolved a method to make a crude photograph by means of a time exposure lasting four hours of a simple barnyard. Niépce began a partnership with the more famous Louis Jacques-Mandé Daguerre, a talented scene painter, in 1829. It lasted only four years. But in this time Niépce transmitted to Daguerre both the basic theory and techniques he had invented for capturing permanently on a solid plane gradations of light by means of chemicals and employing the "camera obscura" technique by means of which a lens condensed and focused an image upon a flat surface. Modern photography was born as the result. Niépce died in 1833, and, by the end of the decade, so-called "Daguerreotype" photography on copper plates had been perfected.

In England, Thomas Wedgewood (son of Josiah Wedgewood, remembered best today for his ceramic discoveries, but an inventor of ingenuity in other fields as well) failed miserably in the early part of the century to produce photographs of subtlety or permanence, but Wedgewood *did* identify silver nitrate as a photosensitive chemical of extraordinary instability. Daguerre's process depended upon residual silver left upon his copper plates, achieved by means of a complex chemical process of development and fixing.

Another Englishman, William Henry Fox Talbot, apparently unaware of both Wedgewood's discovery and the work of Daguerre and Niépce, began working in 1833 upon a photosensitive paper soaked in salt and silver nitrate that, like the Frenchmen, he placed in a camera obscura to produce actual negatives of photographic images and positive prints that were fixed in what we call today "hypo," originally a chemical called sodium hyposulphite. Reports of Daguerre's copper photographs reached Fox Talbot in 1839, and the publication of the news of the latter's process of producing his "colortypes" (or "Talbotypes") shortly thereafter created a good deal of confusion concerning the issue of who actually invented photography. Advocates of numerous claimants to the honor have since attempted to prove that the techniques of *both* Daguerre and Fox Talbot were anticipated by others. Both probably were, but the issue is insignificant. By 1830, developments in optics and chemistry had arrived at a point where photography was a discovery that was literally waiting for its inventor.

The two processes (English and French) naturally left much to be desired, both in methods of taking and developing photographs and in the quality of the resulting image. No end of other inventors around the world modified and improved the inventions. They are still at work, of course. Distinctive contributions to photographic technology were made by such inventive individuals as F. Scott Archer who, in 1851, invented the wet-plate process, by which a nitrocellulose collodion solution coated a piece of flat glass and held in place the various photosensitive chemicals needed to take a picture. This process was used for more than a quarter of a century, despite the fact that the plates had to be prepared, exposed and developed in a matter of minutes, no matter where or when the picture was taken.

Other inventive minds worked out dry-plate methods between the 1870's and the 1890s. In 1887, Hannibal Goodwin (see below) thought of the idea of using transparent celluloid as the (now) "film" medium, creating a bonanza for George Eastman's American Celluloid Company. The result was the eventual invention of the Kodak box camera in 1888, first with its negative paper that was replaced by celluloid film in a year or two. The birth of the Kodak *roll* celluloid film camera in 1891 turned photography into a mass pastime within ten years, although many professional photographers for many years to come kept on using glass and celluloid plates because of their stability and sensitivity.

Capturing color on film had been attempted in France as early as 1848, and we have records of successful color photography during this period. We do not have the photographs, because the colors (like most dyes) faded rapidly.

Further experiments in that country led to the invention of methods of "subtractive synthesis": that is, superimposing separate images on different surfaces of each primary color onto one photograph. By 1912, attempts were being made with moderate success to use a single sensitive silver surface to capture individual colors. In the world of still photography, color was, at first, usually added to photographs by hand, often quite effectively. After World War I, various new methods of printing such hand colored photographs by means of halftone separations (different dots for different colors) and gravure methods (using different plates) were not uncommon, although they were both painstaking and expensive. It was not until the middle 1930s, however, that film manufacturers, most notably Kodak, worked out methods of coating film with three layers of color sensitive emulsions that might produce both negative and positive prints on one surface instead of three, creating a revolution both in color photography and, later, in methods of filming and processing color motion pictures.

Photography and Culture

The technology of still photography was a fascinating and fertile one that affected many different aspects of culture, adding, as any new technology usually does, new dimensions to old ones, rather than eliminating them. Photography's effect upon the press has already been noted. People did not stop *reading* newspapers, they merely expected what they read to be augmented with photographs, and, sometimes, as in the case of the pictorial newspaper or photo-magazine, the balance shifted the other way. They expected pictures to be explained in print. Much the same situation also obtained in book publishing.

Photography also joined the fine arts at the hands of masters like Alfred Stieglitz, Edward Steichen and others, who proved that the camera was a medium for capturing visual images equal in impact and sensitivity to those of any other graphic artist, less because of technological novelty than the ability of the photographer to record accurately his own personal viewpoint of the natural world with selectivity and artistry. Many painters—impressionists, surrealists and others—reacted to the new invention by employing their artistic skills to paint images and visions of reality (some of them bizarre) impossible to see literally in nature and reflecting the artists' own subjective minds-eye vision of the natural world. What had become the highest compliment one could pay a painter or artist in the preceding two centuries ("Your work captures reality exactly!") now became an insult ("Your painting looks just like a photograph!") because of the perfection of photography.

From a cultural perspective, however, it was not the work of photographic artists that made the greatest impression upon society but rather the introduction of photography as a pastime and hobby for the common man in the industrialized nations of the West. From Kodak's first "Brownie," basically a camera obscura employing film rolled on a wooden spool between paper layers, the public, particularly in the United States, responded with vigor to the sales slogan, more or less true, that all one had to do was aim a camera, press a button and Kodak would "do the rest": that is, develop and print the picture and return it to the photographer. In the early years of the century, the popularity of grass roots photography was no less fervent than it is today. The vast majority of still pictures were (and are) remarkably similar: family groups, people on picnics, couples getting married, showing off their new automobile or Uncle Dan simply grinning at the "birdie."

Photography, in a remarkably short time, was assimilated into American life patterns, particularly during the period between World War I and II, when indoor film was perfected. Cameras could produce an acceptable photograph with a minimum of auxiliary lighting, possibly employing a safe "flash" contained in a shatter-proof bulb.

The middle class habit of photographing people almost from birth to death (and certainly at the moments of rites of passage like birthdays, graduations, weddings, etc.) became a family ritual. For generations, albums of photographs were meticulously filled with such pictures, millions upon millions of them, creating a new and lucrative industry. Where did—and do—the albums go, and why is the face of our planet *not* covered with old photographs? The answer is the key to the success of this industry, a success that spread far beyond Kodak's ability to manage it: Most of these photographs, possibly 99% of them, were destroyed as trash each time a new generation cleared away the debris of the former one and began keeping its own "permanent" record.

(For this discouraging reason, let me admit here that I have never in my life taken a photograph of anything or anybody, content in the knowledge that, if I want to remember the visual aspect of any moment, I think I am competent to remember it without graphic help; that if I want a picture of a landscape, I can probably purchase a postcard; and that if I want a reminder of how my son looked when he was two years old, some other fool is certain to have pushed a button and let Kodak "do the rest." I must add, however, that I am a devoted enthusiast of photographic art. Although I have never mastered it, or tried to, I take pleasure and joy—and sometimes sorrow—in savoring the work of its masters like Edward Weston, Walker Evans, Margaret Bourke-White and Henri Cartier-Bresson, among many others.)

The Invention of the Movies: Rapid Photography

The technology of photography joined another technology in the latter part of the nineteenth century to yield one of the twentieth century's most exciting novelties, as well as an instrument of mass communication that was, extremely rapidly, to vie with journalism as the most pervasive medium of communication in the Western world. It also created another cultural institution of industrial proportions and altered any number of folkways, particularly among the young, in many nations of the world.

The "archeology" of the movies, as it is called by the eclectic scholar C. W. Ceram, is absolutely fascinating, confused and slightly insane, a magnificent answer to the arguments of those simple souls who believe in the orderly transfer of scientific knowledge to technological development. Its detailed study is especially delightful for those of us who have never outgrown our children's toys, and take perverse delight in studying and playing with complicated instruments that seem to accomplish little or nothing. People like us, mostly during the nineteenth century, tinkered away at crazy gadgets that brought together various scientific and technological novelties which, in a haphazard fashion, yielded, by the 1880s, something we might recognize today as motion pictures.

The invention of the movies presented to its would-be inventors *two* related, but distinctively different, technical challenges. The first was the *taking* or photographing of pictures in rapid sequence—impossibly rapid, it seemed at first. The second was the development of ways of looking at, or projecting, these pictures to create the illusion of movement. The latter problem was, in some measure, further on the road to perfection than the first until the 1870s. In fact, machines that displayed pictures that moved evolved from various sorts of optical peep shows that had been popular in Europe from the eighteenth century on. A workable magic lantern, with a circular sequence of transparent pictures on a disk was described by Johannes Zahn in the late 1600s. The machine he apparently invented for showing lantern slides became the prototype for any number of slide devices used for entertainment and education during the next century, including elaborate instruments for projecting still pictures (mostly drawn, but later photographed) onto large surfaces with breathtaking effects, often in color.

One genius who stumbled upon the famous "persistence of vision" phenomenon of the human nervous system (not of the eye, as was long believed) that forces one, like it or not, to fuse together into continuous motion a number of discrete continuous images shown rapidly in the same place, was Joseph Antoine Ferdinand Plateau, a Belgian who published his findings concerning the phenomenon in 1829. (Plateau identified the persistence effect occurring if the pictures were shown at the rate of 16 per second. Later studies of this "flicker fusion" phenomenon demonstrated that 16 may be the right number for some people under some circumstances, but that the physiological process depends upon the environment in which it occurs as well as the age and condition of one's nervous system—at a sequence somewhat higher than 16 per second, after which all images fuse for almost anyone.) Plateau called this the "law of stroboscopic effect". In 1832, he invented a machine, the Phenakistascope, that brought together numerous abstract designs drawn on a moving wheel into a single image. The same sort of device was invented at about the same time in Germany by Simon Ritter Von Stampfer who called his wheel the Stroboscope.

Two years later, in England, William George Horner invented the more provocative Zoetrope employing the same principle. This gadget was indeed intended to function as a toy, and was probably regarded as useless by nine out of ten people who played with it. You have probably seen one. It looks something like a large metal wine goblet with slits in it. Hand drawn pictures on a strip are pasted around the inside. When it is twirled at the right speed, you look through the slits, and the pictures appear to move, endlessly repeating the same actions.

Emile Reynaud patented his distinctive improvement upon the Zoetrope in 1877 in Paris. He called it the Praxinoscope, which he built in a number of versions, all still toys, but some quite complex. What he accomplished was the elimination of the slits by using small mirrors. One looked through a peephole and saw the continuous motion of a dancing child or some such diversion swirling around on a central pivot.

Toys these were indeed, but they apparently challenged the imagination of countless tinkerers who had an inexhaustible supply of names for their inventions, all ending in "scope." Most prescient was probably the invention of the enigmatic Baron Franz Von Uchatius who, in 1853, actually invented a *projector* for moving lantern slides. He sold his machine, of which he thought little, to a magician and later committed suicide, apparently because he thought that his important scientific work, the development of armaments of war, had ended in failure. By 1869, however, A. B. Brown in America developed a refinement of Uchatius' invention that utilized a shutter movement. By 1890, magic lantern projectors, displaying continuous pictures on disks, were being produced and used in many countries.

What these instruments accomplished, of course, was to yield but a fraction of the entire sum of technologies that yielded the motion pictures, but they were also critical to their eventual perfection. Most important was not the ingenuity of the toys themselves, although one must admit that they were cleverly built. What they told other inventors of the nineteenth century was an important truth, and they told it by demonstration in the face of common sense: that discrete two-dimensional still images could, under certain circumstances, appear to move continuously in a life-like manner. Now, one begins to see the question that then faced still other ingenious tinkerers: namely, that if hand drawn cartoons and designs might be presented to simulate motion, what about the new photographs on glass and metal that freeze nature? Might they similarly be teased to move? Most sane men said "no." But thank heaven for the screwballs!

An eccentric lot they were: in particular, Eadweard Muybridge and Etienne-Jules Marey, but others as well. Muybridge has become the hero of this development, probably because he was the most colorful of them all, and quite self-consciously developed an heroic, eccentric and inscrutable personality. A displaced Briton, he found himself in California in 1877. Governor Leland Stanford of California's bet with a friend concerning whether or not a galloping horse's legs all left the ground simultaneously has become a legend. So has Muybridge's "proof": his 24 wet collodion plate cameras triggered by 24 threads that took still pictures demonstrating that horses, like squirrels, leap. Muybridge's other "motion" pictures stills, photographed on dry plates after 1881, were not only contributions to the development of cinema, they also indicate his aesthetic talent and keen interest in human motion. And the fact that he found ways to project many of these discrete series of images onto flat surfaces fired other imaginations that dreamed of blending them into *continuous* motion. The answer was near at hand.

In his way, however, Marey, a physiologist, was closer to the latter objective—motion picture photography—than Muybridge. His interest in motion was no less intense than Muybridge's, and, in 1882, Marey figured out a way to take action photographs from a *single* camera built along the lines of a submachine gun (a later modification of Marey's principle) that rotated a plate in a single chamber to make "chronophotographs" at the rate of 12 per second. In 1888, Marey substituted proper strips for the fixed plate and succeeded, with his portable instrument, in making as many as 100 discrete photographic exposures in a second!

Despite his physiological training, Marey had apparently broken the "persistence of vision" barrier without knowing it. His photographs, like those of Muybridge and Ottmar Anschintz (a contemporary German inventor who improved upon Muybridge's methods of photography and projection), were all printed or shown as single pictures, either discretely or by displaying multiple still images of a moving figure on the same print of a picture. Although he recorded only a few seconds of action, Marey had invented the motion picture camera while trying to accomplish something else: fast still photography of motion.

The Invention of the Movies: Continuous Motion

Two technologies now join—in time, in place and instrumentation—and our toy turns into a miracle, while the photographic camera becomes an instrument to perform a service for which it was not originally designed.

Who invented the motion pictures? This is obviously a silly—and useless—question that may be answered with the name of one of (probably) a hundred people who perfected the various technologies that we have been examining in America, in England, in France, in Russia and elsewhere.

As an American, I am chauvinistic enough to prefer our old friend, Hannibal Goodwin, an Episcopalian minister, who, in 1887, devised a way to use celluloid for continuous photography, an invention that was naturally exploited by Kodak's George Eastman. It fell into the hands of Thomas Edison's factory of inventions shortly thereafter. Edison had been experimenting with Eastman's "film" in connection with his early phonograph cylinders and was familiar with its properties. An Englishman in Edison's employ, W. Laurie Dickson, was probably largely responsible for the development of Edison's first motion picture camera in 1888, as well as the first Edison projector the year after, called, respectively, the Kinetoscope and Kinetograph.

In truth, the credits probably followed this line: Goodwin was responsible for the concept, at least, of movie photography; Eastman provided the medium; Dickson invented the gadgets; and Edison served an entrepreneur, receiving credit for all of these steps, in much the same way that the Bell Labs or Du Pont today take credit for the discoveries of their employees. In any event, Edison patented his refined Kinetoscope in 1891, and it became the instrument through which the American public first became acquainted with true motion pictures.

One important point must, however, be made here. At this point in his career, Edison did not appear to believe that the *projection* of motion pictures was a practical idea, despite all he knew about the history of the magic lantern and similar devices. Until the middle 1890s, one peered into a motion picture projector, in much the same way one had done for centuries to see the countless little peepshows that had been invented over the years. This meant that *one* person at a time might view a film. To speak of "audiences" for movies was therefore absurd. Despite Edison's reticence, the next step involved working out methods of projecting images onto a screen. This was accomplished in the United States by Thomas Armat and C. Francis Jenkins with their Phantoscope, quickly acquired by Edison, renamed the Vitascope, and presented to the public in theatres as a vaudeville amusement in 1895. But others were working on similar machines in other places at exactly the same time.

Ignoring the attractions of film projection, Edison apparently continued to prefer the peepshows and tried to encourage their use by means of the early Kinetoscope. A short length of motion picture film, projected at 48 pictures per second, was arranged in a continuous loop that would display a short "movie." Nor did the Wizard of Menlo Park ever really work up much enthusiasm for the idea of theatrical films. Possibly, he did not comprehend how they could return the kind of profits he had reaped from his other inventions.

Dickson did, and he was responsible for Edison's early films. Frankly, the less said about Fred Ott's short performance in the very first of them, *Record of a Sneeze,* the better, or about the first romantic vignette, performers John Rice and May Irwin's *The Kiss,* or *Fun in a Chinese Laundry* and *The Execution of*

Mary Queen of Scots, all Edison productions but made by Dickson and his associates. Their distinction as cinema rests on the fact that they moved—which is more than you can say about some recent films that have been playing lately in American theatres.

Movies as Magic

Motion pictures were, of course, in no way inevitably destined to be projected on screens in front of audiences, and tomorrow's technologies (or today's tiny portable TV sets) may yet justify Edison's early misjudgment. By the end of the century the public was fascinated by the technological capacity of movie film to be "blown up" to screen size by powerful illumination, and with the resulting magic of the larger-than-life image cavorting on a white surface. Indeed, this *was* magic—or very much like the sort of effects that contemporary conjurers achieved, many of whom used magic lantern effects—and elicited wide-eyed wonder from audiences. At this stage in their development, movies found their way, quite naturally, into theatres and vaudeville houses where they brought, in effect, the reality of the outside world into the theatre in a way that the living theatre could not. At this time, and possibly for this reason, stage directors were bending extraordinary efforts to make their scenic exhibitions in the theatre as natural looking as possible. As it turned out, they could not compete with the movies.

The first and best movie projectors were invented in Europe. One of the earliest, built by Louis Aimé Augustin Le Prince, was originally designed in 1888 with 16 lenses and projected glass pictures; its working prototype, however, shown in Leeds in 1889, used one lens and was demonstrated the following year at the Paris Opera for a private audience. Then a strange thing happened to Le Prince: he disappeared—completely, absolutely, and finally. Nothing was ever heard of him again. Apparently a remarkable inventor, Le Prince simply vanished.

In England, the less strange but more pitiful career of William Friese-Greene was getting under way at about the same time. After years of work, this indefatigable Englishman demonstrated a working movie projector in 1891, but Edison had beaten him to the draw, despite Friese-Greene's claim that he had developed earlier plans for a workable instrument and may even have built one; the point is moot. The same year Friese-Greene fell into bankruptcy and ended up in prison. The rest of his life was a disaster, involving wild schemes for balloon photography, color films and inconsequential inventions. He died in 1921, owning only loose change in the pockets of his shabby suit, while addressing the audience of a British film society.

In Germany, two brothers, Max and Emile Sklandowsky, invented, I suppose, one of the most significant and practical of all the early projectors, the Bioscope, that they demonstrated in Berlin in 1895. Max Sklandowsky was probably the technically talented of the two brothers. The other was mainly a showman. The machine they perfected used Eastman film, ran at about 16 frames a second, so the record says, which means that they were running fast lantern slide shows that might—or might not—have seemed to move continuously. At any rate, the Sklandowskys built their own camera and projected movies they had made of a kangaroo, jugglers, dancers and gymnasts on a machine *also of their own invention* for the first time in history. This is their main claim to cinema immortality.

America produced its "first" projector too, the invention of one Jean Aimé Le Roy, about whom little has been recorded. He apparently borrowed freely ideas and equipment from Edison and various French inventors and then started a company that produced equipment for projecting films in the offices of an optical firm in New York City as early as February 25, 1894. He continued showing his moving pictures for two years, charging audiences an admission fee to see his shows.

These pioneers were just a few out of many. We remember them because records were kept of their work. As I look at the names of the multitude of projection instruments patented in the years between 1890 and 1900, I realize that they all must have been invented by someone whose dreams and ambitions and accomplishments have been lost to us. The machines had colorful, crazy names like the Vileocrigraphiscope, Chronophotographoscope, Phantasmagoria and Gettmoneygraph (sic). Nor should I overlook George Demeny's Phonoscope, patented in 1892, designed primarily to demonstrate lip movements to deaf people; or Birt Acres' device, called the Kineopticon, demonstrated in England the following year, that reproduced scenes of golfing, boxing, sailing and "the incredible arrest of a pickpocket" and was shown to the Royal Photographic Society. Because fascination with the grown-up toy was intense, it is not hard to understand why and how motion picture photography was invented by so many people in so many ways in so many places so quickly.

The Lumière Brothers

With regret, we may relegate most of these early adventurous tinkerers to less significant places in the history of today's movies than the more conservative, less driven and less colorful Lumière brothers of France. Auguste Marie Louise Nicholas Lumière and his younger brother, Louis Jean (probably the more creative of the two) ran a photographic supply factory in Lyon. In 1895, they developed a singular instrument, and one which is still a remarkably good idea: a machine which could serve *both* as a motion picture camera *and* projector, eventually called the Cinématographe. In the same year, the brothers screened their famous first film, *Workers Leaving the Lumière Factory,* a short slice of life that is more interesting than Fred Ott's sneeze, at least to my eyes. Other similar films were added to their collection, many of them mini-documentaries, some bits of slapstick comedy, but all of them photographed out of doors in natural light.

The Lumière brothers soon invaded the salons of Paris with their amazing invention. Their famous *The Arrival of a Train at a Station* and *The Sprinkler Sprinkled* (a loose translation of *L'Arroseur Arrose*) have been, in recent years, shown so many times on television and in documentaries on old movies that beginning film students in college today yawn through them. But these late Victorian vignettes were, for their time, remarkably photographed: clear, in focus and providing a life-like, smooth simulation of motion.

By 1897, the Lumières had amassed a collection of 358 assorted films, either photographed in a multitude of countries or with simulated backgrounds. While they did not excel either at photography or art, the brothers were fundamentally documentarians who attempted to record on film scenes of significance in the real world around them. It is fortunate they did, because their existing celluloid strips provide a contemporary record of what boils down to moving postcards, rich in the record they preserved for our eyes of a Europe so long ago—its rulers, common citizens and soldiers, the streets and squares of cities that have since been leveled by warfare and now rebuilt. In total, by 1901, the Lumières had produced the astounding number of 1,299 separate short movies: some as ambitious as a two-part *Faust* and the *Life and Passion of Jesus Christ;* some displaying attempts at trick photography (mainly by reversing film, heads to tails) and shorts on historical figures like Napoleon.

The Lumière brothers displayed their wares in nearly all the major cities in Europe and even, in 1896, at Keith's Theatre on New York's Fourteenth Street, then right on the theatrical main stem of the big city. At first, the sheer novelty of the Lumière movies was enough to attract a crowd. But, in a year or two, Cinématographe features might make up but a single segment of a longer, live vaudeville show.

Movies in Theatres

With this development, a critical nexus was being formed. The Lumières' early films—and Dickson's, eventually, among others—found their way into theatres and were shown to paying audiences who found them exciting, thrilling and amusing. Edison, remember, had resisted this development, probably envisioning his Kinetoscope as a sister or brother of his phonograph. (Many of Edison's early film experiments involved sound pictures, using the phonograph and motion pictures simultaneously and more or less synchronously. They worked, but they were also tricky to operate. Nor could sound be amplified electronically in those days.) What Edison foresaw (incorrectly) was probably a home-sized Kinetoscope in every home parlor in the country next to the phonograph that he thought (correctly) was soon to become a near universal household item. True enough, in a few decades motion picture machines employing incandescent light bulbs instead of the dangerous, hot arcs of the early projectors were to find their way into many American homes, but home movies never competed successfully with theatrical films.

Edison's vision was not to come true, because the cinema was not going to be domesticated in the same manner as his phonograph and electric light. It was, instead, to find its home in the world of the theatre, a world strangely alien to Edison's interests, but one compatible with many—or most—of those other tinkerers who began making and projecting motion pictures as the nineteenth century ran out.

In France and the United States, particularly, it was showmen—or would-be showmen—who recognized the theatrical potential of these jerky, short cinematic amusements. Curiously, also, despite what the Lumières had demonstrated about the capacity of film to capture real history in the making—later called the "newsreel" and "documentary"—the numerous journalists who must have seen this new invention at work did not appear to recognize in it—except marginally and fleetingly—any deep relationship between the movies and the publication of the daily news. Newspapers were one medium of communication, films another, and the two were not to meet for another quarter of a century.

A few cartoonists saw, almost at once, the possibilities of using the films for "chalk talks" before audiences and the opportunity for combining live action on stage with moving pictures. Stage actors and directors looked at the films with an eyebrow cocked; movies had possibilities for them, eventually to be explored mostly by others. It was for the most part theatrical producers who recognized in these early films a form of entertainment at first analagous to the vaudeville theatre and later to the serious theatre. Their talents, their verve and, mostly, their money were to direct this new technology into the theatrical matrix from which it only partially emerged years later with the invention of television.

The Magic of Movies

Magicians, too, looked at these early films. Their visions were perhaps the most inventive and creative of all. First, magicians were theatrical artists, used to performing before audiences. Second, and most important, they dealt in illusion, in technological devices and used special skills to make impossibilities seem real. What they saw in the movies was an incredible technological tool that might manipulate reality: slow it up, speed it, reverse it, fracture it and put it back together again, in ways their cumbersome devices for sawing women in half and levitating assistants had for years operated half as well with twice the effort. The magical mind looked at the movies and saw methods, by means of time-stop photography, for instance, for chopping off heads in full view of audiences, playing tricks on time and space, and a host of delicious illusions literally impossible to achieve by conventional methods. Some of the early and most inventive film makers were indeed professional magicians; one in particular, George Méliès, we shall meet shortly. But the magical mind is not the property solely of professional magicians. Showmen who foresaw the film world and industry they themselves were to create in a few short years were also, at heart, illusionists.

Many, many years later, a young man named Orson Welles was to look at a talking film studio in Hollywood and compare it to the greatest toy any kid had ever been given for Christmas. In those days, Welles was an amateur magician, and it is not difficult to understand his enthusiasm. By 1898, the tinkerers and crackpots had created a toy, the technology of which was rapidly being refined and perfected. Now it was up to the magicians and the young and inventive at heart to play with it. This they did.

An Era of Invention

In another segment of society, however, far saner and vastly more scientific imaginations were building other instruments of the communications revolution in their own methodical way. Their work seemed less spectacular than the invention of the cinema, but it was to bring a change to Western culture that ran deeper into the lives of all men on earth in the years to come than even the movies did.

They did not yearn to see moving pictures on screens. They merely heard voices in the air! This was an age of new technologies, rapid inventions and a naive belief in science that was witnessing, in many domains, the impossible come true. Men were flying through the air in balloons. The invention of the airplane was waiting in the wings. Early automobiles were wheezing along city streets and country lanes. Photographs moved. Man's voice had somehow been captured on a rotating cylinder. Electricity was providing power for seemingly impossible purposes in middle class households. There appeared to be, in truth, no limit to what technology might accomplish, or, phrased better, what the magnificent instrument of the human brain might think up next to conquer the limitation of nature. Painless surgery and dentistry, for instance, were miracles for a generation brought up in a world where once barbers and surgeons were the same people, trained in the same way.

I do not think I digress by ending this chapter with the suggestion that the period from, roughly, 1890 to 1910, was, in the industrial West, one of the most exciting two decades in which to live in history (reasonably well fed and housed, naturally), by virtue of the optimism and hopes that a thinking person might reasonably expect of society as he looked into the future. The limitations of nature *all* seemed conquerable, if not by technology, then certainly by science. The very secrets of the origins of life seemed within the grasp of biologists, so exquisitely had Darwin drawn his evolutionary chart of the origins of mankind. Economics was now a science in the hands of Marx and others, and the perfect social order lay just ahead. And technology was producing, practically day after day, new inventions and discoveries that affirmed man's ingenuity and ability to harness the forces of the natural world and turn the unthinkable into the commonplace.

When I was young, I knew people who had lived through these two decades, and, almost invariably, they spoke of them with a reverence and wonder that puzzled me. Today, I understand. What the scientific-technological genius of this period held out to our grandparents and great-grandparents was a vision of a world in which people would behave like adults and rational creatures, because human intelligence was rapidly illuminating the deepest secrets in nature's bosom. In the end, always just around the corner, was a world of plenty, harmony and, most important, peace on earth forever.

6

New Frontiers: Broadcasting and Journalism

THE INVENTION OF BROADCASTING was part of this great era of technological change, a miraculous invention that burrowed rapidly into Western culture, and, within a generation, touched the lives of nearly everyone in Europe and America, directly or indirectly.

Radio broadcasting—and its offspring, television—is one of the few examples in the communications revolution of the orderly process of a neat transition from the development of scientific theory to a practical technology that exploited theory to its full potential—and continues to do so to this day.

Scientific Beginnings

Towering at the starting point of this history is a remarkable Scotsman, James Clerk-Maxwell, who, working at Cambridge in England (after a distinguished career as an innovator in theoretical physical sciences), published, in 1873, his famous theory, *Treatise of Electricity and Magnetism*. Theory it was, because it relied upon mathematical rather than practical proof. But Clerk-Maxwell, in effect, posited the idea that electromagnetic energy traveled through space in much the same way that light waves did, with the critical difference that it was harder to notice than rays of light. Nevertheless, he maintained in the face of common sense that light and electricity travel in much the same way, and, in their ultimate nature, are almost identical. What Clerk-Maxwell had discovered in his final years (he died in 1879) was that the transmission of signals that were later to be called "radio waves" was *theoretically* possible. As a scientist, he saw little immediate practical application for his enormous discovery.

Neither did the German physicist Heinrich Hertz, born in Hamburg in 1857. He was deeply interested in these electromagnetic "waves" described by Clerk-Maxwell and their relationship to light. He therefore conducted experiments during the 1880s to prove, first, that such waves exist; second, what their sizes and speeds are; and, third, how they behave in different mediums and under different circumstances. By means of demonstrations and through published accounts of his work, Hertz indisputably showed that radio waves were real and that, as Clerk-Maxwell had anticpated, they behaved much like light, although they could not be seen, heard or smelled. Sydney Head, in his study of broadcasting, says that Hertz himself denied that these waves might ever be used for purposes of communication, although he had, without knowing it, invented radio broadcasting and, by means of his experiments, had actually transmitted signals from one place to another. Hertz died in 1894, a few years before he would be proven wrong, not as a scientist, but in his ability to predict the startling usefulness of his contribution to knowledge.

Guglielmo Marconi

The name usually associated with the invention of radio broadcasting is that of the Italian aristocrat, Guglielmo Marconi, a man of technological genius and indefatigable energy. He was born in 1874 and, as a young man, studied the work of Clerk-Maxwell and Hertz. Apparently in his early youth he recognized what neither scientist had seen—that as long as electromagnetism might be sent from point to point through the air, it possessed, like the electric current in telegraph wires, a potential capacity to carry messages in the form of dots and dashes. In Bologna, Italy, he experimented with electromagnetic generators and receivers. At the age of 21 or 22, Marconi had already invented a working wireless telegraph and was quite aware of its commercial implications. Traveling to England in 1896, he patented his invention, and in a year he had made plans to exploit it commercially as fully as he could. Having given demonstrations of his miracle, he started two corporations to produce and market his invention. By 1901, he had even demonstrated the feasibility of broadcasting signals across the Atlantic Ocean.

As is the case with most technology, Marconi's invention was anticipated by others and widely imitated, as various designs flooded patent offices around the world, and other inventors tried to compete with Marconi's attempts to sew up for his company the world's wireless market. In these inevitable ensuing patent wars, he both succeeded and failed, as patent suit followed patent suit and competition popped up everwhere, particularly in the United States. A man of less energy and drive than Marconi might have been defeated by it all. He battled on, however, for exclusive rights to an invention that would soon be so changed and modified by others, and *their* new inventions, that his plans for world monopoly were finally defeated forever—ironically, shortly after he was given the Nobel prize for physics in 1909.

Early uses for radio centered on point-to-point communications, of course, and Marconi envisioned his brainchild as an instrument that might overcome the main physical limitations of the cable telegraph. Its most dramatic functions centered upon marine telegraphy. The story of the wireless operator aboard the sinking *Titanic* in 1912, who stood by his post and reported the tragedy to the world, is a legend. In fact, the legend also includes the fact that his signal was picked up on land by a young telegrapher named David Sarnoff, on duty at a Marconi telegraph exhibit at Wanamaker's department store in New York. For nearly an uninterrupted 72 hours, Sarnoff alerted nearby ships to the *Titanic's* disaster and provided the world's journalists with sensational breaking news as it occurred in the North Atlantic. If anything dramatized radio's role as a communication device, Sarnoff's lucky break did. It also dramatized Sarnoff, who later continued his career in communications as president of RCA until his death in 1971.

What Marconi's invention lacked in its early days, however, was instruments that might better control signal generation, amplification, modulation and reception and keep his radio waves "on the beam." Here the technological picture becomes a bit muddy. Marconi himself attempted to use an early radio tube called a "coherer," invented by a Frenchman, Edouard Branley, in 1890, which was filled with magnetized and de-magnetized iron filings. A far more useful radio tube was perfected by Sir John Ambrose Fleming, a professor of electrical engineering in London, in 1904 and called the "diode." It amplified signals by electricity in a reliable and effective manner.

Lee de Forest

Fleming's tube, however, did not effectively tame and control radio waves with the same versatility and reliability that even a good but primitive crystal detector could. In 1906, Lee de Forest patented his Audion tube, which is, in effect, the grandfather of *all* broadcasting tubes to the present, as well as tiny transistors that today perform many of their functions. De Forest, born in 1873, hailed from the American mid-west, received a Ph.D. from Yale in 1899, and worked for a while for the young Western Electric Company. After a few years of patient invention, he added an electrically controlled grid to the two filaments in Fleming's diode, thereby controlling with great precision the amount and speed of electricity received or sent to or from his Audion. This function was critical to broadcasting's future. Until de Forest's invention, all so-called "detector" tubes could only "detect" whether or not a specific flow of electrons was, in effect, "on" or "off." De Forest's "triode" was able to modulate or amplify electrical currents by means of the grid. Such modulation of the length of radio waves would eventually provide radio telegraph instruments with the capacity to transform into electrical current not only "on" and "off" messages, but impulses that might be translated into voices and music.

De Forest spent much of his life in litigation over his legitimate rights to profit from the use made by others of his invention. The American Telephone and Telegraph Company had paid de Forest a considerable sum for his device in 1913, but only for use in developing telephone circuitry. A year later, AT&T handed him another healthy sum for the radio rights. But even this amount was paltry (in sum, $140,000.) compared to the multi-millions the invention was soon to realize. Various other versions of de Forest's tube were patented by General Electric and the Marconi Company in America and by two German corporations. The matter of patents was further complicated by the fact that Major Edwin Armstrong had worked out for Marconi an ingenious feedback circuit for use with the Audion that de Forest also claimed he invented. Lawsuits involving patents of these circuits continued for 20 years, or until the Supreme Court of the United States decided, at last, that de Forest was in fact the true inventor of the Audion *and* the circuitry allied to it.

A man of remarkable talent and tenacity, de Forest is also primarily responsible for the use of radio signals for broadcasting voices and music—that is, sounds other than dots and dashes. Obviously, both microphones and speakers were necessary for this feat. While de Forest did not invent the first ones, he was responsible for bringing together the equipment necessary to design the first "radio stations," in today's use of the term. For the few sets capable of receiving his broadcasts, he transmitted phonograph concerts from France in 1908 and, in 1910, broadcast a live performance from the Metropolitan Opera House in New York to nearby receivers set up before special audiences. Throughout the remainder of his life, he kept up an active interest in all phases of broadcasting and, later, sound motion pictures. While others grew rich from his inventiveness, he displayed a gutsy talent for claiming full credit (and sometimes the cash) due him, although his business career is one checkered by bankruptcy actions and failures. He died in 1961, legitimately remembered as the "father of broadcasting."

De Forest was a practical scientist and technological genius in the manner of Edison, but he lacked Edison's unusually keen business ability. While the scientific aspects of de Forest's work were not of great importance to him, his awareness of broadcasting's cultural future was. In later years, when he discussed the jammed commercial radio airwaves of the United States and the quality of the nonsense that daily assaulted the public's ears, he asked, in stormy indignation, "What have you done to my baby?"

Radio's New Technology

Two other clever technologists were also closely related to the birth of broadcasting and must be mentioned here. Reginald Fessenden of the University of Pittsburgh developed an electrical generator capable of producing radio waves of high frequency by means of a 50,000 cycle alternator that permitted long distance transmission of signals. He also developed the "heterodyne circuit," utilizing for the first time the idea of broadcasting a continuous wave, interrupted by modulations of various types, especially that of the human voice. In 1901, employing a telephone mouthpiece, Fessenden became, probably, the first man to have actually talked over the radio, although his broadcasts, made between 1902 and 1906, were heard, usually by accident: only by a few startled telegraph operators on ships and in lighthouses. (Confirmed records that Fessenden's broadcasts were actually received by such listeners date back to Christmas Eve, 1906.)

The generator that accomplished this feat was built by another technical pioneer, Ernst Alexanderson, a Swedish-born engineer working for the General Electric Company whose interest in developing high frequency generators, called "Alexanderson Alternators," continued until World War I. Afterwards, he turned his technically agile brain to the development of electric microphones, sophisticated antennae, telephone transmission and receiving equipment and early experiments with television, as well as new methods of ship propulsion.

The development of this technology was rapid, and much of it was redundant— that is, many inventors the world over were inventing the same things differently. In some ways, this activity resembled the flurry of excitement (at about the same time) over the various motion picture instruments described in the previous chapter, But there were differences, and three of them are quite important.

First, this period of invention was the direct result of an advancement in *theoretical* science, mostly the work of Clerk-Maxwell and Hertz. The scholarly discipline of science had, in effect, indicated what it was possible for technologists and inventors to accomplish. And these men followed these clear directions. No such precise scientific agenda were available for the inventors of the movies.

Second, all of the early inventors of broadcasting technology were trained engineers, men either self-educated or taught in universities to pursue the new and exciting—but complicated—field of electrical engineering. I have not cited all of them here; there are too many. But, to a man, they were all specialists of considerable training. The motion pictures were invented by tinkerers with various talents for mechanical engineering and (sometimes) chemistry. Broadcasting was an engineering feat.

Third, inventors of early cinema devices, for the most part, were able to introduce them immediately into culture. Elaborate mechanisms were not necessary to start early Kinetoscope parlors or movie demonstrations. In fact, the movies met the masses during the very decade that a few—very few—people first experienced the miracle of sound transmission through the air. True enough, advances in broadcasting were well covered by the press. But remember that as late as 1912 David Sarnoff was demonstrating the "miracle" of radio telegraphy to the public in a New York department store. A few blocks away "nickelodeon" movie theatres were already doing land-office businesses among the immigrant population of the city. Broadcasting was invented as, and remained, a method of point-to-point communication for some years, a sort of telephone system without wires. It would soon have its day as a mass medium, of course, but complicated technological and industrial problems would have to be solved first. So they were, shortly after World War I.

What we have seen so far in this chapter is, therefore, part of the *pre*-history of mass communications—the development of a highly complex technology that would, much like the early movies, eventually move rapidly into culture and become part of the mass communications complex in Western nations. What is most important to consider, I think, is the chronology of events that marked the beginnings of broadcasting and the cinema. Once again, we are back in that enigmatically vital decade between, roughly, 1900 and 1910 that witnessed, for both media, the technological breakthroughs that eventuated in the development of enormous industries and cultural institutions during the decades to follow. Possibly, the films were a little ahead of radio broadcasting, but perfecting the latter was a greater technical challenge than the former. The notion, however, that radio waves were transmitters of current through the ether moved from theory to invention to practice with almost electric speed itself.

Press Trends in Changing America

Journalism had just undergone—in the pressure of the times—its own great period of technical innovation with the invention of the rotary press and Linotype. These years ending the second half of the nineteenth century were also critical to the direction the entire publishing industry was to take at the start of the next one. Other inventions notwithstanding, the print medium remained the dominant mass medium of communication in the West well into the twentieth century.

During the period from 1900 to 1910, more daily papers (in excess of 2,000) were printed in the United States than before—or since. Weeklies also proliferated, both nationally and locally, along with magazines and books. The only instrument by which the masses might keep in touch with the news of the day and currents of fashion and cultural life remained the print medium. For this period of financial, industrial and educational expansion, it became the one device for which all (or most) of the functions that our modern mass media (radio, television, movies, etc.) serve us today in the 1970s. Except for vaudeville, lecture circuits and amateur entertainments, the press was the average man's theatre, both of fiction and life, and the means by which he maintained his sense of contact with the larger world. It was his source of political and economic news, of jokes and satire and commentary and fashion in its broadest sense. Even if he could not read—or read poorly—others could, would and did mediate to him what they read in the papers.

Under such a cultural burden, the American press could not operate as it had in the immediate past and/or as we have seen it develop. Newspapers, most magazines and even books had been, in the nineteenth century, largely reflections of the personalities who edited and published them. In journalism, the great editorialists, even the elder Bennett, had been men of social conviction and political involvement, and their newspapers spoke for *them*. It is difficult to locate the point, for instance, where Greeley the man ended and the *Tribune* began. By and large, the press of the nineteenth century had responded to ever-expanding, but nevertheless constricted, cultural needs: responsible political and social news and editorial opinion, spiced by just enough entertainment to make the serious palatable and the important enjoyable, as well as to offer a gratuitous tear or laugh to the reader.

After 1880, the American social climate began a rapid change, largely as the result of waves of immigration to the United States from Ireland, Germany and East Europe. These immigrant ''greenhorns'' were not necessarily all tired or poor or oppressed, as we are often led to believe. Some were all three, naturally. But others were intelligent, even affluent; and all were ambitious to make good in their new lives in a new land. Despite their noticeable coagulation into ethnic groups (the lower east side for New York Jews; the farmlands of Minnesota for Scandinavians, etc.), most of them adapted to America's mores with amazing speed, infusing their own culture traits to American culture at the same time.

Literacy in, and the use of, the English language was important to them, and even more important to their children, along with the great hallmark of American respectability: education. They filled night schools and settlement houses to learn their new language. While the ethnic press (in Italian, German, Yiddish and nearly every other European language) flourished in big cities, it was to the American newspaper that the greatest number of these immigrants looked to satisfy their needs for orientation to their new culture. Not only this, but advertisers recognized that the upwardly mobile immigrant was potentially a good customer. The American press either had to meet his or her needs, as well as those of the rest of the population, or die from financial strangulation in new and heated competiton.

A burgeoning population of such ambitious new Americans was not entirely different from the general readership of much of the American press before the 1880s. It was now simply larger and more heterogeneous. The kind of satisfactions, therefore, that the papers could provide the public had only to be pitched to a broader spectrum of appetites or lower common denominators. If the vocabulary of a newspaper or magazine was complicated, it had to be simplified to reach this group. If it was difficult to get ideas across to them—particularly humorous ideas—by means of words, techniques were at hand for the invention of comic strips, and so forth.

More important, the possibility was now wider than ever before for newspapers to expand into big and highly lucrative businesses. Increasing readership meant increasing revenues from circulation and advertising, and, as the shores of the new world filled with new people, the age of the newspaper, magazine and book as a *commodity* in the free-enterprise marketplace started. Fortunes were to be made (and lost) in the world of the press. The age of great editorialists gave way to the age of magnificent entrepreneurs (or industrialists), who seized this opportunity in many colorful ways. Let us look briefly at a few of them. In every respect, they are typical products of their times and places.

To call these men ''press barons'' is glib but not totally inaccurate. The newspapers they managed (and sometimes edited) were their private domains, fiefdoms ruled by iron hands in steel gloves. They were not hereditary monarchs, although some of them were indeed born to money and position.

Joseph Pulitzer and the *World*

The most interesting of them remains an enigma, a personality of enormous contradictions and a man who apparently was little understood, even by those near him in his own lifetime. Today, we may logically trace back to his influence almost everything that is cheap, commercial, meretricious, exploitative and undemocratic about the mass press in America at present. On the other hand, his name is associated with yearly prizes, funded from the fortune he made, given yearly by Columbia University, for excellence in journalism in its finest aspects, as well as for poetry, drama, biography and fiction. One of America's major Schools of Journalism proudly bears his name. All of these tributes are justified, but of such ironies was the life of Joseph Pulitzer compounded.

How appropriate, also, that the full exploitation of the ''new'' America of the late nineteenth and early twentieth century should have been accomplished by a man who was himself an immigrant, who arrived in the United States at the age of 17, hardly able to speak the English language. Pulitzer was a Hungarian, born in 1847, and, from all accounts, he suffered from a frail physique and poor health for most of his life. His parents were well-to-do Europeans. He was given a good private education but ran away from home to volunteer for military service in his native land (rejected), failing immediately to start his chosen career as a soldier-adventurer for physical reasons. He was, however, accepted by the United States Army in Europe in 1864 by an agent recruiter looking for volunteers and exporting them to the U.S.A. Pulitzer, however, jumped ship in Boston and then enlisted in the United States Cavalry.

Pulitzer's military career was less than undistinguished. He subsequently found himself virtually destitute in New York City, unable to get a job because, among other things, of his faulty English and unimpressive looks. Hearing that many German-Americans lived well in the St. Louis area, and speaking German faultlessly, he found his way to the mid-west. Within three or four years, he became an American citizen, studied English assiduously, got a job as a reporter in a German-American newspaper, and began studying law.

What impressed Pulitzer's employers—and everyone else with whom he came in contact—was his driving ambition and apparently endless energy. His normal work day lasted at least 16 hours. Nominated (more or less as a practical joke) by Republicans in a normally Democratic district, Pulitzer somehow got himself elected to the Missouri State Legislature, a position he held while continuing his journalistic activities. He campaigned for Horace Greeley for President in 1872, parlayed a part interest in the *Westliche Post,* the German language paper for which he worked, into a cash sale, and soon bought a broken down St. Louis journal with an Associated Press affiliation for a rock bottom price. He then sold it at a profit almost immediately to a Chicago publisher who had started a St. Louis paper without the AP membership, thereby selling the publisher, in effect, the AP affiliation he needed.

While far from rich, Pultizer now had enough money to visit Europe, look over the newspaper business in New York and return to St. Louis to buy still another newspaper, the *St. Louis Dispatch,* again for an absurdly low sum, and effected a merger with that city's *Post* owned by John A. Dillon. The result was the *St. Louis Post-Dispatch,* born in December of 1878. Pulitzer's partnership with Dillon lasted about a year, after which the latter remained an associate of Pulitzer but inactive in running the newspaper. Pulitzer was more than competent to do the job alone. Part of the credit for the success of the *Post-Dispatch* undoubtedly went to John A. Cockerill, hired in 1890, a tough, nononsense editorial right arm for the somewhat temperamental, artistically inclined, brilliant young Pulitzer.

By now, Pulitzer had mastered English and drove his employees mercilessly and imperiously, but always in the interests of what he considered to be good journalism. His memoranda of these years are legends. "Accuracy! Accuracy!! Accuracy!!!," he wrote, "Never drop a big thing until you have gone to the bottom of it. Continuity! Continuity! Continuity . . . !"

In five years, the Post-Dispatch had become a newspaper to notice, and, as he reached his middle thirties, Pulitzer's eccentric talents were also clearly in evidence. As master of the *Post-Dispatch,* he had developed inscrutable habits, moody, aloof, introverted and unpredictable, punctuated with displays of energy and enthusiasm. Bearded and well over six feet tall, he was now an imposing man with a passion for music and art, matched by deep interests in politics, social matters, economics and, as a matter of fact, everything that might sell newspapers. His two handicaps were poor health and a failing eyesight that was eventually to lead to total blindness. But physical sickness apparently drove him all the harder to overcompensation in developing what was to become a newspaper baronacy.

In 1883, Pulitzer was ready for New York and, as we have seen, New York was ready for him. A near nervous and physical wreck, he bought the 23-year old *New York World* from the shady financier, Jay Gould, who had held it for four years at a financial loss. From St. Louis, he brought Cockerill to New York (the latter having been involved in the newsroom murder of an attorney for which he was never tried in court) to edit the *World.* With much fanfare, Pulitzer launched the "new" *World* on May 11, 1883 and continued much the same sort of highhanded, clever and grandiose editorial policies that had worked for the *Post-Dispatch.*

To say that the *World* was a success is understatement. Circulation rose from 15,000 a day when Pulitzer took over to 100,000 in September of the following year, an occasion Pulitzer modestly celebrated by presenting every employee with a silk top hat and arranging to have 100 guns fired in front of New York's City Hall. Two years later, when circulation passed the quarter-of-a-million mark, a silver medallion was minted by Pulitzer and given to employees and advertisers. He could well afford them. In 1887, an evening edition of the newspaper was published, and, in a short time, the *World*'s circulation led all New York newspapers—including its Sunday edition which sold more than 250,000 copies a week by 1900. In a remarkably short time, it became one of the most popular—and influential—papers in the country!

How did Pulitzer do it? What accounted for the success of the *World,* both as a newspaper and a vehicle of advertising? Again we face a contradiction. From one perspective, Pulitzer took a step *backwards* rather than forward by wisely reviving the formulas that had served the *Sun* and its imitators so well a half-century before in a then smaller city and in a less flamboyant way.

First, he kept the price of the newspaper low, two cents a copy daily, thereby forcing competitors to follow him. And he gave his readers a lot for their money: as many as 14 or more pages daily and from 36 to 44 pages on Sunday. True, much of it was advertising, but the new, affluent population of new Americans read, and apparently liked, much of the advertising copy. And they responded to it. Thus, it continually grew and expanded revenues. Second, he imitated the publishers of the penny-press by exploiting the sensational, the off-beat and entertaining side of the news, always accurately and always well-written.

Like Bennett, Pulitzer sometimes made news intentionally. A *World* fund was set up to collect nickels and dimes from school children to erect the pedestal upon which the Statue of Liberty (a white-elephant gift from France) stands to this day in New York Harbor. Pulitzer sent a reporter, Elizabeth Cochran, nicknamed "Nellie Bly" around the world in 1889 in order to beat the record of Jules Verne's fictional Phileas Fogg in *Around the World in Eighty Days.* She did, completing the trip in 72 days, 6 hours, 11 minutes and 14 seconds. Of such nonsense are empires created. The public loved it, and, as Pulitzer said to Edwin Godkin of the scholarly, low circulating *Post,* "I want to talk to a nation, not to a select committee." At this, he succeeded.

Pulitzer, however, did not merely pour new wine in old bottles. Having built a new building for the *World* (the tallest in New York at the time), he supposedly retired from the editorship of the paper. From 1890 until his death in 1911, Pulitzer spent much of his time at sea on his personal yacht, in Europe or in Maine, now totally blind. But unlike James Gordon Bennett, Jr., in his absentee ownership he still held an iron grip on the *World.* The innovations he had made—the steps taken forward—were well and imperiously superintended from afar.

Frank Mott summarizes these innovations for us. None of them were new, but their novelty lay partly in the expert and professional way they were accomplished.

The *World* was a timely paper with wide and complete news coverage. It was also a crusading newspaper. While its tendency toward sensationalism was inconsistent, its liberal orientation was not, including its attacks on big business trusts, corruption and exploitation of the poor, all of which was reflected in its popularly oriented editorials.

While he had his sight, Pulitzer also gave the *World* a new aesthetic appeal. Columns were clearly set, articles were easy to read and, against his own preferences, clear and well drawn cartoons and illustrations, often printed in the middle of the front page, and copious illustrations were freely used by the *World*.

Nor was Pultizer, or the *World,* overly modest—at least in the eyes of the general public. As reclusive as the publisher himself became in his last two decades of life, so the *World* took the opposite stance, continually promoting its own interests with contests, coupons, public events and schemes to attract attention.

The *World* was also a newspaper that attracted first-rate newsmen, some later lured from it by Pulitzer's great rival, William Randolph Hearst, but men of substance like George Harvey, a politician, S. S. Carvalho, Col. Charles H. Jones, Pulitzer's "publisher" after his retirement, and the veteran journalist, Ballard Smith.

And what of Pulitzer? With his death, the enigma of the private man deepened, and his legacy, largely financial, has probably done exactly what he intended that it should do: encourage excellence in journalism and the arts. The secret, if secret it was, to Pulitzer's success, however, extends more deeply into American culture than his own obvious abilities and eccentric talents for many things, including amassing a fortune against enormous odds.

As a foreign-born American, Pulitzer was able, more clearly than many gifted native-born journalists, to comprehend the new role of the English language newspaper, especially in large cities. He understood the needs of the heterogenous population deeply affected by the waves of new Americans who arrived almost daily with the same sort of ambitions he had nurtured as a young man—to make good in this new land of opportunity. While the *World* was a popular paper with few intellectual pretensions (or distinctions), it was also an *enthusiastic* newspaper, both in the faded pages I read today in the library and in the role it played in New York City as a cultural institution in its time.

Scholars of the press call the *World* the first example of "new journalism." I am not as sure. Other newspapers indeed copied its lively news coverage and editorials frequently and superbly, just as the *World* drew ideas freely from the press around it and from other papers in the past. What the *World* stood for, symbolized both by the golden dome on its proud building and collection of custom made, enormous bronze owls (the paper's mascot) peering down from a low terrace—was a "new *newspaper,*" published, written and edited for a population living in a golden age of optimism, dynamism and self-bestowed wisdom.

(The building is gone, but the gigantic owls remain. For ten years, I worked in a university faculty office at New York University where one of them stared at me daily with silent disdain as I prepared my lecture notes. This formidable outsize bird I grew to hate will, I suppose, always symbolize for me the massive stolidity and keen cleverness of the old *World* and the culture in which it thrived, particularly, I think, the latter. And, of course, Joseph Pulitzer.)

William Randolph Hearst

What Joseph Pulitzer had begun, others would carry to bizarre extremes, even during his lifetime. His great professional antagonist was his opposite number in almost every way imaginable, a man who did not even arrive upon the New York scene until Pulitzer had supposedly retired to his exile, and until the *World* was already established as New York's most successful newspaper.

I am referring, of course, to William Randolph Hearst, a man who was to become an American legend in his lifetime and whose career is probably forever doomed to be intertwined with—and distorted by—the 1941 motion picture, *Citizen Kane,* a movie that many believe is the outstanding artistic product ever to have emerged from Hollywood. Kane's producer and writer, Orson Welles and, in great measure, Welles' collaborator on the story, Herman J. Mankiewicz, intended to create a movie biography merely *based* on the life of Hearst. Their Charles Foster Kane is Hearst in spirit. But it could not be in letter, because Hearst was still alive and could easily have sued for defamation (and prevented exhibition of the movie), if the events displayed in it too closely followed those of his career. What few people recognized or noted, even at the time of *Kane's* release, was that the movie was not merely a film based loosely upon the life of Hearst, but also a *masterpiece* based loosely upon the life of Hearst. The confusion that followed lay in this latter unforeseen mischief. The real Hearst and the fictional Kane tended to become one person, as legend grew and were retold. I doubt that the two will ever be separated.

The genuine Hearst was 16 years younger than Pulitzer, but he might have come from another (and later) generation, as, indeed, he came from another country. He was everything Pulitzer was not. Apparently blessed with abundant good health, he lived to the age of 88 and died 40 years after Pulitzer in 1951. He was born rich—very rich for his time—the son of a distinguished father and doting mother, raised in San Francisco and educated at Harvard—until he was expelled for harassing his professors. Returning home, he was delighted to find that his gold-wealthy father had bought, among other properties, the San Francisco *Examiner*. When Hearst senior was elected to the United States Senate in 1887, "young Willie," as he was called, took over the newspaper at the age of 24.

When old George Hearst died in 1891, William Randolph Hearst became a multi-millionaire by inheritance. Unlike Pulitzer, he never mastered the trick of making money. He was far better at spending it. But, like Pulitzer in his St.

Louis days, Hearst itched to tackle journalism in New York City and compete in a market where the stakes were high. In 1895, he bought an ailing New York daily, the *Morning Journal* (ironically founded 13 years before by Pulitzer's brother) and set himself to undertaking direct and cut-throat competition with the *World*. When all is said and done, Hearst did not succeed in gaining the *World*'s mantle during Pulitzer's lifetime. But the story of his failure—and many others during his lifetime—seems to many more colorful than that of Pulitzer's successful achievement.

Hearst's method of competition in New York was based on the simple principle that good people make good newspapers—or, at least popular ones. With a nearly unlimited supply of money, he was able to lure away from the *World* Pulitzer's best editors, reporters and cartoonists. He was particularly fortunate, in this respect, in attracting to the *Journal* (at first to develop its evening edition) the veteran editors Arthur Brisbane and Morrill Goddard, both innovative, creative talents who possessed the kind of showmanship for which Hearst was looking.

Yellow Journalism

The result was a newspaper "war" between the *World* and the *Journal*, instigated by Hearst. Integral to the war was a relatively innocent bystander, a cartoonist named Richard F. Outcault, who had been drawing a single-panel feature for the *World* entitled "The Yellow Kid." The "kid" himself was a sloppy urchin who lived in "Hogan's Alley," a fictional New York slum populated by ethnic wise-guy youngsters. The kid was yellow because he wore a brilliant yellow and ill-fitting overcoat that stood out against the black-and-white newspaper page like a beacon. Cartoonist Outcault became one of Hearst's many thefts from Pulitzer, because the cartoon was quite popular. In retaliation, Pulitzer hired another cartoonist, George B. Luks, to continue drawing the "kid" in the *World*. For a number of years, then, New York's newspaper readers had two "Yellow Kids," one in the *Journal* and one in the *World*. In fact, they had many more, because the denizens of Hogan's Alley found their way onto the vaudeville and burlesque stages of the city, instantly recognizable and laughable comic characters.

As a result, the competition between the *World* and the *Journal* was soon called "yellow journalism," the reason being the kid's yellow overcoat in both newspapers. The *kind* of competition it turned out to be was determined largely by the peculiarly talented men Hearst had lured away from Pulitzer. The *Journal* led the way. Liberated from the ethical restraints placed upon them by the older and more mature Pulitzer, the *Journal's* reporters and writers and editors could pull out all stops in attracting circulation. The *World* had little choice but to follow.

All in all, the *Journal,* especially its Sunday supplement (first called the *American Humorist* and later the *Sunday American Magazine*), reflected mostly the personality of Hearst writ large. The times were ripe for a flamboyant millionaire of his temperament to swing wide in the world of journalism. One of his slogans was, "While Others Talk the *Journal* Acts." Enormous headlines screamed across the *Journal*'s front page, most of them espousing the *Journal's* position on this or that issue, some of them misspelled if the type did not fit.

Sensationalism in the *World* was mild compared to the *Journal,* especially on Sunday. Pulitzer had pioneered printing comic cartoons, most of them single-panel drawings in black and white. Hearst printed them in color. In fact, he ran front pages festooned with colored drawings. The goriest news was illustrated with gory drawings. Hearst reporters not only covered the police desk, they set about trying to solve crimes. Sometimes they even succeeded. Sex, sports and sensationalism were grist for Hearst's mill, as well as outlandish articles about psychic research, living dinosaurs and phony "scientific" feature stories that peppered the *Journal*'s pages. If one could *not* prove something was *not* true, Hearst was likely to print it! And the *World* was not far behind Hearst. Nor were many other newspapers across the country which, one by one, were attracted to the methods of yellow journalism and the circulation figures that went along with it.

A grab-bag of flashy tricks sold newspapers: Scare headlines, multitudinous pictures, hokum, frauds and poppycock told as news or feature stories, Sunday comics and "campaigns" on behalf of the poor and oppressed all paid off.

Yellow journalism in New York was to reach its zenith between 1896 and 1901, the height of the war between Pulitzer and Hearst. Possibly the assassination of President McKinley in 1900 had something to do with its eventual diminution. The *Evening Journal* had even suggested the idea of the assassination of the President in an anti-McKinley editorial some months before the event occurred. The coincidence may have been too much for the public to stomach. Possibly the public grew tired of the trickery, just as it seemed to interest Hearst less and less as time passed. More likely, however, the virtues of yellow journalism—and there was something to be said for its irreverent energy and originality—were assimilated into common journalistic practice to the degree that neither editors nor readers noticed that it was (and is) still there, while most of its vices quietly died.

Hearst was a fervent American of a kind since passed. Patriotism was an emotion he used to stimulate the glands of his readers, many of them new Americans who took great pride in their adopted nation. He also had political ambitions, and used the *Journal* to exploit them.

The Spanish-American War

Much has been made of the role of the *Journal* (and Hearst) in swaying public opinion to the degree that America was led by Hearst into the Spanish-

American War. If there is any substance to the claim, the Hearst press was not the only guilty journalistic institution that used the three-year period, from 1895 to 1898, to inflame the American public with revolutionary zeal and then play America's subsequent engagement in the war to the hilt. Possibly the *Journal*'s screaming headline, shortly after the sinking of the American battleship *Maine* in the Havana harbor in February of 1898, reflects the temper of the times better than pages of historical prose have since. "The Whole Country Thrills With War Fever," it proclaimed, probably with considerable accuracy. Enter the war America did—for four months. But these were four months that will long be remembered in the history of American journalism. The yellow journalists' efforts, largely, but far from exclusively Hearst's, paid off in enormous circulation figures.

What made the Cuban rebellion so attractive to men like Hearst? In the first place, it was a cause, and a comparatively clear-cut one. A military junta had acted to kick an imperialistic power, Spain, out of the Caribbean and set up an independent government. This action followed the spirit, if not the text, of the old Monroe Doctrine, and even raised hopes in the breasts of men like Hearst that the United States might end up by annexing Cuba. The junta also operated a smooth and efficient propaganda machine within the United States, feeding Hearst and other publishers no end of atrocity stories and tales of dirty dealings on the part of the Spaniards. They sold newspapers. The stories were also well illustrated and lent themselves to the artist's pen in New York or, in the case of the distinguished American painter, Frederic Remington (on Hearst's payroll), in Havana itself. By the end of the war, Hearst even used photographs—real and faked—to dramatize his stories.

Second, the yellow press, and Hearst in particular, was nothing if not patriotic. Publishers saw in the Cuban rebellion a latter-day repetition of the American Revolution of 1776. Local patriots were fighting against a sinister, European imperialistic force, Spain, whose influence in the Americas had been as great, if not greater, than that of Britain more than a century before. Clear moral outrage runs through every edition of the *Journal* up to and including the war period—as it does, admittedly, through the *World, Times, Tribune, Sun* and *Herald.* Only Godkin of the *Post* seemed, in New York, to have resisted the virus of war fever. Hearst's international moralism lasted long after World War I, when, later in life, he turned isolationist in the 1930s. Pulitzer apparently also, eventually, had second thoughts, both about rampant, emotionally directed intervention with every rebellion in this and other hemispheres—and also about yellow journalism.

The sinking of the *Maine,* however, pulled the trigger. America was at war. Whether it was "Hearst's war" or the people's war or President McKinley's war matters little, and is today largely academic. The lesson of the Spanish-American War is today of less interest to journalists than to political scientists and historians. It may serve as an example of how *not* to cover a war in the press, however.

Hearst himself jumped into the fray—along with more than 500 other

American journalists—apparently joining hostilities on horseback and also involving himself in some pointless derring-do from his personal yacht, anchored on the Cuban shore. A virtual armada (the *Journal* alone chartered ten ships at $15,000 per day) was hired to shuttle news stories from Havana to the nearest telegraph station in Key West, Florida. The excitement was intense, so intense that the *Journal* published as many as 40 "Extra" editions a day during hostilities. Everyone felt a bit foolish when the Spaniards so quickly went home, and Cuba quietly began preparing for a tyrannical independence that was to be shattered by another rapid revolution 60 years later.

Hearst in Politics

If war could not satisfy Hearst, politics might. In 1902, he began a short and notably unsuccessful political career, heartening evidence that wealth alone could not corrupt American government, at least during the first part of this century. Hearst was elected twice to Congress, where he served without distinction from 1902 until 1905. His eye was on the Democratic presidential nomination of 1904, but politicians cleverer than he blocked his bid. Hearst then lost the mayoralty election in New York City by a few thousand votes. He ran for governor of New York State in 1906 against the distinguished jurist Charles Evans Hughes. Again, he was defeated. In 1909 he ran unsuccessfully for Mayor of New York.

In effect, Hearst's political career was over before it started. He therefore turned his attention to other matters: a fabulous antique collection as well as the acquisition of real estate, the rise of a chain of newspaper and press services, and later, even radio stations and a motion picture studio he purchased to exploit the talents of his longtime mistress, movie actress Marion Davies. He also built a monument to himself, San Simeon in California—his private castle, museum and fortress—which is today a notable tourist attraction. Among other things, he gave us, via Orson Welles and company, his fictional counterpart, Charles Foster Kane (a cardboard caricature of Hearst, in fact), to add mystery and color to one American whose memory requires nor merits neither one.

The Associated Press

The growth that New York experienced in the world of journalism at the turn of the century also occured across the nation. As far as press services were concerned, the old Associated Press did not have much important competition in America. In effect, membership in the AP permitted a paper anywhere in the United States to have at its command the same sophisticated news gathering force that most New York papers had, except for "scoops" within the intramural battle of the New York press. The AP had neatly cornered the news market for itself by means of an exclusive contract to use Western Union's telegraph wires for its material and was easily able to edge out or excel its few competitors. The AP also wisely and greedily restricted membership in various regions of the country to a limited number of newspapers, and demanded that an AP member subscribe to no other news service. In effect, AP members were at the mercy of seven New York papers that effectively controlled the service—usually holding or delaying the best of the news for their own use. Regional AP groups developed, and competing agencies attempted to break the hold of the AP with its priceless (and expensive) exclusive franchises. But government action was, as we shall see, necessary to clip the wings of this news monopoly on all fronts. In an era of monopolies, the AP was the most notable one in the world of journalism.

Press Across America and E. W. Scripps

Under these circumstances, it may seem surprising that any newspapers and journalists of stature arose beyond the confines of New York, but they did. One of them was the Atlanta, Georgia *Constitution,* best known for its brilliant editor, Henry W. Grady, who led it to distinction between 1880 until his death at the age of 39 in 1889. Grady was a social thinker, a reporter, orator and visionary whose own voice, and that of his paper, were regarded as that of "the new South," for which he spoke both eloquently and sensibly.

More notable for the history of journalism, however, was the rise of the Scripps chain of newspapers. The Scripps brothers were sons of an English immigrant to Illinois, James Mogg Scripps, who was married three times and produced copious children, four of whom were to make journalistic history. James Scripps founded the *Detroit News,* eventually taken over by his half-brother Edward Willis (E. W.) Scripps. E. W. and various other brothers (as well as a cousin, John Scripps Sweeney) also founded the *Cleveland Press.* In addition, and along with various other family members, E. W. gained controlling interests in other papers: the *St. Louis Chronicle* and the *Kentucky Post* among them.

Thus began the famous Scripps chain, a group of well and clearly written papers, generally oriented to the working man's interests and bespeaking a vaguely socialist—or populist—viewpoint. Using his business manager's name as a "front," the Scripps-McRae League of Newspapers sent (and funded) young journalists into likely communities to start new newspapers, usually on a profit-sharing basis, thus cutting the risk capital to the bone. By 1911, the League was made up of 18 newspapers, most of them inexpensive afternoon dailies that followed Scripps editorial policies. Meanwhile, Scripps himself had, during these years, personally and without his "front," began other newspapers in ten cities on the west coast. He even attempted to run newspapers without advertising in Chicago and Philadelphia in 1911 and 1912, but these ventures, like many others of Scripps' daring enterprises, ended in failure.

The Scripps chain of newspapers was the first of its kind in the United

States. While these newspapers were fighting the professional and financial hold of the New York establishment (especially the AP), many of them eventually became big businesses themselves. As we shall see, E. W. Scripps had a long and variegated career in journalism. Personally, he was only slightly less eccentric than Hearst or Pulitzer, at least according to his own autobiographical accounts. He claimed that he consumed a full gallon of whiskey a day (a physically impossible stunt), and his numerous extra-marital love affairs were hardly kept secret, even from his wife, the daughter of a Presbyterian minister. A champion of the poor, he amassed a fortune of about $50 million and died at the age of 71 in 1926, scoffing to the end at public champions of virtue—as far as his own style of living was concerned—and cholerically espousing the joys of vice.

Competition for the Associated Press

I suppose it took a man of E. W. Scripps' temperament to tackle the AP head on. This he did in 1907, apparently out to break the monopolistic hold the AP had on American newspapers. Besides, most AP members were, by tradition, morning newspapers. Most of Scripp's journals were published in the afternoon. He succeeded up to a point, but in his largest objective he also failed. The AP was just too powerful: seven New York newspapers against one determined, but less potent, chain-newspaper magnate.

During the first years of the century, the old Scripps-McRae League became itself a Press Association, operated mostly for his own newspapers. Merging with another service, the Publishers Press in the east, as well as his own west coast Scripps News Service, the United Press Association was founded in 1907. The UP did not operate as a membership club. Rather, it contracted its wares to individual newspapers and drew on the resources of the Scripps chain, less for news than human interest stories and feature materials that were attractive to small city and rural newspapers.

In 1908, Scripps appointed Roy W. Howard as general manager of the UP. Howard was then 25. He would outlive Scripps by many years and eventually assume control of the Scripps chain, involving himself in some amazing adventures that eventually led to the culmination of his career as head of the Scripps-Howard newspaper chain *and* owner of the UP.

Not to be outdone by Scripps—or the AP—William Randolph Hearst himself began his *own* news syndicate, operating on a contract basis, in 1909. The International News Service lived a long and notable life as the spine of Hearst's newspaper chain, dealing, for most of its life, more in Hearst's type of journalistic showmanship than with hard news. Like the UP, the INS could not, in its early years especially, compete with the AP. So its services had to be different. Neither Scripps nor Hearst put all their eggs in one basket, and both developed various distinctive journalistic properties for their own and other newspapers, the best known of which is probably Hearst's King Features Syndicate, begun in 1914, which offered comic strips, poets, jokes and almost everything *but* news to hungry papers that could not afford to develop the kind of talent Hearst, the UP and (later) Scripps-Howard were able to afford on their big city newspapers.

One footnote to the rise of the AP and its competitors may be fairly noted here—but not in a footnote. Smashing the AP's virtual monopoly in hard news awaits a later page in this history, but the eventual merger of Scripps' old UP and Hearst's INS (and their various properties) in 1958 need not. The United Press International born in that year, ended, in effect, much of the cut-throat competition that Hearst had thrived upon in his lifetime. The AP continued on to the present in prosperity, its monopoly broken not by competition, as things turned out, but by government action. But it remains to this day as profitable as ever.

Obviously, by the first decade of the twentieth century, press associations had become a necessity for any newspaper that hoped to satisfy a large readership even in a medium-sized city in the United States. With new papers burgeoning almost everywhere, it was impossible for each one to hire a staff of reporters to cover all the national and international events readers expected to find in daily and weekly journals—*in addition to* writing about local events and political news, usually, the only reason that most such cities required their own newspaper at all, rather than depending upon a big city daily. In addition, newspapers had, by this time, broadened their functions in order to cover in detail various matters that were not understood, for most of the nineteenth century, to be the proper concern of journalists. For these features, specialists and specially trained writers were required. It was, of course, nearly impossible to develop such talent at local levels. The press service or chain newspaper was, of course, the logical answer.

The Twentieth Century Newspaper

What had the newspaper in the United States become by 1900–1910? With the social background of the period in mind, let us remember still that the newspaper was, for this era at least, called upon to perform functions for the average American that movies, television, radio and other institutions fulfill today. No wonder, therefore, that there were so many of them. It was unlikely that the needs of the population in Columbus, Ohio, were identical with those in Cleveland, and within each city different parts of the population looked for different things from their newspapers.

In effect, the modern, all purpose, eclectic newspaper—a vehicle of entertainment, orientation, news, gossip, advice and political razzle-dazzle—was born during these years, necessity being the mother of invention. In few instances—soon to disappear—were these papers any longer exclusively *news* papers, that is, journals of events and political opinion, but rather, in some degree, local and national purveyors of prose and pictures of almost every type, including fiction in many forms and humor printed just to make people laugh.

The changes were notable. Editorial cartoons had become standard fare on the editorial pages. Single panel comic cartoons were now giving way to a new form of topical fiction, the comic *strip,* which was, strictly speaking, entirely "comic" only for the first few years of its life. Sports news was often as important—or more important—than other types of news, especially prize fighting and bicycle racing. Men who were not journalists in an old sense, but short-short story writers with a knack for distinctive feature pieces, originated the daily and weekly "column" or permanent by-lined feature. Such men as George Ade pioneered this type of journalism and were followed by other clever satirical writers like Franklin P. Adams and Don Marquis.

Comic strips themselves followed the lead of one of the first of the genre, Rudolph Dirks' "Katzenjammer Kids," an idea of Hearst's. The "Kids" began their antics in the *Journal* in 1897.

Dirks, incidentally, was hired away from Hearst by Pulitzer during the *Journal-World* war. Another man, H. H. Knerr, continued the strip for years in Hearst's papers, after the courts decided that Hearst owned the strip's title but not the characters. Dirks simultaneously drew the new strip, now called "The Captain and the Kids" for the *World*. So, like the single panel "Yellow Kid," it appeared in two newspapers at the same time. To complicate matters, Dirks' brother then began a *third* version of the Katzenjammer kooks for syndication. The result was that, at one time, it was hard for the average American to avoid meeting Hans, Fritz, der Captain, der Inspector, Momma and company in *any* comic section of *any* newspaper in America. World War I put a crimp in the "Kids' " popularity, because they were all Germans—although oddly living in Africa—but the doughty family survived not only through this war but World War II as well.

With color added, and as part of Sunday supplements, comic strips achieved immense popularity among both children and adults, almost from their birth. Most of the characters in them stepped right off the vaudeville stage (or onto it, like "The Yellow Kid") and indulged in the same sort of antics as characters in the nickelodeon comedies or "one reeler" movies. Do the names George McManus ("Bringing Up Father"), F. B. Opper ("Happy Hooligan"), Winsor McKay ("Little Nemo"), Bud Fisher ("Mutt and Jeff") and the near-genius Fontaine Fox ("Toonerville Trolley") mean anything to newspaper readers today, except those few, like me, still enamoured of the now (apparently) dying form of the comic strip? A few early cartoonists of this period, in fact, devised a distinctly American popular art form—one that was later to share a strangely reciprocal relationship with the motion pictures, each borrowing visual ideas, methods of storytelling and characters, one from the other, during the years to come.

Newspaper photography was also coming of age during this decade, climaxed, possibly, by the dramatic photograph, taken in 1910 by William F. Warnecke, of the attempted assassination of New York's Mayor Gaynor that was run in the *World*.

The Changing Magazine

Photographic syndicates began distributing pictures of national significance, and pictures were also the mainstay of many new illustrated monthly magazines. They offered relatively sophisticated stories, features, drawings and photographs for the price of 10 cents an issue, opposed to much higher prices—as formidable as 35 cents—now charged by *Harper's* and *Scribner's*, as well as the venerable *Leslie's Weekly*. Among the first of these low priced monthlies were *McLure's Magazine, Cosmopolitan, Munsey's, Collier's* and a revivified *Saturday Evening Post*.

A price war developed as the result of this competition. The new magazines eventually raised their newsstand prices and subscription rates, but only after they had severely shaken—and destroyed—many of their older competitors. Whatever else they did, the new magazines also developed a lively, entertaining style in tune with the times. They gave America the formula for the type of family magazine that dominated the periodical market for nearly 50 years, or until television began to lure advertisers away from them in the middle 1950s.

The New York Times

There were, of course, exceptions to these general trends in the American press during this period. There had to be, considering the number of newspapers and magazines published in the United States at this time and their rate of growth.

Most notable among the journalistic mavericks was a Southern gentlemen of German-Jewish extraction named Adolph Ochs, born in Cincinnati in 1858, whose family found their way to Tennessee. Ochs began working in newspaper offices at the age of 11 and, by the time he was 21, was a partner in the *Chattanooga Times,* a paper he subsequently developed, during the next decade and a half, into a valuable property with a new building of its own.

In 1896, Ochs arrived in New York prepared to buy the old and ailing *New York Times,* which had declined severely after Raymond's death, even under the able stewardship of its then managing editor, John C. Reid. Pulitzer's *World,* and even the *Tribune,* were too competitive for the *Times* in a city that did not appreciate a somewhat scholarly journal that still, in effect, was paying homage to Henry Raymond's ghost. Under Ochs, the *Times* would turn this liability into an asset.

A million dollars was a lot to pay for a newspaper with a circulation of about 9,000 per day (as opposed to the *World's* 200,000 at the time), but, to Ochs, it was well worth it. He raised the money from his own personal capital, borrowed funds using the Chattanooga paper as collateral and by selling shares in the enterprise. In fact, Ochs did not own a controlling interest in the *Times* for the first four years of his management. Having acquired the *Times,* however, and with the help of editor Charles R. Miller, he brought circulation up to 75,000 within one year and to 100,000 by 1901. Because of the literate, educated and affluent readership at which it aimed, the *Times* also became a lucrative advertising vehicle.

From the start, Ochs chose to swim against the stream of newspaper popularity in New York. That is, he continued Raymond's tradition by keeping the *Times* a well written, reliable newspaper that conspicuously would *not* indulge in yellow journalism and was, therefore, both different and better than most of New York's other mass circulating newspapers. He did not run comic strips, published few pictures and centered on the civilized presentation of responsible news and opinion in detail. The slogan, which still appears on the *Times* masthead, "All The News That's Fit To Print," constituted Och's deliberate dig at most other New York newspapers that were fighting circulation battles by means of sensationalism. In addition, Ochs cut the price of the *Times* to a penny; the *World* and *Journal* both sold for two cents. The move increased readership and, of course, advertising revenues.

The newspaper that Ochs created (and has remained in his family ever since) is, in many ways, not too different in orientation from the *New York Times* of today. Rather than take for himself large profits from the paper, Ochs put earnings back into its development, the recruitment of a large and capable staff of newsmen and, in 1904, the construction of a home for the *Times* on New York's Forty-Second Street. The building stood in the middle of a traffic intersection in a district that was, at the time, becoming the center of the legitimate theatre. "Times Square," the intersection was named. And so the newspaper began its evolution from a daily paper to a national institution.

Possibly Ochs' luckiest—or brainiest—move was hiring away from the *New York Sun* an Ohioan, Carr V. Van Anda, who, until 1929, was the *Times'* managing editor. Among old-time journalists, Van Anda is considered by many one of America's greatest newsmen to date. He literally lived for the *Times,* seven days a week and usually 12 hours a day on a clockwork schedule. Van Anda was uncompromising in his demands for complete and accurate reporting, skillful copy reading and meaningful headlines. In fact, Van Anda's passion for completeness, entirely commensurate with Henry Raymond's idea of a newspaper that kept the record, is still a *Times* tradition, carried on by printing complete texts of important documents and speeches rather than simply summaries. He was also enough of a reporter himself to know the value of, and relish, opportunities to "scoop" other New York newspapers in covering important breaking news.

The *Times* has been called "good and gray" because of its serious nature and resistance, particularly in its earliest years, to humor, frivolity, gossip and sensationalism. During the first 15 years of Ochs' management, it surely must have appeared somewhat dull when held against other, larger circulating New York newspapers. It was, however, also establishing a national reputation that would, in the long run, turn out to be of greater importance than transitory circulation figures. The *Times* was reliable. It was timely. It was accurate to a fault. It did indeed keep the record, eventually, almost to the point of absurdity: precipitation charts, ship arrivals and departures, fire house calls, marriages, births, deaths, etc. It was also a paper for the cultured man or woman, featuring book reviews, financial news, theatrical news and criticism, and it displayed a cultivated person's sensitivity to the arts. Its conservative format was also reflected in its generally conservative political stance. More strongly than other New York papers, however, the *Times* displayed a lively interest in news from overseas as well as that of American origin.

In the long run, the *Times* survived and prospered because of all these factors: because of Van Anda's perfectionism and because of Ochs' firm purpose in producing a serious newspaper that did not pander to the whims of the public for the moment in order to boost circulation. The *New York Times* is today probably America's outstanding newspaper, despite the fact that many others are excellent in their own ways, and a good number of others boast of larger circulations. The *Times* is now also a rich corporation involved in broadcasting, book publishing and numerous other projects in the field of mass communication and education.

In my lifetime, I have seen the names of the *Journal* and the *World*—along with the *Sun,* the *Herald,* the *Tribune* and other newspapers disappear from the newsstands of my native city. *The New York Times,* however, was there on the day that I was born.

Ochs himself died in 1935, and his paper survived him. It will, I am certain, survive me also. (I can see, in my minds eye, my own *Times*-style obituary, and I am even probably competent to write it.) The *Times* will probably survive you too. The reason, of course, is that Adolph Ochs' aspirations for his New York paper were not momentary strategic responses to immediate needs, but an approach to publishing rooted in a philosophy of *useful* journalism. The Southern gentleman from Tennessee was probably the greatest, if least colorful, of the press barons who competed for the attention of readers when this century was new. His contribution to mass communications was certainly among the most enduring and one whose monument, *The New York Times,* may well last longest.

The All-Purpose Medium

The first decade of the twentieth century was obviously exciting and fervent—if not a distinguished—decade for the American press. Nor do I think that it is hyperbolic to note that it was possibly also the press' most creative period, before or since. Parkinson's amusing law states that institutions display their greatest vitality while they are growing, and much evidence gives credence to his notion. For all its sins—yellow journalism, cut-throat competition, monopoly practices, etc.—during this first ten years of the century, the American press operated without viable competition from other media in an affluent society of readers ready—indeed greedy—for exactly the kinds of experiences that newspapers and magazines might provide for them: not only news, but thrills and laughs and tears and a sense of involvement with a whole expanding nation and the world beyond them. Soon enough the competition would begin: first motion pictures to provide the thrills and laughs, and then radio to bring the excitement of breaking news in far-off places as it happened. But, for the moment, this decade of technological and cultural advancement saw words and pictures spread almost exclusively by means of print.

I do not mean to underestimate the influence of other technologies, especially the railroads, in carrying ideas and men rapidly from place to place, or the novelty of the new telephone, electric lights and talking machines that were being installed in the homes of those that could afford them. Nor do I want to overlook the fact that airplanes began flying during this decade, and that those first, puffing, dirty but gorgeous automobiles made their way down cow pastures and onto Main Street to the amazement and disdain of horse lovers everywhere. But only a small portion of the population could afford such luxuries. Most people saw them, scratched their heads, and settled back with their newspapers and magazines to read more about them.

Newspapers were cheap. Newspapers were everywhere. Newspapers were exciting. Newspapers kept their readers up to the minute. Never again in the United States, I imagine, will they perform so many functions so well for so great a part of our population. Nor, possibly, will any of them accomplish so much with quite the same enthusiasm and zest.

7

Communications for the Masses

THE GREAT MODERN AGE of mass communications in the United States began, I suppose, at about the time that one of its major innovators, Joseph Pulitzer, died. It has yet to end. A new form of public discourse by which very few people speak effectively and clearly to very many describes old yellowed copies of the *New York World* just as it does today the initials CBS.

The mold was set for the growth of modern journalism by about 1910. Today's newspaper, by and large, seems more like a paper of 1915 (over 60 years ago) than a 1915 newspaper seemed like a 1885 paper (30 years before.) Of course, the press also employed new techniques and technologies to carry its services, features, photographs and cartoons to an entire nation. They would soon use others, particularly broadcasting in its many phases, and adapt them to new instruments in the years just ahead: the teletype, the wirephoto and allied devices for the dissemination of messages to the masses.

Integral to this change and period of development was, so we have seen, the photograph and its use by the print media of all sorts—from house organs to bus advertisements to the mail order businesses. From the crude plates of Matthew Brady to the sophisticated cameras of the post-World War II era, the arts and sciences of photography infiltrated every known instrument of mass communication, including broadcasting which was once thought to be impervious to it.

We have already traced the history of the toy that grew into the lucrative curiosity of the street nickelodeon, the early films of Edison, the Lumières and others that attracted audiences merely because they were curiosities. They properly belonged in their carnival environment, as parts of vaudeville shows and as passing amusements that signified how clever were the new technologies of the early twentieth century. We also know that certain other visionaries saw in these early films the germ of an industry, the eventual size of which one day would probably have caused them to shake their heads in wonder.

The transition was not automatic. In the beginning, the nature of what sorts of images a movie could show was limited by the technology at hand, a need for natural illumination in shooting a picture, and the belief that an audience was unlikely to be able to stand more than one reel—or about ten minutes—of continuous action before becoming bored.

Edwin S. Porter

On this latter assumption did Edwin S. Porter, the first American movie maker of note, operate. The result, in 1902 or 1903, was *The Life of An American Fireman,* his first "theatrical" film, probably the first of its kind in America. Considering everything, *Fireman* is not a bad job, better than the Hollywood disaster epic I saw recently at my local Bijou. (Both plots were remarkably similar, except that Porter's was, mercifully, less complicated!) The narrative of *Fireman*—simply a vignette of a fire company answering a call and rescuing survivors from a burning building—is built shot by shot: that is, it is an *edited* film, a great advance over photographs of trains coming into stations. It contains close-ups, is quite naturalistic and achieves some suspense from the rescue of a baby from the burning building. More than anything, it succeeds in telling a story.

Porter's next film, *The Great Train Robbery* (1903) simply elaborates upon these former techniques with a little more dash. The main difference between the two films is that the performers are more clearly individual characters in *Robbery* than in *Fireman*. In fact, one is aware that they are actors, portraying passengers, criminals, etc., suitably costumed for distinct roles. The film even contains a sequence involving a telegraph operator who is captured and bound by desperadoes and released by his small daughter. The bandits are caught, and the film ends with "Bronco Billy" Anderson, having formerly been killed in the action, suddenly coming back to life, and, just for the cinematic kicks, firing his gun a few times at the audience.

In some ways, it is amazing to think of how clearly Porter anticipated many of the characteristics of the film medium as it developed in the years to come in these two films. Mainly, he was thinking in theatrical terms. Unlike the Lumière Brothers, he turned his back almost entirely on the potential of the movies for documenting his times and exploited instead the art of drama. For him, movies were a new way of blending reality and fiction. He also placed his finger neatly on one of two kinds of drama (the other was farce comedy) that remain peculiarly amenable to the art of the film: melodrama. Now, melodrama deals with action, exaggerated and heroic deeds, and, in his planning, he entered into the heart of much of such fantasy: the chase. In *Fireman,* it is the chase of men out to stop a natural holocaust. In *Robbery,* it is the good guys after the bad guys. In order to achieve these ends, Porter's camera is used fluidly, poking its nose here and there into essential pictorial plot points that contribute to a theatrical *whole.* Using his camera, for the most part, out of doors, he was able to demonstrate how the films might liberate the theatre from the proscenium arch of the stage or—better yet—cut back and forth from a stage set (or indoors) to the outdoors. True, Porter's films were naive and simple compared to even the crudest live theatrical performances of his day, but they did illustrate, by means of his "quickie productions" made in New Jersey, what potential this new medium held for story telling in a dramatic mode.

George Méliès

In many ways, the French magician Georges Méliès chose an opposite path from Porter. Although some of Méliès' films were shot in outdoor surroundings, the bulk of his work, accomplished between 1900 and 1906, was photographed in a glass-covered studio outside of Paris, and centered on theatrical and stylized imitations of nature. He too was interested in putting the world of theatre on film, but both comedy and drama were less important to him than sheer illusion, the art he prized most as a conjurer. In a way, his contribution to the technique of film making was greater than that of Porter, because he was able to show what one could do with, and by means of, film that one could *not* do in live performance—without using the complex paraphernalia and special skills of a stage magician.

Indeed, Méliès dramatized fairy tales, took a trip to the moon, re-enacted the Dreyfus affair, the execution of Joan of Arc, traveled to Jules Verne's subterranean universe and to the polar regions. But his stories are less interesting than his legerdemain, and his magic is less interesting than the techniques he invented and used to achieve it. He did not discover "time stop" photography, but it had not been used extensively to perform miracles (as it is today) before Méliès. He wound his films back in the camera to create double exposures that accomplished the impossible. Méliès, full size, talking to his own head in close-up, severed from his body is an outstanding, amusing example. The films, for Méliès were not vessels of reality but theatrical mechanisms for the accomplishment of the impossible. His sets and costumes were not drawn from nature but from his own imagination and the theatre of his time. Méliès' films remind one less of stage drama than of later animated cartoons with live people moving around cut-out set pieces, all involved in an artificial, imaginative magic show.

The story of Méliès' personal fate, his eventual life of poverty as a Paris news and souvenir dealer and final years in an old folks home until his death in 1938 are irrelevant, really, to our history, except to illustrate that the world of communications (especially the films) takes poor care of its own heroes. Porter did little better. He died in 1941, ending his career as a mechanic in an obscure factory, forgotten and unhonored.

Early Films

Both of these men were fascinating innovators. But each made a mistake tragic for those individuals whose talents are involved in technologies that are in the process of growing and changing. Méliès and Porter each indicated clearly the theatrical potentialities of the movies, demonstrated this avenue of development and then continued to repeat what they had already done instead of carrying their concepts further to new imaginative dimensions.

If Porter could tell simple melodramatic tales on films and characterize people crudely, might he subsequently have dealt with sub-plots, more complex themes and richer characters? Might Méliès, having demonstrated that stage magic could be accomplished in new ways by means of film, then turn his attention to using that deceptive art in more elaborate contexts than short, fantastic adventures at the North Pole or on the moon? Probably not. People of this sort are rarely talented at more than the art of innovation. Given an inchoate means of communication, they find artful ways to say what they must say. But their message is usually a crude, simple one. Because their audiences were themselves ahead of Méliès and Porter in their expectations of what movies could tell them, these amusements delighted for a few years and were replaced by ennui. Into the museums they went. In sum, the ideas were used up.

Méliès and Porter are our best symbols of this early period of film production around the world, but they were not alone. G.A. Smith and Robert Paul in England accomplished Méliès-type effects at about the same time he did, and Cecil Hepworth was in the cinematic "rescue and robbery" business shortly after Porter. Ferdinand Zecca, in France, as well as Emile Cohl and Jean Durand, excavated the comic vein of cinema with little farces, camera tricks and jokes that were to open up a whole new world of cinematic insanity.

At Pathé's French studios, the man who was shortly to become the first silent film comedy star, Max Lindner, began his top-hatted, mustachioed career in 1905 and achieved considerable international popularity. Max was the impeccable dandy, always getting into inventive scrapes, fighting an unending battle between the challenges of a complicated world and his own inadequate self. (Some years later a comic named Charles Chaplin was to model his famous tramp upon Lindner's dandy, adding a dimension of pathos to Max's high jinks.) In the early years of the century, however, the most sophisticated work done by film makers came from France, where, after all, much of the development of the film had begun, and where theatrical tradition mated nicely with this new invention and its potentials.

The Film d'Art

What we call today the *Film d'Art* company was simply a desire on the part, largely, of theatre people to move the cinema away from melodrama, farce and magic into the classical tradition of the playhouse. To this end, a French company was formed about 1907 that tried to bring to the screen many of the classics of the French stage repertoire intact, as they appeared in the theatre, but sped up. (All of *Hamlet* was performed by the *Film d'Art* in ten minutes!) Their stage scenery looked exactly like the stage scenery it was. The project was, at first, far from a popular success, although its sponsors, the *Société Film d'Art* kept doggedly at it. Eventually, as we shall see, the films grew longer, and many of them were successful.

The Motion Picture Patents Company

These particular films had a surprising effect upon the trust of businessmen who, in effect, maintained iron control over the manufacture of motion picture equipment in the United States and Europe. The Motion Picture Patents Company meant, and was, a business from start to finish, that displayed little interest either in theatre or art.

The company was born on New Year's Day in 1909 and consisted of nine producers, seven of them American and two French, as well as the distributor George Klein. Each owned various patents on certain types of camera, projection equipment and other cinematic devices. Now they were all joined in a common business pool from which Edison was paid his share as the major single patent holder. Eastman supplied his film *exclusively* to the Trust, and fees were set up for the use of various other types of equipment as well as rentals of all of the films produced by the trust. In effect, non-Trust members who might wish to make, distribute or project their own *or* Trust-made films were frozen out of the game. The Trust's subsidiary, the General Film Company, set itself to controlling all film exchanges, film rentals and exploitation of actors. The Trust lasted intact for less than five highly profitable years, after which anti-trust legislation and the pressure of independent producers forced its dissolution.

Famous Plays With Famous Players

The French *Societé* was one of the independents, in its own peculiar way. Among the international stars to appear in one of its films was the "divine" Sarah Bernhardt, a great romantic stage actress of the period with an international following. Breaking one of the American Trust's major rules, that no picture should last more than one reel, the French *Societé* could not resist photographing so great a superstar as Bernhardt at length. The film she made for them, *Queen Elizabeth,* ran four reels long, or about an hour. *Queen Elizabeth* was a poor last testament to a great performer. It was stagey, over-acted and artificial. But an American ex-fur merchant, Adolph Zukor (later founder of Paramount Pictures), thought that *Elizabeth* would attract Bernhardt's admirers to movie theatres in the United States. He purchased American rights to the film and, unable to convince the Trust to show it in their nickelodeons, booked a legitimate Broadway theatre, the Lyceum, to exhibit it himself. Zukor charged the unheard of price of $1 for admission. Thus began his successful series of *Famous Plays With Famous Players,* started by the aging Bernhardt who found herself, in her sixties, a movie star.

Not exactly. The audience that attended the *Film d'Art* movies from Europe was not made up of the middle and lower class immigrants who populated the nickelodeon theatres in the poorer sections of town. They were, by and large, the same sorts of people who could afford to attend the legitimate theatre. What attraction did movies have for them? The Italian epic, *Quo Vadis,* filmed in Italy in 1912, running nearly two hours, provided a partial answer. In addition to the novelty of films shown in a legitimate theatre, *Quo Vadis* was able to include spectacular chariot races, crowd scenes and a panoramic glimpse of Ancient Rome (or what Italian film makers thought Ancient Rome looked like) that were impossible to recreate on the living stage.

In effect, *Quo Vadis* went the "Famous Play" idea one step further: it employed the unique properties of the film to do even what great naturalistic directors like David Belasco could not do. Its photographers moved beyond the walls of the playhouse, setting its historical drama in an apparently real (or recreated) world.

More than one theatrical artist worried, at the time, about the fate of the living theatre in the face of such potential competition. What others had great faith in, however, was the desire, true even today, of people to see their favorite actors and celebrities in the flesh. If the movies had had it in their power to have killed the living theatre, Zuckor would have been the murderer. As it was, he merely found, in the long run, larger audiences for a new kind of theatre, while patrons continued avidly to fill live playhouses—until other factors (like outlandishly high admission prices and poor plays) began discouraging them decades later.

D. W. Griffith

In recent years, much has been made of the contribution of David Wark Griffith to the art of the film, some of it justified, some of it hyperbolic. Apparently, and in spite of legend, Griffith did not invent many new filmic techniques. (Among film buffs, it has lately become an indoor sport to find prior uses of supposed Griffith "innovations.") The photographic distinctions—and innovation—in much of his output undoubtedly reflects the talents of the cameraman, Billy Bitzer, with whom he worked from the beginning of his career in 1908 until almost the end of his career. (Bitzer's absence rather than Griffith's personal dissipation is often given as the reason for the failure of the latter's final works.) One cannot, however, minimize the artistic and theatrical ambitions that Griffith held for the infant film art, his faith in films as a dramatic medium, the brilliance of his work with actors or his willingness to experiment by carrying the ideas of others to their conclusion, sometimes for the better and sometimes for the worse. Only an egocentric, energetic visionary like Griffith possessed the nerve, showmanship and talent to turn the trick and to succeed—and to fail—so spectacularly.

Griffith was a Southerner, born of an imagined aristocracy and, until his alcoholic demise, a Southern gentlemen as well. As a young writer, working as "Lawrence" Griffith, he journeyed from the professional theatre (where he had enjoyed slight and early success as a playwright and actor) to a series of odd jobs to Edwin S. Porter's Bronx film studio. He appeared as an actor in Porter's 1907 film, *Rescued From an Eagle's Nest.* Then he sold a number of movie stories to the Biograph Studios on New York's Fourteenth Street and soon directed his first film, *The Adventures of Dollie,* in 1908. Having shown his directorial talents, and having helped cameraman Bitzer to exercise his own cinematic ingenuity, Griffith then stayed for about four years at Biograph filming one-reelers, many of them starring his (then) wife, Linda Arvidson. They were shot either in the Biograph Studios or on location along the Hudson, depending upon the season. In them, one sees the slow emergence of Griffith's mastery of the film medium. There were hundreds of early short films, and prints of many survive to this day.

Griffith's art may be summed up—too glibly, possibly—in one sentence: He was probably one of the first directors to recognize that films were, in certain important ways, a new theatrical medium, different from the living theatre of the time—but, incidentally, not as different from it as the theatre itself of the next generation was to be. Zukor's movies had been, indeed, just photographed stage plays, full-length scenes shown from the audience's viewpoint. Griffith's movies were fluid; the audience sat wherever Griffith's camera chose to travel. He used close-ups to clarify emotions, reactions and plot ideas. He directed the audience's attention to whatever *he,* as director, wanted them to see, rather than to what was merely exposed on stage. This was often achieved by turning into a virtue the necessary silence of these early movies, although Griffith did not hesitate to employ titles to provide dialogue.

In effect, his cutting, camera angles and, mostly, *involvement* with the visual action of drama make his short pieces fundamentally cinematic rather than theatrical. To the audience of their time, these short films also appeared *real,* despite their exaggerated acting and (usually) foolish plots. Griffith's lighting was used to achieve emotional effects, as it was in the theatre. Bitzer, unlike most early cameramen, was not merely satisfied by getting enough light into a scene to photograph it clearly, but instead searched for the right play of light and shadow to enhance the mood of the scene wherever possible.

One has to be a devout movie buff to watch Griffith's early films at Biograph and not cringe at most of the stylized acting, foolish stories, contrived suspenses and silly, romantic endings. One may explain these matters away easily enough, considering the technology with which Griffith worked and the dream worlds spun by the nickelodeon audiences he pleased so successfully. What *is* important about these movies is that they are *different* from others being made at the time, and that these differences were copied by others—and by Griffith himself—to be domesticated into the grammar and syntax of the theatrical language that we still expect from a film. The use of close-up symbols is an example: hands, weapons, telephones, a hero, dollar bills, etc. that tell us something vital about a situation or character. In many ways, Griffith was a lucky, talented man working in a pristine dramatic medium with no one experienced enough to tell him what he was doing was wrong or could not be done or might not make sense. In fact, Griffith educated his own audience to understand the vocabulary he himself invented.

Griffith's years at Biograph in New York ended in 1912. He had tried making larger, two-reel films that the Trust released to theatres separately, one reel at a time. Finally, the Trust followed the lead of exhibitors and released both reels together, largely because that is the way audiences wanted to see them. But two reels seemed to be as far as Griffith could push Biograph in New York. In California, he subsequently shot the four-reel *Judith of Bethulia* in 1914. On the heels of *Quo Vadis'* success the previous year, *Judith* was released intact, the first American major movie of (almost) feature length. It was cheered by New York's "uptown" audiences and attracted notice even from theatre critics who, until then, had considered movies frivolities. *Judith of Bethulia* was also Griffith's last film for Biograph.

Griffith's two greatest films now lay ahead of him. For the Mutual Film Company, using the pictorial material carefully based upon old Matthew Brady photographs, he directed his version of a mediocre novel, *The Clansman,* replete with an enormous cast, multiple settings and a fine cast of actors. This famous film, *The Birth of a Nation,* released in 1915, reflects Griffith's Southern background, telling the story of the well-remembered conflict between the states, largely from a rebel perspective. It is biased, inaccurate and mercilessly bigoted in its treatment of blacks (white actors in unconvincing blackface), sentimental and, in parts, just plain dull. But it is also a full-blown cinematic *event,* an historical saga, a personal story and a uniquely effective film—even when viewed today. Its own history, from its early release to the present, has been marred by severe criticism of Griffith's personal version of the Civil War and his attitudes toward the black man. But, all in all, its artistic integrity has neutralized—if not made up for—its historical and social sins.

Spurred on by its success, and smarting under accusations that he lacked tolerance, Griffith attempted an even more ambitious project for his next picture, so enormous that it consumed the substantial profits he had made from *Birth of a Nation.* Called *Intolerance* and released in 1916, it is a movie so "colossal" (a Hollywood word that fits only one or two films) that the film is difficult to describe. Dealing with the results of bigotry in four periods of history from Babylon to modern days (all intercut, one with the other), *Intolerance* is a veritable spectacle within a spectacle: a monumental pre-Christian pagan outdoor orgy, the story of the Crucifixion, an epic of marching armies and a fantastic railroad chase, among other things. It develops four plots at the same time. It is quite safe to say that nothing like it has been filmed since.

Despite its sweep, grandeur and excitement, *Intolerance* did not repeat the success of *Birth of a Nation.* Audiences found it confusing. They still do, and so do I. But it remains, more than *Birth,* the finest example of Griffith's cinematic imagination, verve, vitality and art.

For Griffith, the future was, after *Intolerance,* a trip downhill—at first slowly and then rapidly. His films in the late 'teens and early 'twenties show many signs of the old cinematic touch: *Broken Blossoms* in 1919, *Way Down East* in 1921, and *Orphans of the Storm* in 1922, particularly. Griffith tried to repeat his earlier successes in 1924 with a patriotic opus, *America.* By 1926, he had become an erratic and undependable man who relied now upon obsolete techniques. Griffith had the distinction of directing W. C. Fields in his first film, a contrived circus story, *Sally of the Sawdust,* in 1925. With the coming of sound movies, his career was, in effect, over. Griffith directed a couple of talking pictures and died both sick and broke in Hollywood in 1948. The final two decades of his life provided pathetic and ironic contrast to the creativity and successes of the first 20 years of his career in films.

Griffith, more than anyone else, had turned the films into a valid theatrical medium. His was a people's theatre, not the property of an elite moneyed class, but an artistic theatre within the reach of the common man. Griffith, however, was just one man in a new and rising industry that also produced a dream city devoted to its pursuit: Hollywood, U.S.A.

The Motion Picture Capitol

In the earlier days of the American movies, most films were made in Chicago or New York, particularly the latter. The logic of a New York production base seemed firm enough. The professional theatre, and therefore a pool of acting and directing talent, was readily available in the big city. A larger logic (or combination of logic and larceny), however, sent movie makers scurrying to the Pacific coast of the United States, separating geographically the theatrical and motion picture centers of the country as in no other Western nation.

Why California, or Los Angeles, in particular?

(There was originally no such place as Hollywood, which was just an unofficial section of Los Angeles. In fact, it is almost impossible to locate the authentic Hollywood today. Most of the major film studios were built either in nearby suburbs like Culver City, Burbank or in L.A. proper. The name was, for the most part, a press agent's fantasy.)

In the first place, land for outdoor production was cheap on the West coast of America in those days. The climate was sunny, and whenever possible, natural sunlight was used for filming—a technical factor of cinema production that was soon to change. Many different sorts of landscapes were easy to find nearby. Second, it was about as far away from the Motion Picture Patents Company as the movie producers could get. It was therefore possible to use ''bootleg'' equipment and avoid the hassle of the litigation over matters of who should be paid what for the use of whose patents. And, if caught infringing on patents, a producer could always slide across the Mexican border to let matters cool a bit. In California, also, quick-buck operators managed to squeeze about a week's credit out of their checking accounts in New York banks. And a week was often enough to hire the talent necessary to borrow the money to start a production—using the talent as collateral, of course. Until the rise of California banks like the Bank of America, it took five days to a week for a New York check drawn in California to clear (or bounce), and in that time a lot could be accomplished, as long as the check was paid for against a last-minute deposit (or loan) in New York.

To Hollywood the film makers went—although the business end of the distribution and exhibition of films remained in New York. Hollywood attracted producers, directors and actors, men like Thomas H. Ince, a one-time actor and director turned producer, who developed many of the studio practices—most in the interest of economy—that were to remain standard film production procedures for decades. With his wide background, Ince became, possibly, the first creative film producer—that is, the creative individual in charge of the production of a film, including the work of writers and directors, directly involved in all of the arts and crafts of film making. He is reputed to have developed the idea of the "final shooting script" and "shooting schedule," that replaced the rough "playing by ear" of earlier film makers with precise agenda of what work was to be accomplished by a studio each day. By the early 'twenties, however, the ambitious Ince had burned himself out. His studio, but not his methods, disappeared.

Mack Sennett was another distinctive Hollywood producer of a different stripe. He enjoyed a reputation for production *dis*organization, a legend that he enjoyed too thoroughly to accept whole. Sennett arrived in Hollywood in 1912 after a career as writer and actor. He was a one-time friend of the young Griffith, but he wanted to produce, direct and even act in film comedies. In Hollywood, his Keystone Studios produced the Keystone Kops, a still famous company of clowns and frequently imitated. Much of Sennett's humor was improvised and childish, and much the result of pure cinematic trickery. But it was visual, and it was funny.

In addition, Sennett developed the talents of many comic film actors who were to become great national favorites, individuals about as different from the skilled stage performers who appeared in most serious films as you can imagine. Charlie Chase, Chester Conklin, "Slim" Summerville, Ben Turpin, Mabel Normand, "Fatty" Arbuckle and Edgar Kennedy were all Sennett Keystone alumni.

The energetic Sennett made 140 short comedies in his first year of operation. He stuck to production much as Ince did, inventing, among other things, the custard-pie-in-the-face gag, one of which the public never appears to tire. Sennett continued producing films until 1935. But with the advent of sound movies in 1927, a quality disappeared from his visual humor that he could not once again capture in words. Still, over the years, most of Hollywood's best comedians of later years stopped off at Sennett's madhouse studios at one time or another to learn or perfect their trade.

Charles S. Chaplin

Comedians came and comedians went, but one of them, probably more than any other actor, producer *or* director, made Hollywood the film capitol of the world by virtue of his resounding and startling world-wide success that only a mass medium like the film could provide a theatrical artist. I mean, of course, the London-born clown, Charles Chaplin, about whom more books have been written than most of the leading philosophers of our century. Chaplin was both a hero and a legend in his own day. The public around the world found his screen character intensely funny (and somewhat pathetic) in his own time just as they appear to today. Chaplin spoke an international language of pantomime that appealed to high- and low-brows alike, and to audiences who spoke any language. His memory is today revered even by people who have not seen his movies.

Except me. In fairness, I do not want my enthusiasm for Chaplin's contribution to film art to be misinterpreted. I have watched most of his extant movies. They are mostly mildly humorous, hilarious at times—but inconsistently so. Any number of comics of the silent and/or talking films possessed greater genius for comedy, in my opinion: Laurel and Hardy, Buster Keaton and W. C. Fields to name just three, for instance. Chaplin's tramp character carries but a two-dimensional bag of tricks and is neither an original or rich concept: the trite notion of the funny man with the poet's soul. True enough, Chaplin is both clever and versatile. I think that his later films indicate that he may have been a better writer than a performer or director. He was also a painstaking craftsman. Possibly, he deserves greatest credit for being an unusually protean man of the arts: a shrewd and creative businessman, merchandising his own catholic talents in so clever a way that they, to this day, produce a fortune for him, although he is now old and retired.

Having said this, let us look at Chaplin's astounding career. Coming to America from England as a young man with a vaudeville troupe, he started his career with Keystone in 1913. Gigantic salary leaps from his original $50 per week saw him move rapidly to Essanay Films and to the Mutual Film Company in about three years at a salary, by 1916, of about $10,000 a week, plus fringe benefits. In the transition, after experimenting with various comic styles, he had hit upon the tramp character or "little fellow," as he called him. (Until the end of his life, Stan Laurel claimed that he had originated this tramp character in his vaudeville days with Chaplin.)

The "little fellow" was perfected bit by bit, and, whatever he was, the public loved him. The country went Chaplin crazy: toys, comic strips, dances and other consumer goods bore his name—or at least the name "Charlie" who, for 20 or more years meant only Chaplin. In 1917, Chaplin signed a million dollar contract with First National Films. He was 27 years old, and, as an actor-director, the king of Hollywood, although up to this time his pictures had been confined mostly to short subjects. His only competition for popularity was a little girl star, Mary Pickford, "America's Sweetheart."

The Star System

Pickford and Chaplin—and a few others—had indeed become "stars" in a new construction of the term. By and large, producers and financiers had fought against the star system in Hollywood for the simple reason that neither law nor nature could prevent a popular performer from holding a personal monopoly on his own talents. If you wanted, say, "Bronco Billy" Anderson in your movie you *had* to do business with "Bronco Billy." In effect, he had no competition for his *own* talent, his own face and his own name. Producers would rather have kept their actors anonymous. They tried, inventing such sobriquets as "The Biograph Girl" and "The Imp Girl," with the notion that actors were replaceable units, especially if they asked for too much money for their services. The public would then accept a new "Biograph Girl," not necessarily the current one, say, Florence Lawrence.

The producers were wrong on all counts. Even mediocre actresses like Lawrence were different, one from the other, and the film-going public wanted to know the real (or stage) names of these girls. They ate up bogus biographies that film publicists released to the press about them, especially with the rise of film star magazines that fancifully created illusions about the private lives of these new demigods. But, in the end, men like Chaplin and girls like Pickford were really responsible for the star system. They were indeed unique and *could not* be replaced in movies by other performers without cries of outrage from film goers. They were the sole owners of some of the most valuable properties in the United States: themselves. Thus, they could hold out for fantastic salaries for their services, because they were worth it. The name Chaplin, for instance, meant box office business. There is no question that, in economic terms, stars like him earned every cent they were paid.

Hollywood Hegemony

Chaplin's own star never rose higher than in 1919 when, along with Mary Pickford, Douglas Fairbanks and D. W. Griffith, he thumbed his nose at all the Hollywood producers and organized United Artists, a production and distribution firm with four major assets unique in Hollywood: three top-ranking stars and the best-known film director in town. United Artists was not only responsible for using the talents of its founders. It produced and released other films as well—and continues, under different management, to do so today. For Chaplin, United Artists meant that he now could assume complete control over the production of his films, that he could produce full-length features (like *The Kid* in 1921) and that he could even try his hand at directing a film in which he did not star, namely, *A Woman of Paris* in 1923.

With Chaplin as its symbol, Hollywood prospered in the years before and after World War I. The war itself effectively eliminated overseas competition of European films, especially from Britain, France and Italy. Because titles on silent films could so easily be translated into foreign languages, it was American actors and directors—as well as technicians, distributors and, later, exhibitors—who were able to stamp their distinctive identities upon movies around the world. Hollywood became, in effect, an international export house for movies and film actors who were instantly recognized the world over.

Hollywood also imported European talent. In the case of actors, it was not necessary for them to speak English for silent films—or, for that matter, to be able to speak at all. Directors from Europe (like the enigmatic Erich Von Stroheim, among others) were considered geniuses largely *because* they could not be clearly understood in English. Hollywood was an American phenomenon, but it became also an international melting pot. Even Chaplin maintained his British citizenship all his life, while others became American citizens but maintained their continental ways—in fact, exploited them off screen and on.

The Hollywood Monopoly

By 1920, the films, like the press, were part of industrial America, lucrative businesses directed largely by businessmen in the roles of producers. Many were veterans of the fur and clothing trade in New York City who had vision enough, ten years before, to invest in a gamble that turned with incredible speed from a novelty into a lucrative instrument of mass communication. Artists like Chaplin, in control of their own production units, were exceptions, but actors and directors—most of them from the theatre or vaudeville—made up part of this new monied aristocracy as well. At the bottom of the occupational list were the men who wrote the movies: a place in the film hierarchy, financial and social, that they still, in most cases, occupy.

Among other things, the films as businesses were moving rapidly down the road to monopoly. Hollywood was born, in part, to avoid the monopoly of the old Motion Picture Patents Company before World War I. But there are many kinds of monopolies. The very men who had moved to Hollywood to avoid the old patent laws and their repression were now combining and conspiring in restraint of trade due to their ability to control the production, distribution and exhibition of films in the United States.

Movies and Free Speech

In the meantime, far away from Hollywood, an event—or series of events—took place that probably did not cause much of a ripple in the new movie colony in California. But its implications were felt strongly by movie makers and moviegoers for the next 35 years, and even to the present. This issue, in 1915, centered squarely on a specific point, seemingly abstruse at the time, but critical, in many ways, to the development of the films in the United States and, oddly, elsewhere as well. I shall tell the first part of the story here and, in movie-serial cliff-hanger fashion, conclude it in the final two chapters of this book.

The issue was a simple one. We have seen how and why the First Amendment to the United States Constitution was added in the early days of the new Republic: to guarantee that the Federal Government would not interfere with the rights of free speech of the common people or of the press. Later, after the Civil War, this guarantee was extended even further to ensure that the states were also prohibited from the arbitrary exercise of their powers to silence most forms of speech and print. (Some speech, like defamation and matters of national security, were—and are—excluded.)

By 1915, the question therefore arose concerning whether individual states, in the interests, as they claimed, of their population had the right to license and/or censor the motion pictures. On the one hand, movies are definitely *not* mentioned in the First Amendment; they were not invented at the time it was ratified. On the other, films like *The Birth of a Nation* were *almost* speech. At least, they spread ideas. Continuing our argument, however, *most* movies were in those days pretty crude in the department of serious ideas. They were also silent, and, in 1915, most definitely exhibitions for public *entertainment* and not for public *education* or *enlightenment,* the kind of "speech" to which the First Amendment seems to refer.

In a number of cases in which film distributors protested, in the name of the Bill of Rights, the actions of various states that had either censored or required licensing of movies, the issue was brought to a head. Boiled down, it finally centered upon the issue of whether or not films were or were not "speech," as referred to in the First Amendment. If they were, states had no rights censoring or licensing them. The movies would have, broadly speaking, the same constitutional protections as the press. If they were not, the movies would receive only the legal protections of other growing industries at the time. It was up to the states—and local communities—to decide whether or not particular films might or might not be exhibited, and to whom and when.

This was obviously a constitutional issue that had to be settled by the nation's highest tribunal. Thus, the Supreme Court made its decision on a number of similar cases, the best known of which involved Mutual Films against state censors in Ohio and Kansas. What it concluded was entirely rational for the time—that is, considering the kind of one- and two-reel movies upon which it based its decision—a decision operative until 1952, when still another court, viewing an entirely different kind of motion picture, reversed this decision slyly but absolutely.

What the court decided in 1915 was that the movies were decidedly *not* "speech" in the sense intended by the First Amendment. It reasoned that films were businesses primarily and sheer entertainment second, and therefore no more worthy of a claim to First Amendment protection than any other business or than a circus act. The decision of the high court was unequivocal:

Are the moving pictures within the principle (of the First Amendment) as it is contended they are? They indeed may be mediums of thought, but so are many things. So is the theatre, the circus and all other shows and spectacles, and their performances may thus be brought by the like reasoning under the same immunity from repression or supervision as the public press . . . (The movie industry) is a business pure and simple, originated for profit, like other spectacles, not to be regarded . . . *as part of the press of this country* or as organs of public opinion.

(Oddly, the issue of First Amendment protection for serious stage plays had never crystallized into the kind of issue that would present the Supreme Court with the challenge of determining whether or not the legitimate theatre was legal "speech"—at least until as late as 1975. In that year, the Court upheld the right of the play *Hair* to present on stage a nude sequence after official attempts in Tennessee had been made to prevent the musical from opening. Despite municipal actions against certain sexy plays, particularly burlesque shows, precedent and theatrical history hint strongly that, from the eighteenth century to the present, serious legitimate theatre in America has *always* implicitly been considered a form of ideational expression, hence "speech," and hence protected by the First Amendment. The issue has apparently not required a high judicial test until recently.)

We shall see how this important decision later influenced the growth of the movie industry in the U.S.A. and the nature of the films it produced. Possibly, the wisest part of the court's decision was its recognition of movies as a business, but just how big and powerful a business it was to become, I doubt that the nine Solons of the Supreme Court imagined in 1915, even in their wildest dreams.

Early Radio Years

While the film makers in Hollywood were tooling up what was eventually to become a rich and ebullient film factory, another industry was growing—more slowly and silently. Considering that films were silent and radio dealt in the currency of noise, their simultaneous growth seems paradoxical, but this was precisely the way these two technologies developed between, roughly, 1910 and 1920.

The best that can be said of radio in this decade is that it was a chaos, but a chaos during which certain patterns of use were to emerge as the broadcasting industry in America the way it was to be known for the next 35 years. Men like the colorful "Doc" Herrold of San Jose, California ran self-styled "colleges" of radio broadcasting along with a "station" of sorts that attracted a handful of listeners in the area. "Doc" was active from, roughly, 1909 to 1918 and probably originated many of the stunts later broadcasters claimed as "firsts," at least when his equipment did not blow out.

By 1912, however, it was obvious that some sort of government control was going to be necessary to prevent further confusion than that then rampant on the airwaves. Amateurs, for instance, were broadcasting to ships, and the Navy foresaw (correctly) that it would require certain frequencies to be reserved for its own use. Congress therefore enacted the first radio licensing law. It was duly signed by President Taft and, in effect, passed the buck for the control of broadcasting into the hands of the Department of Commerce and Labor, where it was to stay (at least with Commerce) for about 15 years. Basically, frequencies were allocated to ships, government agencies and amateur broadcasters, with a few of them reserved for experimental purposes, as well as some for universities and colleges that were teaching broadcasting and, as sidelines, transmitting talk and music on the air. Most remarkable was the growth of amateur broadcasting during this decade. Granting a certain amount of illegal radio broadcasting, Barnouw reports that, in 1917, 8,562 broadcasting licenses were issued in the U.S.A. Certainly, some of these "amateurs" were sending into the airwaves radio "programs," as they would come to be known, of a quasi-professional nature.

Sarnoff's "Music Box"

Here our attention turns again to David Sarnoff four years after picking up those faint signals from the *Titanic*. Promoted to an assistant traffic manager of the American Marconi Company, Sarnoff wrote a now famous memorandum to his superiors in which, in effect, he described the configurations that broadcasting around the world was shortly to take. Oddly, considering Sarnoff's own later role primarily as a businessman, the memorandum treads lightly upon the obvious potential of this new medium for making vast sums of money. But this was to come later, and Sarnoff was, at this stage, still a comparatively young and idealistic man.

What Sarnoff suggested was, at the same time, simple, visionary, somewhat unrealistic and startling. Nor can he possibly be the only person alive in 1916 who thought of this notion. He proposed that Marconi manufacture radio receivers that could, with reliability, tune to various different frequencies and provide listeners with radio concerts, recitals and lectures. He called his notion a "Radio Music Box" and indicated that programming might be paid for out of the "handsome profit" Marconi would receive from the sale of sets. Nothing, of course, was done about Sarnoff's idea for four years.

In the first place, World War I intervened. All radio frequencies were taken over by the military forces. Just as the war stimulated the movies, it halted the progress of broadcasting. When hostilities ended, it took broadcasting a year or so to return to the point at which it had been stopped. Second, the kind of receiver that Sarnoff envisioned was shortly to be feasible. Tuning of sets to different frequencies was a difficult matter until, in 1920, A. N. Goldsmith devised a simple receiver the frequencies of which could be controlled by a few knobs, rather like radios today. By this time, Sarnoff had moved (with American Marconi) to the new Radio Corporation of America. Upon seeing Goldsmith's receiver, however, he recognized the instrument that would bring his "Music Box" into countless American homes. What he could not anticipate was that the "Music Box" was also a gold mine.

The Radio Corporation of America

The machinations through which the various electronic manufacturers and the American Telegraph and Telephone Company went during this period to divide the good-sized pie involved, first, in building broadcast equipment, second, sending messages and, later, broadcasting, are too complex to spell out in detail in this history. They are typical of much American business of the period.

Under the guise of preventing foreign takeovers of American broadcasting facilities, Owen D. Young, general counsel of General Electric and American Marconi, formed the Radio Corporation of America in 1919. RCA excluded "foreign interests" from owning more than one-fifth of its stock. Because Marconi's American station had been taken over by the government during the war, Marconi had no choice but to join the plan, which was apparently blessed by powerful men in Washington. Owen D. Young was now Chairman of the Board. Almost immediately, General Electric and AT&T (including its subsidiary Western Electric) agreed to share between them all their patents on broadcasting instrumentation, and AT&T joined General Electric as a major shareholder in the newly created RCA, which then started developing international properties. The move was "dirty pool," probably illegal, but Young got away with it, and it remains history.

Early Broadcasters

Young was not a broadcasting pioneer and neither, for that matter, was Sarnoff. The people who began the broadcasting industry were engineers and tinkerers, men not unlike "Doc" Herrold. Thus, the question of where and when the first radio station began operating is a moot matter, and every time we find one "original" station in the United States, we also discover another that preceded it by months, weeks or days.

Dr. Barnouw mentions Professor Earle M. Levy of the University of Wisconsin and his station 9XM that was operating (in Morse code) in 1917. In Detroit, none other than W. E. Scripps bought his son some radio equipment, and the *Detroit News* was on the air using the call letters station 8MK, later WWJ. Elton M. Plant ran the station, apparently at Scripps' whim of iron, developed a listening audience via the newspaper, and, in 1920, broadcast to his audience the results of the Harding-Cox presidential election.

And, lest other advocates of this or that station's right to be called the "first" American radio station be offended, mention had best be made of Fred Christian's 6ADZ in Hollywood, Ashley Clayton Dixon's station in Montana and Fred M. Laxton's 4XD, broadcasting from Charlotte, North Carolina.

Frank Conrad and KDKA

The first important radio station in the United States was born, however, out of commercial necessity. In the face of much competition, the Westinghouse Corporation had done quite well selling electronic equipment during the war. Now, it looked as if RCA would be able to edge them out of the business. They saw the answer—or partial answer—in establishing a broadcasting station in order to sell receiving equipment. Their choice for operator of the station was Dr. Frank Conrad, an engineer who had broadcast all manner of "programs" from his home for a number of years. Now, he was moved to the roof of the Westinghouse building in Pittsburgh and began, in 1920, a radio service that operated from eight o'clock in the evening until midnight. Its purpose was almost entirely to sell Westinghouse receivers.

Conrad held a Ph.D. and, until his broadcasting career began, was something of an all-around inventor who held numerous patents—some 200—involving everything from electric generators to hand grenades. But he was equally, if not more inventive when facing the challenge of creating a new communications medium out of nothing: radio broadcasting. He had experimented with various formats at his home station, 8XK. He played records on the air, offered live piano music and read news items on the air. Friends and family made up his staff. With financial help and assistance from Westinghouse, he was able to pull it all together into the first American station of national importance, KDKA, Pittsburgh.

That the idea would work had been fairly well demonstrated before KDKA actually opened for business. Horne's department store in Pittsburgh wanted to sell radio sets, and their sales approach depended upon an agreement with Conrad to provide programs for them to demonstrate. The scheme worked, and after the formal beginnings of KDKA, receiving sets began to be merchandised like hot cakes in the area. It was not long, of course, before other retailers (and manufacturers) caught on to the simple fact that if they wanted to sell receiving sets to the public, they would have to provide programs for them to listen to.

One interesting fact about these early radio sets is that they could almost be as cheap or expensive as one wished. Thus they held great appeal for the public. At one end of the price spectrum was the crystal detector, with its "cat's whisker" and earphones that cost next to nothing. A child could make one. Tuning was difficult, because you had to hit the crystal in exactly the right spot with the pin-whisker to receive a signal. But it worked. Kits for building your own sets with tubes and more sophisticated tuners were available, and so were fully fabricated radios that employed either earphones or horns for amplification. Prices started at about $10. For home use, sets were rarely made, in these early days, that cost more than $50. Expensive consoles were to come later: "talking furniture," as it was called by wags.

Concerning Frank Conrad himself, time and circumstances made him the virtual father of American radio broadcasting, a role in history the engineer did not seek or anticipate. From the early roof-top KDKA tent-like studio, Conrad evolved—or invented or re-invented—almost every form of sound broadcasting radio has utilized in its 55-year history. He broadcast news of sports events, political speeches, religious services, dramatic scenes and sketches, concerts, recordings of popular music and market news.

Conrad did not, of course, accept paid advertising, and his programs contained no commercial announcements. His big "sponsor" was Westinghouse. His objective was to sell radio sets. It apparently never occurred to Conrad that radio might be used for any other sort of commercial purpose. Why should it have? His broadcasts did what they were supposed to do effectively, and Conrad's operation was worth whatever expense it cost Westinghouse to sell their reception instruments. Of course, competing brands of radios were also sold as a result of Conrad's broadcasts. For the moment, this seemed unimportant.

Among other things, KDKA became a well-known institution. People talked about it. Newspapers ran stories about it, about Conrad, and, most important, about Westinghouse. With Conrad at the microphone, it seemed as if radio broadcasting in the United States was destined to become an arm of the radio set manufacturing and sales businesses.

The First Stations

For the next few years, as we shall see, radio stations mushroomed across the United States, often without the kind of clear economic base that subsidized KDKA. Accordingly, many failed. In the world of management, however, developments were also brewing that put the power of radio broadcasting into the pockets of certain people, just as they took it out of those of certain others.

The business intrigues of these early radio years were extremely complex, as far as the major interests in American broadcasting and their power plays were concerned. This is surprising, because it is doubtful that any of the competing parties understood clearly, exactly or with certainty what a mammoth industry broadcasting was soon to become. Possibly, the corporations and businessmen involved were as impelled by the adventure of launching a new mass communications medium as by radio's dubious financial potentials. At any rate, for a time AT&T had been pretty well squeezed out of the radio business by the formation of RCA. It held a mere 4 per cent of the stock in the new corporation. The major companies (including Westinghouse, which owned about 20 per cent of RCA) agreed, unlike the early movie moguls, to share their patents to launch this new medium for the common good. But they were not quite certain what the common good was.

Among the new stations that brought the matter to a head was station WJZ in Newark, New Jersey. WJZ was the direct descendant of another station, WJY, which lived but a single day. WJY was the brainchild of Major Harvey Andrew White and David Sarnoff, who attempted to bring to the radio audience, on July 2, 1921, from an outdoor arena, the heavyweight championship boxing match between Jack Dempsey and the champion, a French fighter named Georges Carpentier. (Although you probably do not care, the author of this book was named after Carpentier five years later. The French champion was a personal friend of his parents.)

In 1921, however, both Carpentier and WJY lost their respective battles that day. The jerry-built station, mostly put together from borrowed equipment, at first temporarily succumbed to a number of rainstorms and then responded poorly to the heat of the summer afternoon, which incinerated much of the already overheated equipment. White broadcast a "blow by blow" description of the fight, but most broadcasting historians agree that it was not aired. Instead, the station's technician, J. O. Smith, repeated in a railroad hut what he was able to hear of White's description into a microphone over the air, because he was unable to connect White's ringside wire to his transmission equipment. Some claim that White merely grabbed a telephone, got an open line to Smith, and began talking after his own transmission failed. WJY was, regardless, a brainstorm of Sarnoff and the RCA people, but it did not last longer than Dempsey's fourth round knockout of Carpentier.

Under the aegis of RCA, Sarnoff and the "Radio Group" of broadcasters, WJY, however, was reborn with new equipment as a full-fledged radio station, WJZ, on the following October 5th. It began operations with the successful play-by-play transmission of a World Series baseball game from New York's Polo Grounds. It was a success and, much like KDKA in Pittsburgh, the station stimulated for the broadcasters a listening audience in New York City. Broadcasts of interest to the population of the big town boosted the sale of radio sets, especially when "remote" telephone hook-ups from Manhattan were added to the Jersey station. In effect, WJZ became a dress-up version of KDKA, employing talent from the New York theatre, concert, vaudeville and night club world to attract public interest in this novelty called "radio broadcasting."

Ma Bell and WEAF

AT&T meanwhile watched this activity (and the growth of other radio stations across the nation) with more than casual interest, not quite certain, apparently, of what to do about it. The telephone company finally decided to get into radio broadcasting, starting what was to become one of New York City's major stations in the summer of 1922. Its call letters were WEAF.

AT&T's aspirations for the station seem at first to have been extremely vague. Their executives favored a plan that would make WEAF available to the public, somewhat like telephones. Thus, AT&T stations would be, in a company spokesman's own words, "public facilities over which the general public, one and all alike, may use these services." It now seems quite clear that AT&T did not want (like RCA) to get into the broadcasting business proper—that is, into the difficult business of originating programs, the way WJZ, KDKA and, by now, a host of other American stations were operating. Accustomed as the telephone company was to providing channels of communication rather than content, how and just what did they intend to broadcast?

The solution that AT&T worked out in its odd way opened the door to commercial broadcasting in the United States as we now know it and provided first, radio and, second, television broadcasting with a source—or many sources—of revenue that had not, until then, been seriously considered.

From the perspective of 1922, however, AT&T's executives felt that they were being pushed into radio broadcasting by two circumstances. First, their company held patents on, and were able to build, the best radio transmitters available via one of their subsidiary companies, Western Electric. They were literally inundated with orders for these complex structures—more than 60 in the greater New York area alone. AT&T feared a glut of stations on the air all using their transmitters but receiving no revenue from their use. AT&T favored keeping what they then considered simply "radio telephone service" within their own domain as much as possible. That is, they desired to sell radio broadcasting *services* to broadcasters (who they thought might be interested) rather than sell transmitters to stations over which they exerted neither control nor made continuing profits. Second, it was clear that stations would soon be forming networks, and that direct wire transmission from station to station would probably be necessary. Both electronically and practically, the best way to achieve this end was to utilize AT&T long-distance telephone services. (In fact, the "long lines" department of AT&T was, during this period, in charge of all broadcast operations for the company.) The sale, therefore, of radio time and electronic *services* to broadcasters via their own stations, rather than entering the radio program business, seemed like the logical solution to their problems.

WEAF was therefore to be AT&T's maiden station. It was about the 200th to be erected in the U.S.A. It was clearly, however, the most important, because, if AT&T's game plan worked, the results were most likely to affect broadcasting in America vitally. The plan worked, but not in the way AT&T anticipated—except that the company's long lines telephone service was (and still is) a vital part of network operations for radio and television service in America.

The First Commercials

Sharing time with another station and improvising programming—to provide for their "subscribers" a chance to hear their station—AT&T launched WEAF on August 3, 1922. Various telephone company personnel pitched in to provide programming for a few hours daily. For about three weeks nothing much of consequence happened. Then, on August 28th, one of WEAF's first contributors, Mr. Blackwell of the Queensboro Company, a realtor in Queens County, delivered a ten-minute talk, for which he had paid WEAF $50, concerning the works of the author Nathaniel Hawthorne and the new Hawthorne Apartments, located in suburban Jackson Heights, for which his company was seeking tenants.

That this first radio "commercial" worked seems clear. The company bought five more broadcasts. Other companies followed—modestly at first and then with increasing zeal. The problem for AT&T was how to provide programming. Advertisers were interested in advertising, not necessarily in talking about poets or, for that matter, any sort of broadcast service, as most other stations, say WJZ, were. On the other hand, if it were necessary to provide entertainment along with their sales pitches, most of the advertisers could well afford to do so, within reason considering going rates for talent. Sydney Head indicates that the Gimbel Brothers department store in New York was the first major sponsor to provide its own entertainment on WEAF, fare more elaborate than Mr. Blackwell's talk on Hawthorne.

What was occurring, of course, in the old WEAF studios on Walker Street in New York City, was that American broadcasting was finding for itself the financial base upon which it was to rest for at least the next 56 years—or until the present moment. Two points, however, are slightly odd about the way this evolution occurred.

First, the introduction of advertising to broadcasts was, in its early years, resisted by many (including Sarnoff), who later found themselves in the position of having to defend it. What they were afraid of was over-commercialization of the air-waves—turning the art (or service) of broadcasting into a vehicle of commerce and merchandising. Other countries later resisted this move by turning broadcasting into government controlled or chartered utilities, prohibiting advertising and financed broadcasting by means of taxes upon receivers. The BBC radio service in England remains, in part, an example to this day. In America, there was time to turn back from commercial broadcasting had the public or our legislators wanted to. Nothing forced broadcasters to accept advertising in order to pay for programming, except that, in the go-go economy of the 1920s, it soon became apparent that fortunes might be made quite easily by employing radio as an advertising medium of immense appeal which reached large and receptive audiences.

Second, I find it peculiar that none of the early broadcasters, except AT&T (and then somewhat accidentally), saw in advertising a way of covering costs for providing radio messages, serious or frivolous, for the masses. A model, or example, of this sort of economic arrangement was right in front of them. From their earliest days, newspapers defrayed expenses, and were presently making enormous profits in some instances, not from money brought in by circulation, but from advertising. Of course, by tradition, neither book publishers nor legitimate theatre producers accepted advertising money—although for many years, vaudeville houses had sold advertising space on their asbestos curtains. The movie barons apparently did not need to seek sponsorship to sell their wares at enormous profits. Given the American economic climate of the times, advertising should have been, it seems to me, an early brainstorm solution to radio's economic dilemmas by some broadcaster somewhere, and well before the summer of 1922. The market was abundant with consumer goods. Middle class Americans were prosperous, and competition for customers for nearly identical products was intense. Advertising was needed. Why *not* radio?

Even AT&T officials, however, were dubious about the economic viability of commercial broadcasting at first. It made money, but not much money.

Others, particularly those who envisioned radio as a public service that would be used by cities, educational institutions or even as a home "Music Box," wondered about the propriety of an instrument that would intrude a salesman's voice into the sanctity of the American home. In their wildest dreams, of course, these fastidious people could not anticipate the birth of the singing radio commercial about 15 years later or, eventually, the barrage of goons and creeps who today visit our living rooms in living color to sell us insurance, automobiles, deodorants, detergents and just about everything in the supermarket that was, by the 1950s, to characterize the American consumer economy.

Commercial Broadcasting

Like it or not, however, broadcasting had found a way of paying for its services and, at the same time, turning a reasonable profit for its entrepreneurs. Commercial sponsorship *had* to be accepted, because it was, in the American value system, a "can't lose proposition" from which everyone profited and nobody lost. The public received free radio broadcasts of every kind: music, news, comedy and drama. (Not strictly true: receivers cost money; electricity to run them costs money; advertising charges found their way into the cost of producing consumer goods.) Advertisers discovered new customers for their products. (Not strictly true: In the crazy commerce of advertising, one person will only switch brands or try a new product once every so often. Much broadcasting advertising probably keeps, or kept, people buying goods and services they would buy anyway, but it prevented them from "switching" brands.) Broadcasters and entertainers had created for advertisers a new profession in which to merchandise their talents lucratively and without harming existing institutions. (Not strictly true: Radio—and later television—had a hand in killing off or diminishing other conduits for news, comedy and theatre. Vaudeville died, in part because of broadcasting. Many newspapers and magazines folded, because both audiences and advertisers had deserted them for radio and TV.) Advertising agencies and salesmen of broadcast time, as well as broadcasting personnel made, and still make, a lot of money.

Like the movies, broadcasting grew into another golden goose of the communications revolution in America—as well as in other countries in quite different ways. Of major interest for us in this history is that, in its earliest days, radio broadcasting, unlike movies and the mass press, had few cultural precedents to follow. There could be for radio no "Famous Plays With Famous Players" to stimulate a box office activity, simply because there was no box office involved in broadcasting. Later—much later—there were indeed to be famous plays (or movies) and famous players performing on the vast and ubiquitous broadcasting networks that were to emerge in the years to come.

At the end of 1922, however, broadcasting in the United States had emerged healthily from its first identity crisis.

8

The 'Twenties Soar

THE BURST OF CREATIVE ENERGY that produced the American film industry and the radio broadcasting business was part of a bigger social and cultural phenomenon of the times, one that affected nearly every aspect of American life. It also touched the entire population.

In the years before and after World War I, "mass society" as we know it today was born, infant of new technologies and nurtured by the new communications media that we have seen start to rise into formidable institutions. Henry Ford and his Model A brought the fruits of tangible mass technology to the farm, the home, to the middle classes and even to the poor. Movies—and later radio—did the same for an intangible technology.

Nothing in culture—or almost nothing—remained untouched by the development of the modern age of mass technology and/or mass communications, to say nothing of mass transportation, mass marketing and mass politics. (Regarding the latter, after World War I, twice as many voters as previously were potentially available to cast ballots even for a local dog catcher, once women were given the right to vote.) By the middle 1920s, movies and broadcasting had developed into growing forms both of art and commerce. Neither had many older traditions upon which to fall back; whatever commercial and aesthetic devices they employed or exploited were freely borrowed—and modified— from facets of other aspects of culture that had gone before, some of them, in fact, extremely old.

No gods on Olympus decreed that the films had to, in effect, turn into photographic pantomimes of theatrical conventions and novelistic ideas current during the second decade of this century. *Men* did—clever men who literally found ways of translating the arts of theatre, vaudeville, burlesque, the novel and short story into celuloid fancies that lasted for about 90 minutes, an arbitrary running time based upon exhibitors' experiences with theatre and vaudeville audiences.

Neither Frank Conrad nor a neglected genius "invented," in a true sense, either the news program, the radio concert, the comedy show or the radio drama. Old ideas were poured into new bottles, and the resulting brew tasted new. In spite of the invective heaped upon it in years to come by radio and television critics, neither was advertising invented by broadcasters; nor was it ever carried, by either radio or television, to the extremes of printed patent medicine sales "pitches" that appeared in magazines three generations ago. A man in New York *read* an advertisement for an apartment complex over the air on WEAF, and radio broadcasting had literally thrust upon it a fully developed tradition that continues to this day in television.

Pressures Upon the Press

In no manner should we therefore be surprised that the, by now, venerable institution of the American press responded to the same sorts of culture stimuli that both movies and broadcasting did after World War I. The difference between them lay, fundamentally, in two factors, the significance of which must not be passed over lightly.

In the first place, the press (including magazines and books as well as newspapers) did indeed possess traditions—in fact, more than 200 years of complex traditions—that were borrowed, like all traditions, from other institutions that had long since passed or changed. Journalists and writers felt the pressure of new technologies and of a readership of a size and nature that might now fairly be called "mass." But they tended to continue in their traditional ways, responding every so often to this or that change that modernity was continually hurling at them.

Second, the press (not films or broadcasting) was singled out by the Constitution of the United States to receive special protection from interference by government. In all aspects of life, personal or institutional, when you are granted a privilege, it necessarily follows that you must, nearly always, assume an obligation. Certainly, the press in all its aspects had by the 'twenties, changed in many ways since the late eighteenth century. But unless it remained, in basic function and nature, more or less the same sort of press that the First Amendment had centered its attention upon, it was bound to lose its special status as one of the few institutions in American life that is even mentioned in our Constitution.

The American press, therefore, during the go-go years that saw the films and radio turn into mass media, felt inevitable tensions. On one side, forces of conservatism constrained newspapers, magazines and book publishers to stick to tradition and, in effect, make good the faith that men more than a hundred years before had shown in them as necessary for our democracy to work. On the other side, the success of yellow journalism and mass publicity were enough of an indication that power and wealth lay within the easy grasp of many people who printed words and pictures. Film and radio were, even in their earliest days, media that competed for attention with newspapers and magazines, just as they do today. But, more important, they also served as crude models of how art, commerce and the needs of people to orient themselves to an apparently ever-shrinking world could be exploited to new proportions, reaching more people more profitably than ever before in history.

For the most part, newspapers that would not—or could not—change in some measure with the culture around them died, usually painfully and slowly. In New York City, the *Times* remained an exception. But the question of whether the mass market in even so large a megalopolis could support more than *one* traditional, serious newspaper was asked over and over again for about 40 years. At last, by the 1960s, the answer came, and few people were surprised, because the evidence had been present for a long time. It was, it seemed, ''No.''

The lingering deaths of most of America's old newspapers are not encouraging or pleasant stories, particularly because so many of them are told against a background (except for the 1930s) of social and economic prosperity during which other media prospered.

The Death of the *World*

The fate of Pulitzer's *World* was but one example, and we shall see others pass in their time. Hardly a stodgy or reactionary journal, the *World* was in good health at Pulitzer's death in 1911, and the publisher's sons tried their best to keep up the momentum developed by their father. Editor Frank I. Cobb, Heywood Broun, Franklin P. Adams and cartoonist Rollin Kirby seemed like the nucleus for an unbeatable combination of outstanding journalists to keep the *World* going.

By the middle 'twenties, however, Cobb was dead, and the *World* was well on the path to oblivion. While the economy of the 'twenties soared, the *World* became more and more expensive to publish. A temporary penny rise in price lost loyal readers. Less readers meant less advertising. By the end of the 'twenties, Pulitzer's heirs had lost nearly $2 million on the *World,* which, at the time was still published in morning, evening and Sunday editions.

The story of how, in 1930, Herbert Pulitzer managed to convince a Surrogate Court to override his father's will that specifically stated that the *World* must stay in the Pulitzer family, is a colorful tale but one too prolix (and pointless) for this history. Pulitzer Jr. wanted out. And Roy Howard, E. W. Scripps' protege and partner, had in hand $5 million with which he was willing to extricate Pulitzer Jr. from the financial disaster that was apparently wearing him down to death.

World employees themselves made Pulitzer counter offers, but on the day that the court finally gave Pulitzer the legal right to sell his property, the *World* died. That evening, Howard's successful Scripps-Howard New York flagship newspaper, the *Telegram,* bore a new masthead: the *World Telegram.* So it remained for two decades until the death of the venerable New York *Sun,* when the original mass newspaper's name was added to the *World Telegram*'s masthead. Finally, after another dozen or so years, the entire edifice collapsed. The *World Telegram and Sun* printed its last edition in 1966.

Cross-Media Competition

The fate of the *World,* as we shall see, was to be the fate of many other keepers of newspaper and magazine traditions, at first during the 'twenties, but during the decades that followed as well. Set against the broad picture of American prosperity, the demise of so many journals may seem odd, but the phenomenon was (and is) a byproduct of a new phase of the communications revolution that began, roughly, with World War I. It is still going on.

First, costs of publishing of all kinds rose rapidly as the United States became more and more affluent. Union labor was more expensive, more than non-union labor. Second, readerships grew ever larger, but the people, by and large, did not expand their reading habits to include new or multiple newspapers and magazines. Instead, one or two newspapers became enormously successful in any single market, and others gathered to themselves only small or specialized publics. Advertisers naturally followed newspapers with large circulations, putting their money where readership was greatest. Newspapers and magazines, therefore, found it difficult—if not impossible—to share readership publics. Instead, they were forced to compete with one another or die.

Radio and films also responded to competition of a different kind, but competition it was nevertheless. Moviegoing filled hours many people had previously spent reading newspapers, magazines and books. Radio sent the news into one's home, bedroom or automobile, where it was received free of charge. Radio also interested many (but not all) advertisers who had previously employed print media to sell their wares.

One may find it strange that a city like New York today supports only three daily newspapers (and one or two suburban journals) with its ten (plus) million population. But the factors noted above, among others, began grinding away during the 1920s, and they still operate today. One super-tabloid, one super-serious newspapers, one subsidized liberal journal are all that the economics of newspaper publishing permitted to be produced in this enormous city—tempered by the recourse of a relatively small number of unsatisfied minorities to one national newspaper (*The Wall Street Journal*) and local weeklies like the *Village Voice* and *The New Amsterdam News.* Much the same principles operate in most American cities today and keep the number of competing journals to a bare minimum.

The cultural historian reminds us that what was happening to the American press was and is simply a refraction of what was also occurring to much big business at large in the country. And the cultural historian is right. We have noted that the press, in nearly all its manifestations, changed, in the hands of men like Pulitzer, Hearst and Scripps into big business. Simply because of its special traditions, the press was therefore hardly immune to the same forces of competition, consolidation and control that, say, the automobile industry was subject to also.

(When I was a boy, eight or nine excellent to fair newspapers were published daily in New York, and the city was about half as large as it is today. But, when my father bought an automobile, I must also remember that his choice of American manufacturers was about as wide as—or wider than—my choice of newspapers at a subway kiosk. For about the same money, he might purchase a General Motors, Ford, Nash, Studebaker, Hudson, Willys, Packard, Chrysler, Plymouth, or some other automobile that was made by an independent manufacturer that later disappeared or consolidated with the "big three" automobile companies that dominate the domestic car market today. Similar— but not exactly the same—economic forces were at work as those upon the press, demanding either extraordinary success in the mass market or producing oblivion as the result of modest patronage.)

As the nation grew richer, our *apparent* choice of consumer goods, including automobiles and newspapers, however, grew wider. More brand names appeared on more products that filled our supermarket culture. Men and women with blinders (for instance, Alvin Toffler, the *Future Shock* man) somehow interpreted this change as growth of a diversity of choices. In fact, we, as consumers, readers, moviegoers (and today) as televiewers, are actually doing business with fewer and fewer large corporations as time passes. Their multitude of labels and so called "brand names" encourage us to swallow the fiction that differently packaged breakfast cereals made of oats are somehow different, one from the other, because they are sold under different names—or that apparently "competing" newspapers or magazines, all part of one chain, are, in fact, providing us with different perspectives of the day's news. The hard truth, the cultural historian of intelligence tells us, is that diversity in the American economy in all its aspects began its march to a still lingering death during the second decade of this century. Today it is all but an illusion, ironically sold to us, in part, by the increasingly monolithic paperback book and magazine industries.

Press historians tell us that, after World War I, a period of "consolidation" began in American journalism. So it did. But it was by no means confined to the newspaper world.

The Birth of the Tabloid

Another extraordinary and fascinating factor in eliminating newspaper competition, particularly in big cities, was the invention (or use) of a newspaper format after World War I that simply grew so enormously popular among the masses that competition with it was almost impossible except on its own terms. I am referring to the tabloid newspaper, the first really radical departure from tradition in the basic format of American journalism since its beginnings.

Defining what is, or was, unique about the tabloid is more difficult than at first it appears. One might say that the size of the paper is critical, but small newspapers had been printed in many countries before the tabloid era. Another distinctive attribute is the tabloid's copious use of pictures and photographs. But a count of pictures in today's tabloids will reveal that many of them are less "pictorial" than conventional newspapers. The much discussed sensationalism of tabloids was and is nothing new—especially to an America that had lived, over the turn of the century, through an era of yellow journalism unequalled in vigor before or since.

I find it difficult to resist the conclusion that a tabloid is best defined as a small newspaper that simply displays a certain kind of *attitude*—both towards its contents and towards its readers—that is, the kind of attitude we have learned to associate with tabloids. Now, all tautologies are slightly comic. So is this one. The humor fades, however, when one observes that the largest circulating newspapers in the United States *are* tabloids, and that highly successful tabloids have been responsible for the death of many great and excellent newspapers. They have probably also influenced both the economic status and the output of magazines, radio, television and the films, in one or another way.

The tabloid *format* itself may have been born, via a number of unsuccessful newspapers, in the United States not long after the Civil War. The tabloid *attitude* is a British invention. Of this there is little doubt. And it appears to have sprung full-blown from the remarkable brain of Alfred C. Harmsworth, later Lord Northcliffe, one of the most notable British press barons of this century. Harmsworth began imitating the lively popularized news coverage of Pulitzer's *World* in his London *Evening News* before the turn of the century. He even came to America in 1901, as Pulitzer's guest, to print one edition of the New York *World* in tabloid size, an experiment that fizzled almost as it started. In London, however, Harmsworth's *Daily Mirror,* a tabloid paper in both size and spirit, succeeded and spawned a group of imitators. Its social influence gave Harnsworth his peerage.

The *New York Daily News*

How odd that Harmsworth, by then Lord Northcliffe, should subsequently during World War I, run into an American army officer stationed in England who just happened to be a grandson of Chicago's press scion, Joseph Medill, and who had been discussing plans with his cousin, another Medill grandson, for starting up a new and different newspaper in New York. Odder still because *both* cousins, the Army captain in England, Joseph Medill Patterson, and his partner, the eccentric Colonel Robert R. McCormick, publisher of the Chicago *Tribune,* eventually became, and remained until their deaths, ardent Anglophobes. Both men delighted at hurling invective in their newspapers at Great Britain for the wildest of reasons. (Patterson and McCormick insisted upon being called "Captain" and "Colonel" respectively all their lives. The latter even fancied himself something of a military expert.)

At any rate, it was Patterson who was sold upon Northcliffe's notion of an American version of the *London Mirror* for New York City. McCormick was also enthusiastic about any plan which would first, get his (then) ultraliberal cousin out of Chicago and, second, might extend the *Tribune's* influence to New York. Backed by the fortune the Medill family had made in midwest journalism, the *Illustrated Daily News,* as it was first called, found its way to New York's newsstands on June 26, 1919. As the *New York Daily News* it is still there today, the largest circulating newspaper in the nation at the moment, about two million daily.

Patterson's tabloid *News* was an almost instant success, achieving its status as largest circulating paper in the nation in 1924, when 750,000 copies per day were sold. It was, as we shall see, also one of the most widely imitated in New York. All of the imitations, some of them apparently better than the original, failed, while the *News* goes on and on. To describe or list, therefore, exactly what qualities the *Daily News* possesses that account for its long-term success is both presumptuous and impossible. Were I able to do the job accurately, I would be, I think, in the business of publishing newspapers rather than following their destinies. Let us, however, attempt to see what made- and makes-the *News* tick. Or rather, in all fairness, let us review how Captain Patterson exercised his genius for listening to the public pulse-beat and provided New York with a newspaper its citizens seem to love.

The tabloid size had something to do with the *News'* success, less because it was easy to read on New York's subways than because the small pages accentuated the vivid news photographs, comics, cartoons and other features that stood out less clearly in large papers. The *News* was also a workmanlike newspaper in every respect. It did, indeed, cover the important events of the day thoroughly, if not in as full or detailed way as most other papers. It was well written and simply written, tightly edited (during a series of various nightly editions) so that it looked both timely and exciting. Headlines were succinct, clever and, when appropriate, also amusing. Taking a leaf (or a sheaf of leaves) from the book of the yellow journalists, the *News* accentuated the sensational: crime, gangsters, celebrities, sex, etc. but, almost invariably, told its stories in personal terms. All courtroom trials became high melodrama, and the world of movies, night clubs, theatre and gambling dripped with interesting, colorful people who were photographed, if possible, doing interesting things—or just being their glamorous, colorful selves.

After Patterson outgrew his youthful socialism, the *News* turned (and remained) politically conservative in a city largely inhabited by liberals. Its editorials, particularly when they were written by Reuben Maury, were filled with punchy street-talk. Letters to the editor were edited, or rewritten, into local patois and were invariably amusing.

Captain Patterson, like Hearst, also had a flare for thinking up comic-strip ideas and was able to locate just the right artists to draw them. He put Chester Gould to work on "Dick Tracy," developed Harold Gray's highly political "Little Orphan Annie" and family strips, highly popular in their day, like "The Gumps," "Gasoline Alley," and "Moon Mullins," as well as the adventures of "Smilin' Jack," the aviator hero. In the feature department, he developed a star system for rating movies, a solid "advice to the lovelorn" column written by an ephemeral Doris Blake, puzzles, an astrology column and society and gossip columns for the man in the street, the best of which was written for many years by Ed Sullivan. The sports section of the *News* remained constantly topical, accurate, exciting and possibly the best of its kind, as well as most catholic, in the nation for many years, featuring its own stable or horse race handicappers, columnists and photographers. Sports alone frequently filled as much as a quarter to a fifth of the newspaper's space.

As a lifelong citizen of what we call today "The Big Apple," I have read the *News,* on and off, all my life, and admit that, like many other New Yorkers, I both admire it and feel some affection for it. The *News* is a gutsy voice of a big, tough, energetic city, as realistic and down to earth as most New York cab drivers. It somehow manages to shout loud in the interests of the average man while maintaining a political stance that possibly all of America, and certainly New York, has outgrown. The *News* is against more issues and people than it is for (a characteristic I enjoy), but, at times, it can also be mawkishly sentimental (a characteristic I hate.) It is always readable, lively, hard-boiled, pretending that it tells you much more "inside dope" than its reporters and editors actually know. In the world of journalism, it comes as close to symbolizing the *ambience* of the mass society of our time as any paper I have ever read anywhere in the world. I admire its talent for accurately reflecting the world in which it thrives, a talent that Captain Patterson seems to have brought to the *News* with its birth. It is a hardy institution that has survived and prospered in the heat of the many cross-currents among and between today's various mass media, and for this I also respect its toughness and longevity.

The *Daily Graphic* **and the** *Mirror*

The *News'* most colorful competitor over the years in New York was the famous (or notorious) *New York Daily Graphic* (nicknamed the *"porno-Graphic"*), born in 1924 and died in 1932. Published by the eccentric owner of *True Story* magazines and a batch of physical culture journals, Bernarr Macfadden, the *Graphic* tackled the *News* head-on—and lost. Mcfadden's publishing empire still exists, and he himself was as fit an opponent for the clever Patterson as any man alive at the time. Macfadden was an exhibitionist who posed for pictures in his undies into his remarkably muscular old age, had a well-honed flair for personal publicity and a keen eye for attractive women.

The *Graphic* was edited by a skillful hand: Emile Gauvreau of the *Hartford Courant*. Gauvreau simply tried to do everything the *News* did, but more so. He lacked Patterson's touch for colorful features and amusements, so the *Graphic* was filled with murders, scandals, sex, rapes, and the bizarre affairs of the famous and rich. In the pages of the *Graphic* one might also find "composographs" instead of genuine photographs: that is, faked photographs of any event that *might* have happened. For example, the *Graphic* published a "cosmograph" of the recently deceased motion picture idol Rudolph Valentino entering heaven, and printed it with a straight face.

A *Graphic* gossip column was begun in 1924 by ex-vaudevillian and drama critic, Walter Winchell. His sharp ears picked up naughty whispers concerning the marriages, divorces, squabbles and affairs of the rich or celebrated. Winchell even made up his own colorful language, just as he frequently made up his quantum of gossip out of thin air. On the *Graphic,* he began a long and notorious professional life. In 1929, Winchell transferred his talents to another *News* competitor, Hearst's tabloid, the *Mirror*. A long career involving radio broadcasting and film appearances followed. He was immensely popular with the public, both as a newspaperman and a personality as long as he had the power of the press behind him. Both Winchell and the *Mirror* disappeared from the New York scene in 1963 with remarkably little regret evidenced by most New Yorkers.

The *Graphic's* life was relatively short but colorful, reflective of everything we have been told about the amoralities of New York in the prohibition era. Significantly, it died almost at the moment that alcohol came back into American life—officially, that is. And the *Graphic* left a heritage that lives today. (The old *Police Gazette* owed much to the spirit and nature of the *Graphic,* as did the highly successful *Confidential* magazine during the 1950's.) Today, I suppose it is not unfair to call the *National Enquirer* a modern version, and a slick one, of the old *Graphic.* And the *Daily News* itself always kept one eye on the *Graphic.* Who knows what tricks Captain Patterson learned from his lively competitor?

It would not have been like William Randolph Heart to remain out of the tabloid battle in New York. Hearst had failed with such a paper in Boston. But Boston was not New York, the city where Hearst had given Pulitzer a run for his money more than two decades before. Patterson was no Pulitzer, and, while Hearst was now older (and possibly wiser) than he had been when a young, millionaire crusading journalist, the scent of the tabloid battle was too much for his nose. Even before the *Graphic* was born, in the same year of 1924, another Hearst paper, the previously mentioned *New York Daily Mirror,* was on the newstands.

Almost from the day it was born, if you squinted hard enough, it was difficult to separate the *News* from the *Mirror*. Hearst followed Patterson closely from the start, even characteristically hiring away the *News'* Philip A. Payne as editor. For most of its life, the *Mirror* was neither as cleverly edited as the *News* nor as downright lurid as the *Graphic*. It lived a lot longer than the latter, having been sold by Hearst in 1928 but subsequently bought back by him in 1930. It finally expired long after its publisher's death.

Even in the hands of Hearst's brilliant editor, Arthur Brisbane, in the 'thirties, the *Mirror* lagged well behind the *News* in both circulation and style. At times, I wonder why. Winchell himself was a star performer with a loyal following. None of Patterson's comic strips were as absurdly delightful as Hearst's own discovery, Al Capp's "Lil' Abner." Impressive also was the *Mirror's* meticulous attention to sports, particularly "the sport of kings." Quite frequently, the *Mirror* scooped the *News* in covering sensational news and celebrity gossip, as well as in printing dramatic, arresting photographs. Like the *News,* the *Mirror* caught the tempo and toughness of New York in its pages, but it continually followed well behind its competitor.

At the time that Hearst had three New York papers on the newsstands— the *American,* the *Journal,* and the *Mirror*—it was the *Mirror* that reflected least the eccentricities of the aging publisher himself because of its almost obsessive daily attempt to imitate the *News.* Thus, probably, the *Mirror* was the best Hearst newspaper published in New York in the 1920s.

Other big cities saw their own tabloids also, most of them imitations, one way or the other, of the *News,* but none of them achieved the stature or, naturally, the circulation of New York's little wonder. The *Chicago Times* and later the *Sun* are worth noting in passing, as well as the *Washington Daily News* and other papers that came and went in Philadelphia, Detroit and Los Angeles. In New York itself, the great era of tabloids was the 1930s, a little in advance of our current concerns, but all of these newspapers were all children of the 1920s, as much a piece of that period as radio broadcasting and the dream world of Hollywood.

Results of World War I

In truth, one might say that they were really a part of the vulgarization of American culture by mass communications after World War I, without necessarily intending the comment to be snobbish or disparaging either to America or of mass culture. The sensational world of the popular media of radio and films were reflected in the tabloids, just as a certain revulsion against these same trends may be noted in the early issues of anti-vulgar (or class) magazines like *The New Yorker,* founded in the same period as quiet protests to the tabloid trend. In short, the tabloids were not merely a journalistic phenomenon but a cultural one, much a part of the economic social and class changes going on during the prohibition era and moving into the depression that followed it.

As for World War I itself, it was in some ways *the* event that helped to forge the complex system of news coverage upon which today's modern newspaper depends. Modern instruments of communication were used to transmit stories; wartime censorship, as we presently know it, was institutionalized; press services and "pooling" of correspondents and their coverage became standard practices during the war, although both had, as we have seen, long precedents.

That America would eventually enter the European conflict seemed inevitable by the mid 'teens. In spite of the stand of anti-British patriots like Hearst and pacifist publications like the *Nation,* by 1915 about 500 American journalists representing magazines, news services, newspapers and syndicates were already stationed in Europe, following the hostilities for American readers. Upon America's entry into the war, 40 of our correspondents actually went into combat with the American Expeditionary Forces, representing, in effect, about 2,000 or more American dailies and many more weeklies and magazines. Some were wounded; some were killed. Most are forgotten today.

The military forces themselves began producing newspapers, the most notable of which was *Stars and Stripes,* first published in February of 1918, using the talents of such young men as Harold Ross, future founder and editor of the *New Yorker,* celebrity and journalist-to-be, Alexander Woolcott, and gravel-throated radio sportscaster Grantland Rice. The *Stars and Stripes* died with the end of World War I, but was revived again in World War II and spawned equally famous talents in its reincarnation, most notably those of the young cartoonist Bill Mauldin. The original was not the first newspaper written for and by soldiers actually engaged in fighting a war, but it is the best known in the history of the American press—and probably one of the best written.

Censorship and Propaganda

As in all wars, World War I produced a host of legislation that, in one way or another, prevented the American press from giving aid and comfort to the enemy. The Espionage Act of 1917 was followed by a Sedition Act, passed by Congress the following year. As far as the press was concerned, the main burden of policing these anti-German acts was placed upon the Post Office, although the Justice Department was naturally the main enforcement agency of federal laws. The kind of papers that were likely to give aid and comfort to the enemy or encourage pacifists not to register for the draft were usually sent through the mails, however. A number of such journals were effectively silenced during the World War I period. All in all, however, the American press at home was comparatively free of censorship or government control at this time when compared to the Civil War Period. World War I was, for the United States, both a short and popular war, resistance to our participation confined largely to socialist and pacifist groups, most of which were hardly taken seriously.

More notable during the war than attempts at censorship was the Presidential Committee on Public Information chaired by George Creel, who was able, if he wished, to use legal power to enforce a benign censorship of any aspect of press operations. Creel was also a member of the official Censorship Board created by the Trading-with-the-Enemy Act, one of the offshoots of the Espionage Act. So the CPI, and Creel, had teeth, if they wanted to use them. Actually, the "Creel Committee," as it came to be known, was less a body of censors than a public information arm of the U.S government that spread to the press countless news items, releases and other data designed to activate support at home for our troops abroad and the war effort. (Carl Byoir, later of public relations fame, worked for Creel.)

The Creel Committee poured out propaganda, prepared ads for the sale of Liberty Bonds, raised money for the Red Cross, and, in coldblooded terms, served as a America's propaganda arm during the war, the main function of which was probably to keep home morale at a high pitch. At times, it did indeed have to slap the wrist of such powerful organs as the Associated Press and the *Washington Post* in order to prevent them from printing what were judged to be military secrets—or possibly just negative news—or facts that might injure morale at home.

Although the Creel committee was criticized roundly and widely, especially by political enemies of President Woodrow Wilson, it remains one of the most liberal and least oppressive governmental wartime propaganda and censorship bodies found anywhere on the globe during this century. It died amidst much criticism, consonant with attacks on President Wilson after the war. And World War I had not placed many pressures upon the First Amendment, at least as far as the world of journalism was concerned. Nor was the "World Made Safe for Democracy," as Wilson's battle cry had promised the way things turned out, but that is another story.

The False Armistice

The best known journalistic anecdote of World War I centers on a goof that resounded around the world and was never lived down by the man responsible for it: Roy Howard, then president of the United Press. There have been worse journalistic blunders—many of them—but in 1918, poor Howard had received a report, confirmed by an American admiral, that an armistice with Germany had been signed by the United States in early November. This was fine, except that the report was filed and transmitted on November seventh, four days before the signing of the actual armistice of November 11th. Pandemonium resulted in the United States and elsewhere around the world, first at the good news and second at the revelation of the deception.

Howard had acted in good faith, but somewhere along the line he had been taken in by a hoaxter (a German agent, he claimed until his death) who had managed to get his cable past the offical censor, because the censor had already heard the premature news and gone out to get drunk. By the time Howard, two hours after sending the original cable, wanted to issue a denial, the censor was back at his desk (in his cups), stubbornly refusing to transmit Howard's corrections. The event was a comedy of errors that deserves its private niche in the history of journalistic idiocy. How much damage may or may not have been done by it is impossible to calculate, although one theory maintains that Howard was the victim of a German plot to end the lost war a little early and save lives that otherwise would have been lost—a good idea if it had a chance of working.

Social Changes After the War

We have already seen some of the forces at work in the world of American journalism after World War I. But, possibly, we would be wise to take another look at them now, because they fuse with and refract all other changes then at work in the world of modern mass communications. The consolidation of newspapers and development of chains like the Hearst and Scripps-Howard newspapers were, in effect, models for the new radio broadcasting business which, by the early 1930s, was dependent for program material upon two relatively small but powerful networks—and one larger web more loosely organized. The world of Hollywood had seen its own mergers too—the names Metro-Goldwyn-Mayer and Twentieth Century-Fox symbolizing but two of them—along with a distribution system, that, by and large, placed the enormous output of the California film factories into various chains of theatres almost automatically, just as fast as they came off the production belt.

The soaring 'twenties may seem remote to us today, but, the configurations of the industries that we call today broadcasting, films and the press took their essential form during that decade and have changed little since. All handwriting that indicated what was to become of mass communications in the United States was upon our figurative wall by 1930, with the exception, of course, of future technologies like television that were not, as yet, perfected.

Most important was this nation's determination to go it alone after the war, symbolized by our refusal to join the League of Nations and our rejection of Wilson's plans for international peace in favor of a policy of isolationism. America's interests turned inwards, and we settled for a sustained period of doing what we as a nation apparently did best: development of the technology of mass production along with its bedfellow, mass communication. What this meant, of course, was, as President Coolidge said when the 'twenties flew high, that the ''business of America is business,'' and business we pursued with apparent and, it turned out, deceptive success.

At the same time, other currents were in the air, remnants, I think, of the ideals of enthusiastic socialists who, before the Russian Revolution, had developed intellectually viable arguments drawn from Marx and other Victorian pseudo-scientific social thinkers. These idealists, and there were a good number of them in the United States, did not share the dreams of the majority during the early part of this century to which I have referred in former chapters. Men like Lincoln Steffens and Upton Sinclair, called (somewhat unfairly) ''muck rakers,'' were sensitive to the pressures of technological growth upon the poor, extraordinary powers that fell into the hands of the few and the many prices, in human terms, that capitalist cultures (and perhaps all technological societies) are forced to pay for what they call (or think) is ''progress.''

Some extremists and moderates, like the gifted socialist civil libertarian Norman Thomas, stuck to these guns throughout their lives. Possibly most, like Thomas in his final years, felt that they had fought for a totally lost cause, but their influence was keenly felt in American life at no time, I think, quite as profoundly as in the 1920s, because, in their ways, this social thought helped the country prepare for the depression just ahead.

Concentrating, as we often do, upon the excesses of the prohibition era, post-World War I literary and artistic expatriates and upon colorful gangsters whose lives were glamorized by the movies, we often forget that the 'twenties were also the period in American history during which great antithesis to the old-time capitalist dream began to take shape. True enough, the Clayton and Sherman anti-trust laws had been passed before the war, but they were to become operational in the 'twenties along with new ideas of public utilities and regulated industries. These were concepts that, on one hand, were supposed to provide for our capitalist society the benefits of competition and free enterprise, at the same time that government attempted to control the excesses of big business, where and when large coporations threatened the power of government itself—or exploited their customers or workers beyond reason. Along with these controls, and in a less sophisticated way, the American labor union movement was accomplishing—or trying to accomplish—much the same ends in the interests of their own special constituencies. The boom period of the 1920's was, of course, especially hospitable to the arguments and actions of organized labor— much more so than the depression era that was to follow.

In short, America opted, in the 1920s, seemingly irrevocably, for a modified free enterprise system in the ownership and use of her mass technology, placing her faith in the civilities of government and natural antagonisms that develop between business and labor, producer and consumer and so forth, to achieve this end. And, with a few years out to fight another war, this is indeed the path that we have followed ever since, both in failure and success, thus angering both friends and critics of American society, because we have neither met the objectives of our boosters nor exploded in the class revolution forever predicted by our detractors.

Broadcast Networks

A short look at the world of broadcasting in this era signals for us what was on the horizon.

Having solved the problem of who was going to pay for radio broadcasting in 1922, more or less by accident, the next identity crisis faced by the new radio industry was an organizational one: *Who* was going to run it, and *how* was it to be run? In the light of Sarnoff's "Music Box" idea, a number of answers, it seemed, were possible, including the possibility that the government might enter the broadcasting business, as it was shortly to do in Great Britain in an indirect way via the British Broadcasting Corporation.

AT&T stayed much in the eye of the radio storm as stations multiplied, exceeding 500 by 1923, many of them employing transmission equipment that infringed upon the telephone company's patent rights. Still, Bell refused to sell her transmitters to all comers. She wanted to sell services.

The problem came to a head as existing stations began to form their own network. AT&T discovered, quite correctly, that it had been trying to sell the *wrong kind of service*—one that might be handled better by the new breed of broadcasters who ran RCA and Westinghouse, for instance. At least, this was more or less the intent of the "cross licensing agreement" between AT&T, RCA, General Electric and Westinghouse, when they had divided the broadcasting business in its childhood among themselves.

Things had not gone right, however, largely as a result of AT&T's discovery (via WEAF in New York) that advertising and (almost) advertising alone was, in the future, going to finance a medium of entertainment and news that would be sending programs along telephone lines and literally turning the entire nation into a potential audience for any single sound broadcast. Tentatively, AT&T (again via WEAF) began taking steps in the direction of what was now becoming network broadcasting. Ma Bell had all the long line cables she needed to turn the trick. They required only slight modification to carry radio broadcasting from community to community, and, because she had them, she used them.

A wired program was fed from WEAF in New York to WNAC in Boston in 1923 for experimental purposes. President Coolidge used 22 stations wired by AT&T to air a speech to the nation. Every year, AT&T's network grew. In 1924, six stations used regular telephone lines for three hours a day to hook up six stations, carrying mostly material originated by WEAF. Eighteen stations formed a chain to carry to the nation the sounds of the 1924 Democratic Convention in New York, and a later Coolidge speech (before his election) involved 26 stations.

With profits zooming towards a million dollars by 1926, it looked as if AT&T had hit a jackpot in broadcasting. Under the cross-licensing agreement, and with its concept of billing advertisers to spread their messages, the telephone company could charge broadcasters hefty fees, at the same time that she had sufficient nerve to charge stations run by others for the service of using her telephone long lines to function as a radio network. Eric Barnouw writes, "The power thus exerted by AT&T through its web of cables was deeply disturbing to General Electric and Westinghouse and their sales agent RCA." Barnouw's sentence is a classic of understatement, as the other pioneers in broadcasting, RCA in particular, could do little except to abide by the cross-licensing, patent-sharing agreements made a few years before. While AT&T was figuratively coining money, RCA, in particular, was making nearly nothing, although it was trying as best it could to complete with AT&T's WEAF in the New York area in the business of radio broadcasting.

The Radio Group

From Westinghouse, RCA had bought WJZ, Newark (later New York) in 1922, with studios in the Waldorf Astoria Hotel. But RCA was, in effect, all dressed up with no place to go. Under the cross-licensing contracts with AT&T it had agreed not to use Bell Telephone lines for purposes of networking, nor could it sell its services outright for advertising purposes as WEAF did. In the years that followed, RCA tried every stratagem of which it could conceive to overcome these circumscriptions: long range transmission by telegraph lines, short wave relays, long wave relays. To some degree, they succeeded. By 1926, the RCA network, carrying mostly WJZ's programs, consisted of 14 stations.

Who paid the bills if advertisers were prohibited? At this point in the history of radio, it was still possible for RCA (and its electronic industry) to offer broadcasts in the knowledge that, one way or another, they would be paid for from the sale of radio receivers. So all was not lost. And WJZ hung on, waiting for a brighter future, as did other stations affiliated with RCA's "Radio Group."

AT&T's Crucial Decision

Ma Bell has always been a crafty lady, often taking short term losses for long run gains, right up to the present day. This is exactly what AT&T did—in fact, she acted as one might expect her to. As the leader in American radio broadcasting by 1926, and in the face of mounting profits from her operations, she apparently saw two pictures in her crystal ball. The first indicated that anti-trust legislation was but a breath away from her corporate domain. The second warned her that a telephone company had best stick to the telephone business. (That destiny would, as technology advanced, hurl AT&T more deeply into the world of electronic hardware than she had dreamed, and that a wide-ranging scientific laboratory of corporate dimensions would eventually emerge from her Bell Labs were eventualities impossible to foresee at this date.)

In effect, AT&T agreed to let broadcasters use its wires for networking purposes, providing that the telephone company was paid for carrying radio (and later) television programs by wire or (later) through the air. AT&T also agreed to sell WEAF and almost everything connected with it, to RCA for $1 million.

AT&T's move was not quite as benevolent as it at first may appear. True, Ma Bell was making money in radio, but, as of 1926, she could make far more putting the same labor and resources into the then exploding telephone business. If broadcasting in America was going to be a success, she was also in a position to profit heavily from its fortunes by providing the same lines she already owned and operated for telephones to develop network growth with little or no capital expenditure, just slight modifications to accomodate radio signals. Actually, this was a proposition with no risk involved, not only in developing commercial radio broadcasting and networking, but also in keeping up the company's image as a quasi-public utility.

RCA and NBC

Whatever risks that existed were taken by men with stomachs for them: RCA's David Sarnoff, for one. He had long kept a faith in radio broadcasting, and now, in 1926, it was about to be justified. The ink was hardly dry on the agreement with AT&T, when the Radio Group created its subsidiary, the National Broadcasting Company, half owned by RCA, 30% by General Electric and 20% by Westinghouse. Amidst much publicity, the basic configurations for all "public" broadcasting (meaning privately owned, in the same sense of a British "public" school is) in the United States for at least the next half-century were now drawn. NBC, with its two major stations, WJZ and WEAF, would unite the nation by radio the next year at the beginning of coast-to-coast operations. On November 15, 1926, however, with broadcasts from New York, Chicago and Kansas, NBC's inaugural ceremonies reached the startling number of about five million listeners along a network of 25 stations. Radio, as a mass medium of communications, had come of age.

Most important, two or three relatively old ideas died with the birth of NBC a half century ago. One was that radio broadcasting, or any part of it, might somehow be subsidized by the electronic industry—or any other single industry—or (heaven forbid!) by the federal government, as it was to be, all or in part, in most other countries. Second, AT&T's notion of radio as a service like the telephone that advertisers might use to sell their wares, taking full responsibility for service, was more or less dead. Advertisers NBC would certainly need, and most of them would want to originate their own programs. But this was usually a job done by an advertising agency, and NBC was up to far more than selling a conduit between microphones and the ear of listeners. Broadcasting—owning and operating stations as well as networking them and sharing advertising revenues—was about to become a business, a big one in its own right.

NBC's two flagship stations in New York began, in 1927, to spin off individual networks of their own, building on the arrangements AT&T and the Radio Group had already made with existing broadcasters across the nation. WEAF was the main Red Network station; WJZ the flagship of the Blue, and many major cities carried both outlets on their radio spectrums. During the early 'thirties, the three NBC chimes that identified the NBC network were as much a part of American life as a bottle of Moxie. When Rockerfeller Center was built in New York, the enormous gray office complex was given the sobriquet, "Radio City," because both NBC stations were located in the main building, sharing studios and staff and space in the home office of, by then, NBC's sole owner, the Radio Corporation of America.

The Arrival of CBS

Had radio simply traded off one monopoly—or near monopoly—for another? This was a question the answer to which was postponed for more than a dozen years, largely because a wealthy 26-year old executive of his family's Cigar Company in Philadelphia became bored with cigars and was talked by his family into taking over the presidency of a debt-ridden radio network that had intended to compete with NBC. The young man was named William Paley. The network was called The Columbia Broadcasting System.

Paley was a different sort of personality from David Sarnoff, who later became head of RCA. And CBS was certainly a different kind of radio network from NBC. The former had been organized early in 1927 as the United Independent Broadcasters with the hope of affiliating into a network some of the majority of stations in the country that were involved neither with NBC's Red or Blue networks. Riding along with Paley's deal was also a record company called Columbia Phonograph Records that desired to get radio exploitation for its recordings. UIB, therefore, began the Columbia Phonograph Broadcasting System Inc. The record company soon withdrew from the arrangement, but the name Columbia stuck. It was eventually shortened to CBS.

Paley came to New York and, with fresh funding at his command, took over CBS as well as WABC, New York, its flagship station. Almost immediately, he went into the network business, and, like the inebriated mouse who challenged a cat to battle, took on NBC, its parent company RCA, and all of the sophisticated broadcasters who had been involved in the latter organization since the new technology's earliest days. By means of its rapid success, however, CBS clearly demonstrated to the public and to the government (for the time being) that RCA no longer had a monopoly on network broadcasting in the U.S.A. Sitting on the sidelines, of course, was AT&T, ready to sell its long lines telephone service to any of the (now) three networks that needed them. In effect, Ma Bell had backed herself into the catbird seat!

Radio Becomes a Business

In the years between 1922 and 1928, more than a few organizational and economic changes took place in radio. As Sydney Head notes in his fine book on American broadcasting, it is quite easy to blame commercialism and advertising and large profits for the direction radio took during these years. Too easy! Certainly, much of the spirit—but not the letter—of Sarnoff's "Music Box" idea was dead forever. Radio was fast becoming the "Everything Box," including what seemed to be streams of commercial announcements.

The Radio Group's own original benign ideas of radio as a public service, both specialized and popular, seemed to be shouted down by the vulgarities of a medium that was fast spreading to almost every home—and eventually, automobile—in the nation. Calling so mass a medium of merchandizing as radio a "public service" was (and still is) torturing the term "service" quite a bit. The notion that municipalities might operate some radio stations was strangled by the commercial success of the medium, with one or two exceptions: WNYC in New York, most notably. While hundreds of educational institutions had operated stations in the 'twenties, by the 'thirties, all but less than three dozen were left. They were just too valuable as commercial properties and too expensive for colleges and universities to operate for small audiences interested in what was invariably inexpensive, and usually dull, programming.

In effect, almost everybody in the radio business (and, as we shall see, many in government as well) changed their feeling about what broadcasting *should* be when they found out what it *could* be: a profitable business, a vital force for the sale of commercial goods and services, and, most important, America's newest and eventually best-loved pastime. In other words, radio was a "mass medium" that exploded on the American scene decades before these two words were first used together, or textbooks were written about "mass communications."

The programs that succeeded—that is, attracted audiences and advertisers—were not those soberly understood to be devoted to "public services," like symphony concerts, lectures and debates, but rather, for the most part, what we have come to know since as "schlock" (a Yiddish expression meaning, roughly, "discount or junk merchandise.") Of course, sporting events, news and music (some of it classical) made up a part of radio's repertoire, and some of it was quite successful. In the early years, most commercial announcements were also presented in a restrained way, unobtrusive and in good taste, for fear of offending the listeners' sensibilities, as well as limited in duration and confined to certain times of day.

On the other hand, as Head says, "An accident of history . . . profoundly affected the development of broadcasting in America," the accident being the tempo of the soaring economy of the 'twenties and the "disintergration of the nation's decorous but decaying post-Victorian values of the past generation." This is true, I think. But one must also consider the expanding radio business against the background of Hollywood's film explosion, the burgeoning mass press (especially the tabloids), prohibition and a number of other cultural phenomena that accompanied it. Whatever the cause, as Head notes, "commercial broadcasting just happened to be uniquely in tune with the time," and with the place as well. If the business of America was, indeed, business, the business of broadcasting became advertising, which added up to much the same thing. Bit by bit, broadcasters actually lost control of their own medium. But it is impossible to claim that, as they maximized their profits by turning much programming over to advertising agencies, they were not also giving the American public what it wanted to hear from its millions of radio sets.

The Popularity of Radio

"Amos 'n' Andy" is the radio show usually cited as an example of this early radio fever. It is a good one. Performed by two white vaudevillians named Freeman Gosden and Charles Correll who did a "blackface" act, the program originated in Chicago in the middle 'twenties as "Sam 'n' Henry."

The central characters' names were changed to "Amos 'n' Andy" two years later. Having begun on WGN in Chicago, the pair switched in 1928 to WMAQ and began syndicating (or networking) recordings of their programs. The next year NBC was willing to pay the team an annual salary of $100,000 for their exclusive services, and Pepsodent toothpaste was eager to pay NBC a good deal more than that to sponsor the nightly 15-minute comedy. "Amos 'n' Andy" were on their way to becoming a national craze, wending their way, eventually, into the comic strips, movies and, years later, onto television.

What exactly was this cultural phenomenon that, in most time zones, between 7 and 7:15 P.M., five nights a week, achieved such popularity that telephone operators scheduled their rest breaks during this period, and movie theatres stopped their films to bring by loudspeakers the program to their audiences? Not much, really. And I suppose that is exactly why "Amos 'n' Andy" *is* such a good example of what radio could do best: satisfy low common denominator audience tastes with simple pleasures, skillfully performed and easily enjoyed.

Gosden and Correll usually imitated the various voices of most of the characters in their nightly skits, scripts written so that neither actor had to talk to himself in two roles. The characters were Negroes, residents of Harlem in New York. Much of the comedy was derived from racial (or "minstrel") stereotyping so bland that black Americans, at the time, seemed rarely to take even minor offense at this aspect of the program. If they did, they kept quiet about it. (Sensitivity to racial stereotyping did not peak for 25 years after the birth of "Amos 'n' Andy." When it finally did, it gave the *coup de grace* to this series—along with most of its Jewish, Italian and Irish brethren on both radio and, by then, television.)

Each episode was really an extended joke that moved a thin farce plot slowly along from day to day. Much of the humor derived from the pasteboard, two-dimensional charactors and the complications of their business lives (frequently harmless confidence schemes) and personal problems. The most notable individual in the group was called "The Kingfish" (of the shrine of Mystic Knights of the Sea), played with skillful gusto by Gosden.

On and on the stories went, geared for chuckles, not belly-laughs, at the mispronunciations of the comic characters and the homey wisdom of the more serious ones, notably Amos, who was a good father and family man. Andy, on the other hand, was a bachelor whose romantic exploits provided much of the fun. Little physical action was spelled out or even implied in the broadcasts. Events were talked about more than acted out, a tradition closer to the theatre than to the films, but ideal for sound broadcasting. The pace of performances was usually leisurely, but demanded fairly careful listening for full enjoyment.

"Amos 'n' Andy's" great virtue, if virtue it is, was quite simply that it was a perfect comic vehicle for a mass medium like radio. College professors, bricklayers, housewives, politicians and Presidents of the United States could all chuckle at the "boys" and their adventures without feeling that this innocuous humor was beneath them. Nor was the comedy so complex that a grade school drop-out might not understand nearly all of it. It is possible that half of the American nation listened to ''Amos 'n' Andy'' in its early days, and one is impelled today merely to ask what the other half could have been doing so that they managed to miss it. Pepsodent toothpaste, an apparently non-poisonous dental cream, was, as a result, sold by the ton and stayed with Correll and Gosden for many years until it left them to sponsor a young stage and film comedian who had begun to gather a formidable radio audience. His name was Bob Hope. After Pepsodent, there were to be other sponsors, right into the age of television, when Gosden and Correll bowed out (except as producers and writers), and the characters were finally played by Negro performers.

''Amos 'n' Andy'' was not entirely typical of American radio during the soaring 'twenties, by any means, and, according to certain criteria, it may not even have been the *most* popular continuing radio program in the radio era to follow during the next two decades. But ''Amos 'n' Andy'' became a national habit for millions of Americans for years. Performed modestly without a studio audience for most of its first two decades, it somehow captured the mood of, first, the happy-go-lucky 'twenties, and later, the depression, and finally the war and post-war years for as long—or longer—than any other single mass entertainment presented in the U.S.A., with the possible exception of one or two comic strips.

What killed ''Amos 'n' Andy''? Well, nothing killed them, because they never really existed. The televised version of the radio skits diluted and obscured some of the characters' gentle whimsy. It was simply more fun imagining them than seeing them in person. (Correll and Gosden themselves, in black-face, were not successful in the movies.) Blacks—and many whites—began to resent the Negro stereotypes with which the show was filled, and for the best of reasons. American Negroes were fast ascending social, educational and economic ladders, and the minstrel show tradition, out of which ''Amos 'n' Andy'' came, seemed antique, demeaning and even insulting to more than 20 million black Americans. They obviously did not want to be associated with, when all was said and done, the relatively ignorant buffoons with their typical ''darkie'' dialects played by Correll and Gosden. In a phrase, ''Amos 'n' Andy'' simply was not funny any more, particularly, I think, because they were the creation of white men and not, like the characters played by later Black comedians, authentic reflections of the bittersweet experience of Negro life in America.

Once upon a time, however, when radio announcer Bill Hay said, ''Here they are!'' half of America was listening—including me.

9

The 'Twenties Roar

RADIO BROADCASTING WAS A new and spellbinding medium. Hearing voices and music in the air for the first time was probably not quite as exciting as first watching photographs move 20 years earlier, but it symbolized just about everything for which the technological revolution in mass communications had come to stand. In purveying news, radio was *faster* than the press. It could bring into the living room of the average citizen not only a reporter's version of a far off event but, if circumstances were right, actual sounds of an incident as it was happening. In providing entertainment and cultural fare, the talents of musicians, actors, comedians and others filled one's *own* living room—not a live or motion picture theatre where one sat, isolated by proscenium arch or screen, from the performers. Radio also asked that one use his or her imagination to fill in the pictorial details of an experience created by sound and sound alone.

In another quarter of a century, television would take over many of radio's former functions. But video could not—and has not—achieved the imaginative flexibility of sound broadcasting. And, in my opinion, television may well have taken away from broadcasting some of the excitement that radio stimulated on the listener's "wide screen of human imagination," in the words of an old-time radio writer. The tin horn sound of the early radio sets—and phonograph records that captured on wax the performances of radio celebrities—is the sound that nostalgia buffs now usually associate with the late prohibition years.

Mass communications, by the middle to late 1920s, seem to have gone almost as far as they could go in spreading their influences into society: to homes and automobiles, filling leisure hours and providing for the masses instantaneous descriptions of the great world beyond the little path each person traveled every day. Only the transistor radio receivers invented after World War II would be able to carry mass communications to the more remote corners of culture around the world that had heretofore been missed.

"The Real Tinsel"

The 'twenties were also the years that Hollywood, California began the rise to its greatest era: the 15-year period between 1935 to 1950. On the other hand, cynics like Ezra Goodman have called this new prosperty of the 'twenties the beginning of the "decline and fall of Hollywood," meaning that its supposedly greatest days were just made of what cynics today call "the *real* tinsel." Devoted as it was to show business, press agentry and, in the parlance of the times, "hooey" and "ballyhoo," there *is* something to Goodman's claim, despite the *real* money and *real* fame (or celebrity) that American movies generated also so expertly for so long.

The films remained—and remain—the peculiar property of magicians, true to the spirit of Méliès, masters of the art of fooling the eye with legerdemain, convincing the public that illusions of *all* kinds are true. Ingmar Bergman, the sensitive Swedish film writer and director, devoted one of his best and most mischievous movies, *The Magician,* almost entirely to this subject. Nobody seemed to notice the conjuring at the time—not audiences nor critics nor other film makers. As the saying goes, "It is fun to be fooled," and, I imagine, it is also painful to accept one's own capacities for credulity, gullibility and illusion; that is, to realize how easily and completely we accept as real what is really artful magic. (As a former magician and mind reader, I still frequently contemplate this possibility when I attend good films that fool audiences with their virtuoso conjuring.)

All of this was nothing new to Hollywood by the end of World War I. Foreign competition had been effectively eliminated, and new publics displayed new and voluminous appetites for new movie tricks and for their stars—particularly the stars. No common factor distinguishes these performers during this post-war period, except that they all, in one degree or another, possessed a flair for pantomime. This art was demanded by the silent screen and, apparently, some actors and actresses mastered it and some could not. Beauty or even good looks were not necessary: Buster Keaton, Zasu Pitts, Harold Lloyd and Wallace Beery were awkward, grotesque, pathetic. Other stars were indeed attractive, but each in a different way, one from the other, like Pickford and Fairbanks, Rudolph Valentino, John Barrymore, Theda Bara, Clara Bow and Thomas Meighan. Some exploited their particular talents in distinctively artful ways especially suitable for the silent screen: The superb, grotesque actor and make-up artist, Lon Chaney, was one example of an actor whose extraordinary talents turned ugliness into beauty. His peculiar skill is still visible in revivals of his films.

Erich von Stroheim

Griffith had established movie directing as an art in its own right, different from that of the stage or opera director, professions which themselves were only less than 70 years old. More than anyone, it was probably a bizarre Austrian actor who called himself Erich von Stroheim (his origins remain both complicated and obscure) who carried to lengths never again reached this early concept of movies as a director's medium.

Although he did quite well most of his life playing Prussian villains in films (and even in the Broadway theatre), von Stroheim, at first, displayed his talents by directing *Blind Husbands* (1919), *The Devil's Passkey* (1920) and *Foolish Wives* (1921), all competent and relatively light—even comic—satirical films.

Metro-Goldwyn-Mayer, the great studio with the roaring lion trademark, was created—or patched together—in the early years of the 1920's. Von Stroheim was given a nearly unlimited budget by MGM to film a book by Frank Norris called *McTeague*. The eccentric Austrian tried to do *exactly* that: make a movie of every page of the book with a realism and literalism unknown at the time and rarely attempted since. Exactly what he came up with we shall never know, because the original version of the movie called *Greed* ran about ten hours and was therefore literally unshowable.

Von Stroheim cut it to 20 reels: five hours or so. MGM finally cut it down to ten reels, the version that we possess today. Von Stroheim fumed, but there was little he could do. (The unused celluloid was foolishly destroyed—although the original script has recently been published.) The resulting movie, released in 1924 and shot, for the most part in San Francisco, is a flawed masterpiece of realism, superb acting and cinematic imagination. But, obviously, *Greed* also marked the end of any large studio's inclination to give a director sole authority over the production of any film.

Despite his mercurial temperament, von Stroheim continued to work stormily (and expensively) on a few more Hollywood films, but, by 1928, his reputation for unpredictability and temperment ended his directorial career. He spent the rest of his life as a character actor in the United States and Europe. Von Stroheim died in 1957, seven years after having portrayed a strange caricature of his directorial self in *Sunset Boulevard* with Gloria Swanson, a one-time silent star whom he had actually directed in his last film, *Queen Kelly* (1928), and from which he was fired while it was still in production.

DeMille's Epics

Von Stroheim, in his way, caricatured the growth, extravagance and (there is no other word) ''glamor'' of Hollywood in the 'twenties. The studios were big businesses, involved, as we shall see, in distributing and exhibiting films as well as making them. The people who survived the competition of running them were businessmen: men like William Fox, Louis B. Mayer, Marcus Loew and Samuel Goldwyn. The stars lined "up front," but directors and writers were busy behind the scenes producing day dreams, not for America alone, but for all the world. The economy of the industry ran into the millions of dollars a month.

Directors like Cecil B. DeMille, whose career lasted well into the era of sound movies, literally made Hollywood into a dream factory, and how they did it is still not entirely clear. DeMille himself was one of America's most talented vulgarians in recent history. A fine technician of a relatively sober temperament, he combined Griffith's sentimental sensitivity and experimental drive with von Stroheim's passion for realism and excess, lacking the personal and artistic eccentricities of both. He, therefore, not only survived but flourished in Hollywood.

DeMille's directing career began in 1914 with *The Squaw Man*. What DeMille apparently understood, that others more talented and more intelligent than he missed, was that the films were a *mass* medium, and that anything—literally *anything*—that could be made to appeal to great crowds of people would be considered successful. True artistic quality meant little or nothing. Profits were the only measuring stick of virtue in Hollywood.

DeMille possessed a fine nose for popular fashions and public whims: high comedies with a dash of sex after World War I, and, eventually in the mid-1920's, DeMille's most astounding films, that, for the most part, he kept making and re-making until his death in 1959. I am referring to his corpus of Biblical epics which, from *The Ten Commandments* in 1923 to a re-make of the same name in 1956, I find difficult to describe in English. So are his other films—all of them "big" ventures like *Cleopatra* (1934), my personal favorite and possibly the most vulgar of them all, to *Union Pacific* (1939), *Northwest Mounted Police* (1940), and what may be the most enjoyable film he created, *The Greatest Show on Earth* (1953), a colorful and corny encomium to the Ringling Brothers-Barnum and Bailey Circus.

From the beginning, DeMille quite obviously knew that sex in the form of romance, nudity and sensuality were what most of the world-wide public was looking for in American movies. Others discovered this also, but De Mille managed to find a way, within the limits of a popular art form, patronized by both adults and children who would tolerate only so much flesh, sin and sex and no more, to frame these qualities within acceptable cinema vehicles. (DeMille's earlier films, until 1923, had been overtly reflective of the so-called "new morality" and "anti-Victorianism" of the 'twenties.)

The solution was the "epic," correctly known today as the "DeMille epic," although DeMille had, in truth, merely adapted and extended the notion from the Babylon sequences in Griffith's masterful flop, *Intolerance*. The trick was to locate implications of sin and scandal in the Bible, in history or in legend and then to sanitize them, glamorize them, and show that, in the end virtue, morality and religion—at least, Judeo-Christian religion—triumph by the final reel. Love might also triumph, but personal conflicts ran second in

DeMille's world to the moral tales he told in spectacular dimensions. In fact, DeMille so stylized and glamorized his themes that it was usually difficult to take either their implied depravities or their preaching moralities even half seriously. With a technical grandeur that he developed to extremes over the years, DeMille's world had nothing whatsoever to do with the world in which his audiences lived, and herein, I suppose, lay the key to his success.

Hollywood's Scandals

DeMille's strange type of movie morality was not only good business, it had also become necessary for other reasons. In the 1920s, movie admissions were edging their way up to 50 million a week. Hollywood actors and actresses were much publicized celebrities, cynosures of attractiveness and immensely popular public figures. At the same time, there existed no shortage of reporters and snoopers covering the private lives of these stars, much to the delight, of course, of producers and the actors themselves, whose personal popularity usually assured large box-office grosses for their films.

There was, however, another side to the coin. The movie community of Hollywood consisted of a new-rich group of actors, artists, writers and others. They were probably, morally speaking, neither kinkier nor more free-wheeling than any other group of rich, talented and (mostly) young people at the time. The public spotlight, however, was upon them, and whatever they did was news, especially if it contained seeds of scandal or gossip. Their sex lives, multiple marriages and occasional orgiastic parties were all news stories gobbled up hungrily by the mass audience.

When, in 1921, a popular comedian like "Fatty" Arbuckle became involved in the possible rape and murder of an obscure starlet, or when, in 1922, the talented, handsome director William Desmond Taylor was murdered (and two top stars, Mary Miles Minter and Mabel Normand, were implicated in the dirty work), the problem turned serious. The following year the handsome film star, Wallace Reid, died while trying to withdraw from his narcotics habit. Even the public idol, Charlie Chaplin, subsequently married a 16-year old girl who was noticeably pregnant at the time of the ceremony.

Voices from Washington

Had these events happened in Wabash, Peoria, Chicago or New York, they might have caused raised eyebrows, some slight newspaper melodrama, and subsequently would have been forgotten. But they were happening in Hollywood, the land of the real tinsel. Los Angeles was rapidly developing a reputation as city of sin. At stake, quite literally, was the future of the film business as private enterprise.

Since 1915, committees of the United States Congress had been, from time to time, investigating the moral and the financial status of this new industry. Suggestions had even been made in Washington that some sort of federal control over the film business—and the goings on in Hollywood—might not be a bad idea. In fact, the Hughes Bill of 1915 proposed just that: a five-person Federal Motion Picture Commission, not unlike the Federal Radio Commission that followed it by a little more than a decade. The bill, which was mainly concerned at the time with censoring lewdness in films, might also have had considerable and devastating effects upon the purses of the movie makers, placing them at the mercy of the Department of the Interior which, as licenser of all films, might then place its index finger directly into the middle of Hollywood's rich custard pie.

Now, there was almost nothing that the movie producers wanted (or thought they needed) *less* than government interference in the operation of their private gold mine. Remember that one of the original reasons that the industry moved to the Pacific coast was to avoid patent laws that restricted free and easy "borrowing" of technical devices from their legal owners. That problem had been pretty well cleared up. But a new one loomed: that of monopoly; in fact, monopolies of *two* types.

First, although the major studios competed with one another, they were also quite capable of closing ranks when necessary to keep other competitors out. Eventually, five major studios, Universal, 20th Century-Fox, Paramount, MGM and Warner Brothers, in effect, ran Hollywood, leaving small pickings to competitors that cooperated with their hegemony as the price of their survival. Second, the "big five," as they were eventually known, were making deep inroads during the 'twenties into the distribution and exhibition of films— that is, the businesses of booking movies and the ownership and operation of the most profitable theatres in the country. As a result, an independent producer or smaller studio, say, a United Artists or a Columbia Pictures, *had* to do business with one or more of the "big five" in order to book its movies into theatres owned by the "five" via distribution organizations also owned by the "five."

Monopoly it smelled like, and monopoly it was—or so the Justice Department found out 15 or so years later, and so the Supreme Court decided in still another 12. In the meanwhile, the farther away the federal government could be kept from Hollywood itself, the happier most of the producers were. Hollywood's sudden concern with morality and self-policing during the early 'twenties, therefore, had less to do with the sin and scandal that was reputed to be running wild in Hollywood—or occasional skin shots in "naughty" movies of the flapper era—than the mighty urge of film moguls to keep the Justice Department or *any* bureaucrats from Washington away from their personal monopolistic goose that was able to lay apparently endless golden eggs.

Movies and Censorship

At any rate, by 1923, Hollywood was in the midst of a mighty effort to clean its own houses, both the private lives of the stars and their public behavior on celluloid. True, in a post-war burst of freedom, the movies had become a trifle raunchy—tame by today's standards, but racy enough to keep censors busy in 36 states by 1921, and for a United States Senator to call Hollywood a city "where debauchery, riotous living, drunkenness, ribaldry, dissipation and free love seem to be conspicuous."

One can imagine how the film makers responded to this tribute! Hollywood producers at first fought attempts at legal state censorship, especially in 1921, when New York State established a procedure for licensing films that was to last nearly 40 years. The stakes, however, were too high to fight too hard, particularly in the light of the Supreme Court's decision in the case of *Mutual Film Corporation v. Ohio,* wherein, as we have seen, the movies were *not* given First Amendment protection but were adjudged businesses, pure and simple. Rather than challenge the government and the states, as well as various religious and civic organizations bent on protecting the public from Hollywood's depravities, the industry concentrated on protecting the goose.

Unlike radio broadcasting which, at the time, manifested an uncertain future as a business, Hollywood had already demonstrated that film making was an extremely profitable enterprise both in national and international trade. In order to protect their profits and build a fortress around their growing monopolies, the film makers, good businessmen that they were, compromised rather than take chances. With maximum publicity, they agreed to mend their ways and present, if not a scrupulous image to the public, at least a fairly clean one and to sanitize their output on celluloid so that neither women nor children needed to fear corruption from their local movie palaces.

Self-Regulation

In 1922, the Motion Picture Producers and Distributors of America, or the MPPDA, was organized. It still exists, called now the Motion Picture Association of America, or MPAA. Its history is, in some ways, as bizarre as that of any of the "big five" movie companies. Created as a wedge—and an effective one—between the United States Government and the motion picture industry, it operated as a *self*-disciplinary body and as the administrator of a code of moral behavior on screen (about which more later). It has recently disintegrated (along with the Hollywood of old) into sort of a public relations arm for the people who make movies for theatres and television in California—or for most of them. But, at one time, its muscles were powerful.

The political (or anti-governmental) thrust of the MPPDA was obvious from the start. If a seasoned politician with experience in federal government took charge of what was, in effect, an organization whose *voluntary* membership consisted of *all* of the major producers in Hollywood, these producers could not be up to much mischief—now, could they? The leader or "czar" of the MPPDA, appointed in 1922, was therefore Will H. Hays, Chairman of the Republican National Committee and Postmaster General under President Harding—and a regular churchgoer. Hays was a dignified, lean, conservative gentleman with a dour face who always looked as if he had just been sucking lemons. For many years he presided over the MPPDA or "Hays Office," as it was familiarly known. He was followed by another model of political decorum, Eric Johnston, until his death. The head of the MPAA today is one-time presidential assistant to Lyndon Johnson, Jack Valenti.

None of these men were ever noted either for their intelligence or talent, but they were individuals of moral rectitude. The producers now agreed to censor their own films—although their famous (or infamous) Production Code, and Office of Production Code Administration, was not implemented until the early 1930's. The MPPDA acted as an "advisory," industry supported, private regulating agency that served like a schoolmarm of a bygone period. The caper was as clean as a whistle!

That the MPPDA had been organized as a sort of unspoken treaty with Uncle Sam to stay away from Hollywood is an ironic truth. As years passed, the MPPDA, a creature of the industry itself, became increasingly powerful in its hold over the production of films in the United States. How odd it seems, then, that many producers, directors and others, all represented in theory *by* the MPPDA, eventually fought tooth and nail with it to circumvent its rigorous censorial standards that, by the middle 'thirties, went far beyond matters of nudity and sex to actually prescribing a precise moral code by which film writers and makers were forced to live professionally. For instance, a criminal shown in a movie had to be suitably punished; ministers could not be ridiculed or held up as objects of laughter, and so forth. This was the severe price that the film makers had eventually to pay to preserve their clean image—and keep Washington at bay.

When, in the 1950s, the Supreme Court dissolved the hold of the "big five" on American movies and television began to compete with films, the MPPDA's influence upon American film makers waned, simply because it was no longer necessary. During its most powerful years, however, films with an MPPDA seal of approval on them were almost certain not to create a stir among state censors, parents' groups or religious organizations, thus accomplishing exactly what the producers had intended in the first place. And nearly every film made and released through normal channels in the United States bore such a seal. If it did not, few, if any, distributors would handle it, and fewer theatres would dare to exhibit it. The scheme worked for, roughly, 30 years.

The Silent Films

Of the movies of the early 'twenties, there is so much to say that any treatment I give them here must themselves necessarily be cursory, incomplete and probably unfair. Most of them look odd to our eyes today. But the art of pantomine reached some of its greatest moments in the silent era. The psychologist, Rudolph Arnheim, among others, has noted that just as film makers were perfecting methods of storytelling by means of moving pictures and pictures alone, the invention of the sound film destroyed forever a pictorial medium that promised to develop into a great art. Of course, we shall never know if Arnheim was right, but a study of these old films—or those that still exist— transport one to a silent world of visual illusion quite different from the "all talking, all singing" one that followed it.

From today's vantage point, yesterday's styles and fashions, visualized and exaggerated for the silent camera, may seem outlandish and naive, but most silent movies did not pretend to naturalism—merely to clarity in communicating ideas and emotions. Accompanied by a live piano or organ, the power of many of these old movies—certainly not all of them—to amuse, move and excite audiences may be appreciated today with a little effort—just a desire to look at the world as our parents and grandparents saw it.

Certainly, we must mention the work of Joseph von Sternberg (before his discovery of Marlene Dietrich); the documentaries of Robert Flaherty like *Nanook of the North* (1922); John Barrymore's unforgettable performance as *Dr. Jekyll and Mr. Hyde* (1920); and comedies of Buster Keaton, particularly *The General* (1926); King Vidor's *Big Parade* (1926); James Cruze's *The Covered Wagon* (1923); and Ernst Lubitsch's so-called "touch" of continental satire as seen from Hollywood, U.S.A. Of course, I must also mention the madcap world of Harold Lloyd and the early films of directors who became more familiar to the public during the sound era like George Stevens, Frank Capra, William Wyler, John Ford, Clarence Brown, Rex Ingram and Tod Browning. These men learned the art of film making in the silent era and carried at least its spirit into their sound films during the years to come.

European Films

While some of the popular silent Hollywood films may be termed "works of art" by any standards, other movies that were geared less to the mass public than to an elite audience strove more self-consciously than mass-oriented films to be "artistic." To some, they were—and are—not art but simply "arty." They represent, for the most part, Europe's attempt to compete with the United States in the production of silent films. The main problem that faced the film industries in France, Germany, England and elsewhere, however, was that whenever a superior film director, actor or writer appeared, the lure of Hollywood gold almost inevitably pulled him across the Atlantic Ocean. In fact, he or she did not even need to be able to speak English to become Hollywood's latest European "discovery" in this period of filmic pantomime.

But Europe kept some of its fine actors, directors and writers. While the expert performer, Emil Jannings, sometimes worked in Hollywood, his most notable masterpiece, *The Last Laugh* (1924), was made in Germany, as so was the best work of F. W. Murnau, including one of the first *Dracula* films in

1922. Possibly no movie was more beautifully produced in the silent era than Carl Dreyer's *Passion of Joan of Arc* (1928) which combined the talents of the Danish Dreyer, a Polish cameraman, an Italian star and a German designer. It was made in France, an international effort and a remarkable movie, consisting largely of superb close-ups. The work of Mauritz Stiller and Victor Sjostram in Sweden, and Fritz Lang, Robert Wiene, E.A. Dupont and C.W. Pabst in Germany constitute a mere sample of the superior foreign movies of the period that, one way or another, found their way past the exclusionary barriers the "big five" had erected in the U.S.A. Distributing and exhibiting a foreign film in America was difficult, and remained difficult for many years—unless American interests were involved in its capitalization—but certain independent theatres in big cities frequently managed to offer them to special audiences.

Sergei Eisenstein and the U.S.S.R.

In the Soviet Union, one of the great film makers, Sergei Eisenstein, was to reach his most creative period in the silent era during the 'twenties. Eisenstein's career was a stormy one, less because of his artistic temperament than the power struggles through which this politically sensitive director lived in the stormy days of the U.S.S.R. after the October Revolution of 1917. He was forever, it seemed, trying to make peace with his government by making political-historical movies—and continually failing. History, in the Soviet Union, moved faster than any film director could.

In fact, Eisenstein was not a political animal but a creative one. He had been trained for the theatre, was a talented graphic artist, an excellent caricaturist and competent philosophical aesthetician, all qualities that usually produce poor politicians. Yet, his films were (or had to be) politically oriented to survive in the new Communist state. He nevertheless achieved remarkable cinematic results—some of it much like Griffith's better work (without the American's emotional and subjective sensitivity) and some almost as ambitious as von Stroheim's wild projects, but better controlled and disciplined.

Eisenstein's three major films of the 'twenties literally cannot be described, except to say that, in their way, they all dealt with recent Russian history and that they all were "social" films with strong didactic elements—at times, unfortunately for Eisenstien, the right ones presented at the wrong moment. *Strike* (1924) recapitulates a workers' revolt in Czarist times; *Potemkin* (1925), portrays a pre-revolutionary uprising in the Royal Navy in 1905; and *Ten Days That Shook the World* (also known as *October*), made in 1927, celebrates some of the critical events ten years before during the Bolshevik revolution. *October* centers on the attack upon the Czar's Winter Palace and the overthrow of Russia's brief provisional government headed by Alexander Kerensky.

In all of his films, including those made in the sound era, Eisenstein saw history in epic dimensions. He had a poet's eye for symbols and coaxed unbelievably naturalistic performances from his actors. That his work remains exciting to this day—far more exciting than Hollywood's epics made at *any* time in the American film city's history—is possibly the most telling hallmark of Eisenstein's directorial genius. His later sound films, *Alexander Nevsky* (1938) and *Ivan the Terrible* (1944 and 1958; the second part re-cut and released ten years after the director's death) are formidable sagas told in a (by now) classic tradition, but, to my eye, less astonishing than his earlier works.

Eisenstein, incidentally, managed to get to Hollywood in 1930, where he attempted a number of projects. Most of them, including a version of Theodore Dreiser's novel, *An American Tragedy,* were turned down by his employer, Paramount Studios, before they were started. Under other auspices, he shot some footage in Mexico, where he worked for a year on a film that was eventually abandoned. Upton Sinclair, the novelist, produced it, but ran out of money and into artistic troubles with his colleagues. Eisenstein's Mexican sequences, called *Que Viva Mexico* (among other titles) are occasionally, and unfairly, revived today. Eisenstein had left only scraps of his unfinished project in the United States. He neither edited them nor, probably, did he even view them during his lifetime. This assortment of disconnected scenes makes little—if any—sense, despite some of its pictorial excellence.

Russian cinema after the revolution deserves more than a paean to Eisenstein, because, I suppose, largely of the faith that Lenin, the U.S.S.R.'s first oligarch, showed in movies as an instrument of Marxist public education. Vsevold I. Pudovkin, another Soviet director, was also a master of the epic, having created such films as *Mother* (1924), *End of St. Petersburg* (1927) and *Storm Over Asia* (1928), except that Pudovkin centered his films to a greater degree than Eisenstein upon individuals and the force of events upon them, while the latter told his heroic tales from a more impersonal, almost pseudo-documentary, perspective.

Other Russian film makers also took full advantage of this period of experiment and relative freedom to *use* movies for social purposes. I suppose Dziga Vertov was the first mature documentarian (or newsreel editor) in film history, his lengthy tribute to the revolution itself in 1918 encouraging further experiments in the development of the form. Lev Kuleshov did similar work, and, in 1920, maintained his own studio in which he and his pupils were apparently less capable of producing great films than they were of studying and experimenting with the aesthetics of the silent motion picture. Their work, however, influenced others, including Alexander Dovzshenko, whose *Arsenal* (1929), on the revolutionary movement in the Ukraine, and *Earth* (1930), about life on a collective farm, were full-blown examples of Soviet cinema art.

Steeped as it was in Russian theatrical traditions and the work of directorial giants like Constantin Stanislavski, the more daring Vsevolod Meyerhold, and a roster of recent playwrights of impressive stature, film makers in the U.S.S.R. in the 'twenties could not have been more unlike their contemporaries in Hollywood were they living on different planets! (A Hollywood wag quipped of Dovzshenko's *Earth,* "Boy meets tractor; boy loses tractor; boy gets tractor!") The reasons were many, but the main one was the didactic

Marxist thrust that official decree *demanded* of all movies made in the U.S.S.R. More than one Soviet director, writer and even actor found himself holding a one-way ticket to Siberia—or in front of a firing squad—for "deviationism" from a party line that often swerved quickly, nervously and unpredictably. Second, the profit motive that infused all life in Hollywood was absent in the U.S.S.R. Artists were encouraged to pursue their art for the welfare of the state, and box office statistics were irrelevant. Third, as noted above, a great theatrical tradition was finding its way onto celluloid. Fourth, film makers, like many in the theatrical community of the U.S.S.R., were as interested in theory and philosophy, particularly aesthetics, as in their products or in films themselves.

The Soviet revolution was a great crucible for testing social theory. Critical, social and artistic ideas were plowed and mixed with academic verve. Nearly every director and film artist of stature was also a theoretical writer; Pudovkin, Vertov, Eisenstein are among those most familiar to American film students today. Notions like "montage" may have been invented for the film by Eisenstein, but even he credits the theory of "montage" to Kuleshov's pure experiments (accomplished on a print of one of D. W. Griffith's films, incidentally). This theory, like many others, was then discussed, debated, written about in books and film journals to the degree that, by the end of the 'twenties, possibly no Soviet film aesthetician was able to define "montage" coherently. The Russian proclivity, notable in her novelists, playwrights, scientists and psychologists, to obfuscate simple things by making them appear complex fit well into the cinematic temper of the times and even refracted to the United States where, a generation or more later, American academic "film study" experts appeared to be carrying on this same argumentative tradition that had been given up in the U.S.S.R. (and other European countries) shortly after World War II.

(By and large, movie making and film analysis are still studied as didactic, socially oriented and *very serious* subjects in nations like the U.S.S.R., Poland, Cuba and China. But the dense clusters of abstract theory that surrounded it in Russia in the 1920s has, today, given way to more pragmatic, economical and less prolix approaches—at least, as far as I can tell from an outsider's perspective.)

Phonograph Records

In the meantime, the United States also saw the growth into maturity, during the 1920s, of a technology of communications that had, in sneaky fashion, managed to grow up alongside the motion pictures and radio broadcasting, creating such a quiet revolution that it is treated today only cursorily—if at all—in most histories of mass communication.

I am referring specifically to the record industry, whose output reached true mass proportion with the invention of electrical recording techniques in the 'twenties. These innovations were to influence the film business, most notably after 1927, when sound recording was mated with the silent movie to create the talking cinema. So, let us step back for a moment to reprise briefly the history of this ingenious family of gadgetry, from the first metal foil cylinder records to the disc records of the 1920s. The latter provided for millions a popular form of home amusement and entertainment that vied with both radio and movies for the attention of an affluent public that had, increasingly, been getting used to "miracles" of communication technology popping up all around them.

Thomas Edison himself, and the peculiar stubbornness of this genius of practical technology, are both intimately related to the origins of sound recording. Unlike many other of his inventions, there is little doubt that Edison himself in 1877 designed the first phonograph (called by him the "phonogram"). A prototype was built by John Kreusi at Edison's Menlo Park, New Jersey laboratories. Recording was achieved by the impressions made by a stylus upon a cylinder of metal, wrapped in tin foil. It worked—after a fashion—and we must accept the paradox of a partially deaf inventor—Edison—reciting "Mary had a little lamb . . ." into the thing. According to Edison's own report, he reacted with amazement when his own voice was recreated, as he manually turned the cylinder crank over the scratches he had just made in the tin foil.

Edison was immediately aware of the potential of this new instrument. He even drew up a prophetic list, in 1878, of ten major uses to which the "phonogram" could be put for business and recreation, and all of them are present functions of sound recording. Immersed as Edison was in so many inventions of great scope—particularly his work with the electric light—the phonograph remained but a peripheral interest for the rest of his life. Although he was deeply involved in the manufacture of phonograph machines and recordings during the first and second decades of the century, Edison never gave up his sentimental attachment to his first cylinder recordings—long past the day that they had been shown to be inferior to discs or platter recordings. One cannot help concluding that he regarded the phonograph as an instrument of considerably less consequence than his other inventions. Edison called it his "baby," and he treated it that way.

Other businessmen and inventors also entered the phonograph field, some to compete with Edison, some to cooperate with him. Still others refined the machinery, substituted wax cylinders for the tin foil ones, and by the end of the century had produced a far more workable instrument than Edison's original, although practical uses for it were not simple to demonstrate, so delicate and so difficult to operate was the machine.

The phonograph remained a curiosity. In 1899, Louis Glass of San Francisco took advantage of this fact by installing a number of early cylinder machines in a local amusement parlor. Phonographs did not yet use horns; one had to listen to them through tubes like those on a doctor's stethoscope. But a number of tubes might be attached to *one* instrument, and people, it seemed, could be induced to part with a nickel to listen to about two or three minutes of comedy, song, a lecture or recital played back on a cylinder operated by a battery-powered motor.

By 1891, the Columbia Phonograph Company was to assume leadership in making and reproducing (by crude pantographic methods) these cylinders—the same Columbia, by the way, that fell upon hard luck in the 1920s and subsequently stimulated the formation of William Paley's Columbia Broadcasting System. It was sold by CBS, and eventually, in the 1930s, repurchased to form today's Columbia Records division of CBS. Other companies followed, particularly Eldridge Johnson's Victor Talking Machine Company, an early exponent of new disc recordings.

The sounds that found their way onto these early records constituted a mixed bag, to say the least. John Philip Sousa's marching band was a perennial favorite, and so were instrumental soloists (if their instruments were loud enough to record well) opera and popular singers, monologists from the vaudeville stage, actors and actresses and even politicians. The acoustical limits of the invention prevented much subtle experimentation with sound. Some of the cylinders and early discs do not even list the name of the performers on their labels. Just the words "Irish Stories" or "Sentimental Song" seemed to be enough for amusement park customers and those few Americans who owned home phonographs.

Inventor Emile Berliner's disc recordings—with the substitution of a horn for the ear piece—over a period of a decade domesticated the talking machine. Years before radio, phonographs found their way into parlors across the U.S.A., mostly as novelties, time-killers and purveyors of culture. Edison stuck to his cylinder recordings. But discs were easier to store, to play and—most important—eventually acoustically superior to cylinders. It was also easier to design a disc phonograph that looked like a respectable piece of living room furniture than one using a cylinder, another reason for the success of disc machines. Various companies competed and cooperated with each other in the development of disc phonographs—with Edison standing alone, making cylinder recordings long after he had ceased selling machines to play them, because he felt he owed his customers up-to-date software in exchange for their faith in his former hardware.

The Victor Company, in alliance with Columbia, produced the famous "Victrola" in 1906, along with its magnificent trade mark (adopted in 1901) of a dog nicknamed "Nipper" listening to "His Master's Voice" as it emerged from the horn of a Victor phonograph. By the first World War, the disc recording had unquestionably outpaced the cylinder, and the Victor Company (and Nipper) rode high in the saddle. It had faced and won out against European competition—particularly in the classical music field—by signing such outstanding stars as the Metropolitan Opera's Enrico Caruso to recording contracts. Its shellacked records were durable and reliable, but not especially cheap. Other companies naturally competed with less expensive products. Some, like Brunswick (eventually sold to Warner Brothers), survived. But many did not.

To put things in perspective, by 1923, radio's first burgeoning year as a mass medium and a high point of Hollywood's silent period, the recording industry was about half a century old. It was therefore natural that radio should fall back upon records as a source of programming, which it did almost immediately after the birth of broadcasting. In fact, during the first years of radio broadcasting in America, the record industry suffered near crippling blows. The Columbia Phonograph Company ended up in the shape that Paley found it when he bought it and named his radio network after it. Between 1923 and 1924, even the mighty Victor suffered a 20% setback in sales, a situation so grim that it was said that Victor employees were actually forbidden to keep radios in their homes. After a few more years, the Victory Talking Machine Corporation was purchased by the expanding Radio Corporation of America, symbolizing the way that radio sets were, by this time, being physically mated to phonographs. Victor has, of course, remained an RCA subsidiary to the present day.

Electrical Recording and Amplifier

Another critical change in the recording industry occurred about 1925, after five years of research by the Bell Labs and the British ''His Master's Voice'' company. Up until this time all recording and sound reproduction of records had been achieved by mechanical means: that is, sounds were both etched in grooves and reconstituted by means of mechanical vibration.

By 1925, a method had been worked out for electromagnetic recording. It consisted of a condenser microphone, a vacuum tube serving as an amplifier of sound (now changed into electrical impulses), and an electromagnetic cutting stylus. The playing unit operated in the opposite way: vibrations from a needle were converted to electrical current, strengthened by an amplifier, and converted back into sound waves in an improved speaker. Electrical recording, in fact, combined the mechanics of the record industry with the amplification procedures used in radio. This was, in its way, as dramatic an invention as, say, color photography. One can still tell after a moment's listening whether a recording was made electrically or acoustically, no matter what the nature of the sound is, so great is the difference between the two systems.

Within a year after its introduction to the market place, electrical recording companies made the most of their relationship to radio broadcasting technology. Phonograph manufacturers began producing instruments that could be attached to (then) enormously bulky radios; or one might purchase a combination radio-phonograph in which the amplification facilities of a radio were also used for phonograph records and employing a common speaker.

Both Columbia and Victor profited from the new full sound rer rdings. Cylinders were a dead issue. For a while, it looked as if the two companies would successfully compete with one another. When RCA bought Victor, however, Columbia's fortunes fell through the floor. The company was indeed in parlous condition when, a few years later, Mr. Paley bought it and then, quite soon, sold it.

The Recording Industry

Two major points must be made about phonograph recording in the 1920s. First, most of the most popular records bought and sold were of "hit" songs, popular jazz and show tunes. You would not recognize one in a hundred today. Dance bands with crooners recorded many of them. Some bands, like Guy Lombardo and singers like Rudy Vallee, achieved their greatest measure of fame as recording artists. The names of most of these artists, however,—Meyer Davis was one of the first—are rarely remembered today.

On the other side of the coin, however, there also existed enormous interest in classical music. From one quarter to one third of the recordings sold were classical pieces, performed by some of the finest artists of the day. (The ratio still stands; from a quarter to a third of the recordings sold today in the U.S.A. remain so-called "good" or "non-popular" performances.) Among the first prestigious recordings were the Victor Red Seal series of recordings, featuring, for instance, Leopold Stokowski and the Philadelphia Symphony Orchestra, or a concert by Mischa Elman, the virtuoso violinist. Other recording companies, in the U.S.A. and Europe, also began contracting for the services of the world's greatest musical artists—many of whom had objected to the acoustical limitations of old methods of recording—to cut discs recorded electrically that would now do justice to their talents. (In fact, in the 1930s, RCA even created an NBC Symphony orchestra for the world-renowned maestro, Arturo Toscanini, both in the interests of its radio networks and RCA records.)

Of course, radio broadcasters feared the growing popularity of the recording industry. There is little doubt that RCA was hedging its large investment in broadcasting equipment and facilities when it bought Victor. Little did the RCA executives reckon the absorbtion talents of the American public for mass culture. Phenomena like recordings (or paperback books) do not seem to inhibit the use of what one would imagine (at first glance) to be competing media, any more than radio kept people out of movie theatres or stopped them from buying newspapers, as it was at first feared they might. In fact, recordings broadcast on radio publicized them and the artists who made them, stimulating sales as well as the values of the songs, singers and orchestras as radio artists.

The same was true after the development of talking pictures. Recordings stimulated interest in movies, just as many songs sung and played in movies became hit records, and were, of course, also played frequently over the radio. To stretch a metaphor a bit, with the advent of the electric recording, three hands of popular culture seemed to be washing one another, all at the same time. "Show biz" stars sold records, and many jumped from films to radio to disc. Al Jolson and Fanny Brice are probably among the best remembered today, along with, a little later, Cliff Edwards, Ethel Waters, Ted Lewis, Maurice Chevalier, Helen Morgan, Sophie Tucker and Bebe Daniels. In addition to Victor, other imaginative companies, particularly Brunswick, snapped up the services of cowboy stars like Ken Maynard to record for them. The not-so-new record business had come upon an era of success—except for Columbia, which was beaten by Victor at every turn.

Second, at the heart of this entire phenomenon was the system of amplification used in *both* the recording and playback of sound. This system, either employing a single "pre-amp" tube or some more complex electronic device, traces its lineage directly back to Lee de Forest's audion. As remarkable as the new electric sound seemed in one's own living room, it had other uses that influenced any number of American institutions in addition to music appreciation. Naturally, the fact that *amplified* electronic vibrations of sound might be recorded on a moving disc was important. But equally as important was the fact that amplified sound from *any* source, including the human voice box, could now be transmitted—and made louder—by means of an amplifier and speaker, or system of speakers. Thus, the "public address system" was born with its ubiquitous microphone set ups that accomplishes far more than its name implies. Singers (and later actors) in the legitimate theatre were no longer required to project their voices to the last row of the balcony, as they once did; a microphone was hidden in the footlights. Orators, ministers—even teachers— began to take advantage of a system that allowed them, without effort, to fill an entire theatre with a thin voice or with the low moan of crooners like Russ Colombo and his best known imitator, Bing Crosby.

Sound in the Movies

The possibilities for producing realistic talking pictures had long interested inventors. And why not? The basic technology for making sound films had been available for a generation: pictures that moved and a method of recording and playing back sound. Some of Edison's (and others) earliest films had, indeed, been "talkies," or, at least, sound films. The trick was especially simple to achieve when one controlled manually the playback speed of a phonograph cylinder. One could thus "sync" sound to the film by eye and ear. The main problem with these early talkies was not so much that they worked erratically or could not last longer than a two-minute recording cylinder, but simply that the acoustical sound provided by the phonograph was too faint to be heard even in a small nickelodeon theatre.

With the invention of amplification, this problem was solved. In a remarkably short time, systems for producing loud sound films were invented and in use throughout the Western world. It all started crudely enough: by using available technology. Warner Brothers' famous 1927 film, *The Jazz Singer,* with Al Jolson, using the Vitaphone method of sound reproduction, accomplished just this. It was, for the most part, a silent film. But, whenever Jolson sang, an orchestra came out of the blue and Al's lips moved (roughly) in concert with his loud and resonant nasal voice. At the heart of the process was the amplifier. Jolson had recorded the songs to be played on large discs spun by motors but started by hand at certain "cue frames" in the film. The disc's sound was amplified to fill whatever theatre the movie played in. Jolson's one spoken line, that the audience "ain't heard nothin' yet" was quite prophetic. It was also, of course, also electrically amplified.

Silent films had, as a matter of fact, hardly been silent during their quarter century of life. They were accompanied by everything from live pianists to symphony orchestras with specially written scores, string quartets, organs and harmonicas, as well as sound effects. The sound, however, was invariably live, either ad libbed by a local pianist or organist or played from a score circulated by the distributor with the movie. Some of the first so-called "sound" films —for instance John Barrymore's 1926 vehicle *Don Juan*—simply provided on a recorded sound track the kind of music that ambitious theatre owners had been offering live for years.

The Sound Track

The sound revolution did not, obviously, occur all at once. Phonograph records might be all right for a relatively crude Jolson opus like *The Jazz Singer,* but something else was needed for dialogue and for more sophisticated sound films. Sound, quite obviously, could not originate convincingly from a source independent from the film itself, like a phonograph. Synchronization was too hazardous. It had to ride along with the pictures to synchronize properly with it, thus requiring the production of entirely new types of camaras and allied equipment to make sound movies, as well as film projectors that also might serve as sound sources.

Warner's at first stuck to the original Vitaphone method of using phonograph records, because, for the first few years of the sound era, the sound source mattered little. What *was* important was that amplifiers by the hundred, and many large speakers, were being installed in theatres around the nation. While Bell Labs had developed Vitaphone (not too difficult a task considering the technology they were working with), other inventors had other ideas. Lee de Forest had been working on a photo-electric system of sound on film (the system most frequently used in the years to come) by which sound vibrations were recorded as fluctuations (from black to gray to white) of light that were printed along the side of the visual information on movie film and reconstituted for amplification by a photo-electric cell. A similar system, called Fox-Case, developed by a German firm, Tri-Ergon, may or may not have been developed independently from de Forest's invention. William Fox and Theodore W. Case, a one-time associate of de Forest's, were responsible for the introduction, in 1927, of *Fox Movietone News,* short sound films, mostly documentary or actuality movies, with music and narration but little dialogue.

Between *The Jazz Singer* and the *Movietone News,* enough impetus was given both to film companies and manufacturers of projection equipment to perfect, within two years, viable systems of sound-on-film motion picture production and projection. Cameras made too much noise at first, and had to be housed in "blimps" (rigid sound-proof covers) while sound films were being shot. Microphones were hidden in pots of flowers as two performers played a love scene. Nor did the system work perfectly in theatres with acoustical problems, to say nothing of those with electrical ones.

There seems something of a dispute concerning the issue of exactly what movie was the first *all talking* film. Three reliable and scholarly film histories are now open in front of me. One identifies both Warners' *The Singing Fool* and *The Lights of New York* as *the* first talkie; another stakes a claim for the Paramount movie, *Interference;* the third writer equivocates by including *The Terror* and *In Old Arizona* as possible contenders. All except the last were made in 1928. *Arizona* was produced in 1929, but its claim to fame seems to lie in the fact that it was *both* a sound film *and* made out-of-doors and not on a sound stage. What this dubious distinction means, I am not sure.

Warners profited first and most from the sound revolution, less, probably because of Vitaphone (which shortly found its way from disc to film) than from the early faith it had shown in talking pictures and its readiness to gamble upon them. Once exposed to them, the public expected "all talking—all singing" films and not silent movies. A standardized technology, the optical film track, was to become the method that stored the sound on thousands of movies up the the present day. Optical sound is still employed for most films, although various applications of a magnetic tape strip on the edge of a reel of film have been devised within the past two decades or so, either to add sound to home movies or to utilize one or another method of stereophonic amplification for special movies.

The Effects of Sound

Everybody did not view the new sound movies with equal enthusiasm, however. That a sound track—and particularly synchronous dialogue—would inevitably place certain constraints upon the pictorial fluidity of the silent movie was obvious from the start. The constraints were naturally greatest in the days when the talkies were young. As dubbing methods and sophisticated ways of re-recording the sound of a scene developed—including the practice of recording the sound of musical numbers separately from photographing them—film makers became increasingly adept at harmoniously integrating pictures, dialogue and music. Psychologists like Rudolph Arnheim and writers like John Howard Lawson, however, have fairly charged, I think, that the cinema nearly reached the stature of a fine art form in its silent days by mastering pictorial design and pantomime, when suddenly sound threw the industry back into an aesthetic dark age. Old methods of visual communication employed in the silent films were now obsolete. Movie makers had to begin at the beginning again in devising ways to tell their stories by means, now, of pictures, words and music.

Some film makers, notably Charles Chaplin, resisted the sound revolution for many years by simply refusing to make talkies. Chaplin knew that his great strength lay in the art of pantomime. He did not attempt a film with an extensive use of dialogue until *The Great Dictator* in 1940, although music and sound effects crept onto the sound tracks of his work during the 'thirties. (In later years, Chaplin's judgment concerning his own talents proved to be correct. Pantomime sections of all of his post-1940 films are, to this viewer, far more effective than those containing dialogue.) Other comics of the silent era would often slip back into repeating old pantomime routines for talking films. A number of actors and directors and producers, raised in the silent tradition, seemed intent upon maintaining the movies as a pictorial rather than sound medium, including Walt Disney, whose extraordinary character, "Dopey," in *Snow White and the Seven Dwarfs,* one of his most lovable creations, remained mute throughout the entire cartoon feature.

The claim that the films lost their main and basic pictorial thrust with the advent of sound, is not, therefore, easy to dismiss. To the present day, one cannot follow the plot or progression of most sound films by watching the picture alone. One is usually totally baffled by it, because one does not know what the characters or narrator are *saying*. One *may,* on the other hand, usually follow the plot and identify the action and people in most movies merely by listening to the sound track without watching it. (The sound tracks of old films, incidentally, were played on British "wire service" sound broadcasts after World War II as an alternative to the BBC's limited broadcasting stations. Listening to the songs and dialogue of old Astaire-Rogers musicials was often more enjoyable than anything BBC radio was providing at the time.)

The Radio Act of 1927

One other critical event of the 1920s was also to have repercussions that have not ended to the present day. It concerns the role of the federal government in the U.S.A. in the development of radio broadcasting, and peaks with the passage of the Radio Act of 1927, which preceded in nature and intent another act passed seven years later under which all American broadcasting still legally operates.

That broadcasting was in certain ways a matter of *federal* concern seemed obvious almost from its start. Naval and military applications of radio were obviously functions of national defense, and civilian broadcasting itself, which traveled across state lines, appeared also to be federal issue, at least in so far as the allocation and use of radio frequencies were concerned. The Radio Act of 1912 had plunked control of broadcasting into the lap of the Secretary of Commerce, the job of whom it was to keep an eye on all aspects of interstate trade. The Department of Commerce's exact responsibilities were never spelled out very clearly, however. By 1923, as the result of a court decision (*Secretary of Commerce* v. *Intercity Radio Co.*) it seemed that the Department's responsibility was merely to provide radio wave lengths to all applicants, whether the frequencies existed or not, often by sharing time with another station. By 1926, it was obvious that Commerce could not control how any licensee used his license or do much to protect the rights of old licensees when contested by new ones.

The result was electronic and managerial chaos. Different broadcasters often tried to use the same frequency at the same time. The one with the strongest transmitter won out. Licenses to broadcast were awarded to people who used them for political, religious and self-serving purposes to the degree that, from about 1923 onwards, *both* broadcasters and the Secretary of Commerce (Herbert Hoover at the time) tried to exert what influence they had to get Congress to straighten out the mess. The broadcasters' behavior was quite the opposite, at the time, of that of the movie makers, who were ready to do anything to keep Uncle Sam *out* of Hollywood. Radio broadcasters, however, used every means possible to induce the government to control and supervise the allocation and use of radio frequencies, so that the public would at least be able to locate its favorite programs on their radio dials, or be assured that it would not be drowned out by another station in the middle of a program.

Long overdue, the Radio Act of 1927 was passed on February 23rd of that year and represents, most historians agree, the collective best thinking and the interests of the nation's broadcasters rather than any deep study of a new national resource by the Congress. It was, however, of a piece with the temper of the times—a period that had seen, and was to see, a proliferation of government agencies identified by initials (national "alphabet soup," agencies they were later called) that controlled or competed with this or that aspect of national commerce. The Federal Radio Commission (and later the FCC) was one of many similar agencies in Washington that preceded and followed it. They were all, one way or another, charged with regulating interstate trade in the supposed interests of the people, including, often, the business community. Such is the nature of the ICC, FTC, FRS, ITC, FPC and a host of other executive and other agencies, past and present, like the TVA, AAA, CAB, SEC and NLRB which followed them. In every instance, each agency is (or was) concerned with some national service or resource—railroads, waterways, aviation, power sources, farm products, stocks and bonds—to the degree that federal controls were deemed necessary for this business to operate in an orderly and fair manner, with minimal restraints upon free enterprise. Where restraints occurred, they were, in theory, ceded by the people in their own interests to the federal government.

In the case of the FRC, the business was radio broadcasting, which gained national prominence during an era of increasing government control of private enterprise in what was generally understood to be the best interests of the people at large. Neither the printed press nor the cinema had grown up in such a climate. It is interesting to muse upon their fates had they been babies of the "alphabet soup" period of American history.

The Radio Act of 1927 is not fundamentally different from the Communications Act, passed in 1934, under which broadcasting in America still functions. In the case of the former, a five-man commission (the FRC), at first a temporary and finally a permanent organization, was appointed by the President for a certain period of time, indeterminate at first but specified later, supposedly representing differing interests. It was charged, in effect, with controlling the use of the American air waves.

Now, "control" is a strange word of many meanings. From the start, the FRC was more concerned about *what interests* would be represented on what frequencies (police, Navy, commercial broadcasters, etc.) and *who* had access to these frequencies than in the matter of *what was broadcast,* a situation that still obtains under the Federal Communications Commission today. Too much concern with the content of (then) radio broadcasts might have caused the powers of the FRC to collide with the free press and free speech guarantees of the First Amendment to the Constitution. This issue has always been the single most ticklish and sensitive one in regard to the government's role in American broadcasting, no less true today in the age of television than back in 1927.

In any event, both the technology of, and service rendered by, broadcasting were recognized by the Act as essentially *different* from either the press or films or any other instruments of communication invented at the time—like phonograph records or billboards. Broadcasting was understood to be a public service using channels (frequencies) that belonged to the people of the country and not to the broadcasters themselves. The right of the people of the U.S.A. to receive a type of broadcasting service commensurate with their best interests was therefore superior to any individual broadcaster's right to serve his personal purposes. Access to broadcasting channels had therefore to be selective, and choices had to be made between competing applicants according to the public's need, an issue to be determined by the FRC in the process of awarding licenses to use a public resource.

The Commission, however, did not have (in the name of the people) the right to inhibit freedom of speech as guaranteed by the Constitution, nor, for that matter, any extraordinary powers to limit the use of the air waves by advertisers to sell their wares and to pay broadcasters a fee for this privilege. In matters where these various rights seem to conflict, the Commission was empowered to use its descretion always in the "public interest, convenience and necessity." (Exactly what this latter phrase meant or means has never been spelled out precisely. Or, possibly, it has been spelled out *too* often and *too* differently by different commissioners, broadcasters, jurists and professors to mean anything specific any more, except what some Humpty-Dumpty wants it to mean.)

The FRC was not, however, the final court of appeal for broadcasters. Its decisions on any matters were open to challenge and review by the courts. In all, therefore, the FRC, like many other government agencies, had three main functions *up to a point.* One was legislative: to *make* rules regarding license awards, renewal, engineering matters, etc. Another was disciplinary or punitive: to *enforce* these rules and punish (usually by threatening to withhold licenses) those who did not obey them. The third was judicial: to *select* from between competing interests of any kinds (including those of the American people) the way in which it might best interpret its charge to regulate broadcasting services for the public good as the Commission interpreted it.

Unlike most other government agencies, the FRC and FCC have dealt (and deal) with a peculiarly mercurial and ephemeral commodity, radio—and later television—broadcasting using criteria based upon a vague sentence concerning "the public interest convenience and necessity," rather than precise standards that might be seen, felt, smelled, measured or tested. Both the Commission's many successes and failures may be traced to this peculiar and unhappy state of affairs.

The Civil Aeronautics Board, for instance, has never had too much trouble in determining what sensible and safe utilization of aircraft technology, airports, etc. is, although it does often run into some sticky problems, like jet noise over residential areas. Nor does it need much philosophical or legal talent to determine the precise nature of public safety or comfort as it relates to aviation; or what the public interest is when it awards different routes to different airlines and regulates ticket prices. Disputes can be judged, usually, on the weight of concrete evidence, and problems only arise when one side's evidence seems to be as good as another's: anti-noise pollution groups versus proponents of the SST, for instance.

In regard to broadcasting services, almost *nothing* is easily determined according to hard evidence, including one man's right versus another man's right to broadcast to a given community; or whether one radio or television station is serving the public interest better than another, even if one broadcasts commercial advertising all day long and the other does nothing but play classical music or devote itself entirely to news broadcasting. Claims may be made for the virtues of all parties, as long as people listen and/ or watch their programs. The water gets murkier still when one is reminded that both broadcasters are protected by the United States Constitution's guarantees of freedom of speech, and that the First Amendment does not admit that one type of speech is better than another.

The Federal Radio Commission was, however, something of a social and legal triumph in its time, and it accomplished more or less what it set out to do. The electronic tangle of competing broadcasters on the American airwaves was, in time, unscrambled. As the years passed, the various Commissioners and their legal staffs discovered what the major problems in regulating American broadcasting service were likely to be and devised methods of, at least, containing them reasonably well. If they learned nothing else, they discovered the difficulties in awarding broadcasting licenses and of setting up any highly specific standards for program service.

A station like WEVD in New York (a labor-oriented radio outlet in the 'twenties) might bear down heavily upon social, economic and governmental matters. Another might devote most of its time to farm news or another to symphonic music or jazz, and all might well be serving "the public interest, convenience and necessity," depending on the values of the people doing the judging. Nor could the Commission consider commercial advertisements of and by themselves necessarily damaging to the public interest, because they served as a form of consumer enlightment and apparently had power to stimulate the American economy.

Nothing like the FRC had been attempted before in American history, and, if the truth be told, after the birth of the FCC, nothing like it was tried again, at least to date. In form and function, it is one of the *least* imitated broadcasting regulatory agencies by other countries around the world. It also deserves the distinction of having been disliked almost as much by broadcasters as by the severest critics of broadcasters during its history. But all of this is another story that must await later discussion when the time is ripe.

10

Depression
and Destiny

THE POST-WORLD WAR I YEARS were exciting in many ways. The 1920s have provided grist for the mill of a nostalgia boom during the past few years. Nostalgia is always pleasant, especially if you do not remember clearly what you are getting weepy about.

Looking backwards, the period symbolizes many enviable social and historical qualities. America was proving her mettle as a world power. Her genius at using and exporting the technology she had played with the generation before provided the country with first place around the world in the use and spread of mass production, mass consumption, mass distribution and mass communications. There seemed to be nowhere to go but up. All problems of society were either being solved or would soon be solved. Witness: the war to end all wars that ended in 1918 and the decade of euphoria that followed it.

The Best and the Worst

The seamy side of the roaring 'twenties is all too easy to overlook and/or minimize. It contained moral and social spores of decay that would be spread wide, soon and fast.

Prohibition had become a Constitutional fact of life. As of January 16, 1920, alcoholic beverages were banished from production and sale by the 18th Amendment to the Constitution in the United States of America. As a result, and within a short time, the U.S.A. became a nation of law breakers, as housewives pressed grapes in their cellars, something called ''bathtub gin'' gave amateur pharmacists an opportunity to establish small businesses at home, many, many unlikely people took up the study of distillation, and big-time criminals turned the smuggling of booze into the country into a lucrative industry.

Corruptions wrought by prohibition were nearly ubiquitous. Old-timers still repeat the incredible story (not true everywhere, of course) that, when you drove your Model T Ford into a strange town and were looking for the nearest "speakeasy," the best person from whom to ask directions was the local cop. He would, as often as not, gladly accept a dollar for his good advice.

A number of scandals, including the Teapot Dome oil reserve swindle that involved President Warren Harding's Cabinet—and probably Harding himself—are symbolic of the era. Teapot Dome was more devastating and certainly more extensive an exercise in corruption at high levels of government than the Watergate affair that was to follow it by half a century. Millions of people also lost money in countless real estate swindles. Some of the most notorious and publicized murders in history (including the famous Leopold-Loeb case) filled the newspapers with lurid details, first person eye-witness stories and much solid fiction. A rash of communist witch-hunts bespoke, on one side, a national paranoia and suspicion of everything un-American. On another, there grew a creeping trend towards isolationism and the eternal tendency of Americans— also visible today—to contemplate their navels whenever storm clouds around the world seem too uncomfortable.

And why not? Remember that the 'twenties were also, for the most part, a period of prosperity—at least it was for those who were prosperous, an observation not as redundant as it sounds. Millions of poor people, most of them immigrants, blacks or poor farmers, lived in penury while, mostly in the cities, the growing middle class was discovering new ways to "get rich quick." The trick was to borrow money, speculate in an ever-rising stock and/or bond market, pull in your profits, pay your debts and start out all over again on Wall Street in search of greater wealth.

Uncontrolled by government regulations and propelled by greed, the financial community became the manager of a near nation-wide gambling casino, running a game any number could play. The problem was, for the most part, that this enormous investment in burgeoning American business consisted of capital that was borrowed rather than owned. Profits realized on the stock market and elsewhere were not—and could not be—backed by cash or the real assets of the businesses, banks, mines and other corporations whose shares and bonds zoomed upwards. This last unhealthy state of affairs, touching in some way nearly every aspect of American life, could not last.

The Depression

The show business newspaper, *Variety*'s famous headline, *"Wall Street Lays an Egg,"* of October 30, 1929 tells part of the story, but only part. True enough, the great speculation game of the decade came to an end with a shattering suddenness. But the depressed economy that eventually resulted from it crept into American life bit by bit. Unemployment increased, businesses went bankrupt, banks failed, and many middle class people who had never before known real poverty began to feel its pain.

By 1932, Franklin D. Roosevelt, a new President representing, he said, a "New Deal" of the American deck of cards, was forced to take drastic monetary and regulatory steps to fight the depression. Roosevelt used the powers of the federal government more broadly and extensively than ever before in history to regulate industry and the circulation of money, as well as to create jobs and to feed the needy, whether they were working or not. America had lived through depressions before. But none of them demanded the kind of drastic action that was taken by the federal government in the 1930s in order to bring the United States back to earth from the roaring-soaring 1920s.

A depression or recession, as we are observing today, does not propel the people of any nation into deep concern for the troubles of other countries. The depression of the 'thirties simply continued and exacerbated America's preoccupation with herself to the degree that she became all but oblivious to the harsh fact that America's depression had spread world-wide. It was, for many reasons, literally tearing Europe apart more severely than at home, hurling countries overseas into drastic governmental changes, unfortunately, neither as sane or conservative as those of the "New Deal." Nor were Americans particularly impressed by the rapid industrialization of Japan, nor Nippon's reach, in the early 'thirties into Manchuria, in order to develop the Pacific empire she believed she required to survive. Things were too bad at home! Dictators in foreign countries and the troubles of small nations swallowed by empire seekers seemed remote and unimportant—for a time.

The Press in a Cold Economy

From the perspective of our history, the 1930s wrought one of their greatest changes upon the American press of all the instruments of mass communication we have studied thus far. One reason was, naturally, economic. The lucrative golden goose of advertising that had sustained newspapers and magazines so magnificently for the first third of the century suffered blows similar to those felt by the rest of American big business. Another reason was the fact that, for the first time in American history, the print media—magazines, books *and* newspapers—were beginning to feel the hot breath of competition from other media that performed the same sorts of services that they provided either more conveniently, pleasurably, or most important, more *cheaply*. And within the world of the print medium itself, changes wrought both by a depressed economy and mass technology were also formidable.

Roughly speaking, America's newspapers entered the 'thirties in prosperous, healthy shape. Circulation of the country's more than 2,000 daily newspapers reached about 40 million in 1930. Advertising revenues were pushing $900 million a year. In addition, well over 10,000 weekly newspapers were thriving. Ten years later in 1940, circulation remained roughly the same, but subtle changes had occurred to the American press, changes hidden in mazes of confusing statistics and social factors that were, and are, difficult to observe with the naked eye.

Only in 1933 did newspaper circulation dip as much as 12 per cent. For most of the 'thirties, demand for newspapers—both dailies and weeklies—remained relatively constant, even considering that the country's population had grown about 12 per cent by the end of the period. The main reason of course, was that, by the 1930s, newspapers were regarded as *necessities* of life, *particularly* in a depressed economy in which attention increasingly centered on what politicians, industrialists, bankers and others were up to.

By the end of the decade, this need was apparently not so acute. In large measure, radio broadcasters were, by then, spreading "hard news" to the population, and newsreels were developing their own unique journalistic features. But by this time, the grinding force of the depression was halted, and the tabloid newspapers and their imitators had developed their gossip columns, comics and other diversions so expertly that they now seemed to have gained a permanent place in national life.

Profits were another story. They simply reflected the general economic state of the nation, up one day, down the next—but mostly down. By 1933 or 1934, advertising revenues were down to about half of 1929 high. By 1939, a number of small dailies and weeklies had disappeared entirely. The Hearst, Scripps-Howard and other chains were not severely damaged, although some newspaper magnates who had spread their interests into the radio and the film business gave up these diversions. Most important, newspapers came into the depression era as the main—if not only—mass medium that reached the great bulk of the American people. By the time the decade was over, this was no longer true. Radio and news magazines—including picture periodicals—were now exerting enormous forces upon public opinion, not only because they were able to cover much "hard news" as well as (or better than) newspapers, but because they were also competent to provide editorial comment, analysis and discussion of important issues and special features (like Hollywood gossip) on which the papers had previously held a monopoly.

True enough, few magazines and no radio stations were able to substitute their fare for the sensationalism of the Patterson-style tabloids, or Hearst-style breathless reportage of trivia, or to compete head-on with the full coverage of urbane papers like the *New York Herald-Tribune*. But, by 1940, the American newspaper was simply *one* conduit of news and information for the people and, by then, it was quite possible for an American to have a firm grasp of national and world affairs and never even read a newspaper. Radio, magazines and, to some degree, motion picture newsreels could now do the job.

The Press-Radio War

Hindsight is usually 20-20, and, looking back at the so-called "press-radio" war of the 1930s, much ado may seem to have been made over nothing. There are good reasons, however, as the harsh facts of the depression began to hit home to newspaper publishers, why journalists of all types began to feel threatened by the relatively new medium of radio in an economy of scarcity. The 1920's had been different. Radio and newspapers seemed able to co-exist side by side. But now there was reason for alarm: competition for national attention and, as a result, for advertising dollars.

A copy of a newspaper cost money—not much—but radio service was ostensibly free. That radio was also competing with the printed press for advertising revenue was also a good reason to be fearful. Newspapers' major profits came, of course, from advertisers, who might, at any time, desert them for the increasingly large audiences broadcasters could deliver.

CBS had grown rapidly into a lucrative and highly popular national network. In the face of this competition (and governmental suspicions that they were operating a monopoly) RCA, in 1932, severed its connections with Westinghouse and General Electric, permitting the latter two to compete with them in the production of electronic equipment. This was a dubious victory for Westinghouse and G.E. which, along with AT&T, held considerable fiscal interest in RCA that dated from Owen Young's entry into broadcasting in the early 'twenties and included a number of patents that the three electronic firms (and the telephone company) shared with one another. In fact, in the early 'thirties RCA's monopolistic thrust into broadcasting even included a plan (never implemented) by its then president, David Sarnoff, to take over *entirely* all radio set manufacturing facilities from G.E. and Westinghouse in the interests of what Sarnoff called "unification," a privilege to be paid for with RCA stock.

The United States government had other ideas, however. By 1932, RCA was an independent entity, competing with both G.E. and Westinghouse. To infuse its broadcasting arm, NBC, with vitality, Sarnoff announced that, in cooperation with the Rockefeller interests, RCA would begin construction of a skyscraper called "Radio City" in New York City, part of the new Rockefeller Center complex designed to be a permanent home for NBC's two growing networks, the "Red" and the "Blue." The spectre of radio as a competitor for advertising with the press therefore loomed ever larger. In New York, the *Times* tower on Times Square was shortly to be dwarfed by RCA's home on Sixth Avenue, a structure replete with a multitude of radio studios, production theatres and lavish executive offices. In short, there were few print journalists in the United States who did not feel threatened by competition from local broadcasting in part, but mainly by the two major networks, NBC and CBS.

From its earliest days, of course, radio had been to some degree in the news business. Until the formation of the FRC (and finally, in 1934, the FCC), however, one could easily write off broadcasting fundamentally as an amusement medium and little more. As the concept of radio as a "public service" developed across the nation, however, so did the sophistication of broadcasters as purveyors of hard news. In addition to offering their services free, they exploited advantages over print journalists by virtue of the speed of their operations and their potential ability to broadcast directly from places where the news was actually being made.

Various broadcasters began to gain reputations as newsmen, some with and some without experience in print journalism. H. V. Kaltenborn had been reading his version of the days events over the radio since the 'twenties. Boake Carter, an eccentric British-born commentator, Edwin C. Hill and Lowell Thomas also began to develop wide followings. The weekday 15-minute newscasts of the latter, prepared primarily from newspaper clips and telephone conversations by young Abe Schechter (who later became chief of NBC News) turned Thomas into a national celebrity. All day long, throughout the nation, both local and network radio programming were also punctuated with short news reports gleaned from press association reports and other sources.

Finally, in 1931, on CBS, *Time* magazine sponsored their first *March of Time* broadcast, a dramatic recreation of the week's news in which actors played the parts of famous statesmen, criminals, politicians and celebrities, complete with sound effects, studio orchestra and a ''voice of doom'' narrator (first Ted Husing, then Harry Von Zell and finally the *March's* permanent anonymous spokesman, Westbrook Van Voorhis) who reminded America's radio listeners that, ''Time Marches On!''

What might print journalists do about this new competitor that would, for all they knew, completely change time-honored patterns of journalistic coverage, not only in the U.S.A. but around the world? In the long run, I suspect that most intelligent editors and publishers knew that little has ever changed public habits (or would in the future) because of technology alone. Newspaper owners, however, could, and did, purchase their own radio stations, first for extra profit and second as insurance against the possible and looming obsolescence of the print medium. In the U.S.A., newspaper interests owned roughly 90 radio stations in 1930. By 1940, despite the depression, that number had risen to about 250. Investments were clearly being hedged.

Newspaper publishers also harassed broadcasters in many petty ways, none of which accomplished much in the end. But they did frighten many radio people, as we shall see. Newspapers across the nation frequently refused to print radio station logs even as advertisements: that is, they banned from their pages information concerning what programs were to be broadcast at what times. When such lists were, in fact, printed in the press, they were truncated and/or buried at the end of the paper with the want ads and fire station false alarms.

(This tradition still exists. Even the most prestigious American newspapers give broadcasting—radio *and* television—scant notice considering their popularity in and influence on our cultural life. Radio and television schedules are buried on the last pages with weather reports, shipping news, etc., and most papers devote no more than a column a day—if that much—to any kind of news about broadcasting. One would hardly imagine, reading a daily newspaper in the U.S.A. today, that next to sleeping and working, Americans watch television and listen to radio more than they indulge in any other activity of any sort!)

In other words, the press *could* ignore radio. It tried to.

Starting in the 'twenties, efforts were also made to discourage use by broadcasters of news from press associations, one of the main conduits that carried current events to most American newspapers. In the early 'thirties, Schechter at his NBC telephone, and Paul White, who was starting to organize a news service for CBS, tried to fight this exclusion by seeking alternate sources of news. White even attempted to set up his own echelon of part-time reporters. But soon newspapers began refusing to accept advertisements from sponsors who bought time on CBS news broadcasts and started spreading unflattering publicity about these companies.

The first round of the press-radio war was officially won by the press in 1933. At a meeting in New York's Biltmore Hotel, the networks and their professional organization, the National Association of Broadcasters, met with officials of the Associated, United and International press services to, in effect, surrender. NBC and CBS agreed to go out of the formal news gathering business. Schechter was permitted to keep his telephone at NBC, but CBS's wings were clipped. A service known as the Press-Radio Bureau was then organized to provide the networks with the grand total of about ten minutes worth of wire service news per day.

This solution was obviously unfair and unworkable. All in all, only about 30 per cent of the nation's radio stations even bothered to subscribe to the Press-Radio Bureau. Before long, attempts were made to organize new press services for radio stations alone. One of them, Transradio, serving WOR, New Jersey, a station owned by Macy's department store, was strong enough to survive for a number of years, serving mainly the new and large Mutual Broadcasting System. After a half dozen years of life, Transradio's wires reached some 175 radio stations *as well as* 50 newspapers. By 1935, also, the United Press began violating the "Biltmore agreement." Shortly afterward, the International News Service followed, making their services available to broadcasters as well as newspapers. It was not until 1939, however, that the Associated Press began to provide news for commercial broadcasters, anticipating, possibly, government action begun three years later against the AP's generally exclusionary tactics, rules directed not only against broadcasters but against newspapers that did not qualify, according to the AP, for membership in their "club." At least, the AP recognized broadcasting as a legitimate news medium by the end of the 'thirties. It was quite a step in the annals of journalism.

(In 1945, the Supreme Court itself found that the AP's club-like system of excluding new newspapers from membership unless their competitors agreed—in effect, a method of blackballing new subscribers—to be in violation of U.S. anti-trust laws. The AP was subsequently forced to grant membership to all qualified applicants.)

Looking back, it is impossible, I think, to conclude that either the press or broadcasters won the press-radio war, because the objectives of both sides were so different, one from the other. For a short time, newspaper publishers may well have feared for their lives as the result of radio's *potential* ability to "spread the news" better than print. But the fear did not run too deeply or last too long. It was clear by the middle 'thirties that radio news might eventually influence slightly some time-honored press traditions, like the *Extra* edition that covered briefly important breaking news, or the mad rush of competing papers to print "scoops" and "exclusives." But it was also clear that radio's influence on journalism would not diminish the need most Americans felt for the many and special attractions found in daily newspapers. In fact, it was even possible that radio's superficial coverage of journalistic matters might well whet appetites of newspaper readers for the kind of complete coverage of events that print provided better than sound.

Publishers also eventually discovered that broadcasters harbored no devious intentions of invading journalistic domains more than superficially. Although millions of Americans listened to radio news daily, many sponsors were hesitant to underwrite much of it. They seemed, quite correctly from their viewpoints, to feel that advertising was most profitably placed in and around entertainment shows, comedy programs, sporting events, popular music programs and daytime domestic melodramas (or "soap operas") rather than news programs. When this matter became a fact of broadcasting life, journalists breathed more easily. They even began complaining, when they started considering radio seriously, that few sponsors were interested in serious programming like operas, good drama and classical music and news documentaries, thereby forcing broadcasting outlets to concentrate on trivia. Many newspapers and magazines have hammered upon this theme, off and on, for years.

As the decade moved on and the depression continued, it also became clear that radio broadcasting probably would not make too serious a dent in those advertising revenues upon which both newspapers and magazines lived. Exactly *why* newspaper advertising income remained as stable as it did throughout the 'thirties, in the face of both depression *and* their competition, is difficult to explain convincingly. Suffice it to say that certain kinds of advertisements for local department store sales, amusements and other commodities produced most effective results when placed in print rather than on radio outlets. Others, like laundry soap, cooking oil, cigarettes and beauty products responded well to radio announcements, short dramatizations and finally, singing commercials.

Possibly, also, the depression offered a chance to justify at last the faith that American industry had held for many years in the skills of advertising men, and that, if the nation was to recover economically, private business needed to work its psychological voodoo by advertising via every conduit available. In other words, many businessmen saw widening opportunities for advertising their goods and services as instruments for *ending* the depression. I find it less difficult to fault their logic than the results that many of them achieved by the end of the decade.

In short, the press-radio war was fought neither long nor hard, and both media discovered methods of co-existence. It would be another 20 years before the high costs of broadcast *television* advertising would begin to displace print advertising to the degree that it would severely hurt the press. At that time, it was to be magazines, for the most part, that would be injured by broadcasting rather than newspapers. The latter were, by this time, unfortunately suffering severely their own competitive problems, one with the other, because of a shortage of enough advertising revenue to support one—or at most two—daily newspapers in many communities.

The moral had not yet become clear in the 'thirties, although many anticipated it: Despite their apparent abundance, advertising revenues would not, and could not, support all American mass media (except movies) forever regardless of how they grew; the well was deep—but not endless. Although it might never run completely dry, there were limits to how much water it provided at any time.

Broadcast News Services

I suppose that the main fallout from the press-radio war was the fact that it forced broadcasters interested in news coverage to realize how vulnerable they were to the whims of the people who operated newspaper press services. The war gave them psychological impetus to become, as far as possible, independent of these services. Broadcasters also grew interested in the development of radio as a *different* kind of news medium: a magic carpet that could take the listener to the places where news was breaking to hear voices and sounds that they could only read about in newspapers.

First steps in this direction had been taken by CBS. It is a testament to the foresight of William Paley that, once the excitement of the Biltmore fiasco had died down, he once again encouraged Paul White to pick up the development of CBS news where it had been halted. With one eye on an impending war in Europe, White began employing radio "stringers" as correspondents around the world. In 1937, Paley and White sent Edward R. Murrow to Europe, ostensibly to arrange and schedule educational broadcasts for CBS. Murrow's contacts in England and on the continent eventually grew into a CBS news service with White in control. CBS would, during World War II, amply justify Paley's faith in radio as an important news medium, entirely distinctive but also complementary to that of the printed press.

In this respect, NBC lagged behind CBS. Sarnoff's main interests now centered mostly on complex corporate matters involving RCA. NBC organized its less sophisticated news operation, in part because men like Abe Schechter felt that RCA should keep up with CBS, despite an apparent lack of support at top levels. Schechter in the U.S.A., and later Max Jordan in Europe, managed to hire a talented crew of newsmen and commentators, less clever than those Murrow unearthed for CBS, but one that included a willing group of special events commentators like George Hicks and others who learned fast when challenged by the pressure of events.

At the large and loosely knit Mutual Network, Johnny Johnstone also began a nearly impossible task. Starting with a large but variegated roster of home-bound commentators, he developed MBS News to the point where it sometimes equalled or manfully competed with CBS in getting the big story first and most accurately, despite the fact that Mutual possessed neither the leadership of a Paley nor the resources of an NBC.

Broadcasting and Law

The Communications Act of 1934, under which broadcasting by radio and television in the U.S.A. still operates, also diminished whatever fears newspaper men and women might have had that radio would one day replace print journalism. Following closely the lead of the 1927 Radio Act, the new one reaffirmed the idea that print and radio communications were fundamentally *different* one from the other, not only in technical matters but in legal respects as well. Although the Act stated that nothing it contained should contravene the United States Constitution, its very existence denied broadcasters the same broadside protection that the First Amendment had given America's printing presses since 1791. In effect, the law interposed a federal agency, the FCC, between the broadcasters and the public. This body was supposed, of course, to operate in the interests of the public. In passing the Act, Congress affirmed that radio waves constituted a limited natural national resource. While a man might be free to begin publishing a newspaper as his whim and pocketbook dictated, nobody was able to gain such free access to the nation's airwaves (properties of the people) without the permission of the federal government. The number of possible stations in any community was (and still is) also limited by the electronic spectrum.

Many of the exact provisions of the new law have been changed numerous times during the past 40 years, but its spirit has remained the same. A Commission of seven men, appointed by the President and representing both political parties, serve for seven years each and, in effect, are responsible for licensing and assuring the proper conduct of broadcasters in the United States. While licensees might profit financially from their investments in studio, transmission equipment and programming by means of sponsored announcements, they are also held to periodic review of their licenses.

This three-yearly evaluation was designed to determine in large measure, the quality of each station's performance and to ensure that it maintained certain technical standards. The latter were from the first quite precisely defined, but the former were far more arbitrary—and remain so to this day.

The FCC had no statutory powers of censorship, but it was originally designed to exercise control, in a general way, over the content of radio service in the U.S.A. Should a station choose not to function "in the public interest, convenience and necessity," in the Act's words, the FCC might, first, warn it of its infractions and, second, suspend or refuse to renew its license to operate. This has occurred infrequently in the history of the Commission, both for radio and television stations. When it does, however, broadcasters may take recourse, first, to hearing procedures of the Commission itself and, finally, to the Federal Court system.

The Federal Communications Commission

Like the FRC, the FCC became an all-purpose agency which seemed to exercise either too much or too little control upon broadcasting in America, depending upon how you looked at it. It issued licenses, made decisions in the interests of the public, enforced them, and judged the fairness and equity of the application of (largely) its own rules. Thus, in many ways, it was, and is, a minor legislative body, an enforcement agency, a law court *and* hearing body.

Whatever it is or has done—and it attempted many different things at different times—nothing like the Federal Communications Commission has operated either for newspaper, magazine and book publishing interests in the U.S.A. or for the nation's film makers, at least with the force of law behind it. Thus, because of the FCC's ever-present eye (no matter how cloudy at times), print journalists and broadcasters have been forced, under the law of the land, to operate in distinctly different ways.

Newspapermen and other print media writers are free agents, protected from government interference in their operations by the United States Constitution. They are therefore vulnerable to the same laws that govern other citizens, although the matter of exactly what special "privileges" they might have under the First Amendment as journalists is a matter that has not been, to date, settled entirely by the courts. Broadcasters, on the other hand, remain relatively protected to profit economically from the licensed business of broadcasting. They are understood, however, also to be public servants regarding what they can and cannot (or should and should not) broadcast, simply because broadcasting is regarded by Congress, in the last analysis, as a public service requiring governmental licensing and supervision.

Networks could *not* naturally be licensed, and hence controlled, as stations were and are. The FCC, however, found that it was able legally to limit the number of stations of any type a network could own outright, but it could *not* limit the number of its affiliates. The agency was also able to control the amounts and type of programming that any affiliate might take from a network on certain days and at certain times. From the start, naturally, NBC, CBS and Mutual displayed extreme sensitivities to the workings of the FCC. All three owned profitable stations of their own in the nation's largest cities, and any controls the FCC exercised upon their affiliates affected them indirectly.

In the light of the press' sensitivities to the growing radio industry, and the government's obvious seriousness about radio broadcasting as a public resource, I am afraid I may lead my younger readers (younger than I am, that is) to believe that American radio during the 1930s was something that it was not. If anything seems odd today in the behavior during this period of either the press or the government, it was misplaced faith and/or fear during the 'thirties that radio in America would one day develop into a mature artistic or cultural enterprise, of equal distinction with the press and other older institutions like the theatre, both live and on film. Neither the faith nor fear were justified by the course of future events

Radio During the Depression

Much rot has lately been written about the "*great* days of American broadcasting," mostly, I think, by people who were fortunate enough not to have lived through it—or by amnesiacs. Certainly, a handful of comedians like Ed Wynn, Jack Benny and Joe Penner were passing funny. A *very* few, like Fred Allen were both intelligent *and* passing funny. One out of ten (at most) dress-up radio dramas on *The Lux Radio Theatre, The CBS Workshop,* or for that matter on *The Shadow, The First Nighter* or *Gangbusters,* was either interesting or exciting to some degree. Run-of-the-mill evening programs like *We, The People, Your Hit Parade, Mr. District Attorney, Hobby Lobby* or *Truth or Consequences* were about as good as their counterparts on television today, which does not say much for them.

True, Archibald MacLeish wrote *one* stunning drama for radio called *The Fall of the City;* Rudy Vallee brought some interesting talent to the air waves on his weekly variety hour; Norman Corwin and Arch Oboler came up occasionally with an original and interesting melodrama in sound; and Paul Rhymer's *Vic and Sade* was a rough diamond shining five days a week in the soap opera sewage dump, comparable, if not better than, the more popular comedy program, *Amos 'n' Andy.* But these were all exceptions—vast and infrequent exceptions—rather than rules.

In a preceding chapter I called most American radio broadcasting of this period *schlock.* So it was, and it compares neatly with most—but certainly not all—of America's commercial television broadcasting today—with two important exceptions. Radio's junk quantum was *not* balanced even lightly by a public broadcasting network; nor could it possibly serve as a conduit for disseminating some of the best (and worst) old movies ever made, as video does today.

The main thrust of radio broadcasting, except for one or two municipal stations and a few run by universities, was commercial. If possible, radio seemed even more inundated with advertising than television, because most big-time commercial radio shows were prepared *entirely* by advertising agencies. Stations and networks merely rented their facilities for transmission, and, except for so-called "sustaining" or non-sponsored programs—and most news programs—advertisers called the artistic turn for nearly all broadcasts. The results were pretty much what one would expect. Many critics at the time indicted nearly all radio broadcasting in the U.S.A. for being one long commercial, interrupted every now and then by music, tears or laughter.

Nostalgia, as I say, leads to strange distortions. Much contemporary interest in so much fifth-rate radio is one. We are told, for instance, in many recent books on "media" how Orson Welles frightened the entire nation in October of 1938 with his naturalistic *War of the Worlds* radio drama. Here an interesting legend. But it is largely untrue, generally accepted by many so-called "authorities," *in spite of the fact* that social scientist Hadley Cantril wrote a book on the program and its effects a quarter of a century ago, and the volume has recently been reissued. (See Bibliography.)

Driving, as I was that fall Sunday evening in 1938 with my family along the Henry Hudson Parkway across from New Jersey—the scene of Welles' "invasion"—and listening to the program on an automobile radio, nobody I was with was aware that *anybody* had taken Welles seriously until we read the next morning's newspapers, although we had a perfect view of the Jersey coast and its roadways. Cantril's study makes quite clear that it was *only* the credulous and disturbed who believed even for an *instant* that the Martians were attacking the earth. And only a tiny minority of them—mostly poor souls ready to flip out at the least provocation—who accounted for the numerous telephone calls that harrassed operators at newspapers, radio and police stations at the *one* time of the week, Sunday evenings, when these switchboards were *least* prepared to handle even a moderate increase in telephone traffic.

The matter was indeed investigated by a Congressional Committee that seemed little more than amused that so patently absurd, sloppily acted and haphazardly written a program actually frightened even a rabbit's maiden aunt! (Plenty of recordings of the broadcast exist. Listen to it. The anachronisms and most of the painful line readings were not intentional, as legend has it, but simply sloppy broadcasting. In fact, this performance was no better or worse than most radio melodramas of the time, and certainly no better written.) The main beneficiary of the incident was, of course, Orson Welles, who had neither written nor directed it, but simply muddled his way through as the program's "host" and unconvincing central character, Professor Pierson. The program was really Welles' first serious grasp at national attention in the growth of what has been his erratic career. Like many of the capers of ambitious young men, the Martian hoax smelled in its time—and still does—in large measure of a publicity stunt. How and why it probably worked better than even Welles' press agents thought it would is clearly explained in Cantril's study.

I fear that many—or most—of radio's "great" moments turn out to be spun of the same cotton candy as *The War of the Worlds,* if you take the time to listen to tapes of them today. The game shows—*Dr. I.Q., The Quiz Kids, Take It or Leave It*—are the parents of today's television Juke family, the boob tube game shows. *Information Please,* with its panel of wisecracking experts was an intelligent, amusing diversion—once or twice. So were the more amusing (to me) *It Pays to Be Ignorant* and *Can You Top This*—again, once or twice. The less said about homespun advice-givers like *The Voice of Experience, Martha Dean, John J. Anthony, Mary Margaret McBride* and company the better. Childrens' radio shows like *The Singing Lady* and *The Horn and Hardart Hour* were for the most part, I fear, disasters.

During the late 'thirties, I was a "talented child" who performed occasionally on WOR, Newark, and sometimes the Mutual Network, with an alcoholic former circus hand and ex-acrobatic pianist who called himself *Uncle Don.* Famous for an on-the-air "blooper" he never made, the late Don Carney exemplifies how, in radio, mediocre has-beens and untalented, nervy exploiters could quite easily fool little children and gullible adults. Old Don made a fortune broadcasting six days a week to the kiddies. But eventually he blew his earnings on booze, broads and burned-up beds. Don Carney died in the 1950s in Florida, singing smutty songs for drinks in a cheap nightclub. His story would make an excellent film, but it would be, at least, *Restricted:* for adults only.

Radio as a Cultural Force

At this point, I am hard pressed to single out many qualities of radio broadcasting in these years that are worth admiring. Radio had, indeed, its intelligent moments, and one recalls occasional noteworthy programs. *The Town Hall of the Air,* NBC's Symphony Orchestra (assembled for the great Italian conductor, Arturo Toscanini), much coverage of sporting and breaking news events, CBS' *School of the Air* some *Cavalcade of America* broadcasts, some of the *CBS Workshop's* efforts and a few other programs—very few—come to mind.

Little on commercial radio, however, was more interesting than President Franklin D. Roosevelt's "Fireside Chats" to the American people, or the work of broadcasters who later covered World War II in Europe, the result of the labors of men like Murrow and Hicks. Milton Cross (and Texaco) brought America the *Metropolitan Opera of the Air* every Saturday. W. C. Fields spent a few great moments at the microphone. Many news commentators like Quincy Howe, Elmer Davis and Raymond Gram Swing talked intelligently to the public about serious issues. And, for a few years, a young man named Henry Morgan ad-libbed on a local New York outlet some of the most delightful daily quarter hour exercises in *non sequitur* ever broadcast.

As a service supposed to operate in the public interest, many observers agreed at the time that radio, like television today, left a good deal to be desired, but few of them had any idea of what to do about it. Like television, radio was also immensely popular and therefore financially remunerative for many people. Radio was also ostensibly a free service. It was a pleasant and effortless diversion. The most profitable programs were those that relaxed their audiences, diverted them, and therefore enhanced their receptivity to the sponsor's message.

Quite quickly, broadcasters discovered the low common denominator of public tastes and interests in broadcasting. Everybody laughs at the ridiculous; nearly everybody weeps at the troubles of other people; and everybody likes to feel surrounded by reliable friends. (Radio, like television, offered one hundreds of bogus "friends.") In these respects, radio may indeed *have* performed a public service. But the chances were slim that, at any moment that you tuned your receiver, you would hear anything more stimulating than popular music, romantic drivel or weak comedy.

There was little, however, that the FCC (or anyone else) could do about this type of popular cultural democracy, even if they had wanted to. Broadcasting seemed to hurt nobody; its success could be measured by the rating services and, most important, it seemed to sell soap. The term "the public interest" seemed to be taken to mean "whatever the public is interested in at the moment," and so it remains, for the most part, to the present day when applied to both radio and television.

News Magazines and Henry Luce

The depression also gave impetus to other changes that upset a few print journalistic apple carts in the 1930s. Serious news magazines were, of course, not new in the United States with this decade. We have seen that such journals were published in the nineteenth century: *The Nation, Harper's Weekly* and others.

In 1923, however, two recent Yale graduates, Henry Luce and Briton Hadden began a fresh new magazine called *Time*. Published weekly, *Time* was written in a readable, clever, punchy but literate style. It threw to the winds many an old journalistic notion of objectivity in favor of an editorial stance later known as "interpretive reporting." In a way, all of each issue of *Time*, from political to cultural coverage, was one big editorial, various editors rewriting the news of the past week in such a way as to place current events into what they regarded as proper backgrounds and perspectives. Hard news and features were, therefore, dramatized by lively writing, and much background and editorial comment.

During the 1920s, *Time's* popularity grew. It was, however, after the failure of one other ranking serious news magazines, *The Literary Digest,* in 1936 that *Time* really came into its own. (*The Literary Digest* had predicted that Alfred Landon would beat the incumbent President, Franklin D. Roosevelt, by a landslide. It smothered from the splatter of egg pushed into its face election morning.) Circulation of *Time* rose to such a high mark that its publisher, Henry Luce, decided the time was ripe for a mass circulating magazine that might find for itself even a larger public than the relatively highbrow *Time*.

Hadden had died years before. Now, Luce imperiously managed his own publishing firm that, by 1930, included the monthly business magazine *For-*

tune, an expensive, successful, highly specialized publication. Using the name of a defunct humor magazine, Luce launched *Life* magazine in 1936 to unexpected and enormous success. He even had trouble finding sufficient printing presses to meet the demand for the more than a million copies of *Life* that were being sold weekly within a year and, eventually, the two million copies by 1938. Quite a triumph in the middle of a depression!

Life was as dramatic and as editorially slick a publication as *Time,* except that it said what it had to say in pictures, not words. Luce hired the best news photographers—and some of the best portrait and artistic photographers—in the world to work for *Life.* He sent them to the places in which people were interested with orders to bring back photographs—multitudes of photographs—out of which the best would be chosen for that week's photo stories in *Life,* told with a minimum of captions. *Life* would "go to a party," visit celebrities, sit with statesmen, cover disasters, and even, in a celebrated issue, stick its lens into a hospital delivery room to watch the birth of a baby. *Life* was as timely as *Time* but far easier to read, more graphic in its presentations, and interpreted the word "news" a good deal more broadly.

Luce's success with *Life* naturally encouraged numerous imitators, one following the other almost like cheap Chinese firecrackers. Each tried to be just a bit more dramatic, more pictorial, more sensational than the other. This they managed to do, but, unfortunately for them, the quality of the photographs they published were almost invariably poorer than *Life's.* Stories about criminals, call-girls, burlesque queens or murderers kept them going for a time, but eventually most of them died. Names like *Pic, Quick, Ken, Glimpse* and *Peek* appeared at thousands of newstands. But only one of *Life's* competitors survived. It was *Look* magazine, begun in 1937. *Look* reached a circulation of one million in three years. Somewhat less "newsy" and slightly more "wordy" than *Life, Look* began as a bi-weekly journal, oriented to a family readership and, for many years, enjoyed notable success.

In the end, television killed both *Life* and *Look,* as advertisers deserted their still pictures for moving ones on the television tube. *Look* suspended publication in 1971 and *Life* in 1972. Neither seemed much missed by its erstwhile readers. But lovers of superior still photography remember *Life* in the 'thirties (and 'forties) with affection, and many recall *Look's* affable, lively first decade or two with admiration for the young magazine's pictorial zest and irreverance.

Luce's publishing empire showed its strongest muscles in the 1930s because of the sensational and rapid success of *Life, Fortune's* social influence, and *Time's* pithy journalism, as well as the Luce Empire's weekly and monthly entry into radio and film, *The March of Time.* A new type of journalism seemed to be emerging from Luce's efforts: *Life* and *Time* with their electric, exciting print and arresting pictures were counterbalanced by the weekly radio dramatics of *The March of Time,* (described above) and a monthly filmed documentary *The March of Time,* shown as a short subject in thousands of the nation's movie theatres.

The March on film was usually devoted to one or two feature subjects, such as New York's Mayor Fiorello LaGuardia, the rise of Hitler in Germany or broadcasting in America, and was narrated by the same stentorian voice as the radio show. On celluloid, it was much like many of today's television documentaries, except that *The March of Time* was more ponderous and pseudo-serious, dealing in considerably more hokum than we are accustomed to now. In addition to using real people (who played themselves as they do in today's video documentaries), *The March of Time* frequently hired actors to impersonate common citizens who were then directed to act as amateurishly as possible in order to look as much like real people as possible.

For a period, it seemed as if Henry Luce might be assaulting news communications from all sides—print, pictures, radio and film—and somehow gaining a toehold in each domain using the same basic method: overdramatization (or melodramatization) of news events, simplification of issues, super-patriotism and the exploitation of colorful people. As the 'thirties ended, however, no dramatized news program on radio could possibly compete with the genuine drama in the war clouds gathering in Europe. Radio's *March of Time* died. Television killed off the screen's *March* during the post-war period, just as it was to lead eventually to *Life's* death in 20 or so years. Louis de Rochemont, the filmed *March of Time's* producer, attempted to use his pseudo-documentary methods for a couple of fiction films with some success. But his tricks had become, by the 1950s, open secrets that passed openly from Luce's hands into those of the television industry at large.

Henry Luce's apparent publishing power never again gained the head of steam it seemed to be brewing in the 'thirties. A colorful character, Luce was a latter-day Hearst, but more professionally genteel, well educated and urbane. His wife was the charming Clare Boothe Luce, a witty playwright, politician and eventually an Ambassador. Luce himself directed his variegated empire from offices in Radio City and later from a super-modern skyscraper on New York's Avenue of the Americas.

Time Incorporated, of course, is still going in its somewhat undisciplined way, responsible for *Time, Sports Illustrated, People, Money, Fortune* and *Architectural Forum* in the magazine world. The company now also underwrites, produces and distributes films, television programs and materials for educational use. It publishes pictorial encyclopedias (many of them using old *Life* feature pieces) and runs a book club, among other things. *Time* no longer marches on, but it still gets around, a good deal less stridently than it once did in the 1930s. In the world of communications, however, Time Inc. still produces about one surprise a year, some of them successful and some egregious duds. All of the originality and vigor have not yet been drained from its veins.

Paperback Books

Another communication innovation of the 'thirties was to cause almost as big a stir (in its way) as *Time* and *Life*. This idea also found its way out of the granite fortresses of Radio City (or Rockefeller Center.) Inexpensive paperback books had long been familiar items on the European continent, and the British *Penguin* series had been successfully published and printed for years, consisting of numerous soft-cover fiction and non-fiction reprints of books sold at prices a good deal lower than their previous hard-cover editions. In America, Random House's *Modern Library* books of hard-cover reprints of notable volumes of many kinds had utilized mass production techniques to merchandize a highly successful series of well bound volumes of many kinds at reasonable prices. Spurred on by the success of the *Modern Library,* Pocket Books' Inc., based in Radio City, began its own tentative entry into the mass book market in the late 'thirties. It started a revolution in book publishing in the U.S.A. that continues today.

Four characteristics were distinctive of these first *Pocket Books,* aside from their charming and ingratiating logo, a cartoon kangaroo, eventually known as "Gertrude." First, *Pocket Books* consisted mostly of reprints of proven successful products: books that had been outstanding best sellers in hard cover, like Agatha Christie's mysteries and James Hilton's *Lost Horizon* and *Goodbye, Mr. Chips,* William Henry Hudson's *Green Mansions,* as well as non-fiction like Dale Carnegie's *How To Win Friends and Influence People.* Second, the books cost 25 cents each—in an era when most weekly magazines sold for a nickel or a dime. Third, these were not, strictly speaking, *paper-backs,* but rather fairly sturdy volumes, bound in cardboard, laminated with celluloid and therefore rugged and permanent. (A few that I still own from the period are today in curious condition. The individual pages of some have turned brown and tend to crumble as they are turned, but the covers remain colorful and intact.) Fourth, they were not distributed through conventional book outlets—that is, bookstores and book clubs—but rather in the same places magazines were sold: newstands, street corner kiosks, and tobacco stores as well as some places where magazines were not found like drug and grocery stores.

Pocket Books themselves were an immediate and enormous success, gaining their greatest impetus in the years during and immediately following World War II. Today the firm is a part of the giant Simon and Schuster publishing enterprise. But, more important than their success was the multitude of imitators they spawned. At first, other competing companies also specialized in reprints. Then some of them began publishing *original* volumes of all sorts, including reference books, biographies, mysteries and cook books in *relatively* inexpensive paperback editions. By this time, however, the price of them all had doubled. Finally, even prestige publishers capitulated, and all manner of paper editions of all sorts of books—texts, limited edition art books and many, many others—began to appear. Again, prices rose.

At the present writing, you are, of course, aware that only a few paperbacks, even the old one-time 25 cent Agatha Christie classics, sell for much less than $1.75 each. So many paperback books had flooded the market by the late 'fifties and 'sixties, in fact, that, in large cities and college towns, bookstores began popping up one after the other that specialized in *nothing but* paper editions—not a hard cover in sight. As a direct result of the paperback revolution, of course, the book you are now reading has been published (in its first edition) in *both* paperback and hard cover formats, the former largely for students and casual readers and the latter mostly for permanent libraries (personal, public and academic).

Sadly, I must report that today's paperback books cost, by and large, about the same as hard cover volumes did in the 1930s! Inflation, American affluence and rising publishing costs (despite technological changes like computerized typesetting and offset printing) caused this phenomenal price rise, which I sadly calculate at about 700 to 1000 per cent. Hardcover book prices have also risen, but not quite as steeply. A new best seller which might have cost $2.50 in 1937 probably retails today for $10 to $12, an increase of only 400 or 500 per cent, if it is to realize a reasonable profit for its publisher and author. A book like this one would, in 1937, not have been published in paperback at all. And the hard cover edition would cost, at most, about a quarter of the price I hope you paid for it. (Let me add, however, that professional writers of fiction and/or non-fiction are, in general, no wealthier—or poorer—by and large, than they were 30 or 40 years ago. My impression is that publishers, however, have grown somewhat fatter.)

World War II slowed up the "paperback revolution" in the U.S.A. a bit, although multitudes of inexpensive paperbound books were printed for the Armed Services during the war. In the post-war boom years more American books were circulated to more people in America, Europe and even the Far East than ever before in history—everything from millions of copies per year of the perennial paperback best seller, Homer's *Iliad,* to such startling recent popular literary landmarks as Xaviera Hollander's *The Happy Hooker.* Whether or not this revolution has either encouraged the publication of superior fiction and non-fiction, or encouraged a new love of reading and literature among the rapidly growing population of the world, I cannot pretend to know. Frankly, I doubt it, as do many others who judge the results of "revolutions" by their observable influence upon the people in the societies in which they occur.

Music and Movies

A revolution of sorts was also occuring in the American film world at about the same time. It began with the 'thirties, but is, I think, a bit more difficult to pin down as neatly, say, as the growing pains of radio under FCC supervision, new kinds of publications like Henry Luce's magazines, or the sudden growth of the paperback book industry. A number of factors contributed to it, and, as we examine them, we shall also see what its results were in the American cinema's world-wide influence.

A short time after Wall Street laid its egg, the American movies—or at least Pathé's cinematic mascot, the rooster—were crowing full tilt. As of 1930, the silent film was an obsolete novelty, suitable for occasional revivals and home movies. Actors in "talkies" talked, but this was only part of the sound film metamorphosis. Tentatively, background music was soon added to sound track. It was usually, at first, an outgrowth of the action of the film: a fiddler played beneath a window during a love scene, or somebody turned on a radio to provide a reason for music in a scene, a convention of realistic stage drama of the period. (You can still observe these little motivating shots that intrude weirdly into movies, made in the first four or five years after the age of sound pictures began, on late night television. They are hard to miss, because, although they were intended to increase the naturalness of movies in their day, they now stick out like artificial sore thumbs.) In time, directors discovered that sources for movie background music did not need to be identified visually— that mood music introduced arbitrarily was perfectly acceptable to an audience of filmgoers that had been trained to accept it.

Movie musicals, of course, brought a new community of talents to Hollywood that radically influenced all types of films. Drawing upon theatre traditions, musical selections in films like *Footlight Parade* (1933), *Forty-Second Street* (1933), the various *Gold Diggers* musicals of Warner Brothers (a series of five films begun in 1933), or the *Broadway Melody* movies (begun in 1929), often came out of nowhere—as a character broke into a love song while walking in the park, or as a rehearsal pianist's lone accompanyment to a Dick Powell's singing might suddenly expand mysteriously to symphonic proportions.

Fred Astaire, a popular, talented theatrical dancer of the 'twenties who arrived in Hollywood in the 'thirties, made a notable contribution to films in this respect, both as a dance director and performer. Starting with his first movie, *Dancing Lady* (1933), Astaire's infectious, easy-going romantic character (one he continued playing until the 1960s) might spontaneously whip into not only song but also an elaborate and invariably clever dance at any time and in almost any place. Reality had nothing to do with it, because there was nothing real about the musical world that Astaire and his imitators inhabited. But somehow it was all strangely believable nevertheless.

In the films Astaire made with Ginger Rogers, the U.S. Navy might look like a Miami resort hotel or the city of Venice might be designed by an illustrator of children's books. Nobody cared. In their most delightful film—in my opinion, *Top Hat* (1935)—you swallow whole a crazy, complicated plot that ends with Astaire and Rogers dancing into cinematic eternity up a flight of apparently endless stairs. To his credit, Astaire's peculiar genius for fairy tale magic found its way into the musical scenes of countless movies. The noted choreographer, Busby Berkeley, also possessed much the same touch, but today his work, and that of his imitators, look less like romantic imitations of life than exaggerations of peculiar and bizarre artistic fashions of a bygone period.

Sound in Movies

Most talking films were not, of course, musicals. In a remarkably few years, however, sound was tamed and cleverly integrated into film making—

not only for dialogue, but for sound effects, background noises, voice over narration and a host of other effects. None were entirely original with the movies, but all became closely associated with the art of sound cinema.

In fact, in my opinion, movies which had, in the silent era, been developing a distinctive aesthetic character, now moved closer in style to the living stage. The history of live theatre is, in large measure, the history of the *dialogue* of plays that have been written since Ancient Greece. In silent movies, dialogue was naturally minimal, confined to pantomime, symbols and titles. With the coming of sound, the *major* theatrical device for communication, dialogue (and monologue), found its way on to the screen. Movies had long been called "photoplays" in the silent era. They were, it seems to me, really "photo-pantomimes" for the most part, some of them superbly produced and acted. With the coming of sound, they *did* indeed become, for the most part, "plays," in a far more theatrical sense.

The Movie Makers

Actors, directors, producers (and even writers) responsible for this transition—responsible, that is, for the taming and domestication of a new theatrical form—are, these days, receiving more than their due share of adulation in the current nostalgia market. As these folk are dying off, they spend their days writing (or dictating) endless biographies, compiling picture books of their works and even participating in video series on Public Television. Most of these artists were theatrically trained in New York or Europe, although some others, like Frank Capra, Joan Crawford and Clark Gable had had minimal stage experience before beginning their film careers.

Most, directors like Reuben Mamoulian, actors like Humphrey Bogart, and actresses like Ruby Keeler (and many others), succeeded first on the stage and made a transition, not always swift or permanent, to films. Comedians like Eddie Cantor, the Marx Brothers and W. C. Fields were trained on the New York stage in vaudeville and burlesque. So were most of the best character actors in the movies of the 'thirties. Writers came from the legitimate theatre or the world of fiction, for the most part, although a new breed of screen writers, without much experience in theatre or with literature, was also spawned. Film scripts often represented the collaborative efforts of many scribes, each of whom possessed one or another particular sort of dramatic talent.

Some film artists migrated to the U.S.A. from Europe. The rise of the Nazis in Germany impelled directors like Billy Wilder, Fritz Lang, Josef von Sternberg and performers like Peter Lorre, Conrad Veidt and Marlene Dietrich to desert European cameras for England and Hollywood. Because their crisp speech and superior vocal training were often attractive to American audiences, a good number of British performers also settled in Hollywood—people as different one from the other as Ronald Colman, Charles Laughton, Boris Karloff and Merle Oberon. The most famous British-trained director in Hollywood was (and is) Alfred Hitchcock, whose flair for slick and crisp melodrama delighted audiences around the world.

Hollywood also raised its own flock of talented writers, performers and directors—as well as scene designers, costumers, choreographers, musicians and other talented artists and craftsmen now necessary to employ in order to produce a film. While Europe—and particularly the Soviet Union— was also developing film communities of formidable talents, Hollywood led the movie world in this period. Directors like Capra, John Ford, William Wellman, Lewis Milestone and many others displayed artistic skill unequalled anywhere else. The same may be said of many Hollywood performers—Astaire, of course, but also such serious actors and actresses as Paul Muni, Katharine Hepburn, Spencer Tracy, Fredric March, Marie Dressler, Bette Davis and others.

Movie Audiences

One real-world obstacle that Hollywood had to face in the 'thirties was, of course, the depression. The financial holocaust had peculiar effects upon the film community, and it reverberated wherever films were being made in the West. They were peculiar troubles, indeed, first, because film attendance remained fairly high in the United States during the depression, despite the two factors that might lead one to predict that it would have fallen drastically: competition from free radio broadcasting and a shortage of money among the public to spend on luxuries. The need for escape from the general gloom of the American landscape, however, impelled millions weekly into the dream world of the movie palaces. Some of the unemployed slept, and virtually lived, in theatres during inclement weather.

For the admission price—25 cents until 1 P.M. at first-run houses; as little as 10 or 15 cents at second or third run theatres; a quarter at night—one was served a large and diverting entertainment meal. This was the period of the double, and sometimes triple, feature, two or three full-length movies, a couple of shorts, a cartoon, a 10- to 15-minute newsreel and possibly a live Bingo game. One might even receive a dish or a water tumbler as an added inducement to attend. Features changed at most local theatres twice a week, as exhibitors happily consumed Hollywood's output of grade A and B and C movies, good or bad, in mammoth gulps.

Meanwhile, Back in Hollywood . . .

The story is not so sanguine, however, when seen from the perspectives of the studios themselves. Attendance simply would *not* remain high unless admission prices remained low. Sound technology had increased production costs, as did the public's growing appetite for more and more lavish productions. Among the highest salaries in the nation were those of cinema stars, directors and producers. The movie industry accounted for more than 1/300th of the national economy during these years. It was, for the most part, a generally unprofitable industry, however, not unlike selling $5 bills for $4 and doing a tremendous business. For this reason, many of the studios went bankrupt and/or fell into the receivership of banks, some to California's Bank of America and a number of others to eastern institutions.

By the middle 'thirties, many of the most critical management decisions in Hollywood were being made by financiers, not movie makers. The money men, of course, operated at a considerable distance (real and psychological) from the movie capital. (A clever minor comedy of 1937, *Stand In,* was written and produced by a major studio that was in receivership during this period. It concerned a movie studio run by a "square" banker out of his depth in Hollywood, and featured delightful light comedy performances by Leslie Howard, Humphrey Bogart and Joan Blondell. The studio—both the real and fictional one—was Warner Brothers.)

The bankers, of course, wanted to make money, and they could not afford to let the film industry die of starvation. They appreciated Hollywood's exquisite monopoly on production, distribution and exhibition and its potential for profits in the future—and even at the present moment, if the organizations were well run.

Hollywood had, by now, devised methods for keeping even the relatively few independent exhibitors in line by, as we have seen, literally funneling its entire output through the five major studios who split the market between them. Such exhibitors would be forced into the practices of "blind buying" (accepting films without knowing their titles, actors or stories), "block booking" (taking the entire line of a single distributor, both good and bad, in order to get a crack at the most profitable ones), and "designated play dates" (waiting until producer-owned first-run theatres had creamed off the most profitable, first-run audiences for superior films.)

With the end of the depression and the war economy of the 1940's, the banks retreated from Hollywood, except to finance individual films, and the studios once again became their own masters—for a time.

Depression Films

The depression also found its way *onto* celluloid, as a number of studios began making films about the effects of contemporary poverty, unemployment and demoralization upon American life. Called "social" films, most of these movies were melodramas, some versions of stage plays like *Dead End* (1937), or *Golden Boy* (1939), while others were original films. A few were comedies like *It Happened One Night* (1934), and *My Man Godfrey* (1936). Some were as somber as *The Grapes of Wrath* (1940), one of the many versions of the Bonnie and Clyde Barrow story, *You Only Live Once* (1937), or any number of gangster films in which essentially decent people turned either to crime or the ministry (or both) because of the pressure of America's failing economic system.

While, for the most part, Hollywood steered clear of them, the 'thirties also saw the growth of documentary movies, a form of journalistic cinema largely created in the United States during the silent era by Robert Flaherty and in England by John Grierson. Often funded by an agency of government, a foundation or even a large corporation, these films proported to demonstrate, in narrative non-theatrical terms, the impact of the social and economic climate upon the quality of life at home and abroad. They centered both upon rural and urban themes, many of which still seem fresh today: conservation, flood control, health care and agriculture, as well as other sensitive topics. Outstanding among them were those made by Pare Lorentz like *The River* (1937), and Willard Van Dyke's *The City* (1939). In effect, these movies were poetic, longer and more liberally oriented statements, but many were not unlike Luce's *March of Time* short subjects. Most were exhibited by clubs, labor unions, service organizations and at fairs and expositions, rather than in movie theatres.

Color Cinema

This decade also saw the perfection, during the early 'thirties, of a fairly realistic method of shooting and printing movies in natural color. Until, roughly, 1934, a number of color film processes existed, but none of them were able to reproduce all natural colors with fidelity. "Cinecolor," for instance, could not achieve a true red hue but substituted a bright orange instead.

For many years, a clever inventor named Herbert Kalmus had been working on a patented invention he called "Technicolor." Having started work in 1918, his color process, using two of the primary light colors, was at one time tried for a few silent movies. But it was not until movies were well into the sound era that he unveiled his perfected system for recording the three primary colors of light (yellow, blue and green) with consistent and natural fidelity.

At first, Walt Disney used the process for his animated cartoons, *Silly Symphonies,* in which the colors might be carefully controlled and corrected, if necessary. Finally, MGM produced a musical short, *La Cucaracha* (1934). The next year, the first full-color Technicolor feature, *Becky Sharp* (with Miriam Hopkins), was released. It was a sticky version of Thackeray's *Vanity Fair,* but the color photography, as I remember it at the time of its release, was dazzling.

The coming of color, however, added still another monopoly to the Hollywood scene. It lasted until the late 1940s, when both the pressure of anti-trust action upon Kalmus and Eastman Kodak's development of a new film stock for 35mm production which was able to compete with Technicolor, ended it. Until that time, however, Kalmus had controlled all the major patents connected with the Technicolor process. If a studio wanted to make a Technicolor film, it was necessary to *rent* Kalmus' cameras (and cameraman), buy the film from Technicolor Inc., allow them to process it and finally to supply all color prints for distribution. In addition, any studio shooting in Technicolor was forced to hire Herbert Kalmus' wife, Natalie, for a formidable wage as a consultant, although her work was often nugatory. (Watch for the credit: "Color consultant: Natalie Kalmus" on *all* American—and European—color films made before 1949 when they are shown on television!)

Herbert Kalmus was repaid handsomely for his dogged tenacity in perfecting the Technicolor process over a 15—or more—year period, but he kept an iron grip on his invention until forced by law and competition to let go. Kalmus was one of the few people in Hollywood during the 'thirties before whom even the mightiest movie moguls figuratively cringed, simply because they needed him more than he needed any one of them. Here is another story that would make an interesting movie!

The Production Code

Many movie makers remember the 1930s primarily as the time when Hollywood was forced to institute extra legal procedures to censor its own output. We have seen how the Motion Picture Producers and Distributors of America was organized in the early 'twenties. In 1927, a vague series of guidelines for "proper" decorum in movies had been drafted and accepted by the MPPDA. Little attention, it seems, was paid to it.

By the early 'thirties, however, a good number of films had gotten pretty racy. Sound, as unlikely as it seems, was largely the culprit, not the moving pictures themselves. Actresses like Mae West were able to turn innocent phrases into risqué invitations by a simple vocal inflection. Themes of many serious movies, while remaining quite innocent pictorially, often treated openly such themes as adultery, prostitution and pre-marital sex. What was even worse to many bluenoses was that such behavior was often condoned, as well as other controversial matters, most notably certain quasi-criminal activities. Costumes in musicals had indeed grown pretty provocative for their day—hardly brief or revealing enough to raise even my old eyebrows now—but, in their time, scandalously revealing too much, thought many.

Under movie "Czar" Will Hays, the MPPDA, responding most immediately to pressure from lay Catholics and some churchmen (who were eventually, in 1933, to form their own Legion of Decency, directed mostly *to* Catholics), began revising the old Code. The Rev. Daniel Lar, S.J. and publisher-author Martin Quigley Sr. drafted a new Motion Picture Code in 1930, as clean as a bride's fingernails, that would pass muster at anybody's Sunday School—unless he or she had too many scruples about violence. The Code alone meant little until the MPPDA gave it teeth: in effect, an agreement among the producers themselves to abide by it—and no nonsense.

The result was the Production Code Administration that had power to fine any producer and/or prevent any film from distribution that did not stick to the Code in letter and spirit. This meant submitting to the Code Authority the book, play or story from which a film was to be made; adhering to its suggested guidelines for filming; permitting the Authority to read the shooting script, and, if necessary, sending a censor to the set where a scene was to be shot—as well as reviewing the finished film and finally giving it the MPPDA Seal of Approval. The Authority began operating in 1934, and its effect upon Hollywood remained, for nearly 20 years, deep and devastating.

Stories were sanitized. Mae West was watched most carefully. The safest films a producer might make were obviously the most puerile and innocent. It is no coincidence that the Production Code Authority was followed by the exploitation of the child prodigy, Shirley Temple, to stardom and a never-ending stream of revoltingly "wholesome" pictures about dogs, horses, children and clean-cut American families. MGM's "Hardy Family" series (note the name) was the prototype for many of these latter movies. In fact, nearly everybody and everything in Hollywood became clean-cut.

If, for instance, the issue of adultery had to intrude necessarily into the plot of a film, it was necessary to imply or signal it by means of a series of seemingly innocent symbols to which most audiences quickly became privy. (When a scene faded *out* on a couple in an embrace showing a man wearing a jacket, and then faded *in* on the same set, say, an hour later, and the gentleman had *removed* his jacket, his shirtsleeves now symbolized that the pair had had sexual relations during the interim. Incredible, but true! Take a look, for instance, at Warner Brothers famous love story, *Casablanca,* the next time it is on the tube.)

The Production Code survived the depression. And so did Hollywood. With the MPPDA loudly crowing their new slogan, "Motion Pictures Are Your Best Entertainment," the demoralizing decade turned. Now, all of America, including Hollywood, turned its attention to the serious business of two wars that were beginning to the West and East of the United States.

11

At War with the Media

MOST OF US HOPE THAT World War II will be remembered mainly because it was the single most devasting man-made holocaust in history, and for this reason alone. As years pass, our world will never again be able to afford another period of devastation deeper or more searing than this conflict, I fear. Recall its casualties, direct and indirect: six million Jews, Gypsies and others incinerated in the ovens of Nazi Germany; the near destruction of the beautiful cities of Cologne and Dresden; the merciless bombing of the City of London; over six million Russians dead defending their country; nearly five million German and Japanese killed in battle, victims of their leaders' megalomania; atomic bombs exploding over Hiroshima and Nagasaki killing roughly 120,000 Japanese—no one will ever know the precise number; and other horrors that might continue for pages.

The United States did not suffer the worst devastations of the war. Hitler invaded Poland and began the major conflict on September 1, 1939. It was not until the Japanese attacked Pearl Harbor two years later, on December 7, 1941, that America was drawn into hostilities in Europe and the Pacific. Germany finally surrendered to the Allies on May 7, 1945; Japan on August 14th of the same year. Except for the destruction of naval bases in Hawaii, little damage had been done to American soil. The American armed forces, however, made up an enormous fighting force, third only to that of Germany (20 million) and China (17 million). Sixteen million United States military personnel were involved in hostilities, but casualties were relatively light when held against other nations: 671,000 American wounded and 292,000 killed.

The overall number of dead and maimed soldiers and civilians left by

World War II is not worth totaling on our calculators, so immense and sickening a number it is. And one dead man, woman or child of one race or nationality or political persuasion is much the same as another. Death, particularly mass murder on the scale of modern warfare, is a great democratizing force that makes all men and women indeed equal. No, the world we know cannot afford a third World War. This fact seems even to have made some impression upon the consciences of politicians, dictators and demagogues during the generation that has passed since V-J day, the end of World War II.

Extraordinary destruction was not the only reason that this war was a unique experience in the history of mankind. While the idea was not new, and its roots may be traced into ancient history, this was a war fought with an unusual objective: *unconditional* surrender rather than a *negotiated* peace. For many of the countries involved, excluding those of North and South America, it was also a *total* war, involving not only military forces of the combatants but also the civilian populations of the hostile nations, mostly victims of rampaging, conquering or retreating armies, objects of merciless, continuous air attacks and other kinds of unbelievable devastation.

Historians may quibble about definitions, but World War II was probably also the first nearly *global* war in history, involving, one way or another, almost every inhabitant of our planet, even those insulated by arbitrary "neutrality," like the Swiss and Swedes, or those in remote corners of the earth whose isolation was broken by modern technology and transportation that intruded even into remote Pacific Islands and the Arctic tundra. If any inhabitant of any country of the world was not, in one way or another, touched by this war, the reason was his (or her) psychological isolation from reality rather than geographical or military factors.

World War II was also the first major war to enlist, almost from the start, the technologies of mass communications as instruments of combat. By and large, the press, radio and films around the world served three major functions for those nations involved in hostilities.

Media as Persuasion

First, they functioned as propaganda instruments for the civilian populations, whose assenting opinions and support were invariably necessary for the conduct of hostilities. To this end, Adolph Hitler in Germany probably anticipated the so-called "morale" function of the newer mass media before any of the other combatants. In the 1920s, he had appointed his alter-ego, a doctor of philosophy in drama named Joseph Paul Goebbels, as his propaganda minister with the mission, broadly speaking, of bringing together all of the instruments of print, radio and film in Germany, and later in nations conquered by Germany, for service to the Nazi party. How Goebbels (at the direct command of Hitler) accomplished this end is a long and complicated story. But even before hostilities had broken out in Europe, it was clear that total war included, in the fourth and fifth decade of the twentieth century, the use of *all* instruments of mass communication available to national leaders in order to achieve unity and support of military aims and objectives on the home front.

That Hitler was far ahead of both his allies and adversaries is a testament to his diabolical cleverness and, to some degree, the power of the mass media. As early as 1934, Hitler's cinema photographers, directed by a talented, young former actress, Leni Riefenstahl, were photographing one of the most impressive and frightening propaganda movies ever made, *Triumph of the Will,* released in Germany two years later. *Triumph* is an important and seminal film. It was not the first nationalistic propaganda movie ever produced; we have seen that such projects had been attempted earlier in the U.S.A., the U.S.S.R. and elsewhere. It is, however, the *best* in many respects, mostly because of its unwavering success in portraying in documentary fashion Adolph Hitler himself and the Nazi party as political and mystical saviors of Germany. The message of the film's power as propaganda was clear: If nationalistic persuasion had become a weapon of modern war, the hardware to deliver it was housed in the mass printing press, the radio station and the motion picture studio. Look at *Triumph* today if you can. You will see that it was as much a weapon of the Nazi's war against civilization as the burning of the German Reichtag.

Media as Instruction

Second, mass communications might also be employed as an instrument of military instruction and propaganda directed at fighting forces in training and in the field. The United States, for instance, employed all of the mass media effectively, both by the armed forces and in cooperation with the professional world of mass communications. A radio network (Armed Forces Radio) served as an instrument of entertainment, morale building and indoctrination for U.S. troops stationed around the world. Various mass publications, most notably *Stars and Stripes,* were distributed to fighting men in the various theatres of war. Few members of the American military services were not innundated by training films, some superbly and professionally made, some amateur and foul, that seemed to cover about every topic in the soldier's manual of arms from cleaning rifles to the perils of patrol duty.

Some of us remember various of these training films to this day, particularly the gory clinical realities, lovingly photographed, in one or another famous ''VD scare'' movie, but also some superb British films on streetfighting, mine and booby-trap detection and other rugged arts. I clearly remember viewing a fascinating short film on how to disembowel a hostile person with a bayonet in fast and (supposedly) painless fashion. The lesson was so well taught that it has remained with me for well over 30 years.

More significant, possibly, were American movies directed to soldiers and sailors that explained historically their nation's role in the war. None of these were, in the opinion of many, as effective as somewhat similar efforts like

Triumph of the Will in Germany, which, although it was directed to civilians, stimulated fighting blood in German troops as well. In the U.S.A., Frank Capra, the noted Hollywood director, edited an impressive series of movies called *Why We Fight,* made between 1943 and 1945, that chronicled for American soldiers and sailors the complex and baffling historical realities of the conflict in which they were engaged. All of them were salted with heavy doses of propaganda. Subsequent studies showed that these superbly made documentaries apparently had little long-term effect upon the attitudes of American fighting men, but they, and others like them, certainly did the U.S.A. no harm. It is also impossible to determine the deterioration of morale among soldiers and sailors at times of temporary military setbacks and losses in combat had they *not* been extensively utilized by the armed forces.

Media on the Front

Third, mass communications entered the battlefield itself in new and unusual ways. In former times, when an army, regiment or group of fighting men captured or liberated a city or town, their first move was invariably to occupy the center of government: a city or town hall, executive palace or mansion, or military command headquarters. In the era of mass communications, this tactic changed to the occupation of the local radio station and possibly the offices of the local newspaper, followed by military and political installations. Mass communications had become weapons. People responded to radio voices, be they voices of conquering heroes or the voices of resistance groups.

In the latter respect, the incredible work of the British Broadcasting Corporation had much to do with the resistance of the English to Germany's nightly air bombardments during the Battle of Britain, despite Hitler's attempts (via renegade propagandists like the well-known "Lord Haw-Haw") to undermine civilian morale. Radio broadcasting had a good deal to do with the determined defenses of Stalingrad and Leningrad against Nazi forces by the U.S.S.R. In nations captured by both Germany and Japan, propaganda broadcasts and local newspapers were responsible for much demoralization among the occupied populations. Of course, in nations such as France, Holland and Denmark, underground newspapers (and broadcasters) mushroomed among resistance fighters. Poets and philosophers like Albert Camus and Jean Paul Sartre spoke and wrote eloquently for the resistance forces, fighting, in effect, a propaganda war in tandem with their underground guerrilla actions.

Media and the Civilian Population

In modern warfare, communications play a new role on the home front, a fact perfunctorily recognized 25 years before World War II with the creation of the first World War's Creel Committee, that acted as a government censor of all news in print about hostilities that circulated in the United States. Its function was designed primarily to guard military secrets, but it could not help but play also a role in building up home front morale and, in a way, therefore serving as an instrument of psychological warfare.

The task that had faced the Creel Committee was exacerbated many times when World War II began, largely because mass communications technology had grown so enormously in the quarter-century between the two wars. As we have seen, dimensions of warfare had themselves expanded in scope and deadliness, no longer involving isolated battlefields in strategic locations but "theatres of war" where civilian populations as well as military personnel were effected.

Mass Communications at Work

Of all the nations involved in World War II, the United States was probably the last to begin actively the kind of activities that the various propaganda ministries of other countries—including its allies—had been busily organizing as war clouds gathered. The need for them, however, was enormous and obvious. Almost immediately after Pearl Harbor, President Roosevelt created various new government agencies to direct and control the powerful forces of mass communications for many functions in the coming conflict.

The basic needs of the U.S.A. were three in number, and all of them, to different degrees, ran against the grain of American traditions of a free press and relatively libertarian broadcasting and film industries. In their different ways, these temporary agencies ran obstacle courses around the First Amendment of the United States Constitution and its guarantees of free speech. The Supreme Court, incidentally, had determined during World War I that the First Amendment's freedom principle might—and should—be abridged (or possible disregarded) where and when a "clear and present danger" to the safety of the nation existed. If necessary, therefore, all instruments of communication (even interpersonal ones) might be controlled by the government in time of war, *if* such a danger existed.

The trouble with the Supreme Court's criterion of a "clear and present danger," however, was that its application necessarily depended upon both guesswork and opinion. Nobody is able to prove incontestably what a "clear and present danger" is until *after* it has caused its damage. Then it is naturally too late to stop it. When a nation is at war, however, all kinds of dangers—real and imaginary—seem more threatening then during peacetime. Little opposition was heard after the bombing of Pearl Harbor to the formation of government agencies that would, in effect, control and censor all American instruments of mass communication, including the press, so that they might cooperate to the fullest degree with the war effort.

What was required of newspapers, magazines, broadcasters and film makers fell into three different general categories, as I have noted.

Military Censorship

First, there existed a need for censorship and control among those media which disseminated war news. This centered largely on tactical military secrecy in regard to battle plans, troop movements, etc. but went so far, sometimes, as underplaying bad and exaggerating good news. On all military fronts, therefore, for newspapers, radio broadcasters and newsreel photographers, the censor, representing a military security bureau, was ever present. Newspaper stories might be datelined "Somewhere in Germany," broadcasts from combat zones were recorded first and censored later, scripts were carefully monitored, and the words "military secret" became part of the country's common language. None of this interference with open communications seemed unnecessary or unusual, however, because even personal letters that soldiers and sailors wrote to their families from military zones were carefully screened. Sections of words or paragraphs that might leak strategic information were cut or inked out.

Propaganda

Second, the mass media in the U.S.A. obviously had the task of serving as propaganda in its broadest sense, to boost what was called "home front morale" for the purpose of obtaining the widest possible civilian support of the war. (We have seen recently what a war that is *not* supported at home by civilian popular opinion is like: Vietnam was a superb case study, and a tragic one!) Americans had to be exhorted, not only to cheer on fighting men in their own circle of acquaintances and families, but to work hard and long hours at the production of military materiel. They had to be encouraged to observe rationing laws governing consumer goods and price controls made necessary by the war, to buy war bonds and, if possible, volunteer for one of many war-related, home front service-related jobs. Thus, in America, many thousands of civilian air raid wardens (who would never be needed) were pressed into service, women collected old clothes for our allies, and children went from house to house gathering scrap metal to be turned, they hoped, into guns and bullets.

Psychological Warfare

Third, as we have already seen, mass media had become instruments of war of and by themselves. Germans were broadcasting their propaganda to the U.S.A. nightly. Tokyo Rose, a popular Japanese-American female disc-jockey, was peculiarly effective in directing her pro-Japanese radio messages to Americans in the Pacific theatre. The British Broadcasting Overseas Service was dishing up a nightly bag of tricks on news broadcasts to Germany and Italy. In 1941, only America was not yet ready to join the propaganda war on the airwaves, to broadcast to our enemies our version of the truth in the hope of undermining morale and of reassuring our allies of our good faith.

The Voice of America

To meet these needs, in part at least, the United States Government first organized a Foreign Information Service. Concerned mostly with broadcasting, in January of 1942, it started the famous *Voice of America* that continues to this day as an overseas arm of a peacetime agency begun in the 1950s, the United States Information Agency.

By June of 1942, the Office of War Information had been created, under the direction of Elmer Davis, a veteran newsman, one-time Rhodes scholar, staff reporter for the *New York Times* and CBS news commentator. Heading the *Voice,* under Davis' control, was Pulitzer Prize playwright, Robert E. Sherwood, a tall, dour man who had ghost-written speeches for President Roosevelt and whose recent Broadway plays centered, with strong anti-Fascist zeal, upon the war in Europe. Also involved in the OWI were poet (and later Librarian of Congress) Archibald MacLeish and Colonel (later General) "Wild Bill" Donovan, who eventually headed America's war-time spy network, the Office of Strategic Services. The latter unit, incidentally, became the father (or grandfather) of the present, and now infamous, CIA. Davis' associate director of the OWI was Milton Eisenhower, brother of the General who was eventually to command all allied forces in the European theatre.

The Office of War Information

The authority of the OWI intersected that of many other agencies—Army and Navy intelligence, censorship and public relations units, for instance—but, because all were working to the same end, this fact appeared to matter little. The OWI's domestic section was, in fact, one enormous news bureau with hundreds of employees responsible for communicating safe but reliable war information to newspapers and radio stations across the nation. In itself, the OWI was an enormous public relations agency with one client: the American war effort. To this end it attempted to produce and coordinate massive releases of news, advertising and campaigns for the sale of war bonds, rallies and similar activities.

It may seem cold blooded to observe that it was the job—successfully accomplished—of Davis' domestic agency to "sell" the war to the American people. But that is the way it now seems, looking back at the OWI and what it accomplished. More sentimental observers may emphasize the role, as Emery and Smith do in their history of the press, of the OWI in telling the American people "the truth and nothing but the truth" about the war. In their way, they are right. Compared to Dr. Goebbels" Propaganda Ministry in Berlin, the OWI was the epitome of virtue and honesty, but its major home front thrust, never-theless, was to make the best of however the fortunes of war turned: good, bad or indifferent.

On the foreign fronts, the OWI operated a little differently under Sher-wood's direction and assisted by Joseph Barnes, an experienced newspaper hand. The agency's output consisted of not only radio broadcasts addressed to our enemies and allies but news reports for the foreign press, feature stories, photographs and eventually motion pictures, pamphlets, magazines, books and many other types of materials utilizing many media.

In addition, the *Voice of America,* which constituted about two-thirds of the OWI's overseas operation, dabbled (with some success) in propaganda broadcasts—or what has since been called "psychological warfare" against our enemies. Notable propaganda victories, especially on programs aimed at enemy army and naval units on the verge of defeat, have been claimed (in various ways) against Italy, Germany and Japan. These broadcasts were often coupled with such unorthodox mass communication procedures as dropping thousands of leaflets from aircraft upon enemy troops, claiming that the war was lost for them and the game up, urging surrender and promising kind treatment for pris-oners of war.

Propaganda Movies

The OWI was not the only agency involved in any or all of these activi-ties, of course—merely the largest one. The United States Army Signal Corps and the Navy contracted with professional film makers, including even Walt Disney of Mickey Mouse fame, to produce movies for their specific needs, mostly the sorts of training films mentioned previously. Some movies were made by military film units.

When the OWI did indeed begin contracting for its own movies, a number of them, mostly documentaries, turned out to be outstanding projects. The best were made towards the end of the war and exhibited in occupied nations over-seas. They set themselves simply to showing the positive side of American de-mocracy: our methods of voting, the America's free library service for chil-dren, our educational system and other simple subjects told in meaningful human terms. Other short movies explained the causes of the war and its im-pact upon the people of the nations most affected by it. Some were also re-leased in the United States and shown in schools where they, and their British counterparts, constitute to date, much of the best documentary work ever done in either country. None of these films were, unfortunately, as impressive as Hitler's *Triumph of the Will.* But he who makes the best movies—or even uses best other instruments of mass communications—does not necessarily win wars—although I have met idealists who believe so, in spite of enormous evi-dence against them.

How trite to observe that warfare brings out the best and worst in people, but also how true! Most particularly, World War II illustrated, in many contexts, the ways that the newest and least tried medium of mass communication might rise to new artistic heights in the United States in spite of (or, some say, because of) its commercial domination for nearly two decades. I am referring of course, to broadcasting, sound broadcasting in these days, and the influence that radio had upon the entire experience of warfare as the people of the U.S.A. felt it from 1941 to 1945.

Edward R. Murrow

One hardly knows where to begin. We have seen how Edward R. Murrow began his wartime vigil in London (and, at times, on the battlefield) for CBS News. Since his death in 1965, Murrow has been lionized, immortalized, biographed, and today stands as a figure of near mythical stature in the world of broadcasting, partly because of his extraordinary work during the European war in his radio days and partly because of his later courage in beating out new trails in television broadcasting and sticking to his guns in the heat of controversial matters after the age of video had begun.

Most living Americans remember Murrow best as he appeared on *Person to Person, CBS Reports* and *See It Now*—his spaniel-like countence looking forever sad, even when smiling, the inevitable cigarette curling smoke from his fingers into the black and white television image that seemed to reflect his distinctive serious demeanor so well. His voice was the audible reflection of his visage; colleagues called him "the voice of doom," because, even in casual conversation, what he said was punctuated by such resonant and superb elocution that even an insignificant comment seemed important. It was both his blessing and curse that, on the air, he seemed to lack a sense of humor, that he sounded middle-aged in his twenties, old at 50, and somehow personally "doomed" himself by 53. Those who knew him even casually could not escape the sense of intensity in life as he lived it, as if the only enemy he really feared was time.

Murrow is a legend, and there is little to say, even in histories like this one, about such recent legends. He was also a human being with a human being's weakness and petty sides. Possibly, these matters had best be left to future biographers who will be free to write about him without worrying about the feelings of living men and women, and after Murrow's ghost stops stalking the passages of CBS' newsrooms, as it does today. This time will come.

Many of us remember Murrow best as a reporter, a war reporter who had never cut his teeth in a newspaper's city room and had never (to the best of anyone's knowledge) covered a beat for a print journal. His medium was radio. During World War II, he evolved almost single-handed a type of verbal news reporting that remains today unique. Its flavor cannot be captured in print, although I, among others, have tried to include sections of Murrow's broadcasts in books with little success. Murrow's words were written to be spoken—by

Murrow—and they constitute a type of war reporting combined with blank verse poetry nearly impossible to describe.

What did Murrow tell the American public? First, he described the Battle of Britain, the terrible bombardments the English were taking nightly at the hands of Hitler's bombers. Rather than cover the action entirely from the street, Murrow, for the most part, actually found ways to interview himself—attempting to share with the listener back home his own reactions to the enormous resistance the British were putting up against the merciless pounding London, in particular, was taking from the heavens. True, he would often speak from a setting of dramatic interest, but wherever he was—on a rooftop during a London air raid, walking down a deserted street at night, or traveling with combat troops—his broadcasts were personal messages between himself and his listeners. His famous broadcast of April of 1945, after the allied troops had liberated the German concentration camp, Buchenwald, was carefully scripted and read from a broadcast installation. It was, nevertheless, fresh, moving and honest, because Murrow had surpassed the art of mere "on the spot" radio coverage. He had evolved a new type of audio journalism which, unfortunately, was so much a part of his talent that it apparently died with him in 1965.

Broadcasters and the War

This is not to say that many other radio reporters did not serve notably and admirably during the war. George Hicks of NBC stationed himself atop a naval craft during the D-Day invasion of Normandy and risked his life (possibly unaware of his vulnerability at the time) to bring to the radio audience an eyewitness account of his experience. Hicks spoke into a recorder, similar to that used for movies, operated by means of an electric eye controlling a light beam photographed on film. (The broadcast historian Eric Barnouw says that Hicks used a wire recorder, an improbable statement. Wire recording was a German invention, that had not been "liberated" from the Reich by allied troops at the time. Hicks verified this bit of common sense for me about ten years ago.)

The broadcast is a classic, as is Charles Collingwood's D-Day interview with naval public relations officer Jerry Danzig on the beach in Normandy while squadrons of planes were flying overhead, and both men shared a simultaneous sense of history and bewilderment at the dramatic start of the Allies' invasion of Europe.

Other World War II broadcasters are still at work on television today, for the most part no longer reporters but armchair pundits. Eric Sevareid, then of the *Paris Tribune,* gave America its last broadcast from Paris, as Hitler's storm-troopers entered the city in 1940. Winston M. Burdett was at the microphone in North Africa, and Howard K. Smith had been broadcasting from Berlin until the outbreak of hostilities, sensitively describing the growing European conflict. Having escaped from Germany, Smith continued his analysis of the tangled European holocoust from Switzerland and elsewhere. Others, like Larry Leseuer and Richard C. Hottelet were familiar voices from the European theatre, and others, like Tom Traynor, were killed in the conflict.

Radio reporters in the Pacific were less well known, but many of their broadcasts were also exceptional: Bert Silen's account of the Japanese bombing and invasion of Manila, General Wainwright's own broadcast to his troops telling them of the surrender of Corregidor, Pat Flaherty's NBC report of the liberation of the Philippines, Don Pryor of CBS' description of the siege of Okinawa, and many other radio accounts that were given by nameless Army, Navy and Marine reporters who literally risked their necks to bring the American public some of the most moving and important on the spot news reporting it had ever experienced.

The War Commentators

Radio's task during the war, however, was not only to bring to listners news from the battle sites—Atlantic and Pacific—but also to create for listeners a coherent picture of the conflict from the perspective of the home front.

I have already mentioned the news reports of H.V. Kaltenborn, who maintained long vigils at the microphone before and during the conflict. Able to speak fluent German, he and William L. Shirer, both of CBS, were particularly adept as the analysis of the many political and military aspects of the conflict. In addition, Shirer had personally covered on radio Hitler's march through Europe before the U.S.A. entered the war.

Other analysts like Raymond Gram Swing, Major George Fielding Eliot, Quincy Howe and, before his OWI days, Elmer Davis, kept America informed concerning the larger issues created by the conflict. Some, like Gabriel Heatter and Walter Winchell, all but turned the war into a circus on their broadcasts, exploiting its sensational aspects, dealing in melodrama, overstatement and lurid sensationalism, but possibly performing the service of keeping American morale at fever pitch, even when the tide of war seemed temporarily to turn against the allies during the first and final years of the conflict, both occasions when the Axis forces fought most fiercely and desperately.

Home Front Radio

Like almost every other American industry, radio broadcasting was affected deeply by World War II. Without much urging from the OWI or any propaganda agency, radio dramas, and even comedy shows, began to develop themes having to do with the war. While Hollywood dealt with the big picture, radio concentrated mostly upon the home front. Characters in soap operas like *The Goldbergs* were sent to war (especially when young actors were called into the service), and wartime themes wended their way into most radio broadcasts, even and especially commercial announcements. Women were urged to save cooking fat, look their most beautiful for the day when their service man would return and so forth. War bonds and stamps were "plugged" continuously by the networks. Certain special programs, the work of such old-hand radio writers and directors as Norman Corwin, Arch Oboler, William N. Robson, Robert Lewis Shayon, Orson Welles and other luminaries of the period, gathered together enormous casts of Hollywood and theatrical stars who would broadcast one or another type of spectacular program that beat the drum hard (and often too long) in order to sell war bonds and boost civilian morale.

Most of these programs read—and sound—like tenth rate *ersatz* poetry today. Most of them were. But one must remember that they were set against the highly charged emotional backdrop of the U.S.A. at the time, and that they indeed raised both blood pressures and raised formidable sums in the sale of government bonds. Out of hundreds of them, only Norman Corwin's *On a Note of Triumph,* broadcast by CBS on V-E day, might today be worth the time spent to listen to it. But even this jubilant, unrestrained and synthetic hymn to victory oozes hokum, pretentiousness, and sentimentality. (Archibald MacLeish's dramatic poem, *The Fall of the City,* produced before the war in 1937, succeeded far better in both its didactic and poetic goals than *On a Note of Triumph.* In its day, however, *City* unfortunately attracted far less attention than the more pretentious *Triumph* eight years later.)

Largely because her efforts were studied in depth by social psychologist Robert Merton, Kate Smith is remembered for her radio marathons (something like today's "telethons") during which she spent hour after hour in front of a microphone imploring her listeners to send to her pledges for war bond purchases. She was but one of the many who gave both their time and talent to wartime radio in the U.S.A.

Listening to an evening's output on a network radio station during those World War II days, as I have recently, clarifies for one how totally integrated into the nation's life was the *fact* that America was at war, how fully all institutions in society cooperated with the war effort, and how, heaven help the word, "popular" the war itself was! Male guests on quiz shows were almost always servicemen, if possible. Celebrities in uniform spent their leaves—and sometimes most of their military service—using their prestige to speak to the American people in exhortatory terms. Glenn Miller's entire orchestra, somehow or another, turned up as part of the Army Air Force. Miller was killed in a plane crash, but his music went marching on through the war and into peacetime. Old-time radio shows like *We The People* and *The Cavalcade of America* suddenly exploited war-time themes and propaganda messages for their audiences.

Here was a new kind of total war on the home front: total innundation by radio. I well remember being awakened daily at 5:30 A.M. by the voice of Arthur Godfrey on his early morning broadcast, piped through an Army base's public address system, the "ole red head" speaking his daily morale message to those of us in uniform. Quite a change from the traditional bugle calls of old, but so were USO shows, replete with film and radio stars touring Army and

Navy training camps and installations overseas, and the general attitude of a nation of civilians who, indoctrinated by radio to Ed Murrow's famous "sign off," never said "Goodbye" to you if you wore a uniform, but substituted the phrase "Good luck."

Despite a considerable shortage of consumer goods on the American market, radio prospered during the war years. Competition between purveyors of essential goods and services was considerable, even in those in short supply. Other manufacturers with little to sell—like automobile and electrical device manufacturers—realized that the war would not last forever, and that Americans would once again in the future be choosing between brands in a competitive market. For the record (and lest we forget), home front consumer shortages centered upon gasoline, meat, butter, sugar, coffee and rubber goods (including automobile tires), for which rationing procedures, in one way or another, were applied by the government. In short supply were all imported goods like Scotch Whisky, chocolate and tea, as well as other luxury commodities such as cigarettes. While shortages were both ubiquitous and noticeable, the American economy, standard of living and way of life was not changed severely on the home front when compared, for instance, with Britain. Wages were high and money, as always, was all that one needed to buy almost anything—if he or she wanted it badly enough. Our "war time economy" was more a psychological than social reality. Of all the major belligerents in World War II, there is little doubt that the U.S.A suffered least in material terms.

Broadcasting Monopolies

One aspect of American economic life, however, deeply affected radio broadcasting during the war years, while World War II itself was in no way affected by it. I am referring to the tendency of many industries, previously noted in the film world, to form monopolies, and for large companies effectively to exclude competition from smaller ones.

We have seen how and why NBC and CBS had, by the outbreak of the war, become the most potent forces in the broadcasting industry—NBC with two networks, the Red and the Blue, and CBS with one. Mutual, a loose affiliation of many stations that had started by sharing recordings of broadcasts of *The Lone Ranger* from WXYZ in Detroit, followed a poor third, unable to sign up affiliates in many communities served by CBS and NBC. Nor did it attract those stations to which the FCC had assigned powerful clear-channel wave lengths, that is, stations that would not encounter interference at any time of the day or night with other outlets using the same frequency at some distant point.

The problem of a two-network monopoly was clearly one for the Federal Communications Commission, which began its probe of the matter in 1938. While CBS was involved in some dubious enterprises and exercised considerable control over its affiliated stations' use of their own broadcast time (in favor of that of the networks), the FCC, under the chairmanship of James L. Fly, really centered its attack upon RCA, the owner of NBC's Red and Blue radio networks.

The FCC took three years to issue its "Report on Chain Broadcasting," so incendiary a document that it was immediately attacked, damned and villified by the broadcasting establishment, its industry organization, the National Association of Broadcasters, and its mouthpiece, *Broadcasting* magazine—all of which were (and still are) powerful business-controlled organizations. The reaction was justified. The Report, accurate and devastating, hit the broadcasters right where they lived: in their pocketbooks. Ironically, the Report hit the broadcasting scene just as the economic uncertainties of war were begining to cloud the nation's horizon, compounding the hysteria.

What did the Report say? It was a complex document centering largely on the degree and nature of the controls that the networks exercised over their affiliates; the extraordinary power of NBC; the way in which the two major networks, particularly NBC again (although CBS was also culpable), managed to worm into the talent agency business, acting as artists representatives for the broadcasters they themselves employed; and other, less significant concerns.

Following the Report, the FCC's newly written and quite severe "Chain Broadcasting Regulations" were adopted by the Commission. In the face of much opposition from the industry and their many friends in Congress, the Supreme Court of the United States then upheld the validity of the Commission's new rules.

Despite their bravado during this period, the networks had noted the handwriting on the wall. Both CBS and NBC quickly slid out of the talent bureau business in 1941, before the Regulations were tested in court—almost as if they were children caught raiding the cookie jar.

New regulations, giving affiliated stations greater option over their own broadcasting, were then subsequently enforced. NBC was forced to sell one of its two powerful networks. It chose to get rid of the Blue, which, in itself, was quite a feat. Both NBC networks had used the same studio facilities in their major production centers, especially New York's Radio City. Dividing up the hardware, studios and staff was no mean task.

A New Competitor

Edward J. Noble, who had made a fortune manufacturing Life Saver candies, bought the Blue network for $8 million give or take a bit. The deal was consummated in 1943, but the vivisection of NBC was difficult and painful, particularly with a war going on. By 1945, however, Noble had changed the name of the one-time RCA property to the American Broadcasting Company, and was well on its way to moving the new network out of Radio City and into quarters of its own.

At the time, and for a number of years thereafter, Cassandras predicted that Noble's ABC could not make a go of it considering the competition from

NBC and CBS. But they were wrong. America ended the war with four national radio networks, NBC, CBS, MBS, and ABC, each providing essentially the same type of service, but each also organized, capitalized and run quite differently. NBC and CBS still led the industry. MBS was large, but its affiliations were loose. ABC was suffering the first of its many identity crises. Smaller networks also dotted the country, operating in various regions. But they could not compete with the giants. Some large network stations were also affiliates of the smaller webs, and they came and went. Some of the other networks, like Westinghouse, purposely avoided operating outlets in highly competitive areas. The Don Lee Network, the Rural Radio Network and others shared programs in haphazard ways, but they went out of their way not to tackle the big competitive markets.

Hollywood Monopolies

That the same sort of governmental forces directing themselves against monopolies of big businesses like radio networks should also be aimed at about the same time at the motion picture industry is not a coincidence. No federal agency, of course, controlled or licensed the movies the way that the FCC did for broadcasting. Government watch-dogs (and the people at large) could not, however, help but notice that the monopolistic growth of the American film industry was amazingly similar to what was going on in RCA's Radio City and CBS' headquarters slightly uptown on Madison Avenue.

That the films seemed to be unmistakably in the grip of a monopoly of *some* sort despite their well-publicized financial failures during the depression seemed to many odder still. How could an industry just recovering from receivership, as the movies were apparently able to do, pay some of its executives and stars the largest salaries in the country? How did they keep nearly all foreign competition at bay? How were they able to fill the nation's theatres with *four* new Hollywood products each week and to convince upwards of 50 or 60 million Americans to see at least one double feature every seven days? This miracle was also wrought, at the time, by an industry in which supposedly competing studios clearly sustained cozy relationships, one with the other, and the tentacles of which obviously but mysteriously ran into the film distribution and exhibition business. Certain theatres played films produced by certain studios and no others. Why? It was all puzzling.

In 1938, the Department of Justice decided to take a long hard look at film making in America. They finally saw what many people had known for many years.

Within a short time, the government discovered that the film companies were enmeshed in monopoly structures that made the hold of the big broadcasters on their affiliated stations look like child's play. What was going on was fairly obvious. The Hollywood "Big Five" motion picture companies—MGM, Warner Brothers, 20th Century-Fox, Paramount and Universal—had a near stranglehold upon the American film industry. This was *not* because they had cornered the market in production (although they used their power frequently to control the use of major talents in Hollywood), but because they had an effective life or death grip, by means of allied companies, upon both the distribution and exhibition of films in the U.S.A. That is, the major producers owned *both* the companies that booked their own and other studios' films *and* many, or most, of the theatres in which they played. One part of their individual organizations, therefore, might lose money while other parts more than made up the losses. Through the largesse of the ''Big Five,'' also, the so-called ''Little Three'' companies—Columbia, RKO, and United Artists—were held contractually to doing business exclusively with ''Big Five'' distributors and exhibitors in localities where one of the ''Little Three'' did not own its own facilities or services.

Independent studios, of course, like Selznick, Monogram, Republic, Disney and others might be permitted to produce their own movies. But if they wanted to release them in America (and some overseas theatres), they usually had to do business with the ''Big Five.'' Independent theatre owners might also make a reasonable living, but only by signing exclusive exhibition contracts with one of the major distributors. The price, as we have seen, was that the independent owner had to submit to the tyrannies of ''block booking'' (accepting a lot of unwanted movies in order to exhibit a winner), ''blind buying'' (taking movies for exhibition sight unseen), and ''designated play dates'' (accepting a movie *after* a competing studio-owned theatre had syphoned off its first- and often second-run audiences.)

In effect, these practices and the power of the big studios assured a lucrative market for Hollywood films from cooperating studios, excluded foreign movies from the U.S.A., and brought into all of the nation's theatres everything Hollywood made—good, bad or indifferent—in enormous quantities.

The film audience did not seem to care much. Movies were exploited vigorously, and moviegoing was a habit of millions of Americans, regardless of the quality or nature of the product. Hollywood producers could therefore be assured of a market they controlled entirely, and that, no matter how foul their films, all would all be shown in theatres and a large number of addicted people would pay cash to see them. Filmgoers were satisfied—in the sense that a dog who does not eat meat is satisfied, even though he has never tasted and is never fed meat!

The Department of Justice was not. By 1940, action had been taken to request the ''Big Five'' to stop purchasing new theatres. Under court order, they agreed. But the Justice Department did not possess the same kind of licensing power over the motion picture that the FCC maintained over radio station owners. Twelve years were to pass before the government could accomplish, by means of court actions, consent decrees and mountains of litigation, the virtual dismemberment of this complex monopolistic structure. Only with the force of a Supreme Court case, known best as the ''Paramount Decision'' in 1951, did the whole structure finally crumble. Starting in 1949, dogged government actions caused parts of the empire to fall away. By 1953, MGM, the largest and most powerful studio, distributor-exhibitor of them all, was split into different production, distribution and exhibition companies.

What the Hollywood studios had accomplished in their Byzantine way over-the years was to weave a series of strange vertical and horizontal monopolies. The various film companies had, in effect, conspired, one with the other but in different degrees, to maintain the film capital's control over movies in America. This was horizontal monopoly. The feeder operations that moved films to studio-owned distribution organizations and theatres were vertical ones. Both types of monopoly squeezed out independent producers who were un-cooperative, distributors who wished to handle and select diverse films from different studios, and exhibitors who did not want to live at the mercy of dis-tributors who forced their full line of products upon them.

Not until after the war could the federal government really face up to the powerful legal forces and lobbies of the movie people. But once they began, the system was doomed, obstructed to the last minute by a Supreme Court case that, more or less, eventually confirmed what had been obvious for many years: in the wake of their rapid growth, modern mass media tend to stimulate modern mass monopolies.

The eventual results of the disintegration of the film industry will be dis-cussed in Chapter 13. They were neither as devasting as many gurus of Holly-wood had feared, nor as devasting to the rich and powerful cinema magnates of California (and New York) as many—including the United States Attorney General—had hoped for many reasons, all of them unpredictable at the time.

Hollywood at War

The movies themselves "went to war"—from the comfortable balcony seat of Hollywood, California. War fever was in the air, and one might even have sniffed it as early as 1939 in the dialogue of David O. Selzick's all-time monument to cinematic grand scale soap opera, *Gone With The Wind,* (credited on the screen to playwright Sidney Howard but probably written—or dictated to a secretary—by an all-purpose handyman of popular culture, ex-newsman Ben Hecht.) Inane dialogue about why men fight, the mystique of the land and its spell upon mankind and the evils of fascist-like tyranny creeps in and out of this endless Technicolor epic. More directly, the Warner Brothers, who ran proba-bly the most actively war-oriented studio on the coast, produced an execrable anti-Nazi film the same year, *Confessions of a Nazi Spy.* War themes, one way or another, not only ran, but virtually galloped, through almost half of the mov-ies Hollywood produced. The motives for making these movies, however, was less patriotic than the simple fact that the war, in its various aspects, provided plenty of exciting material for the kind of action adventure stories, love stories and even comedies that movie audiences appeared to adore.

Were I to cite and annotate the major war movies that emerged from the Pacific coast from 1940 to 1945, this book would be filled with nothing but the list from here to the end. Some of them turn up today on television. Let me assure you that almost *none* of them, with the possible exception of Clarence Brown's *A Walk in the Sun* (1945), in any realistic manner reflected what the war was like from the viewpoint of the men and women who were really involved in it.

On the other hand, these movies constituted a *smorgasbord* of oddities, from outright propaganda to moving melodramas. Even such subtle social statements as Samuel Goldwyn's over-praised *The Best Years of Our Lives* (1946) were enormously successful. This movie concerned the experiences of three combat veterans returning home after the end of hostilities and drew a reasonably honest picture of how the war had upset the personal lives of many Americans. Particularly notable was the moving performance of Harold Russell, in his one film performance, as a veteran who had lost both of his hands in the service. Russell himself had been the victim of just this mutilation as an American paratroop sergeant, and the realism of his screen presence may have coldly exploited his misfortune, but it also provided a highly moving and realistic dramatization of the fruits of victory to certain victors.

The range of better movies of the period runs from Charles Chaplin's ill-timed spoof of Hitler and Mussolini, *The Great Dictator* (1940), in which the great comedian finally played a *speaking* part, to Warner Brothers' weeper, the famous *Casablanca* (1943), in which Humphrey Bogart relinquishes his true love, Ingrid Bergman to the war effort, and heads out to the battlefield with one-time traitor Claude Rains. From Warners also came the peculiarly embarrassing *Mission to Moscow* (1943), a panegyric to our Soviet allies, in which a Russian workman explains to American Ambassador Walter Huston that there really is no difference between the American and Soviet economic systems—with a straight face!

Some moviemakers, at least, tried harder than others: Dudley Nichols' screen play and Charles Laughton's performance in a film about the French resistance, *This Land is Mine* (1943), was a superb job simply as a sentimental, professionally made adventure story. MGM's highly touted *Mrs. Miniver* (1942) constituted an absurd, stiff-upper-lip salute to the bravery of our British allies that certain cynics hoped, at the time, would not cause England to declare war upon Hollywood. Old chestnuts like *Waterloo Bridge* (1940), an early play by Robert E. Sherwood, then a 1930 film, concerning a Canadian soldier who falls in love with an English prostitute, was updated by means of flashbacks. It was not bad. (*Waterloo Bridge* is indestructible. It was remade once again in 1955 under the title *Gaby,* and is probably being shot again somewhere right now!)

Every movie hero went to war—on the screen. The names of the films they were in are irrelevant, but Errol Flynn, Paul Muni, Gary Cooper, Dana Andrews, Robert Mitchum—even Abbott and Costello, Sherlock Holmes (Basil Rathbone) and Orson Welles—found themselves in war films of one type or another. Women—stars and starlets—waited at home for their loved ones or, one way or another, got themselves involved in hostilities.

Of the home-front movies with war themes, made before V-J day, only one remains kindly in my memory. It is William Saroyan's *The Human Comedy* (1943), made, oddly enough, by MGM and featuring Frank Morgan and Mickey Rooney. It is a simple story of an aged telegraph agent who is forced to send his messenger boy to deliver to his own home a telegram announcing that the boy's older brother has been killed in action. Here was a remarkable little film, made, I imagine, by accident. It did, as I remember, poor business at the nation's box offices. No action, no sex, no excitment!

Films From Overseas

Two of the most interesting movies that emerged from World War II did not come out of Hollywood and had, in story and theme, nothing to do with World War II. One was a French film, made with French peversity as an answer to Hollywood's *Gone With The Wind* at a time when Paris was occupied by the Nazis. The actors and crew literally had to scrounge for food, and the last project you would imagine a film maker would want to attempt under these circumstances would be a nineteenth-century costume epic about theatrical life in Paris in the 1830s. Filmed in black-and-white and released in 1945, the movie was *Les Enfants Du Paradis* (*The Children of Paradise*), directed by Marcel Carne and starring the superb French performers Arletty, Jean-Louis Barrault and Pierre Brasseur. It was a wildly theatrical, beautifully produced romantic drama that could not help but receive world-wide acclaim upon its release after the war, even in the United States where, as we have seen, distribution of foreign films was all but impossible. In a way, it said more about the indomitable spirit of the French during wartime than dozens of Hollywood's action epics did. Whatever else its half-fed, politically harassed and defeated cast of actors and crew were saying in the film, they were also sending the world a remarkable message of hope.

Britain produced many war films, some of them quite good. Documentaries like *Target for Tonight* (1941), concerning the Royal Air Force, were tough and exciting, produced with skill by the Crown Film Unit under government supervision. Noel Coward, usually remembered for his light entertainments, wrote, produced and directed a brilliant studio-made drama, *In Which We Serve* (1942), about the British Navy. It centered upon a captain of an English destroyer that is torpedoed at sea. Coward played the leading role with fine realism and restraint.

The most remarkable British film of the war years, however, was another historical drama, made in an environment slightly less oppressive than German-occupied Paris. Shot in color and directed by its star performer, Laurence Olivier's movie version of Shakespeare's *Henry V*, released in 1944, in no way reveals that it was produced in the middle of a devastating war. In my opinion, it is the single most imaginative translation to celluloid of any of the Bard's plays produced in the English language. Olivier's production is a visual, musical and poetic treat, a bit heavy on the glory of fighting for England, naturally, but a film, nevertheless, of epic scope and theatrical integrity. One wonders how Olivier coped with the difficulty of finding male actors not in service, wartime shortages, air raids and other distractions. Like *Les Enfants Du Paradis, Henry V* was a message to the world that England's indomitable spirit had not been diminished by five years of devastating warfare.

Stars in Uniform

In the U.S.A., Hollywood's public relations experts made much of the fact that numerous film actors were drafted or enlisted in the armed services. Clark Gable's tenure in the Air Force was marred by the constant attention he received from both military and private publicity personnel. Not being able to use him for much else, the Army assigned him to make a film in England, a project that was finally aborted. James Stewart fared better as an Air Force officer. The talents of men like Melvyn Douglas were wisely turned to what they knew best: providing entertainment, live or by radio, for the troops. Actor Lee J. Cobb spent most of his service career performing in a play, Moss Hart's *Winged Victory*.

Other film performers were utilized for recruiting purposes and to sell war bonds. Comedian Bob Hope maintained his civilian status, although he began his many years of performing for troops overseas at this time. Others who went overseas included Marlene Dietrich, Al Jolson and Bing Crosby. The latter was known by servicemen as "Der Bingle."

Military Journals and Journalists

As far as the press is concerned, special service-oriented newspapers emerged almost immediately after Pearl Harbor. In April, 1942, the old World War I newspaper, *Stars and Stripes,* was revived. An edition was produced at various locations in Europe, and a Pacific edition was also printed that was eventually established in Tokyo after the final victory. Another service publication, *Yank,* was edited largely in New York. Both journals utilized the talents of newspapermen who had been drafted into the service, and certain civilians (like cartoonist Milton Caniff), who also contributed their talents. Millions of Americans still remember Caniff's female heroine, Lace, in his strip *Male Call,* Sergeant George Baker's *Sad Sack,* and Sergeant Leonard Sansone's G.I. with a wolf's head whose only interest in life was women. Many smaller military papers were also printed, including the Marine Corps' monthly, *Leatherneck.*

The one major talent to emerge from World War II journalism was a youngster named Bill Mauldin who began drawing cartoons in the *45th Division News,* one of the smaller service papers. Transferred to *Stars and Stripes.* Mauldin became a battlefront artist, following combat troops in Europe by jeep

and drawing single panel cartoons, often under combat conditions. These drawings he called "Up Front." His central characters were two tired, ragged "dogfaces" or foot-soldiers, enlisted men named Willie and Joe who epitomized the
fatigue, cynicism, boredom and filth of battle in their personal unheroic war
against both the Germans and their own officers. Willie and Joe did not appear
in all Mauldin's cartoons, however. Some centered upon stuffed-shirt officers,
like the two who, admiring a pretty sunrise, wondered if there was one for
enlisted men, or ridiculed others—a cavalry officer about to shoot his broken-
down jeep as he would a horse.

Mauldin's cartooning genius reached its heights during the war. He continues his career to this day, one marked by consistently superior work recognized by numerous awards. Willie and Joe, however, disappeared with the war,
as, of course, they had to, and were revived only as figures in memory. Since
they stood for everything that soldiers have to endure in battle, I fantasize that
Mauldin's two fictional, pen-and-ink dogfaces were killed in action, neither
more or less heroically than my other friends who lost their lives in the insanity
of warfare.

One cannot talk about World War II journalists without also mentioning
Ernie Pyle, the Scripps-Howard syndicated columnist, who began, in 1942,
sending home dispatches from overseas describing the war as he thought it appeared to the men who fought it. From North Africa through Europe, Pyle's
dispatches centered upon the personal lives of our fighting men—little stories,
not heroic reports. The result was, at first, a large readership, followed by nationwide fame and, in 1944, a Pulitzer Prize. His work was warm, emotional,
authentic and intensely human. When the war in Europe ended, Pyle went to
the Pacific theatre where he was killed by a Japanese sniper in April of 1945. A
movie was made about his adventures. But the impact of his work can best be
summed up by noting that his death was as much a blow to the soldiers and
sailors about whom he wrote as to the American public for which he was writing.

Pyle was the outstanding print journalist of the war, but others, in their
own way, are also notable—for many reasons. Writer Ernest Hemingway
managed to serve a stint as an overseas correspondent—and a good one—until
an automobile accident in blacked-out London incapacitated him. Frank Mott
gives an historian's salute to Henry T. Gorrell of the U.S. for his personal
heroism during an air attack on Greece, and his "scoop" in sending to the U.S.
the first dispatch from France after the D-Day invasion; to Vern Haughland of
the AP, stranded, after bailing out of a plane over New Guinea, in the jungle;
to Leland Stowe's remarkable dispatches to the *Chicago Daily News* while he
lived on the U.S.S.R.s front lines after the German invasion; to Quentin
Reynolds' articles and overseas reports for *Collier's* and numerous others.

Richard Tregaskis, William L. Shirer, W. L. White and others turned their
experiences—and dispatches—into best-selling books. Photographers like Joe
Rosenthal, who took the original still picture of the flag-raising on Mount
Suribachi on Iwo Jima in 1945, found countless opportunities to record the

drama of war on still and newsreel film. This was hazardous journalistic work, because, unlike print reporters, cameramen had to travel into the heart of the action, wherever it was. Much of the best of it was accomplished by anonymous Signal Corps servicemen. But *Life* magazine's photographers, including Margaret Bourke-White, also produced some remarkable photographs that would have received enthusiastic approval from Matthew Brady.

Journalists at War

All in all, 1,646 people were accredited as news correspondents by the Army and Navy during World War II, representing all of the media—press, radio and films. In addition to the news services, 12 magazines and 30 newspapers sent their own exclusive correspondents into the fray. History had never before seen such an inundation of journalists into any war. If we add the thousands of "public information" officers and enlisted men whose service jobs were largely journalistic, it almost seems that one of the major activities of World War II was, for the first time in history, linking the various combat areas with the world's networks of mass communication. On an international basis, this task was, of course, monumental.

Notable goofs also occurred, naturally. Edward Kennedy of the Associated Press broke the story of the signing of the European surrender of the German army at General Eisenhower's headquarters on May 7, 1945, in spite of an official pledge Kennedy had taken not to release the story until given official permission by Eisenhower's Supreme Headquarters. As it turned out, this release was to be delayed two days at the request of Josef Stalin who wanted time for all the allied leaders to disclose it to their countrymen before the newsmen filed their stories.

Having heard that the German radio had already broken the news, Kennedy filed his dispatch, an "exclusive" of course, from Paris to the London AP office by telephone one day early. Only one-fifth of his report got through, but it was enough to travel immediately to the AP wires and then to American newspapers and radio stations. Kennedy was now responsible for one of the great "scoops" of the century, but he had also seriously violated journalistic ethics. He found himself disgraced, and most other journalists were irate at his behavior. A Senate investigation later exonerated him. To the end, Kennedy kept maintaining that he was in the right and would do it again, although his career as a journalist was, for all practical purposes, ruined. He ended up as managing editor of a minor California newspaper.

World War II had its "false armistice" too, a little less dramatic than Roy Howard's blunder in World War I, but an event that embarrassed the United Press once again, nevertheless. Somehow or other, on August 12, 1945, two days before the Japanese forces capitulated, a "flash" appeared on the UP wire that President Truman had just announced that Japan had accepted the Allies' surrender terms. Unlike the World War I goof, the origins of the release remain obscure to this day, and the whole thing was probably a practical (or malicious) joke. The UP offered a sizeable reward for the identification of the culprit, but he or she was never found. Fortunately, the news did not get into any newspapers, because it was sent only as a "flash" (or alert) that a news story was soon on its way. The story, of course, never followed. A number of radio stations, however, primed for news of V-J day, did jump the gun and announced the end of the war. Little harm was done, but the UP smarted severely because of memories of its "false armistice" during World War I.

Mott summarizes the casualties suffered among newsmen during the war. They were light, considering the number of American correspondents in the field: 37 were killed and 112 wounded. He notes, however, that the rate is about four times that of the military forces, but, as anyone who has served in a modern war knows, most military personnel are stationed in positions that back up fighting forces rather than participate directly in combat. Newsmen and women were primarily interested, and therefore engaged, in the hostilities themselves. War reporting was, and remains, a hazardous form of journalism, regardless of the medium for which a reporter is working. This, I imagine, for various perverse reasons, is exactly why it is so attractive to good writers, photographers, cameramen and broadcasters. War is hell, but it is also exciting. This may be one of the reasons the human race has spent so much of its time, energy and resources on it.

World War II and the Media

World War II was the first "mass communications" war, in that much self-consciousness and a sense of "history-in-the-making" impelled the military forces of all the belligerent nations, and most especially those of the U.S.A., to go to great pains to record for posterity as much of it as accurately as possible. Between World War I and World War II, all of the countries involved had indeed become oriented to, and aware of, the need for public relations and propaganda in the modern world to interpret the hostilities, not only for a civilian public at home, but for posterity as well. In the 1960s, the new medium of television was to intrude into the Vietnam war, creating still another dimension of electronic, mass-media coverage of hostilities: the near immediate transposition of combat to millions of home television screens in a matter of hours after the events themselves had occurred.

In spite of the censorship imposed during World War II, no nation in history was quite as up to date on the progress of any war as the American public during World War II, and this included much bad as well as good news. In Germany, particularly, tight censorship prevailed in spite of the Nazi's coverage—comparable to that of the allies—of all hostilities. The people were told little except good news. But, after a time, Hitler's lies began to catch up with him. Defeated soldiers returned to the Reich from the East Front in Russia. The people expected to hear stories of the great victories about which they had read in newspapers and heard on the radio. Instead, they were told the truth concerning the ravages of the Russian winter, the uselessness of German tanks on Russian terrain, the battles of Stalingrad and Leningrad, and the hordes of German dead and wounded left on Russian soil.

The credibility, therefore, of the German news services, newspapers and radio broadcasters was injured. Upon the threat of death, many Germans and others therefore risked their lives to listen to the short-wave broadcasts (in German) from the BBC and the *Voice of America* to hear the truth.

The military lesson of Germany's experience was simple. Mass communications and public relations may indeed function as important instruments of persuasion and propaganda on the home front, but only as long as they deal in truths and do not try to deceive the civilian population, at least in important matters. Words, news stories and films (and, today, television) are critical to the conduct of modern warfare, particularly the kind of "total" war that World War II was in Europe. Words and pictures, however, are not substitutes for military victories, and, in effect, actions speak more loudly than words. Mass communications may *support* a victorious army and navy, cheer and/or raise morale at times of temporary setbacks. But they may also backfire, if the messages they deliver are not verified by the course of events.

Certain wars—and phases of wars—have been accused of being "phony" or mere "propaganda wars." The charge is often true, but only up to a point. In the end, words must eventually give way to military action. Psychological warfare is a reality, but it is a limited and specialized type of weaponry. No war in history of which I know, including the ambiguous Vietnam engagement, was been won or lost on psychological grounds, or because it was popular or unpopular with a civilian population, or because its information officers did not do their jobs properly, or because of the kind of the press coverage it received.

Our *military* forces won World War II for us. I mean the generals, officers and soldiers of all the allied forces. In Korea, in the 1950s we fought to a stalemate, because the military forces of the United Nations were strategically hampered in the scope of their operations—the reason also that an obstinate General MacArthur was relieved of his command by President Truman. (Generals want to fight with all of the power at their command; and who can blame them?) The U.S.A. was almost totally unprepared for the kind of guerrilla-civilian hostility into which it charged in Vietnam. The political and ideological demoralization *followed* the fact that we had barged into a tactical situation that we were simply unable to handle.

World War II was a remarkable event, however, hurling the human race to some of its most heroic moments, and some of its most base, in all of history. Just as the mass media communicated heroism and glory to people all over the world, they also, in their neutrality, told terrible stories of Hitler's extermination camps, the slaughter of prisoners by nearly all of the belligerents, *including* the U.S.A., Germany and the U.S.S.R., and finally the still controversial barbarity of the two atomic explosions over Hiroshima and Nagasaki that ended hostilities in the Pacific.

The latter, I think, were the greatest stories of World War II, events that mankind will remember longer and more clearly than anything else involved in the enormous conflict. On an August day in 1945 the atomic age began in the most horrible way imaginable. Nothing has been quite the same since for the entire population of the earth. On that day we discovered that men now had it within their power to destroy their own race, and many and ubiquitous instruments of mass communication around the globe spread the news to every corner of the earth and have reminded us of it continually ever since. In this manner, possibly, they have served us quite well, because the news stories of August, 1945, have, I think, diminished somewhat the blood-thirsty aspirations of many who have since had cause to consider tactically the awful consequences of total war as it has been re-defined since August of 1945.

12

Novelty and Normalcy

THE EVENTS OF THE YEAR 1945 are written in fire in the memories of nearly everybody old enough to remember them. Roosevelt's death . . . Hitler's suicide . . . victory in Europe . . . the atom bomb . . . V-J Day . . . parades, celebrations, elation!

What most of us remember, however, is but a reflection of an environment, not the environment itself. To the soldier in Europe, the end of the continental war arrived in a clutter of confusion and rumors. To an American at home, V-J Day meant getting drunk at a roadhouse or in Times Square or at home. What *is* real is the *memory* of the media: the instruments of mass communication that transmitted the news to the public—newsreels documentary films, radio broadcasts and newspaper headlines.

News of Victory

Today, the newspapers seem to me to capture the frenzy of the past best: the incredible drama of history as its shock waves reverberated into the personal life of millions. Some of us recall that year as a great time, a wonderful time. Others look back at their own naiveté, at remembered emotions of tragedy, irony and loss. The wisest of us somehow knew, on that August day of 1945 when World War II ended, that nothing in our lives would ever be the same again and that our country—and other nations—had been effected in ways that we could not understand, but were changed indeed inevitably and permanently.

I have just listened to a tape recording of announcer Robert Trout at CBS' New York radio studio receiving the news of the end of the war: his confusion and elation as the news staff begins to celebrate victory as if it were New Year's Eve. Trout, rarely at a loss for words, is nearly speechless as he gropes for something to say that will sound neither trite nor banal.

CBS had previously treated the victory in Europe with pompous dignity months before, as we have noted, by broadcasting (and re-broadcasting) Norman Corwin's overblown prose-poem in dramatic form called *On A Note of Triumph*. *Triumph* sounds today either funny or sad, as you wish: the phony baritone narration of Martin Gabel and the smug, self-satisfied attitude of the free verse, the music, the voices and the entire approach, a self-conscious attempt to treat the event with intelligent dignity—and failing. Trout's spontaneous elation and confusion is more authentic and therefore more moving. In a way, he spoke for all of us. Where do we go now? What will *really* happen to us now that victory is won?

In the world of mass communications, war did not end with a clash of cymbals, simply because World War II itself did not so much end as unwind. Young people, for instance, are often amazed when told that the War Emergency, declared by President Roosevelt after Pearl Harbor, has not *yet* ended, 35 years after the fact. Nazi war criminals still linger in jail in Germany and points east. And, in much of the world, vivid scars of World War II are still visible, national antagonisms are still burning, and, in some ways the war goes on. Old hostilities die slowly, if ever.

Americans thought the war's end meant a return to normalcy. It did not, possibly because nobody knew what normalcy was. The great depression had ended, artificially subsumed into a war-time economy in which money was plentiful but consumer goods and services were not. True, it took a while for the local butcher to learn *not* to say, "Don't you know there's a war on, buddy?" when you complained about services or prices. Conversion of our industrial machine to peace-time pursuits took a couple of years, and, in the meantime, the U.S.A. lived in large measure on faith and hope.

Slowly but surely, many of the old threads of national life were once again picked up. Technologically, the war, however, had stimulated lasting changes in a number of areas: transportation industries almost immediately began making use of radar and sonar. The wire recorder, stolen from German inventors, appeared on the market, followed by sound tape recording. Antihistamines invaded our pharmacies, much to the relief of hay-fever sufferers; miracle drugs followed by developing their side effects into families of mood changing (or psychoactive) drugs. Jet aircraft made a rapid transition from military usage to commerical transportation. But, much to the disappointment of the American public, new post-war automobiles remained almost carbon copies of pre-war models. In fact, in fundamental design, the American automobile remains to this day much the same as it was in the 1930s; some say the 1920s.

Long-Playing Recordings

CBS Labs perfected the microgroove, 33 1/3 r.p.m. disc recording in 1948, and the next year, much to the puzzlement of the public, RCA announced that it would henceforth produce records to be played at 45 r.p.m. Slow-playing phonograph records were an old story to radio broadcasters, but such "electrical transcriptions," as they were known in the 'thirties, were enormous in size, cumbersome and heavy. Engineers at both CBS and RCA had found ways of utilizing small, etched grooves, pressed close to one another, so that, in CBS' case, long-playing recordings were no larger than old three-minute ten-inch 78 r.p.m. versions of decades past. RCA's little records were smaller, automatically changed on special players more frequently, but their technology was much the same. Plastic was substituted for the old shellac discs. Records were still breakable but sturdier than they had been; fidelity was better and prices per minute of playing time no higher.

The problem that faced the consumer was an interesting one: two types of turntables and pickup arms were required to use both systems. With tape recording nudging the record business from the rear, a compatible way of handling the problem was eventually evolved. But, in the late 'forties, the phonograph industry looked like a total mess, not because either its technology or sound output was poor, but rather because it was equally as good at two different playback speeds: CBS' and RCA's.

Major Armstrong and FM

Frequency modulation (or FM) radio was also a post-war technological phenomenon, the history of which was over-dramatized almost from the moment that its feasibility was shown publicly in 1946 to the present day. Called "radio's second chance" by some enthusiasts in the middle 'forties, modulation of the *speed* of radio waves rather than their *size* was, in fact, a technological development that dated back to the early days of the century.

Part of this pseudo-drama centered on the personality of Edwin H. Armstrong. Armstrong was a young inventor when, in 1922, he sold a new type of radio circuit receiver he had invented to RCA and suddenly found himself rich. Wealth and talent often breed eccentricity, and Armstrong was then both eccentric and talented. At Columbia University, he began work on a static-free radio transmission system based upon the idea of frequency modulation. By 1933, the invention was ready for testing. Demonstrations were subsequently given, and numerous contemporary accounts report these broadcasts as being nothing less than the eighth wonder of the world. I doubt it.

Armstrong believed that RCA would now develop and market his invention. He was wrong, however. David Sarnoff and company were indeed developing an interest in modulating frequencies, but only in order to develop further the still crude British invention of television. RCA and most other broadcasters, as well as the FCC, seemed to be content to leave the broadcast radio wave spectrum where it was: on amplitude modulation and short wave bands.

In short order, the cause of FM broadcasting turned into an obsession for Armstrong. In 1939, he opened a New Jersey station WQXMN. A number of electronic firms showed considerable interest in the system. General Electric, Zenith, Western Electric and other companies planned to build special FM receivers, but the war interfered. Armstrong turned his invention over to the military forces, and it was used by them for a number of purposes.

By 1945, both FM's strengths and weaknesses seemed quite clear. On the plus side, the fidelity of FM was nearly unbelievable when compared to AM, *if* proper allied equipment was utilized in reception. Second, FM was virtually static free. Its limitations were two. First, an FM signal, in general, could not travel farther than the horizon, because it was propagated horizontally and moved in a straight line. FM's range was thus limited to about 50 miles. AM signals followed the curvature of the earth and, with sufficient power, might travel many hundreds or even thousands of miles. Second, FM signals showed a tendency to "slip" or "slide" from their assigned spot on the radio spectrum, requiring frequent retuning of receivers.

Assigned a specific place on the radio spectrum in 1940, Armstrong charged ahead nevertheless, and, by 1942, 30 FM stations were on the air—with virtually nobody listening to them. Special radio receivers were required to pick up their signals. With peacetime, the FCC permitted existing radio broadcasting outlets to acquire an FM frequency for broadcast purposes and simply to duplicate their AM service on FM.

The advantage of Armstrong's invention at this point, therefore, boiled down to the fact that it was static-free, not much of an incentive to purchase a special receiver or one capable of receiving both AM and FM broadcasts. In many ways, RCA had been pretty high-handed with Armstrong (including the cavalier theft of the method of FM sound transmission for its television broadcasts), and, in 1948, Armstrong instituted suit against Sarnoff's company for his share of profits from his invention. The lawsuit dragged on for years, unsettling (and unbalancing) the now obsessed Armstrong apparently beyond the point of sanity and bleeding him dry financially. On the verge of a million dollar settlement with RCA, but unaware that it would be soon consummated, Armstrong, in despair, committed suicide in 1954.

Armstrong was not much encouraged by the actual fate of FM broadcasting in the post war years. Most FM licenses were held by AM broadcasters as a form of insurance, *in case* anything happened to their rights to AM transmission. By 1950, the few stations that attempted to broadcast on the FM band alone were, for the most part, out of business. A paucity of receivers among the public was the reason, as well as the odd fact that FM fidelity was actually *too good* for most speakers and amplifiers then used in inexpensive receiving sets. Whether a program was broadcast on AM or FM, therefore, made little difference to one listening in his home or automobile.

It was only with the advents of the high fidelity fad of the 1960s that FM finally came into its own, followed by an FCC ruling in 1965 that AM stations owning FM outlets in medium to large cities had now to program each service separately. FM also became the natural conduit for transmission of stereophonic sound by radio, by, in effect, breaking one electronic signal into two discrete components. By this time, however, the public was willing to invest in necessary FM and stereophonic equipment sophisticated enough to receive clearly and properly transmissions broadcast in stereophonic, high fidelity sound.

The Technology of Television

That Sarnoff and company were not too interested in FM radio broadcasting during the middle 'thirties seems perfectly natural and sensible. Conventional AM served its purpose nicely for domestic broadcasts in the U.S.A. Ships, police, fire departments and long distance transmissions were assigned to short waves. Something more exciting—and entirely feasible—was visible on the far horizon for RCA. Sarnoff was quite right in sacrificing the development of static-free high fidelity radio for the development of television, sensing that he was in a race with others to perfect this new pictorial medium of communication, and that, if RCA could turn the trick, it would gain the jump upon other equipment manufacturers in the United States and elsewhere. As a matter of fact, RCA's main competitors in the development of video were not, in these early years, Americans at all but rather the British, as noted above.

The idea of transmitting pictures electronically goes back to the nineteenth century. A Bostonian named George Carey, in 1875, figured out a way to break up the elements of a still picture into electrical signals and subsequently to reconstitute them. Within ten years, after some other early experiments in the USA and France, Paul Nipkow patented a device in Germany that was remarkably sophisticated for its time and remained at the heart of all television experimentation from 1874 until RCA entered the scene in 1930. A method of so-called "image scanning" was invented by Nipkow that depended upon a rotating disc. This device broke an image up into electrical components at one end of an apparatus, and another disc reconstituted them on the receiving end. Mechanical scanning procedures were thereafter understood as the *only* way to change light images into electrical waves for many years, the notion of the rotating disc having been borrowed from then burgeoning experiments in rapid photography—which themselves led to the development both of the motion picture camera and projector.

Rotating discs with small holes punched in them were, incidentally, not bad ways of breaking a picture up into small light and dark elements—18 lines in Nipkow's case. Nor was the resultant information too difficult to code electrically and send by wire. (The wireless, of course, had not been invented at the time.) A photoelectric cell, made of selenium, was necessary to change light into current and vice-versa. The problems presented by this method of crude video transmission centered on the necessity to synchronize the two rotating discs most precisely, although they traveled at very high speeds and upon the fidelity and sensitivity of the selenium "electric eye."

Nipkow proved that it was indeed possible to transmit pictures (small pictures, crude pictures) by electric wire. A German, K. F. Braun, then invented a "cathode ray" screen, a fluorescent surface that glowed when it was activated by an electric current. Further experiments during the next 19 years were to produce a glowing glass tube that showed great photoelectric sensitivity to different amounts of electric charges. In the meantime, Boris Rosing, working in Russia in 1907, figured out a way to use such a screen as Braun's with a mirror system to transmit crude shapes by electricity. In England and the U.S.A., J. A. Fleming's and Lee de Forest's work on modulation and amplification also opened up new possibilities in the development of video technology.

J. L. Baird and the BBC

Over the next two decades, a number of electrical engineers in Scotland, England and the United States constructed instruments and drew up plans for instruments which clearly indicated that *radio* transmission might be employed for sending images from point to point without wires. Most notable was the workable (but unsuccessful) system of Charles Jenkins in the U.S.A. who, between 1925 and 1930, actually built and began a company to start television transmission that soon unfortunately failed.

It was J. L. Baird in Great Britain, however, who, in 1926, presented a demonstration of motion pictures transmitted in this manner that could truly be called "television," as we use the term today. Baird's images were shaky and uncertain, made up of 30 horizontal lines on a fluorescent screen that changed ten times a second to produce an image that looked like early flickering movies on a tiny, dim screen.

Baird's demonstration was convincing enough for the British to begin perfecting Baird's system under the direction of Sir Isaac Shoenberg. After an experimental period that began in 1929, the British Broadcasting Corporation inaugurated the world's first open circuit television system in 1936. By this time, English video employed 405 lines in such a way that 25 full pictures per second were transmitted, well beyond the number necessary to create a smooth looking image above the nervous system's "persistence of vision" limit. The one weakness of the BBC's working system, however, was its necessity to employ mechanical scansion, that is, the old synchronous rotating wheels that were at the heart of Nipkow's original method and remained quite unreliable at high speeds.

Vladimir Zworykin and RCA

Enter RCA in the United States. Vladimir K. Zworykin had patented a tube he called the "iconoscope" back in 1923 that, in theory, did away with the mechanical scansion system and substituted an ingenious electronic method for accomplishing this purpose in both camera and receiving set. It took Zworykin a number of years to develop his idea into a practical model. In 1930, RCA gathered a group of some 40 engineers to work under Zworykin's direction in Camden, New Jersey on electronic television in order, RCA hoped, to beat the British. With General Electric and Westinghouse cooperating in the project, the iconoscope tube was perfected by 1932. For the next seven years, RCA experimented with the new video medium, setting up a demonstration broadcasting system in New York City in the late 'thirties.

The record tells us that regular television service by RCA began when its experimental television station, WQXBS, intruded its electronic nose into the opening of the New York World's Fair on the afternoon of April 30, 1939 at Flushing Meadows Park in Queens, New York, about half a mile from where I am writing today.

A Personal Note

While television has obviously made much progress since that historic afternoon, I have not. I was among the crowd of eager spectators, one of many 'teenagers at the event, straining to watch Sarnoff, President Roosevelt, Grover Whelan and other dignitaries take their place before the now familiar iconoscope cameras, rushing into the RCA exhibit both to see how they looked on the tiny 10-inch (I think) screens, then back again to the locus of the live action. I wish that I could say that I had a feeling that I was watching history being made, but I cannot. The World's Fair itself seemed so much grander than this one technological device. My head was in the clouds, mostly because I really believed in the theme of that fair, "Towards Peace and Freedom." Nineteen hundred and thirty-nine was, of course, the year that the cannons of Europe began thundering.

I had earned my skepticism that day, however, because, a few years before, under circumstances I do not recall, I had already witnessed a television transmission in New York City from WQXBS, and I imagine that I was one of the few Americans who did.

Various RCA executives had installed receivers in their homes and, for one reason or another I forget, I found myself as a guest at the Sarnoffs' lavish Park Avenue apartment one afternoon in the middle to late 'thirties, watching a demonstration of experimental video on David Sarnoff's personal receiver. While the circumstances are cloudy, the experience is not.

The set itself was enormous, about the size of two of today's largest hi-fi consoles piled one on top of the other. The screen was about six to ten inches square and located above eye level on a flat surface of what looked to me like an outsized phonograph. Slanted over the top, a hinged cover was open, and a mirror was so placed that it reflected the tube image in order to, first, reverse it (early American video images were inverted when reconstituted by a home receiver) and, second, made visible to a good-sized audience seated in front of it. The program involved a variety show, as I recall, and nothing about that experience smacked of the miraculous either. Movies looked better; radio sounded better. I remember riding home in the subway predicting to myself, with childish confidence, that television was a mere flash in the pan without a future. I was, of course, right—for the next dozen years or so—but for the wrong reasons.

Other Technological Developments

By no means was RCA alone in its development of video in the U.S.A. It was, however, responsible for major developments in the medium, the work of Zworykin, and the considerable publicity—and faith—with which it eventually stimulated interest in the new invention.

Philo Farnsworth had invented components of television systems that would later win for him a patent suit against RCA. Allen B. DuMont had been experimenting with video in association with Lee de Forest and Westinghouse since the early 'thirties. DuMont developed a type of receiving tube that later put him into both the business of building receivers and into broadcasting. Many of DuMont's receivers found their way into the American marketplace before his competitors, but his early television network, delayed by the war, was soon edged out of the market by competition from the former radio networks. Nor was CBS content to let RCA run alone with the video ball, having experimented itself with the new medium over station W2XAB in New York since 1931. Little noticed, CBS was on the air with commercial television programs the same day RCA inaugurated its own service. But its problems in competing with RCA were just beginning, as we shall see.

One major problem was the electronic compatibility of the various systems in use, that is, the need for cross-industry agreement upon the number of lines the television video picture had to be made up of and the number of frames, or discrete pictures, displayed on the receiving tube per second. *Three* systems were first found acceptable as standards by the FCC—one compatible with sets made by RCA, one with DuMont receivers, and one with receivers built by the Philco radio company.

Sarnoff hit the ceiling. In 1940, he began a high pressure sales campaign to sell RCA receivers in areas where experimental telecasting had begun. The FCC (and Congress as well) went back to the drawing board, mindful of the fact that their odd catch-all decision jeopardized the work and research of many competing organizations. RCA had invested the most money in video: $9 million. But the total investment of its competitors was far greater. Each company had a stake in its own system and instrumentation, each of which transmitted a different number of lines and a different number of picture frames per second.

In a way, the FCC solved the problem by satisfying nobody, although they left the door open for NBC's method of electronic synchronization to become eventually the industry's standard. In 1941, black-and-white television was given an assigned place on the Very High Frequency electronic wave spectrum consisting of 18 channels. FM radio transmission (that also traveled at these frequencies) was chosen as the method of audio transmission, as well as a video transmission system of 525 lines at 30 pictures per second. These are, in general, the electronic video standards still in use in the United States.

Many other countries, particularly in Europe, selected a system utilizing 625 lines and 25 pictures. In the U.S.A., as well, quite a bit of programming is today accomplished (particularly by public television stations) at different standards on the Ultra High Frequency electronic band. Each different method of transmission displays certain advantages and disadvantages, the least successful to date being the latter UHF signals, because they seem both unstable and unpredictably weak when compared to slower frequencies, according to many electronic specialists.

The Growth of Video

Barnouw reports that by May 1940, 23 television stations were on the air in the U.S.A., including an outlet in Los Angeles, where the Don Lee Radio Network had been experimenting with the medium for nearly a decade. To those less cynical than I was when young, it looked then as if the television age was about to begin.

The war, however, interrupted this growth with apparent finality. Production of all receivers halted in April of 1942, as the electronics industry turned to military pursuits. Only a half-dozen video outlets continued experimental transmissions during the conflict, nearly all of them entirely subsidized by electronic firms.

At these stations, some in New York City, one in Schenectedy (home of General Electric) programming was desultory: little theatre groups and drama schools provided live entertainment for minuscule audiences. Performers were roasted alive by incandescent floodlights, as feeble iconoscope cameras strained to capture a creditable image. Old movies were repeated again and again.

At war's end, the nation's return to normalcy was, as noted, neither dramatic nor immediate. Electronic equipment remained in short supply for quite a while, and some confusion attended the spectrum allocations given television stations by the FCC before the war as well as new ones issued shortly after it.

The wide UHF band had been explored further during the war. It now seemed possible that *all* video broadcasting might sensibly be moved from VHF broadcast channels to UHF. Many applications for building permits and spectrum allocations were received by the FCC, but the agency was in no hurry. CBS Labs had, by this time, also developed a scheme for color television broadcasting that, it felt, would perform better on UHF than VHF. It was not until 1947, however, that the FCC finally decided to ignore the then unperfected CBS system and, in effect, simply return to its pre-war standards.

New camera tubes known as image-orthicons had also been developed by now. These instruments did not require the intense lighting that the old icono-scopes did, and fluorescent lamps were substituted for many of the old per-former-burning photofloods—but not for all of them. At any rate, television production techniques cooled off enough to make live broadcasting humane and comfortable. By 1948, video was definitely a part of the American landscape.

Early Television Years

The latter year was a critical one for the growth of the new medium. Over 40 stations were now on the air in the U.S.A. serving more than 20 cities. Network broadcasting had begun on a spasmodic basis. When actual relays could not transmit programs live to remote places, methods of photographing video on motion picture film—the well-known *Kinescope* or *Television Record-ing* procedures—were developed to permit delayed transmission. Millions of receivers were sold just as soon as producers of electronic equipment were capable of making them. Most showed little advancement over pre-war models. The old mirror had indeed gone. But the screens were tiny, and some of them were round-looking like portholes on a ship.

Video receivers attracted attention wherever they appeared, because they were among the first post-war "miracles" available to the public. Private sets were by no means cheap: prices started at $300 for the cheapest receiver. For this reason, a television set became, for many, a status symbol. The rich, the up-to-date, the young in heart were the first to embrace television. The sale of antennas, in fact, far outstripped the sale of receivers, because many status-conscious individuals mounted aerials on their roofs, although they had no in-tention of buying television receivers in the near future. Passing neighbors, however, would *think* that they owned one!

Crowds gathered in front of electronic stores to watch the free show where sets were demonstrated. It was like viewing a movie standing in the street. Owners of bars and cocktail lounges installed receivers for their patrons, except the most exclusive, intimate bistros where the customers were more interested in each other (and drinking in darkness) than in entertainment. A sign in the window of a saloon usually announced the presence of a television set. Many who could not afford a receiver at home gathered nightly at a neighborhood bar to look at television. Boxing, wrestling, other sporting events—and a peculiar sadistic contest (reminiscent of the suicidal game in the recent film *Rollerball*) called a "Roller Derby"—were odds-on favorites among the beer drinking crowd. Admission was cheap: the price of a brew—and the penalty one suf-fered from an hour's televiewing was a mere stiff neck from craning one's head to look at the small screen mounted at the end of the bar. (Sitting on a different barstool the next night usually reoriented the pain.)

This was the period when *New York Daily News* columnist Ed Sullivan in-troduced his variety show to the country and became the first "TV personality,'' which is to say he manifested a cool, calm approach to entertainment so nondescript that his program, virtually unchanged, was to please family audiences for decades. Milton Berle, a Hollywood flunk-out but Broadway and nightclub favorite, suddenly dominated the tube with his ancient, endless burlesque and vaudeville routines. This was also the era that the new Zoom lens was perfected, and television cameramen and directors could not resist playing with it *ad nauseam* on shows like the *Kraft Television Theatre* and others featuring such favorites as the comic team of Sid Caesar and Imogene Coco. Popular programs included *Garroway at Large,* the first *Lucy* shows, and, in time, much good, original television drama courtesy of Philco, Goodyear and General Electric. Because they were ideal performers for the new medium, a nearendless parade of puppets also found their way onto the tiny screen. All but Kukla, Ollie and their friend Fran (and, of course, Burr Tillstrom) were forgettable. And, of course, video offered plenty of old Hollywood movies, many of which are still visible on television today in the early morning hours.

In these early years, those of us who remained skeptical about the future of video were heartened by the fact that television in its early days did not—and could not—show a financial profit. Although, by 1950, about 10 million receivers dotted the land, video's losses, including those of its experimental years, had been so great, that making money was difficult even for a medium of such obvious potential (and current) popularity. NBC had earlier predicted that it would sustain an $8 million loss from video operations between 1946 and 1950, and was apparently not far from the mark. Production and transmission were both expensive—far more expensive than radio had been, and commercial advertisers could not be expected to pay the astronomical costs of many programs that frequently cost as much to produce as a Broadway play, if not more. The poor economics of video at this time drove a number of early, small networks and broadcasters from the airwaves, notably the ambitious Dumont network in 1955.

Radio Versus Television

The large networks, however, had their ace in the hole. All three, NBC, CBS and ABC, recognized that television would, one day, replace network radio as the dominant free broadcasting medium in the U.S.A. (They did not, incidentally, foresee the future strength of *local* radio as a communications instrument, but recognized only that big-time broadcasting was moribund.) In the meantime, however, before video sets and stations saturated the U.S.A.—an eventuality that was not to occur until, roughly, 1958, when television sets in use just about equalled the number of American homes—radio could and would be milked of its last dollar in order to pay for network expansion into video, and, if all went well, it might even yield broadcasters a profit as well.

The middle 'forties, therefore, saw a gigantic last gasp of network radio broadcasting, marked by intensive competition between the broadcasting giants. In general, NBC was the loser and CBS the winner of the game. By holding out clever tax-dodges and using capital gains as the bait, CBS literally raided NBC's stable of talents like Jack Benny, *Amos 'n' Andy,* Edgar Bergen and Burns and Allen, among others. ABC snared the immensely popular Bing Crosby from NBC by encouraging the leisure-loving singer to tape his programs at his convenience and, after while, to plug freely a frozen orange juice corporation in which he had a major financial interest.

Their new talent hoard proved doubly profitable for CBS. When Benny and company finally made the switch from radio to video, they did so on the CBS network. NBC was in the position of having to develop its own new talent, but the organization was both cocky and confident in those days. Milton Berle was actually signed by NBC to a *lifetime* contract, so confident was the network that Mr. Television would dominate the medium forever. The public tired of Berle's slim talents, however. He gave his last performance for NBC and his sponsor Texaco on June 14, 1955, except for an occasional nostalgic return to video.

As the 'forties ended and the 'fifties began, network radio, however, turned into a bigger and better carnival than it had ever been. For financial reasons, much serious and cultural programming was dropped from the air, and, for a short time, audio and video competed with one another for the American mass audience. Quiz shows were proliferating, soap operas were going strong, Arthur Godfrey seemed ubiquitous on both radio and television. Bob Hope, Benny and other perennial favorites were doing well, and so, in new formats, were old timers like Eddie Cantor and Groucho Marx. NBC even launched the last of the network radio "big shows" called, appropriately enough, *The Big Show.* It was written by Goodman Ace, starred Tallulah Bankhead of Broadway with music provided by Meredith Wilson, later writer and composer of *The Music Man.*

In a remarkably short time, the carnival was over. *The Big Show* survived a few seasons and died. Cantor, Groucho, Benny and Burns and Allen, among others, made the transition to video successfully. Some could not. Nearly all of the radio soap operas died. The driest, wittiest and most intelligent successful radio comedian, Fred Allen, was never able to find his place on the television tube. But we are getting ahead of ourselves.

Hollywood After the War

The post-war period was also a boom era for Hollywood movies and, in a way, a last hurrah for the old studio system as well. By the end of the 'forties, the Hollywood's exhibition-distribution-production monopolies run by the big studios were coming apart at the seams, a fact difficult to notice from the vantage point of the local Bijou on Main Street. Hollywood kept up a brave front, coining a new slogan, "Movies are Better than Ever." The public evidently believed it.

Weekly admissions during the late 'forties fluctuated between 90 and 100 million a week. The old double-feature, two programs a week, continuous-showing system was working full steam. In the background, however, hovered millions of tiny television screens, some of them even set up in lounges of movie theatres for patrons to watch while waiting for seats. It would, in the end, turn out to be television that would change Hollywood more trenchantly than all the anti-trust legislation the government hurled at it. Smart operators in Hollywood foresaw this, but most remained silent. For the moment, the old goose was laying 22-carat eggs, and movie people took advantage of immediate opportunities. Little did most of them think that they were, in fact, busily engaged in providing the program material upon which the new medium of video would eventually feed for years to come, right up to the present time.

In some measure, with an apparently conditioned audience that salivated at whatever Hollywood produced, the studios during the post-war years, fell back upon the device of imitating their own past, their own best moments and best movies. How sad to watch the career of the Marx Brothers (as a team) end with *A Night in Casablanca* (1946), or observe the once dashing Errol Flynn start his dissipated road to his grave in *The New Adventures of Don Juan* in 1948. The era of genuinely scary horror films was over at Universal. But Frankenstein's monster kept meeting the Wolfman who met Dracula who eventually met even Abbott and Costello. MGM tried to keep the Hardy family going despite the approaching middle age of star Mickey Rooney. These sorts of shoddy pictures were all "sure things." They sold the comfort of pre-war nostalgia as well as actors and actresses (and stories) all familiar to the American public.

Many performers—light and dramatic—indeed reached their prime during this period. Fred Astaire worked in some delightful fantasies like *Blue Skies* and *Easter Parade*. Films like *Crossfire* (1947) and *Home of the Brave* (1949) attacked the social problem of bigotry in American life with plenty of dramatic verve, even if such movies, like most of Hollywood's social epics of the 'thirties, offered pat solutions (like love and sympathy) to such complicated problems as anti-Semitism and anti-Black prejudice.

Post-War Movie Drama

With peace in the air, Hollywood assumed a liberal, forward-looking stance, as it occasionally centered upon American life in its serious aspects. This was nothing new. During the depression, more than a little left-wing rhetoric had crept into films like *Dead End* (1937) and *The Grapes of Wrath* (1940). Some post-war cinema was simply realistic and more or less non-political, for instance, *The Lost Weekend* (1945), the story of a man suffering from alcoholism and *Boomerang* (1947), a movie that, despite political overtones, was simply a good mystery-thriller shot on location. Other films straddled a middle ground between social statement and old fashioned melodrama: *Naked City* (1948) directed by Jules Dassin is as good an example as any.

Various notable serious American movies of the time centered upon how the American dream had gone wrong for certain people. They were neither as exaggerated nor frenetic as many socially realistic movies of the 'thirties. Some simply found themselves mysteriously caught up in their own twists and turns of plot. *All the King's Men* (1949) was one, as was *The Snake Pit* (1948). The former reprised weakly the career of Huey Long, ex-governor of Louisiana, and the latter centered superficially upon a woman's mental illness. Hardboiled melodramatic films like Billy Wilder's *Double Indemnity* (1944) and *Sunset Boulevard* (1950) were more to my taste, as was *The Postman Always Rings Twice* (1946) with John Garfield and John Huston's *The Treasure of the Sierra Madre* (1948). (I count the latter, made just before the Hollywood "Red Scare" closed the door on greed for gold as a viable film topic, one of the best performed films made in Hollywood, especially the point-counter-point virtuoso acting of Walter Huston and Humphrey Bogart.) They *were* melodramas, of course, but spiced with neat naturalistic flavor and crisp dialogue.

Bohn and Stromgren, in their history of the films, list some other films of the period as "dark movies." What they mean is that certain of these movies were very somber melodramas, generally bereft of social meaning, but intended clearly to frighten and shock. Many were good, and nearly all were excellent box office attractions. I remember particularly the grim story of carnival life, *Nightmare Alley* (1948), *Somewhere in the Night* (1946), *Kiss of Death* (1947) and *The Spiral Staircase* (1945). Most of these pictures, like the many film versions of mystery stories by Raymond Chandler and Dashiell Hammett, lacked any but the most cynical social message—usually "Don't trust anybody!"—but they were nearly all good hokum and fun, welcome relief to a public weary of war news and world-shaking events. They were also well acted and usually directed with expert exploitation of sinister, deadly and a surprise little twists in plot, especially trick endings. Such films, for better or worse, are rarely made any more. The studio which made some of the best of them was Twentieth Century-Fox: movies like *Laura* (1944) and a number of films that employed the acting talents of the versatile character actor, Laird Cregar, whose career was cut short in 1944 by an untimely death.

Communists in Hollywood

I think it is today fair to characterize the social film of post-war Hollywood as "bent" slightly to the left, or at any rate, in the direction of the kind of liberal social thinking that was fashionable those days among well-fed, well-paid artists and intellectuals. In no sense, could most of these movies be called "un-American." In fact, if anything, they were given to concocting impossible solutions to socio-economic troubles and materialized last minute affirmations of God, country and the American flag. The closest that Hollywood had ever come to flirting with communism was a few frankly propagandistic movies about our Russian allies during World War II, and these features came from major studios which, as we have seen, were bastions of nineteenth-century capitalism.

It is common, these days, to associate the "Red Scare" of the post-war years in Hollywood with the now infamous Senator Joseph McCarthy of Wisconsin. But it is also incorrect. McCarthy's mischief was of a sort similar to that which hit Hollywood in the 'forties but did not gather steam until the West Coast witch hunt was practically over. Nor was Hollywood's problem caused entirely by the House of Representatives' Committee on Un-American Activities which, in a rather silly and naive way, was trying to fulfill a charge given to it years before by Congress to seek out enemies of the state wherever they might be, including Hollywood.

No, the two main culprits, I think, were even more shady and unsavory characters: invisible men, in the sense that G. K. Chesterton once wrote about the postman who was not noticed as he makes his rounds, because he had become so familiar. First, in centering its attention upon Hollywood, its writers, stars, actors and directors, the HUAC was simply selecting one of the few cities in the U.S.A. where the largest crowd of gossip-oriented newsmen and women per thousand of the population was centered day and night. The Committee, second, played to the grandstand of public opinion by calling as witnesses *genuine* movie stars, writers and directors, not mere labor agitators or college professors, but the people who made American *movies,* a medium supposedly as American as mom's apple pie. Public curiosity did the rest. News of HUAC's hearings filled newspapers and radio newscasts. Because they knew the cast of characters, the public inevitably applauded the show and asked for encores.

Congress Investigates Hollywood

The whole episode, begun in October of 1947, was disgraceful, but it was to be repeated as HUAC and other investigating committees moved to other American institutions. The witch hunt started with the movies but spread to the television industry, the professional theatre, universities, the Army and into government service itself. Once the public's appetite for subversive blood was whetted, the press—broadcast and print media—followed their instincts both to feed it and, most disgracefully, to exploit it. This was, many said, the price the people paid for freedom of speech. True enough, but very few journalists, the broadcast or print kind, were willing to use their precious freedoms to attack with vigor the Roman circus of the Hollywood communist investigation in the late 'forties and their sequels in the 'fifties.

By way of direct public response to this outrage, I remember only two sane, notable voices: those of radio-TV commentator Edward R. Murrow and playwright Arthur Miller. Some teachers and professors I myself knew made brave noise in the safety of their classrooms, I must admit, but such whispers took little courage on our parts. We excused our own apathy as a consequence of our "academic detachment"—even as we saw colleagues broken, fired and disgraced for crimes they had not committed by kangaroo courts, like the House Committee, that possessed no legal punitive powers but had, nevertheless, the power to punish by destroying reputations and employability.

Novelty and Normalcy

The famous "Hollywood Ten," mostly writers, were blacklisted from the industry as a result of their (supposed) communistic leanings. They were eventually also jailed for pleading the Fifth Amendment (the right not to testify against one's self), which was interpreted as contempt of Congress. For others, the problem centered upon the Committee's demand that they swear under oath that they were *not* communists, an act abhorrent to many who believed that politics are—or should be—a matter of personal conscience in a democracy. Thus, were actors like Larry Parks, the aforementioned Dassin, and directors like Joseph Losey rendered immediately unemployable. Some sought refuge overseas. Others, writers like Miller, Lillian Hellman and Dalton Trumbo, continued their fight in the U.S.A. For a number of screen authors, an ignominious solution was the clever ploy used by the talented Albert Maltz: They simply wrote under pseudonyms, accepting, of course, diminished stipends for their work because of their deceptions.

There *were* certainly some communists and communist sympathizers in Hollywood during and after the war. Friendship towards the U.S.S.R. had run high nearly everywhere in the U.S.A. from 1941 to 1945, and it was impossible for many to switch their ideological gears overnight. Others were not sympathizers but simply *not* anti-communists. This was, and remains, another matter entirely. All of these important distinctions had been eliminated, however, by the early 'fifties in the HUAC investigations.

Worse, the HUAC never even realistically tested the possibility that Hollywood movies may *well have been* a subversive force in American life for years. It apparently did not occur even to one of the witch-hunting investigators of Congress to examine closely the bulk of American films themselves that had been *made* in Hollywood to determine whether or not they contained communist propaganda. (Naturally, the movies did not, except in instances so rare as to be negligible.) Instead, the Committee concentrated upon *people*—the stars and those who worked with them—who, they knew perfectly well, made good newspaper copy and created broadcasting hoopla that the public, the ultimate victims of their mischief, would gobble up.

The result of the Hollywood Red Scare was to demoralize an already fractionalized, dispirited community in many ways and add just one more burden to all of Hollywood's troubles at the time; anti-trust actions and impending competition from television.

The films of the late 'forties and early 'fifties themselves took on a frantic quality. A popular 1945 musical, *State Fair* was a harbinger of the kind of movie that producers and exhibitors considered absolutely safe from every perspective. It was a musical with plenty of harmless hokum. It affirmed American values in the American way and could not be misinterpreted by anyone. Neither could biographies of song writers, war melodramas, or most gangster movies.

Problems of censorship now not only centered upon matters of sex and personal morality but intruded into any ideologies motion pictures might imply. Safe stars in safe movies were the order of the day. Nor, apparently, did the public care much. Box office receipts climbed to an all-time high in 1949. The public, let me add, seemed in no way displeased with Hollywood's "house cleaning." The "Red Scare" was not to end for more than half-a-dozen years, and, when it was finally put to rest, it was not the public or the communications industry that turned the trick but rather the Congress of the United States itself.

Post-War Cinema Overseas

The European cinema that arose from the rubble of war also deserves attention for a moment. Exhibition was still difficult in the U.S.A. for films made overseas. But conduits of distribution were opening, especially for a number of extraordinary movies made in Italy by a few new and talented directors.

These films, called by film cultists "neo-realistic" (whatever it means), were delightful, sad, poignant slices of life, often utilizing the talents of both amateur and professional performers. Scripted or ad-libbed, they had about them a quality of improvisation, partly because they were made with crude equipment and shot on location under difficult conditions, centuring upon what their directors and actors knew best: their own country in the turmoil of post-war life, the futility of combat, poverty and the simple joys and sorrows of a poor and desperate people. Roberto Rossellini was probably the first master of these movies. His *Open City* (1945) and *Paisan* (1946) remain classics of this type of work. Vittorio de Sica's *Shoeshine* (1946) and *The Bicycle Thief* (1948) combine a skilled professional directorial hand with the peculiar warmth that young children, well directed, bring to the screen.

Unfortunately, the Italian neo-realists were not able to carry the freshness of their post-war liberation into the 'fifties, and the style of Italian films changed with the new prosperity of the new decade. While many of these later films were excellently performed and directed, none could once again capture the magic of the early post-war years.

British film makers emerged buoyantly from the war with such superb movies as David Lean's *Great Expectations* (1946) and *Oliver Twist* (1947). (The latter was unmercifully cut in the U.S.A., so that close-ups of Alec Guinness as the hateful Fagin would not offend the Anti-Defamation League of the B'nai Brith organization and other Jewish groups that were, and remain, sensitive about screen portrayals of Jews.) Carol Reed gave us the crackerjack melodrama, *Odd Man Out* (1949), as well as Graham Greene's immensely popular *The Third Man* (1949). Other British movies in color experimented with stories told as ballets. The indefatigable Laurence Olivier was busy adapting his superb Shakespearean performances into admirable film productions that he directed himself. Others have attempted Shakespeare on film before and since. But, during this period and largely as a result of his movies, Olivier established himself a the world's outstanding interpreter of the Bard.

Almost all British movies exported during the five years from 1945–1950 displayed considerable vigor and originality, born in the glow of wartime victory, that, for many reasons, only partially continued during the decade to come and died almost entirely after the early 1960s.

British comedy also experienced a period of post-war vigor with the emergence of genuinely funny, subtle films that capitalized on an English proclivity often to laugh at what others usually take seriously and vice-versa. Alec Guinness played eight roles, including that of a woman (all of whom are murdered), in the delightful *Kind Hearts and Coronets* (1949), setting off a string of Guinness' satirical comedies in which larceny, other crimes and even death itself served as the focus of the humor. Alexander Mackendrick's *Whisky Galore* (1947) (also known as *Tight Little Island*) was also a unique gem set on a Scotch Island whose residents run out of their booze supply.

On the continent, with the exception of Italy, most of the combatant nations in World War II moved quite slowly back into the movie business. As in Japan in the East, the devastation of war itself forced film makers to put first things first, and reconstruction of a ravaged continent was the immediate imperative. By the time film making in these countries moved into full production, conduits for distribution in the U.S.A. were at last open for foreign films.

Immediately after the war, Hollywood movies had inundated all of Europe to such a degree that quotas were placed on nearly all American imports that were, in effect, working exactly in the opposite fiscal direction of the United States Foreign Aid program, known as the Marshall Plan, that was pouring money and food into the war-torn continent.

In 1950, Hollywood still led the world in film production—383 movies were made in California that year; in England 125 were produced; in France, 117; and in Italy, 98.

France, incidentally, was about to produce a new wave of young film makers whose work was to attract world-wide attention. But, during this period, only a few movies, like *Symphonie Pastorale* (1946), *Devil in the Flesh* (1947) and Jacques Tati's delightful *Jour de Fete* (1949) and René Clair's *Beauty and the Devil* (1949), gave any indication of the movies to come from the post-war French generation of film makers.

Hollywood's Last Fling

Back in Hollywood, the old safe studio-made films were whooping up their last hurrah. Gene Kelly, Frank Sinatra and company cavorted in *On the Town* (1949), and it was quite impossible to predict the shape of things to come, a shape to be determined by the rapidly spreading television screens that glowed in millions of American living rooms. Hollywood was to begin a search for any type of movie that was simply too big, or too wide, too deep, too colorful or too loud to be compared with video and which might successfully compete with the new home entertainment medium.

Many people suspected that such competition was absurd, no matter how the technology of film production and projection might be called to the service of novelty. Only a few were aware, however, that new multi-millions were to be made by means of cooperation rather than competition with television, and that film production and television might co-exist comfortably side by side— just as long as one was not regarded as the natural adversary of the other. The movies might well have killed vaudeville and burlesque, but the cinema itself seems to have been made of hardier stuff than even the living popular theatre. Hollywood simply refused to lay down and die, and its prosperity arrived in an unexpected way.

The story of what became of Hollywood in the era of television takes us, naturally, to the present day, because the old film factory is, at the moment, alive and well and, although changed, more prosperous than ever!

The Post-War Press

Immediately after the war, the Americn book publishing industry received great stimulus from the G.I. Bill of Rights that entitled any veteran to return to school for at least a period equal to his or her military service. At first, all book expenses for veterans were paid directly by the government, a period during which many of us gathered libraries of expensive books freely placed on course reading lists by sympathetic professors in universities and colleges across the nation. Abuses were notable, and soon the money allocated for texts was set at a reasonable stipend per term. Nevertheless, textbook publishers particularly benefited enormously from the arrival of so many ex-soldiers and sailors on American campuses paid for by what were, in effect, large-scale government scholarships. Military programs had kept many universities in business during the war, particularly institutions for men. These programs, mainly the Navy's V-12 and the Army ASTP training efforts, had strained the publishing industry's hard-pressed resources of paper and binding materials to its limits. With peacetime came continued prosperity.

The end of the war, however, was not such a fortunate period for some newspapers and many magazines. No matter how one feels about it, warfare remains the biggest journalistic challenge newspapers and magazines can possibly meet, and battlefield stories remain the ultimate test of a newsman or woman's skill in communication. Big stories indeed followed the end of hostilities: the peace treaty with Japan, the signing of the United Nations' Charter, the Bikini atom bomb tests, the formal surrender of Japan, the founding of the State of Israel, and the beginning of the "cold war" between the U.S.A. and the Eastern European Communist nations, among others. From a purely journalistic perspective, however, they were almost all anti-climatic. Even the upset election of Harry Truman in 1948, when he confounded the pollsters and beat a sure winner, Republican Thomas E. Dewey, captured only momentarily the old dramatic journalistic vigor of the war years.

Editorial writing was simply not as trenchant, political cartoons less vitriolic and newspapers less stimulating than they had been in recent memory.

Picture journals like *Life* magazine had brought the art of photography to new heights during hostilities. Its editors spent the generation after the signing of the armistice attempting either to reach *Life's* old levels of distinction or find a new identity for the weekly publication. In the end, for many reasons, all these attempts failed.

Superficially, however, all seemed well with the American press. But this euphoria was, it turned out, an illusion. Columnists like Walter Winchell and Leonard Lyons kept shouting away—now, with little to shout about. Much distinguished writing, particularly the commentary of Walter Lippmann and other socio-political analysts like the team of Stewart and Joseph Alsop, appeared almost daily. But the public was tired of serious writing. It was searching for novelty and normalcy.

Comic strips remained popular. "Joe Palooka," "Smilin' Jack" and even "Superman" came home from the war. Comic books had been the overwhelmingly favorite reading matter of the men who fought World War II. Their enthusiasm for the funnies continued in peacetime. Al Capp's inventive brain introduced the "Shmoo" to "Lil Abner." (The Shmoo was a balloon-like little animal who symbolized peace and plenty by dropping dead and turning into a plate of pork chops or a chicken dinner just because it wanted to please people.) Milton Caniff wisely quit drawing and writing his old strip, "Terry and the Pirates," in 1947, the rights to which were owned by the Chicago Tribune Syndicate. He began drawing a new feature, "Steve Canyon," copyrighted by Caniff personally. His move was followed by other new cartoonists, who wanted to own all rights to their creations themselves. "Pogo," "Barnaby" and even *Yank*'s "Sad Sack," appeared in the nation's newspapers. The comic pages—both daily and Sunday color versions—seemed to have become a vital part of the American scene that was here to stay. Old favorites, "Dick Tracy," "Little Orphan Annie," "Barney Google," "The Gumps," "Flash Gordon," "The Katzenjammer Kids," and "Mutt and Jeff" went on and on, although many of their original artists had deserted them or died. At about this time, also, more than one or two odd-ball sociologists, psychologists and critics began to take the comics somewhat seriously. By the time these academics took the comics *very* seriously, and began studying them in depth, most of the old cartoon strips were moribund or dead.

The familiar family magazines seemed healthy and well, deceptively well. *The Saturday Evening Post, Liberty, Collier's, Look* and *Life* seemed to be American institutions that would certainly continue publication, it was thought, for generations. The *Reader's Digest* spread its influence into a multi-lingual empire by means of a baker's dozen foreign language versions. *Time* magazine produced Latin American and European editions. Prices rose a bit: magazines like the *Post* and *Liberty* cost 5 cents before the war and now rose to 15 cents, but all costs were up, and a new prosperity for all was just ahead. Countless special interest journals sprang up as well: magazines for children, magazines for the newly created 'teenage market, magazines for sports enthusiasts, racing car drivers, nudists, cooking enthusiasts and other hobbyists.

As the old grocery store gave way to the new supermarket, so did the distribution of women's magazines change. *Woman's Day* found its outlets at first through the A&P chain stores, simply because A&P owned it. Later, antitrust action forced A&P to quit the publishing business. But the magazine remained on its check-out counters, as did *Today's Woman* and other competitors that were now sold, not mostly by subscription or by news dealers, but along with the week's groceries. Newly formed diaper services started circulating free magazines along with their sanitary services. These latter publications were (and are) supported entirely by advertising and are supposedly avidly read by exactly the right target audience for vendors of baby care products.

Economic Publishing Problems

A disturbing trend was noticeable in the air, however. Newspaper circulations grew to enormous totals, nearing the 50 million-per-day mark. But, the overall number of discrete daily publications was falling, to about 1744 in 1945, an all time low for the half century. The reason, boiled down, was largely that the journalistic giants were getting bigger and bigger, making it more and more difficult for other papers of moderate circulations to survive.

Newspapers were also becoming expensive to publish. So were magazines. Not only were costs of newsprint and machinery rising, in large and medium-sized cities labor unions insisted that printers, distributors and reporters had the same rights to decent wages and job security as other workers. Most notably, the International Typographical Union and the American Newspaper Guild flexed their considerable muscles during the immediate post-war period. As a result, many newspaper prices were forced up, just as some other newspapers were forced out of business. In the 1950s, not more than 300 newspapers in the U.S.A. were sold any longer for less than 5 cents.

A snowballing tendency towards the merger of newspapers was also well under way by the time the 'forties ended. In New Orleans, Minneapolis, Dayton and Springfield, Ohio and elsewhere, formerly competing papers joined forces to cut overhead, meaning that now one newspaper existed where two or three had been published previously. In Minneapolis, for instance, the *Star* and *Times* were married. The new newspaper was therefore the only paper in town, by 1947, that competed with the *Morning Tribune*. But it mattered little, because both papers were owned by the same publishing company headed by John Cowles. Such multiple ownership of papers within a single city was not uncommon, and occurred in Dayton and Springfield, Ohio, Worcester, Massachusetts and elsewhere. (In the latter metropolis, the competing newspapers, both owned by the same company, written largely by the same people, set by the same typographers and printed on the same presses, consisted of a morning and an evening journal, one titularly Republican and the other Democratic, thus giving the citizens of Worcester a "choice" of political news sources.) The number of "single ownership cities" was not enormous in the 'forties, but it continued to rise to the present, as we shall see.

For economic reasons alone, chain newspapers prospered, while independents, by and large, had a difficult time. Chains like Scripps-Howard, Knight, Hearst, Gannett, Cox, Ridder and others were able to cut overhead by, in effect, utilizing feature writers, editorialists, photographers and even compositors economically—somewhat like a small press service. Most chain papers were quite uniform. Front page stories were often identical in all the papers, and, if they were copied verbatim from the news ticker of a press service, *exactly* the same as most other newspapers' front page stories. The reason, of course, was that it was far cheaper to depend on a chain alliance and/or news service like the AP, UP or INS, to buy syndicated features, such as comics, columnists, cooking articles, crossword puzzles and even editorials (on either side of any fence) than to originate them locally.

Some years before the war, an aging publisher of the old school lamented that, on a train trip across the U.S.A., one was sold in different cities at each stop the identical paper with different mastheads. He was right, and this trend was to continue. It was not laziness or a lack of journalistic enterprise that caused the problem. It was the hard truth that newspaper economics, except in a few instances, were undergoing mighty changes that made it difficult to print a newspaper profitably unless one depended upon syndicates, news services, or unless a paper was part of a chain.

Marshall Field III

One of the most interesting press barons in American history emerged in the early 1940s. By the second half of the decade, and despite some spectacular failures, this man had established himself as one of the most colorful and idealistic publishers in American history. He provides us with an interesting series of personal contradictions.

Marshall Field III, a third generation department store millionaire in Chicago, decided, in 1940, to get into the newspaper business and to start at the top. No publisher since William Randolph Hearst had displayed quite this much nerve. Field was, however, cut from quite a different pattern from Hearst. Quiet, unassuming and oriented towards the political left, the liberal Field at the age of 47 decided to invade the New York newspaper market place—made up at the time of the *Times, Tribune, Sun,* Scripps-Howard's *World Telegram, three* Hearst papers (the *Mirror, Journal* and *American*) and the extraordinary *Daily News,* among others—with a new type of newspaper.

The paper was a tabloid journal, rabidly left-wing for its day. Some identified its political orientation with that of the *Daily Worker,* the Communist party journal then also being published in New York. Geared to the masses and written simply, clearly and well, Field's paper was called *PM.* It was indeed unusual in many respects.

Backed by Field's millions, for its first six years it accepted no advertising, a symbol of its independence from big business interests. *PM*'s editor was Ralph Ingersoll, a one-time publisher of *Time* magazine, who found Luce's magazine incompatible with his liberal sentiments. At times, *PM*'s ledgers even showed profits. But it was ultimately dependent upon Field's largesse, even when it began accepting advertisements—and accordingly lost Ingersoll—in 1946. Many New Yorkers liked both its novelty and near childish simplicity. For a time, news articles were even accompanied by cartoon symbols indicating "good news" or "bad news" (from *PM*'s point of view), and many of its staffers were excellent journalists. Louis Kronenberger, *Time's* drama critic, wrote for *PM*, often panning the same play he had anonymously praised for the Luce magazine. Walter Winchell pitched in during presidential campaigns, working free for *PM* under the by-line "Paul Revere Jr."

PM died in 1948 when Field, disenchanted with the way his baby had grown, sold it to other interests. They tried, for the next half-dozen years, to keep it floating, first as the *New York Star,* then as the *Compass,* as it passed from owner to owner. Much about *PM* that was good persisted in American jounalism, from its sharp social and political satirical muckracking to some of its comic strips and the cartoons of Johnny Pierotti that enlivened its pages. Many of *PM*'s writers, embittered by their experience, ended up teaching journalism, feeling that in this way they could best keep *PM*'s old spirit alive.

Field had tasted newspaper ink, however, and eventually achieved his greatest success in Chicago, where his grandfather had amassed a fortune as a merchant. The *Chicago Sun* appeared three days before Pearl Harbor, and, after a few years of publication, backer Field himself took over as working publisher. Less liberal than Field's *PM,* the *Sun* was a somewhat sensational but reliable newspaper. In 1947, with his son, Marshall Field IV to help him, Field acquired the *Chicago Times* and eventually joined it with the *Sun.*

Opting originally for the tabloid formula of the *Chicago Times,* the *Sun-Times* grew into a leading American newspaper within a decade. In 1959, Field the younger bought the *Chicago Daily News* to "compete" with his successful *Sun-Times.* He thus was able effectively to oppose the tremendous influence throughout much of the mid-west of Colonel Robert R. McCormick's old, conservative *Chicago Tribune* which, even after the death of the Colonel in 1955, continued exploiting McCormick's personal conservative political quirks (that sold newspapers) but also provided excellent local news coverage.

In this process, naturally, the Field family moved from department store barony to newspaper barony, mainly because there seems to be no end of Marshall Fields. The *Sun,* in its early days, was locked in heated competition with the *Tribune.* Part of the battle centered on the fact that, under existing AP regulations, the *Tribune* could (and did) block entirely Field's newspaper from membership in that press association. AP bylaws stated, in the early 1940s, that, in a city with one AP member, a second newspaper's application would only be considered if the applicant paid the AP 10 percent of *total* AP charges in that locality *from 1900 to the present*—in the *Sun's* case, an initiation fee of $334,250.46—unless its competitor waived this fee. The *Tribune,* of course, did not waive it. The *Sun* (or Field) refused to pay.

Field, encouraged by support from the incumbent Democratic party for which his paper spoke, started monopoly action against the AP under the Sherman Anti-Trust Act. He would probably rather have attacked the *Tribune* directly. The action had to be taken, however, in New York, the home of the AP. A district court agreed that the AP's regulation was indeed ''in restraint of trade'' and ordered the press service to rescind its rule. On appeal, the case finally found its way to the U.S. Supreme Court where, for the past decade, the AP had not fared well. Once again, the AP was rapped on the knuckles. the judgment against it was sustained in 1945, and the AP duly admitted the *Sun* and other papers excluded under the same rule to membership without gargantuan admission fees.

According to Frank Mott, the decision eventually did the AP more good than harm. He claims that, as a result, the spectre of the old AP as a closed club and private monopoly for the privileged was at last put to rest. So it seemed. AP membership was now open not only to all newspapers that could afford its services but to broadcast stations as well for use on radio and television programs. So extensive was AP's service to the various media, that, in recent years, other news services have had difficulty in competing with it. So a circle has, in some measure, been completed. If its competition is indeed put out of business in the future, the AP may once again find itself in the journalistic cat-bird seat, although effective competition from the UP-INS and *New York Times* news services, for the most part, keep the AP presently on its toes.

The U.S.A. at Mid-Century

Slightly before New Year's Day in 1950, *Time* magazine singled out for a cover story Winston Churchill as ''the man of the half century.'' In stentorian tones, the Luce magazine reminded us that ''he launched the lifeboats'' that saved civilization for the remainder of the twentieth century, not once but twice: against Hitler in the 'thirties and Stalin and the U.S.S.R. in the 'forties.

Whether or not *Time* was correct in its choice of heroes seems to matter little today, more than a quarter of a century later. But the year 1950 was a critical one for the Western World in many ways. Churchill or no Churchill, few people shed tears as the 1940s passed into history. The decade had seen barbarities, tortures and cruelties beyond belief, none of which were lessened by the victories and dubious justice to which they ultimately yielded. The 1950's stood, at least, for a new chance.

A new chance, but for what? This was the uncertain question that faced an uncertain nation full of uncertain people as the half-century mark passed. It is no accident that the favorite literature of the young generation to mature in the next decade turned out to be science fiction! Such stories provided answers to these questions, probably incorrect ones, but they were better than no answers at all. And one fact about the growth of modern technology was certain: whatever the future held, television was certain to be an important, and possibly critical, part of it.

13

The Fabulous Infant

SOCIAL ANALYSTS OFTEN LOOK at technological change as a mixed blessing. On one side, new technologies usually bring material, social and cultural benefits to more people more cheaply than ever before. On the other, they are almost certain also to produce unwanted by-products or "fallout" that is certain to influence—or kill off—older, time-honored ways of doing things. Knowing this, many people are neither overly enthusiastic—nor entirely pessimistic—about new technological breakthroughs in modern society. Their reasons center, as I have already noted, on the inability of *anybody*—even our wisest historians or clever "futurologists" and other kinds of fortune tellers—to predict the ways in which a technology will distribute both its blessings and curses, much less determine how it will change other institutions—that is, whether it will stimulate them, leave them alone or kill them off.

Hundreds—possibly thousands—of examples in the history of Western society illustrate this point, but none more clearly than that of television during the 1950's.

Turning the clock back 27 years, we might now responsibly predict that video will eliminate all commercial radio in the United States and that it must inevitably send all motion picture theatres to oblivion. On the other hand, we may also discover few reasons to believe that television should have much of an effect upon print media like magazines, book publishing and newspapers.

All things being equal, these would have been good guesses. But all things were not equal—or the same—during the 'fifties, nor have they been since. Predictions like these were (mostly) wrong, because they could not possibly take into account other cultural, economic and countless types of events that, one way or another, would accompany the introduction of video screens into nearly every household in the nation by the end of the decade, and would, ever so slowly, cause changes in the way the population of the entire nation lived and thought.

Video in the Early 'Fifties

While many historians look back at the 'fifties as a time of stability (compared to the restless years that followed them) they were also a time of hasty decisions and irresponsible, angry and nervous commitments for thousands of people who, by now, were, one way or another, caught up in the destinies of the mass media communications industries in the U.S.A. Only the insensitive and dense could not recognize that they were living through a period of considerable and deep transition. Understanding the *nature* and *direction* that these changes would take, however, was another matter! Here the wisest of us caught ourselves tripping over our own best predictions and removing egg from our faces every few years.

The sale of television receivers began, in 1950, a rapid acceleration, that continues almost to the present, for a number of reasons. First, more and more interesting programs were turning up on video. A large library of old movies, some of them excellent, were available on the television tube. Second, many nervous radio performers, and some nervous film celebrities, were also staking out early personal territories in videoland. Large publics followed them. Last, the price of receivers was falling, as mass production methods were introduced into the television receiver industry. Video screens were also getting larger and reception somewhat better. Between 1950 and 1952, the sale of television receivers in the U.S.A. doubled from about 10 to 20 million per year, at a rate of increase that has not leveled off much in the period since then.

What kind of programs were carried by the three networks in those days? Well, most of them, except for the old movies and cartoons, were telecast live. Systems of recording a video image were still expensive and far from perfect. Dramas were rare but popular, and, during this period, some of them were shot on film exclusively for television distribution. New talents at the networks were freely exploited. Ed Sullivan (*Toast of the Town*), Dave Garroway (*Garroway at Large*), Lucille Ball on film (*I Love Lucy*), Milton Berle (*Texaco Star Theatre*) and Arthur Godfrey in many incarnations were among the first of them. Godfrey, incidentally, continued his career in radio at the same time by means, mostly, of "simulcasts": programs that were both televised and broadcast on radio at the same time.

Few people will, I think, challenge my judgment that the best television show of the period was the live coverage given the Senate Committee hearings in 1952, conducted by Estes Kefauver, into organized crime in the U.S.A. This pseudo-news event (that actually accomplished little or nothing) starred a cast of irate Senators, a flash-in-the-pan, vigorous prosecuting attorney, and a parade of colorful real-life gangsters. They included Mafia boss Frank Costello (whose objection to television coverage of his face caused cameramen to center upon his nervous but eloquent hands), a real-live gun moll named Virginia Hill, and a more than slightly crooked ex-mayor of New York City, William O'Dwyer. (When hearings ended, O'Dwyer thought it wise to move his law practice to Mexico City, where he remained for years until the heat cooled and could safely return to the U.S.A. without fear of being hauled into court for perjury as the result of his television appearances.)

Kiddie shows, cartoons and puppets appeared in the early evening and Saturday mornings. Most of them were not too different from their counterparts on television today. NBC began its *Today* show, featuring Dave Garroway and a chimpanzee named J. Fred Muggs. Philco, Goodyear and Kraft experimented, as sponsors, with live video dramatic works written especially for the new medium. You may hear nostalgia buffs speak of these particular broadcasts as the "golden age of television drama." These sentimentalists have many nay-sayers to contend with, expecially those of us who actually suffered through many of these slim dramas by Paddy Chayefsky, Reginald Rose and others. Most were poorly written, under-rehearsed and roughly comparable to second-rate summer stock theatricals. Actors forgot their lines, and production goofs were numerous. Directing was mostly unimaginative, and the less said about many of the scripts, the better. (Some, indeed, did make creditable films after considerable re-writing—usually with different actors.)

Most of these programs were fresh material when compared to the old movies that preceded and followed them. And, like much live television in the early 'fifties, they communicated, at least, a sense of spontaneity. This meant that you never knew when an actor might drop a prop, draw a blank, when a door on the set might stick or a director might punch up the wrong camera. Today's daily televised daytime soap operas continue some of these amusing traditions of early "golden age" television drama.

Whatever was happening on the video screen, it *was* popular. Last night's television became grist for the mill of the next day's conversation at the office, on the bus or at lunch. The saloon set favored competitive athletic events, although a never-ending procession of bizarre, staged wrestling "contests" seemed to hold enormous fascination for the audience, as well as other kinds of legitimate athletic contests that included baseball, football, basketball and horse-racing. The greatest challenge to the first television commentators covering these events was, in fact, learning how and when to keep their mouths shut. Most were graduates of radio broadcasting in which, of course, every move had to be described in detail. Now video did much of their descriptive work for them. The challenge to their skills lay in exercising judgment concerning what *not* to say and how to clarify what the viewer saw but might misunderstand or misjudged.

The FCC "Freeze"

The growth of television broadcasting in the early 'fifties must, however, be set against the background of an FCC regulation that, in effect, impeded the growth of the video industry but, at the same time, permitted broadcasters to concentrate upon developing new program formats and to straighten out the dim—or dubious—economic future of a new medium. The introduction of television had cost the radio networks millions of dollars in cumulative losses because of the difficulty in finding advertisers willing to pay the high costs of producing television programs.

In September of 1948, the FCC placed a so-called "freeze" upon new applications for television station licenses that was to last until April, 1952. The FCC's motives centered upon doubts that the 12 available Very High Frequency channels then (and now) in use would (or could) adequately meet the nation's needs. The FCC was also unsure that these frequencies might turn out to be electronically satisfactory for the transmission of color signals, if and when color video technology was finally perfected. These VHF channels had been assigned years earlier, when alternate broadcasting spectrums, like the Ultra High Frequency band, were not yet considered feasible for television, and VHF video station licenses had been given out more or less freely to (mostly) radio broadcasters.

A major question facing the FCC was whether some licenses should be withheld for non-commercial broadcaster—say, cities, school systems, universities and other cultural institutions. Many, like FCC Commissioner Frieda Hennock, campaigned vigorously for the reservation of certain video channels for what was known then as "educational television," mindful of how radio broadcasters had years before overlooked, for the most part, opportunities for using sound broadcasting for purposes of teaching in their early rush to commercialism. The fault, Hennock and others believed, lay in the FCC's regulations which had not encouraged the growth of educational radio.

Organizations like the Joint Committee on Educational Television were formed, fired with missionary zeal, to support Hennock in her eventually successful battle to reserve some channels for educational (now "public") broadcasting. In all, some 242 VHF and UHF frequencies were finally reserved for non-commercial use as the result of these efforts—for both better and worse, it turned out as the years passed. In respect to cultural and educational matters, television, it seemed in 1952, was now off to a better start than radio had been in 1934.

The UHF-VHF Problem

Aside from the breathing spell it gave the industry and the reservation of educational channels, the end of the freeze on licenses (the FCC's Sixth Report and Order of 1952, called by historian Sydney Head an "historic" document) accomplished in the long run less than it appeared to at the time. The old 12 VHF channels were retained for commercial and some educational service, and 70 UHF frequencies were added to the *possible* spectrum of television frequencies. The latter indeed seemed then like a spectacular change that would increase the number of stations on the air in the U.S.A. immediately and dramatically. It was not and did not.

Most television receivers built then, and those manufactured for the next dozen years, could not receive any UHF signals. Without additional transmission power—and expense—UHF video signals did not compare favorably in fidelity to the old VHF transmission system, nor do they in most cases today. Nearly every UHF station opened in the wake of the freeze eventually went out of business for lack of viewers, until, in 1962, the United States Congress required that the electronic designs of all new television sets include the capacity to receive UHF signals.

Manufacturers, of course, complied because they had to, and this capacity has been built into all sets since then. But little was accomplished by this move. The outlook for UHF was, and remains, bleak. Of the 80 or so UHF stations operating in the early 'seventies (and discounting public television stations) only about half managed to operate in the black, and, of those, profits, by and large, averaged a mere five per cent of those realized by the most successful VHF stations.

The Networks

The end of the freeze, in other words, simply reactivated the old scramble for profitable VHF outlets. It was also becoming increasingly clear that, despite the fact that certain independent stations (especially in big cities) might survive without network affiliation by operating on a syndication basis—that is, by buying programming from private sources—a network affiliation was vital to the economic prosperity of a video station in America. The networks, while fiercely competitive one with the other, taken together, held in their hands a virtual monopoly on certain *types* of national video service, and the entire industry could only afford to support three of them—for the next generation, at least.

The early Dumont television network died in 1955 after five years of feeble competition with the giants, NBC and CBS. The Mutual Broadcasting Company wisely elected to remain in the radio broadcasting business. This left NBC and CBS, as well as the one-time upstart Siamese-twin of NBC, the American Broadcasting Company. ABC moved into television on a shoestring in 1948 and, five years later, joined a wealthy conglomerate headed by the now independent theatrical part of the quondam Hollywood Paramount Pictures monopoly.

There followed no shortage of competition between the three video networks for advertisers' dollars or for audiences. But one network pretty closely imitated the other, particularly in regard to programming, with ABC's functioning as a sort of a "discount house" during the 'fifties. Some observers blame what they consider the "decline" in the quality of American television during this period (and to the present) on ABC. I think they are wrong. The quality of programs on all three networks is about the same today as it was 20 years ago; and so are the programs, scripts, plots and jokes.

Like all other new mediums, it took ten or more years for television to become fully assimilated into the daily lives of the American mass audience. Some 500 (later, nearly 600) stations joined the networks as affiliates. The largest network was NBC, the second CBS, and ABC third. This distribution of programming leveled off at what was a point of economic balance and limit.

Television and Radio Broadcasting

Predictions that video would kill radio broadcasting were, of course, entirely wrong. But radio broadcasting in the U.S.A. underwent some remarkable changes.

Network radio—"big time" radio—as we had known it, died a slow and frustrating death during the 1950s. One by one, the large network shows, Bob Hope's program, Fred Allen's comedy show, *Gang Busters* and the rest of the hardy perennials of the sound broadcasting era, bit the dust. Then the soap operas began to fold. Gone were *Ma Perkins, Our Gal Sunday, Life Can Be Beautiful* and *Mary Marlin* along with countless others. (Only a few programs, like Arthur Godfrey's weekday chatter and song show, managed to hang on. Godfrey, who continued his radio program until April, 1972, was one of the last hold-outs on CBS, and Lowell Thomas, one of the first radio newscasters, said goodbye to his listeners in May of 1975.)

To the casual observer, radio was indeed visibly dying. In fact, radio in the 'fifties was in the midst of a boom that would simply change the nature of sound broadcasting services in America, so that it would not—and could not—compete with television.

During the new video era, radio broadcasters now required a network affiliation for one thing only: news broadcasts, in particular, national news. Otherwise, most radio broadcasters could accomplish cheaply what television broadcasters could not do at all without incurring financial losses. That is, radio was now free to provide inexpensive *local* services of all kinds, mostly the old staple of recorded music for local audiences via an army of disc jockeys who would play this or that number, requested by "Al, Harry, Arlene and all the gang at the Red Horse Pizzeria." 'Phone call talk shows run by voluble loud-mouths were cheap and popular too.

Radio did not require one's total attention the way television did. It provided background music in diners and barber shops, invariably accompanied automobile journeys, served as electric alarm clocks, and, for many Americans, as the age of rock 'n' roll gained momentum, provided at home wall-to-wall noise to distract one from his or her own consciousness. Battery operated, portable transistor sets helped too. (As a teacher during this period, I discovered that certain students who I thought wore hearing aids were attending my lectures and listening to baseball games at the same time!) This meant, of course, that radio advertising might be offered quite inexpensively to local businesses, an opportunity at which many local businesses avidly jumped.

Everything about radio broadcasting seemed to grow in size as a result of the death of big broadcasting. In the 20 years after 1948, the number of radio stations in the U.S.A. tripled from about 2,000 to about 6,000. Radio advertising was indeed now a local—and fairly cheap—medium, but, added together, tt also became a surprisingly lucrative one. Network revenue diminished to almost nothing, as local profits of individual stations began to rise to new highs by the end of the 'fifties. New interest in high fidelity broadcasting encouraged FM station operators, even those owning AM outlets, to expand and improve their operations. Stereo transmissions, feasible only on FM, soon gave them a further lift. Many new "FM only" outlets appeared.

More radio receivers than ever were sold per year, now cheaper than ever before. Between 1951 and 1955, about 12 million receivers were produced by various manufacturers. By the 1965–68 period, the number had risen to about 23 million. It was calculated by then—and it is still true—that, in the U.S.A., one working radio exists for every man woman and child in the population—*at least*. This exceeds the number of flush toilets, the number of working automobiles and of every semi-permanent object manufactured for personal use with the possible exception of toothbrushes.

As radio localized and expanded its dimensions, so too did it seek out new and specialized audiences. The bulk of sound broadcasting was directed to the young and consisted, as noted above, of popular recordings. But ethnic stations spoke to Blacks and to other special populations in foreign tongues. Classical music outlets directed their programs to highbrows. Special tastes of all sorts were catered to—along with advertising designed to interest these specific markets.

While radio broadcasting no longer constituted a vast national enterprise— and networks were reduced to "feeders" that provided some stations with periodic news and commentary—it was, and remains, a healthy local business, employing a good-sized work force of engineers, writers, announcers, disc jockeys and others. And the word "local" is more than a rough slogan. In farm areas, special reporters talk endlessly about agricultural condition and the prices of farm products, cover cattle auctions and even accompany the farmer on his tractor into his fields. In cities, some stations broadcast mainly to intellectuals, non-conformists and almost every type of specialized minority. Compared to the old days, this is small-time broadcasting. But, from a national perspective, radio has grown into a new and healthy national institution, after its temporary setback in the early 'fifties.

The Recording Business

One phenomenon related to radio's eventual reaction to video was the sudden expansion of the record industry beginning in the 1950s. After 1948, recordings designed to be played at 33⅓ or 45 revolutions per minute paved the way for increasingly naturalistic home reproduction systems for music, popular and classical, including, eventually, stereophonic sound. Transistorized electronics simplified the construction and lowered the prices of truely fine high fidelity phonograph equipment. Tape recorders of various kinds also added a "do it yourself" dimension to sound recording. Not only might one now record easily his own voice (or harmonica solo), he or she could also plagiarize anything broadcast on radio for the price of the tape alone.

For reasons that remain economically unclear, all of this, including the plagiarism, gave the recording industry an enormous boost in the early 'fifties. It has continued until today. Sydney Head reports that American record sales reached a quarter of a billion dollars by 1953, and that a fourth of this came from the sale of classical or serious music. (One must *not* assume that one-fourth of the total *purchasers* were devotees of symphonies or operas. Classical records were, and are, more expensive than their popular counterparts. Collectors of serious music tend to invest more in their enthusiasm than the younger public, to whom pop music appeals, invest in theirs.)

At any rate, the recording industry grew, not only in size but institutionally by allying itself with broadcasting companies, and with the new conglomerates that now included one-time motion picture producers, print publishers and electronics manufacturers. In its way, television had somehow liberated industrially still another communications medium, one that had for many years lived almost entirely under the heel of the broadcasting establishment.

Video: A Distinctive Medium

Until about 1955 or so, much of the American public—and even some broadcasters—cosseted the notion that television would eventually grow up to be a medium best described as "big time radio with pictures." For quite a while, this was indeed the direction video seemed to be taking. In the first place, television broadcasting in America, largely because of its technology and method of distribution, had fallen into the hands of radio broadcaster: networks and individual stations. Both video and radio were, after all, methods of "broadcasting" as it was (and is) defined. Second, it was therefore assumed that the economic structure of video broadcasting would probably be similar—or identical—to that of radio.

Advertising would, for the most part, pay for a free (or nearly free) television service provided to the nation as it had in radio's heyday. It turned out, however, that there was a great economic difference between radio and television. Boiled down, it was simply one of cost, both capital costs of building television studios and transmission facilities and the running costs of production.

Comparisons between radio and television expenses are difficult to show, because the value of a dollar has not remained constant during the post-war years. A radio station, nevertheless, in the 1940s might cost, at most, $100,000 to build. It cost about three to five times as much to construct a primitive video installation at the time, and it would cost at least $2.5 million to build a similar one today. (And, as of present writing, a television installation costs about fifteen times as much as building a radio station!)

Displaying differences in the costs of programming between radio and television is almost like comparing Jello with sirloin steak. The difference is formidable: far more that just the matter of adding pictures to sound. While it is not easy to pin down the cost of a former network radio program, few of even the most elaborate shows consumed in excess of $20,000 per half hour, including commercials. Most cost far less. Television prices are variable too, depending on personnel, the type of program, whether it is filmed or taped, etc. But costs of $70–100,000 per network half hour are not unusual.

Unlike radio, moreover, the price of television commercials themselves far exceed the price of programming, often by three or four times for a single half-hour. Commericals, of course, may be shown more frequently and on more stations than may programs. From another perspective, however, *the total amount of money spent on commercial broadcasts far exceeds the cost of video programming of all types*—for reasons that are not difficult to figure out if you compare the two closely, merely in terms of production extravagance.

Whatever their surface similarities, network broadcasters and others had to conclude that the basic economic rules that governed radio would have to be changed for television. Few advertisers could afford to "sponsor" video shows as they had radio programs. This meant the necessity to devise an entirely new method of production, sharing costs among different advertisers. In the radio era, advertising agencies had served as production arms for single sponsoring corporations by writing, casting and preparing all sorts of radio shows. The agencies had now, obviously, to quit the production business, because various advertisers represented by different agencies might share the costs of a single video show. (Exceptions like the *Hallmark Hall of Fame*, the *G.E. Playhouse* and a few other programs continue to this day, but they are rare birds.) At any rate, advertising agencies now had their hands full simply preparing television commercials on film and tape and booking "spots," or time, for them locally and on network broadcasts.

Programming still had to come from somewhere! In the early 'fifties, it was provided by a combination of network talent, advertising agencies still acting as producers and a new breed of "package producers" who made series of programs live, on film and later on tape. These parties then split the pie between them in an interesting ratio, considering later trends. In those days, the networks were responsible for roughly 30% of the total station output; advertisers about another 35%; and package producers the remaining 35%.

At present, advertising agencies are nearly out of the production game. The networks' share has dropped to 20%, much of it news, documentary programming and talk shows. Package producers are responsible for almost all of the remaining 80% of the material that appears on video screens across the nation. Of course, local stations also prepare a small amount of material, mostly news, but it is negligible.

During the early 'fifties, therefore, much trial-and-error experimentation centered upon the obvious proposition that *somebody* was going to have to provide programming for television broadcasting, lest the new medium simply become a device for replaying ancient theatre films over and over. Many in the old Hollywood motion picture establishment, on the heels of the Supreme Court's disintegration of the "Big Five," had overlooked this fact when they consigned movies to the scrap heap in the wake of video's new competition. They were nearsighted almost beyond belief. Some, however, also noticed the obvious: that, although radio people were, for the most part *running* television in the U.S.A., video was quite unlike radio in almost every respect except the way it was distributed and received in the home. Television was, however, similar to the movies—in fact, in many ways identical with them.

This nearsightedness of the Hollywood pessimists may not even be blamed upon myopic interpretations of the so-called "distinctive" nature of television's voodoo by the academic squirrel, Marshall McLuhan. He was not around at the time, and nobody was yet foolish enough to take his writings even half seriously. Television was simply regarded as an elaborate form of radio broadcasting and thus irrelevant to film production.

Movies versus Television

Hollywood's panic sent film makers running in two directions: one, to try to produce for the motion picture theatre screen a type of movie that simply could *not* be shown on the small home video receiver. The early 'fifties, therefore, was a time when a number of movies were shot in a three-dimensional process that required the viewer to wear Polaroid glasses and gave one an illusion of depth or, as it was called, "3-D."

The basic optical process was as old as the nineteenth century stereopticon. And, in the 1930s, movies of this sort were made by separating a picture into two images, one red and one green, that were fused together when one wore cellophane lenses of red and green, one color over each eye. Polaroid lenses separated the images in a different, more complicated way than colored celluloid. The illusion of depth it produced was not bad, but the cardboard glasses were uncomfortable (particularly if you wore them on top of regular eyeglasses.) The movies, made in the 3-D process, fare like *Bwana Devil* (1953) and *House of Wax* (1953), were miserable. Clearly, 3-D was not going to save Hollywood!

Fred Waller's *This Is Cinerama* (1952) offered a more interesting experiment that succeeded as a film but hardly revolutionized the movie industry, as some pundits predicted at the time. Waller's system used three conventional movie cameras and projectors. The resulting picture on a wide-wide screen was spread out into a long, high and curved color image that provided a partial illusion of depth. For the next years, Waller's system was used for various features. Most of them, except *How The West Was Won* (1962), were travelogues that explored colorful and spectacular scenery, usually by airplane or helicopter.

The introduction of Cinerama was followed shortly by Twentieth Century-Fox's Cinemascope process in 1953. A new version of an old invention, Cinemascope simply squeezed on to one conventional 35mm movie frame, both shot and projected through a special anamorphic lense, a wide and thin picture eight times as long as it was high. Other film makers followed with their own versions of wide-screen movie processes: Warnerscope, Superscope, Panascope, and Vistavision. The latter employed a film, the frames of which were 70mm in width. All of these processes utilized stereophonic sound tracks. And all were difficult to project properly in certain theatres, often miraculously sliding out of focus either around the edges of the picture, in the center or both.

By the end of the 1950s, wide screens had become old hat. The public seemed to like them well enough, but they influenced little either the quality of movies then being made or the rapidly declining attendance of the film audience, and, except for a brief spurt around 1955, declines in box office revenue as well.

Theatrical movies were eventually to make something of a comeback among the public, but not until about 1965 and for an unanticipated reason: Movies, by this time, had begun to direct their appeals to adults, because, by now, they were freed of the old censorial restraints that had encouraged the people who made them to remain as young and foolish artistically as they had 50 years before.

Televison Rescues Hollywood

Televison, however, *was* both young and foolish in the 'fifties. If video replaced any national pastime, it was not radio listening, attending picnics, bowling or sex, but instead addictive attendance by millions of people a week at Grade B and C films—just the sort of fare that Hollywood had, for years, produced most efficiently, economically, expertly and profitably.

An anthropologist once called Hollywood a "dream factory" during its heyday. I suppose it was. But, more important, it was also a "junk factory." The latter fact came to the rescue of the film industry in the 'fifties and subsequently brought it to new prosperity with the advent of video broadcasting on a national scale. The dreams had vanished. But the junk on film, as we shall see, continues to this day to roll from the American movie capital's production lines as profusely as it did in the busiest days of the old Hollywood monopolies.

Television entrepreneurs faced the tremendous problem of simply feeding their fabulous infant. Because every station demanded 12-, 18- or even 24-

hours of programming a day for 365 days a year, television's ongoing consumption of prepared and specialized material was far greater than that of any medium of mass (or class) communication that had preceded it. True enough, many radio stations offered 'round-the-clock services, but, because of the absence of pictures, feeding its appetite was not too difficult. One disc jockey, one engineer and a pile of records might keep an all-night station going with a minimum of cost, preparation and effort. Nothing like this was possible for video, unless one was content to replay *ad nauseam* a limited backlog of ancient movies that viewers would tolerate seeing more than once. Live television of even the most primitive sort was difficult to produce, and, when one got right down to it, a modest daily half-hour soap opera could generate in three or four days as much dramatic writing and acting time as an entire feature film once did, consuming a production period lasting from two weeks to two months!

Hollywood naturally was not able to solve entirely the problem of television's insatiable appetite. It could, however, do a lot to decrease its constant drain upon the resources of broadcasters. As we have seen, during the 'fifties, more and more television broadcasting began emerging from so-called "package producers"—that is, production organizations that provided a complete product (a program or series of programs) for a fee, to a network or advertising agency that it, in turn, might then sell it to sponsors, local or national. At first, these packages were mostly live performances of dramas or panel shows. Or their first performance of a program was live, but this would be recorded on film (or "kinescoped") for transmission to other stations beyond the range of a network, or because of time differences throughout the U.S.A., or for later broadcasting. Finally, package producers found that they could, quite economically, film their programs (usually in Hollywood) or, after the introduction of videotape technology in the late 'fifties, electronically record them, store them, and lease them to networks and independent stations as needed, either for first showings or as reruns.

By far the slickest, surest (and most expensive) way of packaging a television show was, and is, to film it, either in front of a live audience or on a conventional Hollywood sound stage—with or without audience noises like laughter and applause added later to the sound track. This technique of production was, and is, not exactly the same as making a movie for theatrical production, although the entire film might be shot on a sound stage at a movie studio like Universal or 20th Century-Fox. The difference between the two centers largely upon the production speed of the operation, the use of continuous characters and scenery in series programs, and the ratio of film shot to that actually used in the final production: often about three to one for television film, as opposed to ten to one for certain theatre films. The great similarity between the two— and the major advantage of film over tape—remains the manner in which filmed material may be cut and edited, the sound track manipulated, and various optical effects produced in the laboratory that are difficult (and sometimes impossible) to achieve by means of videotape.

From the early 'fifties onwards, smart film makers caught the scent of money in videoland and recognised that the home receiver and the new mass medium might eventually be their salvation instead of their assassin. Most of the major film producers set up "cheap and dirty" television subsidiaries that began grinding all manner of items for the home screen. Columbia Pictures, Paramount, Warner Brothers, Universal and the others certainly possessed both the know-how and equipment.

The Film Factory Prospers

In fact, only modest changes in some of their old working procedures were necessary, because, as filmgoing patterns changed, Hollywood's one-time market for near endless Grade B formula-films dried up. The old formulas, it turned out, were good enough for television. So plots, dialogue, actors and sets (and horses too, probably) that had once fed America's twice weekly double-feature movie habit kept on grinding. Instead of feature films, however, series like *Have Gun, Will Travel, Peyton Place* and *The Beverly Hillbillies* emerged from the old movie lots. And many old Hollywood hands, including writers, actors and directors, were quite aware that nothing had really changed much for them.

Or had it? The need of television for good, reliable Grade B and C movie corn also stimulated a number of new production firms to start making their own television films in their own studios. Some simply rented studio space from large companies and produced features with their own stars, written by their own writers, and directed by their own directors. The best known of these production companies was Desilu Productions which, largely as a result of the popularity of their filmed *I Love Lucy* series, finally bought RKO's film studio and set it to shooting nothing but television shows. (In the 1960s, CBS even purchased the old Republic Studios, home of countless theatre westerns and "cheapies" of the past, in an unsuccessful attempt to develop its own captive source for video film *along with* a production firm to produce theatrical films at the same time. This overly ambitious venture failed.)

At any rate, many of the popular television programs of the 1950s were just "quickie" versions of old Hollywood "quickie" movies: *Father Knows Best, Wagon Train,* the *Schlitz Playhouse, Gunsmoke, Lassie,* as well as formula comedy shows like *Burns and Allen,* and even quiz and audience participation shows shot on modified movie sound stages.

In 1954, one of Hollywood's shrewdest and most enigmatic showmen burst into television with an entire retinue of time-tested characters, stories, songs and talents. Walt Disney brought the *Mickey Mouse Club* to the nation's television screens (on film), juxtaposing live action with his established cartoon characters, paving the way for another series, *Disneyland,* which became a household word, years before the opening of the amusement park with the same name near Hollywood.

As a result, the Disney organization was soon busier than it had ever been, preparing a daily and weekly video program and, also on its sound stages, shooting live-action theatrical movies, one after the other. Only Disney's old-time animators suffered from any shortage of work, as the cartoon short and feature business dried up, and new animation studios (some employing Japanese and Mexican labor) began producing cheap and dirty "limited animation" movies for youngsters watching television. While these animated films were crude compared to the old Disney theatrical features and shorts, one could hardly tell the difference when they were transmitted by video. Disney's cartoon operation soon adopted their own time- and labor-saving methods of limited animation as well.

While less people, therefore, found their way into movie theatres each week during the 'fifties than they had for the previous two or three decades, Hollywood film makers, as a group, did not suffer severely. In addition to making video films, the 'fifties was also a period when many movie moguls delightedly discovered that the land that they had bought 40 years before for next to nothing was, it turned out, one of the most oil-rich territories in the U.S.A. Up went derricks and cranes!

A population explosion in and around Los Angeles also turned many acres of motion picture property into prime residential real estate. Housing projects grew where once *ersatz* cowboys had chased phony Indians for movie cameras, but neither the studio owners nor happy stockholders in the motion picture companies, for the most part, let sentiment interfere with their profits.

Even though their roles as producers of hit television shows grew more and more important, the film companies themselves were not able to gain a foothold either in the actual ownership or management of the three major television networks. The numerous package producers who used the facilities of the film producers stood in their way. These packagers were owners of their own products—that is, the most popular titles, stars and production concepts in video. Not even the biggest of Hollywood studios, like the ever-growing Universal, could attempt for long to compete with this television production establishment. It made far more money by cooperating with the packagers, and half a loaf was better than none.

Theater Films on Television

In 1955, the first of the major film companies also made available for telecasting a number of theatrical movies produced during the previous seven years, a period "off limits" for television by virtue of agreements between the film producers and the various labor unions involved in film production. The first valuable library of recent movies was offered for sale by RKO, already out of business as a film producer. Soon other companies followed their lead, negotiating favorable contracts for the video release of their post-1948 films, the broadcasting of which would no longer interfere with profits from theatrical distribution.

All old Hollywood films, however, were not released *carte blanche.* Some, like *Gone With the Wind* and *Snow White and The Seven Dwarfs* have not yet appeared, except in segments, on television, because they still have life in them at the nation's movie theatre box offices.* Some others, like MGM's *The Wizard of Oz,* are released for video only periodically (usually once a year) at an increasingly large rental fee to one or another television network because of their special and enormous appeal to successive generations of children who have not seen them before or who want to see them again.

After 1955, nevertheless, hundreds of recent Hollywood films were available to the nation's broadcasters. Viewing choices were widened somewhat for the public, but the insatiable appetite of the new medium hardly seemed slaked. There seemed to be no shortage of continuous entertainment of the, then, black-and-white television tube. But a good share of it, particularly during the summer months, consisted of kinescopes and films that one had probably seen before.

The Communist Hunt in Videoland

It remained for real-life drama of the broadcasting industry to find its way onto the home receiver in a number of extremely unpleasant ways.

Television historian Eric Barnouw devotes a formidable part of his coverage of the early years of the video medium to the blacklists and communist witch hunts of the early 'fifties that, in retrospect, seem to have literally terrorized broadcasters. These executives, whose livelihoods depended upon the public's favor, feared boycott, reprisals—or worse—if they hired anyone who may even have been slightly connected with the once formidable communist movement in the U.S.A. during his or her lifetime. In effect, the House Un-American Activities Committee's persecution of so-called ''Reds'' in Hollywood discussed in the previous chapters, now a few years later, reached the headquarters of the radio and television networks in New York, but in an illegal, more insidious and devilish way than it had arrived on the West Coast.

Whether or not this disgraceful period is, in the long run and examined alone, as important as Barnouw believes is probably irrelevant. The climate of opinion that the broadcasting blacklists created in the radio and television industries may have paved the way for the coming era of Senator Joseph McCarthy's investigations and the publicity given them by broadcasters. The latter turned themselves inside out to cover on video his scandalous senatorial inquisition of the Army, the State Department and just about everything else in sight. McCarthy succeeded, in part, because he provided good newspaper copy, but, more important, he also attracted people to their television sets.

The junior Senator from Wisconsin had little, if anything, to do personally with the ''Red Scare'' that literally terrorized the broadcasting industries—and the Broadway legitimate theatre as well. In fact, one school of thought regards

* *GWTW* was shown on national network television divided into two segments on consecutive evenings, as I was correcting the final manuscript of this book in November, 1976.

Hollywood's tarring and feathering of token communists, the witch hunting that ran through the radio and television industries, and the Senate Investigating Committee headed by McCarthy (which centered its attack mostly upon government and the military agencies) *all* as the *results* of *one* spasm of social panic in the air at the time. Others disagree.

By the end of the 'forties and in the early 'fifties, remember, many sincere Americans indeed shared some realistic reasons to fear the insidious spy-plus-propaganda network of the U.S.S.R. at the time. All of their concerns were not paranoia, as it seems to many today. Important atomic secrets *had* apparently been transmitted by agents in the U.S.A. and Britain to the Soviet Union. In England, the threads of a network of Russian spies, highly placed in the foreign services, *was* starting to unravel in an astounding, almost unbelievable way. A number of American intellectuals, writers and others, began to reveal, loudly, publicly and apparently honestly, the actual complexity of Soviet espionage activities in the U.S.A. during the 1930s, a network that included individuals who had later risen to trusted government positions—or so it was believed and shown in court rooms at the time.

True or false (the matter has not been settled to this day), cause indeed existed for a certain degree of apprehension on the part of Americans who were sincerely worried about the influence of communists in the U.S.A. upon our communications institutions and government agencies. It was exactly this sincere concern that demagogues with a flair for showmanship, like the late Senator McCarthy, took advantage of to their own ends to gain headlines and personal power. Because men like McCarthy so exaggerated this threat, in time they were quieted down by both censure and public revulsion, but not before much damage had been done to innocent people—and doubtless a few not-so-innocent ones—along the way.

Were I to search for a moral in these purges that ran through the entertainment industries (and elsewhere) at this time, I would attack them less as matters of principle, the way liberals like Barnouw do, than for their journalistic sloppiness, irresponsible exploitation of well-meant fears by broadcasters, and the sheer mischief of many newsmen and women in overdramatizing what was, and remains, a perfectly natural and honest area of public sensitivity: the threat of subversion. The entire blacklisting episode may seem silly and stupid today. It was also silly and stupid yesterday. But, looking backwards, I do not believe that the many fine, innocent people who were caught up in its thrust and ruined or driven to their deaths were just victims of witch hunters. They were also victims of editors, reporters, executives and performers in all the media who squeezed every last bit of sensational publicity out of this unsavory era to pander to the appetites of a public that was, with considerable justice, both frightened and confused!

Sadder still was the sorry fact that the Red Scare hit the broadcasting industry without even the force of governmental power—or *any* real power except industry hysteria—behind it. A number of sleazy ex-FBI men began printing a newsletter called *Counterattack* in 1947. Then a book, *Red Channels,* appeared. Both were published by the same rascals—and others. The function of these journals was simple. Identified by name were radio and television actors, directors, writers and others (151 alone in the first *Red Channels!*) who were supposed either to be communists or sympathetic to communist causes.

In no uncertain terms, *Counterattack* and *Red Channels* directed their message to broadcasting producers and sponsors. It was, "Fire these people!" Backing up these threats were the sentiments of various (in large part) well-meaning Americans, including some individuals who merchandised products sponsored on radio and television. They exercised considerable pressure against sponsors, advertising agencies and networks to blackball "suspicious" artists, who, for the most part (but not entirely), were people who had refused to state openly that they were against denying anyone, including communists, First Amendment rights of the United States Constitution. But the issue, unfortunately, was not completely one of right and wrong or black and white, as some tell us today.

The original list, in all fairness, *did* contain the names of a few Communist Party members in show business. Whether, as actors or directors, they in any manner constituted a threat to the welfare of the U.S.A. is another question. Most of the people cited, however, were simply liberals who, at one time or another, had expressed sympathies towards the U.S.S.R. during the war. In fact, the list was, for the most part, made up of entirely loyal Americans whose only error might have been their hyper-enthusiasm for certain dubious liberal causes and American-Soviet friendship.

This did not matter. The odd thing about *Counterattack, Red Channels,* the other publications that followed them—and a rumor mill that was likely to chew up any professional career in broadcasting for the oddest of reasons—was that they worked. For a number of years—particularly as Senator McCarthy's bombast about communists in government was avidly snatched by newspaper editors and given front page coverage—all critical personnel at the networks and other employers of artists required an arbitrary and mysterious "clearance," either by the editors of these newspapers or someone else who set himself up as an expert on communists to keep their jobs or get new ones.

What might someone do who found himself listed as a "communist sympathizer"? For all practical purposes, very little. In some instances, it was possible for a performer and/or writer or director to declare in public and print that he or she was *not* a communist, never had been, and so forth—and then, usually, as a token of faith, name a few colleagues who *had* been communists. Those unwilling to abase themselves in this manner were forced either to look for different kinds of employment or leave the country. Some grovelled. Some left.

Actors Sam Wanamaker, J. Edward Bromberg and others went to Europe. Some found other ways out. The harassed actor, Philip Loeb, committed suicide. A fine actress, Mady Christians was, it is said, literally heartbroken to the point of death by the fact that she suddenly found herself unemployable. Many careers were finished for good. Individuals were consigned to obscure marginal employment in show business, including the delightful comedienne (and fine lady) Minerva Pious who had once achieved enormous popularity on radio with comedian Fred Allen. Some stuck it out and survived; others even prospered in later years. Unemployable in radio and television, they worked when possible in the theatre, summer stock and at universities until the dust settled.

The Fate of Blacklisting

How and when did it end? The story is complex. Little by little, the cause of anti-communism seemed personified by one man: Senator Joseph McCarthy. Senator McCarthy was himself, in large measure, a television-made personality, with considerable help from the press coverage given his wildest accusations. As chairman of the Senate Permanent Subcommittee on Investigations, he centered his attacks upon the government, mostly the State Department, the Army and Navy and the United States Information Agency—whenever possible via televised hearings.

McCarthy quickly learned how to take advantage of the video medium during the four or so years he rode high, badgering witnesses, indulging in sarcasm and often giving attorneys for his witnesses, and the witnesses themselves, little or no opportunity to defend themselves. Eventually, all irresponsible anti-communistic crusading in the U.S.A. became known as "McCarthyism," a misnomer because of the influence of the Wisconsin Senator. And the witch hunts of one sort or another spread, not only into broadcasting but to universities, big business, publishing and, of course, into the government itself during the first four or five years of the 1950s. Those who are hurled to fame by the mass media seem often doomed to be destroyed by it, I think. Richard M. Nixon launched his national political career with his soap-opera-like 1952 "Checkers" speech on television, answering charges of corruption regarding the funding of a previous congressional campaign. Eventually, his dissembling was exposed for all of the U.S.A. to see on video when the Watergate hearings and their aftermath splashed all over the tube. McCarthy was, in effect, also a creature both created and done in on video, but over a much shorter period of time. The Senator's end came more quickly, however, than the protracted finale of Nixon's career.

Murrow versus McCarthy

The man mainly responsible for silencing McCathy, and possibly McCarthysim, was Edward R. Murrow, himself listed in *Red Channels,* but a subtle and even-tempered warrior against McCarthyism from its beginnings. Murrow's major move was made on March 9, 1954, when, on his *See It Now* television program, he telecast one-half hour of fascinating—and devastating—film clips, carefully edited, displaying Senator McCarthy at his worst and in action.

The late Gilbert Seldes, later and correctly, observed that Murrow's *See It Now* program was a hatchet job, hardly fair in any respect to McCarthy—biased, slanted, inaccurate in parts and editorially distorted. I agree with Seldes. My own feelings at the time, however, were the same as they are today: that there are rare occasions when fire must best be fought with fire. Murrow's treatment of McCarthy was no crueler than McCarthy's treatment of numerous innocent witnesses before his committee, and the damage eventually done to McCarthy was pretty much the same sort of damage he had done—or tried to do—to many others.

Murrow and CBS, of course, offered McCarthy "equal time" to answer back the program. This McCarthy did a few weeks later. But it was like giving a fly equal time to attack an elephant. McCarthy did not possess Murrow's production know-how or even the funds to produce a response in kind. All he could do was to deliver a dull, ineffectual speech.

In effect, though, the fat was in the fire. Public opinion began to turn against McCarthy. Murrow kept up his attack at a somewhat diminished level. McCarthy subsequently conducted a particularly terrifying 36-day hearing centering on certain Army and civilian so-called "subversives," during which he locked horns with Boston attorney Joseph Welch. The latter's keen legal mind and gentle civility showed up McCarthy for the boor he was.

Later that year, on December 2, 1954, Senator Joseph McCarthy became the second man in the history of the Senate to be officially condemned by his own colleagues. Stripped of his power and publicly disgraced, McCarthy, a heavy drinker, then faded from the public scene. He died, a victim of liver disease associated with alcoholism, in 1957. McCarthy was dead, but McCarthyism was merely dying.

The Slow Fade-out

The thrust of McCarthyism continued long after the Senator had faded from the scene, just as, in one degree or another, one can still sniff it in the air here and there even today. In 1956, the famous blacklisting by CBS of news commentator John Henry Faulk took place. Faulk then sued *Aware Inc.*, the descendent of *Red Channels* that had pointed its finger at him. After many years of litigation, he finally won his case but did not get back his former position with CBS as a newscaster.

For a long time, one's open or personal political affiliations were not irrelevant to whether one might not be employed in the broadcasting industry, particularly by the networks. The issue remained important longer in broadcasting than it did in the motion picture industry. Broadcasting, however, was a growing, highly unified institution during the 'fifties, while the film industry was disintegrating and undergoing great changes at the same time. By 1955, Hollywood was a good deal more worried about survival than politics. On the other hand, the television industry, at the time, was concerned vitally about its national image and how the public felt about the enormous control that the three networks exerted over their affiliates. Broadcaster's' sensitivities to criticism were, and remain, far more acute than those of movie makers.

Most broadcasters claim today that blacklisting of any kind for any reason does not exist any longer in their industry. This is probably hyperbole. But the nightmare years of McCarthyism indeed faded as America turned into the 'sixties. We are reminded only occasionally of them today in books and (surprisingly) on television documentaries. Most of us are also certain that they will, and can, never return again. In this matter, I think most of us are dead wrong. Much history tells us that the potential victim of *any* kind of witch hunt is never more vulnerable than when he is convinced that he is entirely safe and secure.

Dirty Work on the Quiz Shows

The late 'fifties also saw another kind of scandal shudder through videoland and move from there to high places. While many people took it seriously, it was, for many others, pretty funny while it was happening. To some, it even looks more foolish (in many ways) from today's perspective. Loosely known as the "quiz show scandals," it is a story of human greed run wild, show business ethics gone crazy and public opinion at its loudest and most irresponsible. Here was a peculiarly American phenomenon, similar in its trivial way to the many political scandals that preceded and followed it up to the present writing.

The insanity started in 1955, when Louis G. Cowan, an independent program package producer, thought up the notion for a live video program called *The $64,000 Question.* The show was based loosely upon a former radio hit, *Take It Or Leave It.* On the latter program, a guest could parlay his winnings, by answering various questions correctly, to the grand total of $64. It was a clever little program. It was fun. On Cowan's television version, the stakes were raised a thousand times. The contestants (unlike the radio version) were carefully selected for their peculiar televison appeal: a shoemaker who was an expert on opera; a Marine with a supposedly fantastic knowledge of cooking and other anomalies. Dr. Joyce Brothers, a pretty young psychologist, appeared from nowhere as an expert on boxing, for instance.

A nice honest-looking young man named Hal March asked the questions that were prepared by scholar Dr. Bergen Evans and his staff. The show was tricked out with all sorts of visual dramatic devices: an "isolation booth" in which contestants (for reasons yet to be determined) might commune with their intellects while thinking up answers, a vapid looking bank manager who repeated weekly a nonsense speech about the super-security given each question.

The program was enormously successful, both for CBS, Cowan and for its sponsor, Revlon. Cowan soon joined CBS as a network executive. But, as *The Question* began to spawn offsprings like *The $64,000 Challenge,* imitators on other networks, such as NBC's *Twenty-One,* all nearly as (or more) popular, it was probably possible for him to read the prophetic handwriting on the wall. The first hint came when Cowan, instead of glorying in his success, slipped away from CBS to become a university professor. Meanwhile, the stakes kept rising—to as much as one genius' $160,000 winnings on *Challenge*.

By 1958, the golden boy of the quiz show contestants was a likable, somewhat shy young academic type named Charles Van Doren, a Columbia University instructor and member of a distinguished family of scholars. Van Doren appeared on the Barry-Enright NBC program *Twenty-One*. He seemed to know almost everything about everything. One after another, he demolished contending contestants in this quiz show version of the card game, blackjack. Audiences apparently loved him. When he finally stumbled on a comparatively simple question (involving living royalty in Europe), he finished his stint on *Twenty-One* $129,000 richer for his trouble and moved from Columbia University to a lucrative job as a television broadcaster for NBC.

Next, the lid was blown off the entire pot by a gutsy young veteran of *Twenty-One* named Herbert Stempel. The whole caper, it turned out, had been a fake! There followed an agonizing series of disclosures, denials, charges and grand jury hearings. Investigations even reached a House of Representatives subcommittee on legislative oversight. Finally, some of the culprits, including Van Doren, told the truth. This led to an exposé of all the big money quiz shows, including CBS' *$64,000 Question*. All of them were, in one degree or another, fixed, and, in many instances, more carefully rehearsed than video's soap operas. None of the contestants, it seemed, was nearly as brilliant as they seemed (with one or two exceptions), and the programs were as carefully manipulated as puppet shows.

The problem actually centered upon a strange clash of ethics. The producers and most of the contestants were caught up in the carnival morality of show business. In this world, a magician may say, "There is nothing up my sleeves," and be lying—but for a good reason: to entertain. All actors, pretending to be people they are not, in a way, lie. What is important, is that the audience understands that these are simply entertaining *performances*. So also did most people involved in the production of these quiz shows think of their successes in terms of audience suspense, excitement and, of course, viewer ratings, all issues having to do with *performances*. The audience at home, on the other hand, seemed to be functioning by different ethical guidelines. They, naturally, believed that they were watching real contests of intelligence, and that the outcome of each program remained in doubt. Such ethics are those that we assume guide athletic contests, which, in many ways, these quiz shows resembled. Both the behavior of the producers and the subsequent outrage of the viewers at their trickery is therefore simple to comprehend. What is harder to explain is how and why men like Van Doren allowed themselves to become involved in these shady dealings. They have offered many explanations over the years, but the most likely one is simply that they were greedy.

The scandals passed, but not before they had done their damage. Van Doren probably suffered the most. He left both broadcasting and the academic world to become, eventually, an editor for *The Encyclopedia Britannica*. Others, like Dr. Brothers, weathered it all and came out of it all smelling of roses—somehow. Still others, particularly, those involved in the actual productions (and more-or-less innocent bystanders like actor Hal March), found their careers aborted. Cowan had long been safely out of the picture. Revlon concentrated for a time upon print advertising. The high brass at the various networks claimed to be "shocked" at it all and swore vehemently that their upper echelons knew nothing about this hanky-panky in their organizations, claims impossible to disprove but difficult to believe.

Quiz shows on television, however, did *not* die. Prize money awarded on those that remained, however, suddenly shrunk by many multiples. Emphasis was now placed more upon quiz masters like Groucho Marx or celebrity panels such as the weekly *What's My Line*. Paradoxically, these "safe" shows were probably not run one bit more honestly—or dishonestly—than the infamous *Question* and *Twenty One*. But the competitive element and financial aspects of them were so underplayed that it did not matter. These days, audiences seem to understand that television quiz shows abide by show business ethics rather than those we employ for athletic contests, race tracks or in gambling houses, where gaming must be at least honest by tradition and/or law.

Educational Broadcasting

Despite the money involved in them, the quiz shows of the 'fifties displayed American television at its cheapest and shoddiest. The programs achieved large audiences and pandered to the public's silliest whims in every way possible, at the expense of the sort of basic honesty even children understand. The same period, however, also saw the birth of educational television, which, in its zeal to avoid merely satisfying public appetites and imitating commercial video, ran into no end of problems of its own, none of which were as devastating or well publicized as the quiz show scandals.

As the results of the efforts of the Joint Council on Educational Television, we have seen that, at the end of the station "freeze" in 1952, some 250 or so channels were reserved by the FCC for educational use. Only a third were on VHF frequencies. To reserve channels was fine, but the problem remained of who was going to support these stations if they were built, who might build them, and what sort of programming they would carry. These questions were not definitively answered in the 1950s and, by the end of the decade, prospects for their eventual resolution did not look healthy.

Many universities and other educational institutions certainly wanted to construct and operate stations, but these were tremendously expensive undertakings, even in that period of national affluence. And all educational stations, by charter, were to be prohibited by the FCC from indulging in anything but nonprofit, non-commercial broadcasting. That is, they could not be funded the way commercial channels were, by the sale of air time to *anybody,* except, under certain circumstances, to other non-profit organizations or by donations from private citizens or profit-making corporations.

The JCET, a well meaning cluster of educational bureaucrats, naturally looked around for a suitable sugar-daddy. They found it in still another, larger bureaucracy, The Ford Foundation. Ford was set up to do good works and spread good words by the heirs of millionaire Henry Ford. The Foundation dripped so much money that it was necessary, for administrative reasons, to dispense with it in large globs. Educational television looked like a good cause, and it needed enormous amounts of cash. By 1961, Ford's Fund for Adult Education alone had sunk $12 million into educational video. Other arms of the Foundation spread its wealth over various schools and school districts for experiments in educational broadcasting to the tune of many more millions. Within a few years, little or nothing done with or about video for non-commercial purposes could not be traced back, by one route or another, to the largesse of the Ford philanthropoids.

KHUT in Houston, Texas was the first permanent educational video station—on the air in 1953, operated by the University of Houston. Others followed, most of them associated with universities. Some, like KQED in San Francisco (opened in 1954) were community operations. In time, the JCET gave way to another, slightly more flexible bureaucracy, eventually known as National Educational Television that helped to provide films and kinescopes for programming. By the middle 'fifties, about 25 educational video stations were on the air in such cities as Pittsburgh and Boston. By the end of the decade, the number had more than doubled.

The stations, however, faced numerous difficulties. First, their lifeline to Uncle Ford might be cut off at any time without cause; Uncle Sam would have been preferable. Second, much of their programming was poor. Attempts were made to reach children in school and students in class at universities, good ideas in theory but lukewarm ones at best in practice, as bitter experience has many times shown since. Instruction (or something) was, of course, offered homebound youngsters and pre-school tots. Many programs of a strange nature concerning such esoteric arts as paper-folding and yogi may best be described by the meaningless academic term "adult education." Third, hardly anybody watched educational stations broadcast on conventional VHF channels, and *nobody* but school and station administrators looked at the few operating on UHF.

Ford's money appeared to be flowing down an open drain. The future of these stations appeared doubtful. The foundation was obviously achieving far more in the domain of do-goodism simply by underwriting a weekly Sunday series of programs called *Omnibus*, produced by Robert Saudek and the Ford Television Workshop. *Omnibus* even paid part of its own way by accepting commercial sponsorship. It lasted, under Ford aegis, from 1952 to 1957. Free from Ford, it could not work up its own fiscal steam and finally withered and died.

Omnibus was never immensely popular, but the size of its Sunday afternoon audience on numerous commercial stations was impressive. Productions were impeccable—and expensive. The programs were held together by the urbane talents of Alistair Cooke, an American of British origins, who always seemed to be on the verge of leading the viewer to an experience of immense cultural significance. And *Omnibus,* true to its name, turned its cameras at various times on almost anything and everything: *Oedipus Rex,* Dr. Johnson of dictionary fame, Lincoln's youth, ballet programs, a cat giving birth to kittens (yes!), and any number of oddities, sacred and frivolous, but more of the former than the latter.

Omnibus was highbrow television on a commercial channel. It simply could not survive without the Ford Foundation's help. Advertisers were not interested in it, and so it disappeared. I missed it then, and I still do.

The Ford Foundation, however, had by no means cut off its lifeline to the educational channels, nor has it entirely to the present day. Others were to join Ford at the quasi-philanthropy of educational broadcasting in less than a decade. By then, the old name "educational television" was thrown on the scrap heap. In the 'sixties it emerged as "Public Television," a new rubric. No matter what it was called, non-commercial video had, nevertheless and eventually, to face the same old problems that had dogged it in the 1950s.

14

New Voices;
New Tunes

THE 1950s ARE OFTEN CALLED by historians "the Eisenhower years." Today, they seem to provide for the nostalgia market an unending stream of published memories. To the student of mass communications in the United States, however, they are remembered mainly as the beginning of the age of television.

By 1950, the U.S.A. had turned the corner from wartime austerity to peacetime prosperity. As we have seen, the arrival of video did not *displace* much in American life, but, looking back, it seems as if *part* of almost every aspect of our culture slid somehow onto the television tube. By this I mean that part of the film industry, part of the radio business, part of the theatrical world and part of the advertising game (in the world of mass communications) were gobbled up by television. But, more than this, television exerted distinctive influences on America's attitudes towards the Korean War, upon reactions to political conventions and campaigns, upon consumerism, upon the behavior of the disaffected young (known then as the "beat generation"), even upon education and a new desire of nearly all Americans, it seemed, to become college graduates, part of the general optimism of the time.

Many agreed that the country's most serious problem of the decade was our need to catch up with Russian space technology that was surging ahead of ours, an issue wrung dry both by video and print pundits and television documentaries. True, the voice of the ecologist was also heard in the land, but only faintly on television. Come to think of it, a nation which took so seriously the quiz show scandals could not have been concerned about too many more serious things! Scandals, particularly trivial ones, are luxuries of the affluent and self-satisfied.

We have seen some of the direct effects of video upon the film world and Hollywood in particular. We have also observed how, in the early 'fifties, fate was particularly cruel to the film industry in America by destroying just about the neatest national monopoly since John D. Rockefeller's old Standard Oil Company. Hollywood's turmoil resulting from these matters alone was enormous. But, in some ways, the major blow to movieville's once beautiful body was generated by a power more subtle, more lethal and more insidious than anti-monopoly legislation and/or video competition. I am talking about changes in the moral codes and standards of behavior, and the subtle way they crept into custom and law during the 'fifties and 'sixties.

Movies and the First Amendment

Please recall that, shortly before World War I, the Supreme Court of the United States had determined that motion pictures were excluded from the protection of the First Amendment as part of a free press or free speech. Fair enough for 1915! Most silent films of the period, even after the release of *The Birth of a Nation,* were simple entertainments or novelties. The court compared movies to circuses, citing the fact that film making was a business (not unlike the toy business), and found little about them that deserved the same sort of protection as the press or speech, as both were understood by our founding fathers. The film industry might therefore only claim those constitutional protections that other businesses received. In fact, there remains some question to this day about whether the films, had they been equated with the press in 1915 and given First Amendment protection, would have been quite the same vulnerable targets they were for the Justice Department's anti-trust busters 30 or so years later.

That latter point remains moot. As of 1952, Hollywood's three-sided monopoly was officially over. Movies were definitely still businesses, but they had, of course, also changed their functions as instruments of communication since 1915. They were now full-blown theatrical mediums capable of dramatic and/or documentary statements of extraordinary power. They talked, they sang, they accurately imitated the facts of life and death (sometimes crudely) and dealt in a wide currency of ideas and emotions. Many claimed that some art films closely resembled printed book—fiction or non-fiction—with characteristics of newspapers, magazines and other print communications thrown in as well. Educational and training films had helped the Allies to win a war. Films were now used as text materials in classrooms from kindergarten to professional schools. Were they still to be denied the protection of the First Amendment of the United States Constitution? Were they not, by this time, speech—or comparable to print—as means of communication?

To test this point somebody, somehow had to create an issue in order to be decided by the courts, particularly the Supreme Court of the United States. The old Hollywood of the 'twenties, 'thirties and 'forties was not the place to look for issue makers—not as long as the business barons of Hollywood production were busy covering up countless monopolies. In 1952, however, with Hollywood suitably disintegrated and foreign films circulating in American theatres, the question now arose, "Are movies *still* beyond the protection of the First Amendment?" This question had been quite unnecessary to ask about most of the pure, Code-approved, non-controversial Hollywood claptrap movies of the decade before.

The test fortunately first centered on religious freedom, a fundamental, bedrock guarantee of the First Amendment. An Italian movie called *The Ways of Love,* consisting of three short featurettes, opened in New York City in 1951. One of the sequences called *The Miracle* was considered offensive by some state Catholic pressure groups. The entire film, however, had previously been provided with a state license (standard practice since 1915) indicating that it was fit for New Yorkers to view. Not only this, but *The Miracle* had also been reasonably successful when shown in Rome, and it had received acceptable notices from the Vatican's film reviewer. New York's Catholics, however, felt differently about it.

The film episode in question was hardly a masterpiece. It centered upon the delusion of a retarded Italian peasant woman that her illegitimate child, to whom she discreetly gave birth on screen, was the Christ child. Catholic pressure was somehow great enough to force the New York Regents (who licensed films in their spare time) to rescind their permit to display the movie. The distributor, Joseph Burstyn, challenged the issue in court. *The Miracle* found itself eventually before the Supreme Court of the U.S.A. in May, 1952. The point the Court was asked to determine was whether the Regents had a constitutional right to rescind its state license.

The Court actually decided *only* that *this* film could *not* be censored by the New York Regents as blasphemy in the interests solely of a Catholic minority, because of our constitutional American tradition of free speech and religious freedom—not an earth-shattering conclusion. In his opinion, written to explain the unanimous decision, Justice Tom Clark, however, added a sly observation that was, in the next decade, to nullify completely the old 1915 *Mutual* v. *Ohio* (one of the many names given a number of cases all tried at the time) decision. Said Clark, among other things, "We conclude that expression by means of motion pictures is included within the free speech and free press guarantee of the First and Fourteenth Amendments. To the extent that the language in the Ohio case is out of harmony with the views here set forth, we no longer adhere to it."

Quite a statement! Justice Clark, naturally, was supposedly only talking about a religious matter: blasphemy. The reason for the inclusion of the Fourteenth Amendment in his statement was because of its specific wording that no *state* is permitted to make any laws that contravene those of the federal Constitution. Despite this implied limitation upon *The Miracle* decision, the path was now clearly open to test whether or not all movies might receive the same protection as the press and speech *in all respects,* and whether the 1915 interpretation of the movies as businesses or circuses was, *in toto,* obsolete.

Within the next decade, however, a number of cases, about a half-dozen in all, whittled away all state and city licensing and censorship of movies. By 1961, only 14 local censors (some city, some state) were left in the U.S.A., and four years later most of them had disappeared. By 1966, the Mutual decision of 1915 was, for all legal purposes, as dead as a dodo.

With each of the High Court's decisions, the principle enunciated so modestly by Clark was re-affirmed. And each repetition was important. Movies were speech. Movies were similar to the press. Movies deserved the protection of the First Amendment. Neither states, cities or any other agencies of government might censor them within the country.

This did *not* mean, on the other hand, that films were now free to show or say *anything* that they pleased, any more than a newspaper or book publisher is. Libel and other forms of defamation (including certain kinds of invasion of privacy), plagiarism and subversion are not, nor have they ever been, included in the First Amendment according to judicial interpretation. Nor, to this day, (1977) is obscenity considered speech or protected by law—that is, if you can *prove* that something is obscene, a difficult trick right now. Motion picture makers also maintain the right to censor themselves if they wish. This meant the old MPAA code which, in 1952, was still adhered to scrupulously by most Hollywood producers was in no manner unconstitutional.

Films Outgrow the Code

Times however, were a-changin'. The Code's days were numbered for many reasons. Its teeth had been extracted by the government's anti-monopoly action against the film makers. Now a Hollywood film maker could locate a distributor whose organization was not a mere subsidiary of an MPAA member-producer. This was especially important for an increasing number of small, independent Hollywood producers.

The irrascible director-producer, Otto Preminger, released *The Moon is Blue* (a silly comedy with some innocuous jokes about virginity, pro and con) in 1953 without Code approval. To the amazement of many Hollywood watchers, the world did not come to an end! The film did a healthy business—partly because audiences thought it was going to be more risqué than it turned out to be. In 1955, Preminger's *The Man With The Golden Arm* told a grim story of heroin addiction, a Code no-no. It was also released without Code approval. There was little anybody could do about it, especially in the light of its serious nature—and success—and the honesty with which the theme was developed.

The next year, Elia Kazan's version of a Tennessee Williams play, *Baby Doll,* containing some fairly erotic material, packed audiences into theatres mostly *because* of the absence of the Code seal. (I can think of few other at-

tractions it possessed and remember most clearly the repulsive performance of
the leading lady.)

Because of *Baby Doll,* the Code was doomed. In the next decade, it became a Hollywood antique. Private censors like the Catholic Legion of Decency and the National Board of Review kept on rating films, but their disap-
proval often called attention to certain movies that were then avidly patronized
by people in search of "kicks at the flicks." Censorship of all kinds was heading for the rocks.

No Censors: New Films

By the middle of the 'sixties, it fell apart almost entirely. The only remaining relic of the Code in evidence today is the MPAA rating system which
is supposedly "suggested" to exhibitors. Strictly speaking, their ratings only
apply to Hollywood films. Distributors and exhibitors also use the G, PG, R
and X ratings, however, for other movies, like non-Hollywood-made exploitation pictures (today's "pornies," for instance) and foreign films, as a public
convenience and protection. Frequently, they are also employed to quiet protests by local pressure groups. (X ratings are also useful to help pornographic
film enthusiasts identify their special cinematic interest. Quite unofficially,
many exhibitors bill these works of art as "rated Triple-X," a phrase that means
either nothing or everything, depending upon how one's tastes run.)

In 1973, however, another and later United States Supreme Court, presided over by the conservative Chief Justice Warren Burger (who had replaced
liberal Chief Justice Earl Warren), swung the pendulum a few degrees back in
the direction towards old-time film censorship. The case of *Miller* v. *California*
(also called the *Paris Theatre Case*) affirms that individual communities maintain the right to decide whether or not a movie is obscene *for that community.*
They may therefore prohibit the film's exhibition in their particular bali-
wick without contravening the First Amendment.

Miller's logic stands up pretty well as law, because obscenity, as we have
noted, is not given federal or constitutional protection. In practice, since 1973,
surprisingly few communities (taken usually to mean a city, county or state)
have shown any inclination to hunt out obscene movies one by one and use
their rights to censor them, although the *Miller* decision was, at first, treated as
a national disaster by civil libertarians—and by chronic patrons of X-rated
films. On the other hand, *Miller* has not been tested yet in more than a handful
of communities and obviously presents both judges and juries with difficult and
tricky decisions.

Changes in the Film Business

What it all means in terms of the kind of movies that are shown in the
U.S.A. is recent history. This segment of the cinema's development has not

yet, of course, come to an end, or even turned a corner. Hollywood's hysteria in the face of television's competition was, however, over. So was its endless production of Grade B movies for motion picture theatre consumption, the mid-week double features, and those 90 million (or so) admissions once sold at movie theatres every week. The Grade B factory continued to turn out drivel, but its nonsense formula, westerns and "quickie" claptrap was now revised into video formats. They provided (first on film, and later on film and video-tape) an endless series of programs that filled the nation's video screens for years: *Lucy, Star Trek, Bonanza, Alfred Hitchcock Presents, Gunsmoke,* etc. etc. etc., all B films in new clothing that now occupied prime time on Ameri-can television.

Movie exhibitors, of course, could not hope to charge money for the same thing that television was giving away free. There followed a noticeable decline in the number of operating motion picture theatres in the U.S.A.: a drop of from nearly 19,000 in the U.S.A. in the cinematically glorious year of 1949 to 13,000 or so between 1963 and 1968. Attendance fell to roughly 20 million or so admissions per week from the heights of the boom years. Simple arithmetic told an apparently hopeless and sad story about the fate of the cinema in America.

Simple arithmetic was—and is—quite wrong. What happened in the 'six-ties was simply that the American film business underwent enormous changes in an attempt to create a new identity for itself in the age of television. Whether it succeeded or not we cannot yet be certain; but there is another side to the story.

Drive-in theatres, with their own peculiar attractions (not all of them film), *rose* in number quite steadily across the nation from 1948 to the present from about 800 to 4,000. After reaching an all-time low of 12,000-plus cinemas in the middle 'sixties, a new trend in theatre construction started. Many of the old, big and medium-sized city popcorn palaces, seating a thousand or so cus-tomers, were either destroyed or remodeled. In their place, "mini-cinemas" sprung up in urban areas as well as in semi-rural and rural shopping centers. Seating a few hundred people, these theatres were neat, modern and small, often employing one projection booth to serve a "Cinema I" and "Cinema II," each offering a single different feature (no more double bills) at a rela-tively hefty admission price. In the decade following 1966, the *number* of movie houses in the U.S.A. actually *rose* by about 2,000 theatres. Today, about 15,000 movie houses operate successfully in the U.S.A., many of the most lucrative ones located in areas near colleges and universities.

Changes on the Big Screen

Obviously, the movies themselves had to change also. We have examined all of the forces—competitive, financial and legal—that broke down the old studio system. In name, all of the studios continued operating: MGM, Twentieth Century-Fox, Paramount, Warners and so forth. But, by the 'sixties, they had become very different sorts of businesses from what they were in the 'thirties and 'forties. Many—or most—had either become, or joined, industrial conglomerates with varied interests inside and outside show business: record companies, mail order businesses, real estate firms, gambling casinos and others. Movies were still made on sound stages, but, as we have noticed, many were simply co-productions produced with video packagers for television, and many were entirely independent productions—that is, film capitalized individually by non-studio producers who paid star performers with a percentage of the "action"—using the studio facilities of the once-great Hollywood giants for production.

The big studios tried to mount their last hurrahs with spectacles, musicals and old-time historical horse and elephant operas. The final enormous major epic was probably the 1963 disaster, *Cleopatra*. Some, like *My Fair Lady*, (1964), *How the West was Won* (1962), and *It's a Mad, Mad, Mad, Mad World*, (1963) displayed a bit of the supercolossal Hollywood spunk of days gone by.

The last holdout among the studios was probably Twentieth Century-Fox. Fox had achieved enormous profits with *The Sound of Music* (1965). It tried to repeat the trick with *Dr. Doolittle* (1968) and *Hello Dolly* (1969), both of which, while moderately successful, could not even hope to recoup their $20 or $30 million production costs no matter how good they were.

Studio movie extravaganzas died in the 'sixties, although the *illusion* of super-productions did not. Audiences were rarely privy to how much money was actually spent on a film, and, by the late 'sixties and 'seventies, independent producers and others had worked out ways to produce movies with a big production "look" or façade at quite moderate costs. Examples were *Airport* (1970), *Planet of the Apes* (1969), *Funny Girl* (1968), and recent disaster films like the *Poseidon Adventure, The Towering Inferno, Earthquake, The Hindenburg* and their imitators, all variantly popular during the early and middle 'seventies. The trick was accomplished in clever and subtle ways: piling star performers, past and present, into the casts, simulating enormous disasters and bizarre events, often by clever camera work, the use of miniatures and models, location shooting, and the legerdemain of countless optical effects available in film processing laboratories. More than anything, intensive and heavy exploitation made even a thin film like *Jaws* (1975), for instance, seem a good deal more substantial a production—and more elaborate—than it turns out to be upon close examination.

The 'fifties and 'sixties, however, also show other new trends in film-going, some of which have diminished in recent years. One was a short-lived American preoccupation with foreign films, particularly those made in England, France, Sweden, Italy and Japan. Many of these movies were extremely successful when released, and, because most of them cost less than Hollywood movies, were also profitable for their American distributors. I cannot begin to list them all. The British movie, *Room at the Top* (1959), Peter Sellers' various comedies, the Beatles' movies, Ingmar Bergman's Swedish excursions into the dark corners of sexuality, Federico Fellini's circus-like contemporary dramas—particularly his superb *8½* (1963)—Alain Resnais' French films, romantic but mature and realistic stories like *A Man and a Woman* (1966), *The War is Over* (1966), and a series of Japanese directors who followed closely the work of Akira Kurosawa come immediately to mind.

The reason, I believe, that Americans were, in the early and middle 'sixties particularly, attracted to these films was that they dealt more or less frankly with adult problems like marriage, sexual relationships, fear of death and other serious matters, at the same time Hollywood was still producing the same kind of whipped cream that had proved such safe and profitable fare two decades before. When American writers and directors, now independent of the studio system, turned their attentions to equally adult themes, interest in these sorts of foreign films declined.

Without the lucrative American market, therefore, many outstanding films were produced overseas that did not even reach American shores. They were replaced by such "adult" American movies (meaning movies of interest to anyone with a mental age of over about 14 years) as *The Graduate* (1967), *Easy Rider* (1969), *Bonnie and Clyde* (1967), *Midnight Cowboy* (1970), *Five Easy Pieces* (1970), and the virile melodramas of Sam Peckinpah. They literally shoved aside many foreign films of the sort that had found favor in America by virtue of their maturity and willingness to show on the screen reasonable approximations of what really happened to people in life.

Such American films—most of them made by independent producers— could never have found distributors under the old Hollywood MPPDA Code during the 'forties and 'fifties. Nor would many of them have been produced, had movies not found their way under the umbrella of the Constitution's First Amendment, a change that eliminated, bit by bit, state and local censorship entirely by the middle 'sixties, leaving only a voluntary rating system in its wake.

Sex and the Cinema

Some claim, not without a bit of justification, I think, that equating the films with speech and the press and giving them the First Amendment's protection has turned out to be a mixed blessing. Throughout the 1960s, movies, obviously, were not only growing more adult in orientation. They were also more frank, much colorful but vulgar language crept into them, and, in a word, they were also becoming increasingly "raunchy." Most established film makers used their new freedoms with moderation. Italian director Bernardo Bertollucci's *Last Tango in Paris* (1973) is about the most "adult" X-rated movie I have seen made by a noted film maker featuring a star performer, the aging Marlon Brando.

Younger, less well known independents, however, many of them former producers of exploitation pseudo-sex films, "nudies" and similar "quickies," slipped rapidly into a new pornography market. As the 'sixties turned into the 'seventies, "sexy" was not even the proper word to describe many of their movies. In 1968, a Swedish mish-mash, *I Am Curious: Yellow,* attracted considerable attention because of its frank cinematic love-making. Americans, however, were not to be outdone by Swedes. A new school of American "hard core" pornography was born out of the "soft core" exploitation sex movies that preceded them by many years.

In the interests of scholarship, I have followed this trend in X-rated films and must admit that *some* of these films, made by certain independent film makers, have certain unique cinematic qualities besides raw sex to recommend them to the adventurous. Russ Meyer's movies tend to concentrate on physically gifted females; so did much Greek statuary. Gerard Damiano's *The Devil in Miss Jones* tells an honest and highly provocative story, and the work of California's Mitchell Brothers is sometimes strangely both bizarre and depraved in an interesting way. The best "porny" film released to date, in my opinion, is a French import, advertised as *Talk* (1975), a delightfully irreverent spoof. But I do *not* recommend it for your mother-in-law or your minister's wife or even to you, unless you are broadminded and over the age of, I suppose, 18 or 21, depending upon your place of residence.

Such movies naturally create controversy, and, in the case of *Miller* v. *California* (1973), the Supreme Court clearly affirmed, as we have seen, that communities possess rights to censor them if they wish, just as they may (presumably) censor print or speech that offends a majority of their residents. (The latter is a relatively untested matter at the moment.) At any rate, the recent growth of the pornographic film industry does not seem to have destroyed the moral fabric of the U.S.A., as many predicted it would. Nor do I personally note that the sexual morals of the college students I teach seem notably different from 25 years ago, in an era when movies were as clean and as well scrubbed as a hound's tooth.*

At the moment, it also seems possible that as much of the public is growing bored with the profusion of films simply displaying near endless sex (or homo-sex) just for sex's sake. The fact that little variety or imagination has been employed in producing most of these cheap and dirty productions may, in the end, eliminate them or diminish their current popularity to nearly nothing. In the meantime, they are, at least, doing their bit to keep audiences going to movie theatres, because it is highly unprobable that "Triple-X" movies will, in my lifetime, ever be shown free on prime time, open-circuit television.

---

* As the teacher of a college course on movie and literary censorship since the late 'fifties, I have lived through a period of enormous change in print and film permissiveness. I am able to conclude only that the notions of privacy and candor with which I personally grew up are dead or dying—*on the verbal level.* Students, professors and others may *talk* more freely about sex these days, and they may well curse more than they once did. But young men and women *behave* more or less as they did when first I taught this course, or so it seems to me. Nor am I even convinced that liberalized abortion laws and new contraceptive devices have changed young people's sexual *behavior* much since my own youth, and that antedates and overlaps the period of World War II.

The Changing Press

The 1960s were also the years that saw changes occurring, or about to occur, in the world of newspapers and magazines from which there would be no retreat or return. In previous discussions, we have noted how many of the old, great newspapers, particularly those in New York City, eventually went out of business or merged one with the other during these years.

Life, Look, The Saturday Evening Post, and other once great magazines had died—or were on their way to oblivion. Reasons were many: unionization and high labor costs, competition for the public attention from non-print media and a host of other factors. But the main cause centered on advertising. Large advertisers were loathe to spread their big promotions in big cities among a large number of newspapers. They chose those with the highest circulations and with the greatest number of avid consumers among their readers. National advertising in magazines and magazine sections run by chain newspapers had to compete with commercials on television that could, in the advertising men's vocabulary, "deliver" a larger audience more cheaply than print ever could and, in many instances, achieve more substantial effects than the older medium.

The irony of this situation lay in the fact that many magazines and newspapers died despite quite respectable, even some gigantic, circulation figures. But these readerships could not compete in number with the masses who watched national (and sometimes local) television. Except for certain specific products, there seemed few special incentives to advertise in print. Television's effect on viewers was apparently direct and indisputable: it was able to sell almost anything to anybody, or so the advertising departments of broadcast stations and networks claimed. Thus, major advertisers deserted the print medium in droves. The result sharply curtailed a number of older publications that had depended largely upon advertising for their modest margins of profit.

New Trends in Newspapers

Tastes, however, change, and certain successes in print journalism are also notable during this gloomy era. Despite the failure of its West Coast edition, *The New York Times* established itself as the closest publication America had to an eclectic national daily newspaper. Jet airplanes now circulate copies across the nation in hours.

The once modest *Wall Street Journal,* however, achieved even more remarkable results without many airplanes. The conservative financial daily, begun in 1898 by the Dow Jones News Service, broadened its horizons after World War II and turned into a peppy, eccentric and amusing newspaper with well over a million and a quarter circulation. It was to be printed eventually in ten locations across the United States and delivered like lightning to any American's breakfast table anywhere in the U.S.A.

When I call the *Journal* "eccentric," I mean just that. Still providing complete coverage of America's daily financial news (that extends far beyond Wall Street, New York), the *Journal* carries almost no photographs (except in advertisements), covers only the news it apparently wishes to cover—including many excellent feature stories—does not run "departments" like obituaries, women's pages, sports sections, etc. But it *may* cover the death of a celebrity, *may* suddenly print a recipe, *may* review a book, a movie or a play, or it *may not* run any of these items, depending upon editorial whims, I suppose. A front-page feature story may delve into the exquisite details of mink farming, discuss how to beat casinos in Nevada, or argue the case against extra-sensory perception, again, apparently at somebody's whim.

One never knows exactly what he or she will find in the *Wall Street Journal.* This is precisely, in my opinion, one of the newspaper's greatest attractions for the public and the secret ingredient of its current success. It is well written, peppy, irreverent and, while politically conservative, seems to open its pages to unorthodox ideas of almost every kind. Nor is the *Journal* over-loaded with advertising. Its local editions permit it to carry both regional and national ads at a formidable fee, but much of its income comes from its gigantic daily circulation.

In 1962, Dow Jones started a less successful Sunday edition of the *Journal* called *The National Observer. The Observer*'s range of interests is no smaller than the *Journal*'s, but it is less oriented to financial news and is more a cultural periodical. Slow to gather a following, the *Observer*'s circulation hovers around the half-million mark, one of the more successful new journalistic enterprises of the 1960s.

The Suburban Press

Suburban newspapers were established institutions at mid-century in the United States. Many that are still published go back to, or before, the Civil War. The death of so many large city newspapers in the 'fifties and 'sixties, however, meant the death as well of local news coverage for many suburban areas. Some large city newspapers therefore attempted, and still attempt, to fill in the gap by running regional editions. But the 1960s saw a resurgence of interest in papers that centered their interests upon suburbs and even in some cases, like New York's *Village Voice* and its imitators, upon special neighborhoods within modern metropolises like New York, Chicago, Los Angeles, Philadelphia and San Francisco.

Ernest C. Hynds in his illuminating book, *American Newspapers in the 1970s,* notes that studies show that the number of suburban newspapers jumped by more than 50 per cent between 1950 and 1968, their greatest gains naturally, centering in the largest metropolitan areas, expecially those that had recently lost local dailies that covered local news and carried local advertising.

Hynds pays particular attention to the phenomenal success of Long Island's (New York) *Newsday,* a newspaper begun in 1940 by a relative of the *New York Daily News-Chicago Tribune* family, Alicia Patterson Guggenheimer and her husband. Mrs. Guggenheimer died in 1963, but *Newsday,* purchased eventually by the Los Angeles *Times-Mirror,* drove out nearly all of its major daily competition in the area. It settled back with its more than half-million circulation and well-filled advertising pages into what seems to be permanent suburban prosperity, although a few other daily newspapers still serve local regions of Long Island and adjacent sections of New York City.

Some weekly suburban newspapers are little more than advertising broadsheets; some provide timely community news. The range is quite wide and the number of these papers is enormous. Hynds reports that more than 100 newspapers are published in the San Francisco Bay Area alone. A good number of them are weeklies.

The average suburban newspaper today in the United States is a modest operation, run by a handful of versatile editors and reporters who double in brass as the advertising department, and is published once a week. It is probably also tabloid-sized (for ease of printing and delivery) and both sane and conservative in the way it covers local events, sticking close to the interests and biases of its most important constituents, local advertisers and local political leaders. While its lead headline may not replicate the drama of the fabled prototypical suburban news story, CAT LOST ON MAIN STREET, much of its coverage is likely to be little more pithy than this. The newspaper probably depends, in large part, upon public relations handouts for much of its copy about such local events as new movies, shopping center fairs and the arrival of visitors of note. In the void created by the death of big city newspapers, suburban journals thrived in the 'sixties, their number rising to well over a thousand—possibly to more than the number of dailies printed in the U.S.A. (Suburban papers appear difficult to count definitively; they come and go so rapidly.)

The Underground Press

In addition to the rise of suburban newspapers to national importance, the 1960s witnessed the development of one other kind of newspaper geared mostly to young people, called the "alternate" or "underground" press. Those who would like to pin the origins of the underground newspapers in America upon the rebellious younger generation of the Vietnam War period are incorrect. The daddy of most of the underground papers of the 'sixties was founded in 1955, almost in the middle years of "Eisenhower prosperity," in New York City. It was the aforementioned *Village Voice,* less a journal of rebellion than one that echoed the dissatisfactions of a group of "hip" young men (and a few women) with the then reigning Greenwich Village neighborhood weekly, *The Villager,* which *was* (and is) more concerned about lost cats than with the colorful folkways of New York's Bohemia.

The *Voice* still exists, but it has "gone square," having recently been purchased by Clay Felker of *New York* magazine, who has spent a fortune trying to extend its readership into all of New York and to the nation's middle class.* In its earliest years, the *Voice*'s founders (who included novelist Norman Mailer at his wildest), hoped that the *Voice* would become the spokesman for the young, the disaffected, the revolutionary and minority groups in New York. In a way, it succeeded for a number of years, encouraging new and interesting talents and viewing the established arts and politics of New York from a sarcastic, critical and youthful perspective.

As the 'sixties wore on, however, other Greenwich Village newspapers came and went, *The Realist* and *The East Village Other* among the most successful. These upstarts bespoke even more liberal—even radical—views than the older *Voice*. In effect, the *Voice* was considerably muted by its own offspring, until it. was finally forced financially into its present unbecoming respectability.

There was, however, little respectable about most of the underground papers that mushroomed around the U.S.A. during the 1960s. At first, most of them started in little "Greenwich Villages" across the nation—the lion's share in college towns, where they merged with campus rebellions that marked the final years of the Johnson administration and the early Nixon years. *The Berkeley Barb* and the *Los Angeles Free Press* were among the best known. Most were weeklies, militantly pacifist, anti-establishment, erratically and confusedly socialistic, and blatantly free-wheeling in regard to sexual discourse and morals. If they were governed by any philosophy or ideology, it was, I suppose, a loose interpretation of the confused musings of social critic (I guess) Herbert Marcuse whose curious Freudian Marxism seemed to provide extrasensory messages, ink-blot style, for many of the student rebels of the 'sixties.

The papers were against more things—all sorts of things—than for them, and most made for lively, if indecorous, reading. It is my belief that these newspapers, however, had precious little effect upon most of the student insurgents of the time, mainly because these college youngsters—like those immediately preceding and following them—apparently read little of anything, neither their textbooks nor newspapers nor magazines. They did, however, look at pictures!

The most popular items found in the underground press were, therefore, comics and cartoons, most off-color and reflective of the drug culture, the "hippie" culture and seething with the alienation of both. The one comic artist of genuine talent that they produced, to the best of my knowledge, was the eccentric, irreverent Robert Crumb, whose *Fritz the Cat* went on to fame in the first X-rated animated movie. Crumb's Fritz in newspaper comic style was more convincing than his cinematic counterpart, and Crumb's other work (since

---

* During the winter of 1976–77, Felker was pushed out of his growing publishing empire by Robert Murdoch, a rich Australian-English press baron. As I correct proofs, therefore, for this page, the future of both *New York* magazine and the *Voice* are in doubt. The *Voice*, however, has been having severe editorial problems ever since Felker took over a couple of years ago.

widely imitated) displays an earthiness that is as amusing as it is relevant to the interests of many young people.

A number of exceptional publications emerged from the underground. The most notable, possibly, was *Rolling Stone,* started in 1967 as a rock music journal, but which shortly turned into a general interest weekly with wide readership across the nation. At first, it catered most to the young, but later many older people read it as well. Its "new journalism" or subjective reporting of writers like Hunter Thompson was distinctive, crisp and highly readable. Thompson did not hesitate to attack large issues in politics, foreign relations and/or anything else that struck his fancy. As the *Stone's* editors aged, so its initial orientation to youth culture broadened to include a wide spectrum of other interests, and the weekly grew in circulation and prestige during the 1970s.

Another successful journal that University of Missouri professor of journalism John Merrill refuses to call a "newspaper" (possibly because he has never read it) started in the late 'sixties largely as the results of monomaniacal interests of its editor and founder, Al Goldstein. Called *Screw,* its popularity is today nationwide, and its circulation, says Goldstein, exceeds 50,000 per weekly issue.

Goldstein is a blatant pornographer and a robust, unsubtle wit, who proudly advertises his connections with every aspect of the smut market and "tries to prevent *Screw* from displaying any socially redeeming characteristics," in his own words. In this latter attempt, he fails, peppering his not-so-cheap but dirty tabloid with political vitriol, movie criticism (even of non-pornographic films), book reviews, biographical stories, consumer news, classified ads (that defy description) and other matters of interest to the sexually obsessed. If success is determined by imitation, *Screw* and its homosexual brother (sister?) *Gay* are both raging successes, although their imitators have not mastered Goldstein's trick of transferring to print its publisher's egomania and public stance as a professional bad boy.

In his strange way, Al Goldstein is the William Randolph Hearst of pornography. *Screw's* managerial interests involve at present a number of magazines, books, motion pictures and, for all I know, assorted massage parlors. Of all the underground papers of the 'sixties, *Screw* remains the most outrageous, in my opinion, and therefore for the broad-minded the most fun—in small doses. Goldstein, quite seriously, regards his newspaper as the vanguard of America's sexual revolution. He is, in fact, a far more perceptive, thoughtful and generous (although no less gutsy) individual than he seems in print. Whether he is correct in his assessment of his, and *Screw's,* place in modern culture, I leave to journalism experts like Professor Merrill.

The Black Press

Newspapers oriented to Negroes have a long and honorable tradition in the U.S.A. going back to the first third of the nineteenth century. But in the 'sixties, the national movement for Black identity on the part of many of the nation's 22 million Black citizens, particularly young people, gave them a degree of nation-wide attention they had never before received. The number of Black newspapers rose from 150 to about 300 between the end of World War II and the end of the 'sixties, and the publication of many Black magazines followed.

The Johnson publications, begun in 1942 with *Negro Digest,* generated a publishing empire which, during the 1960s, changed its orientation from mere imitation of white magazines to a number of publications reflecting the new ethnic identity of the American Black, born in the civil rights movement of the 'fifties, but which reached new heights of significance in the 'sixties. Based in Chicago, Johnson's *Ebony* and *Jet* now have circulations in the millions; their other publications appeal more to special interest group Blacks and are less successful.

Among America's Black newspapers, a number are notable publications. New York's *New Amsterdam News,* the *Los Angeles Sentinel,* the Philadelphia *Tribune* and the Chicago *Daily Defender* are among the leaders, both as spokesman for Black communities and in terms of their circulations. By far, the most popular Black paper in the U.S.A. is *Muhammad Speaks,* a national weekly published in Chicago by the Black Muslims, that circulates well over half a million copies per issue. The popularity of *Muhammad Speaks,* started as a phenomenon of the 'sixties, reflecting new Black racial pride heard in the eloquent voices of Black leaders as different in political orientations as Martin Luther King Jr., Malcolm X, and Eldridge Cleaver, among others.

Black periodicals and newspapers have faced a difficult row to hoe in the U.S.A., but the outlook for them improved considerably during the 1960s, a function largely of a small but noticeable rise in the social and economic status of many Blacks. Black publications for the most part depend, like their white counterparts, upon advertising. Here, magazines like *Ebony* maintain an advantage over newspapers, because they can frequently interest white advertisers, particularly those that sell products used nationally, to expose their messages to Black readers. Black newspapers are less fortunate, depending more than the magazines upon local advertisers in Black communities, who often have only limited budgets for advertising.

Total circulation of Black newspapers during the 'sixties is difficult to estimate, but it probably reached about four million, or one newspaper for every five Blacks in the U.S.A. Considering that about one out of four members of the population at large purchase a daily newspaper, this number (including weeklies) is a formidable one. One must remember that an undetermined number of Black readers—probably a major percentage—purchase white newspapers. Thus, Black publications not only compete one with the other both for readers and advertising, but with the enormous circulations of the white press as well.

In spite of this, the 'sixties saw both growth and expansion in this segment of the minority press in the U.S.A. The rest of it remained relatively stagnant or declined, particularly the number and circulation of foreign language newspapers. Most experts agree that, whatever the fate of the Black press, it will continue to reflect the social, economic and educational status of Black communities in the U.S.A. As time passes, it must either center its interest upon interests and institutions that separate Negroes from white communities, or, as some Blacks desire, upon trends which integrate the two educationally, economically, socially and, in time, racially as well. In the long term, biology will probably determine the fate of the American Black press. In the meanwhile, the issues upon which its attention are centered are largely ideological, political and, in urban areas particularly, social.

Successful Magazines

The death (or death-throes) of so many of America's best-loved magazines during the 1960s by no means infers that they all succumbed to the competition of television and expired. Those that were somehow unique or *could* compete with television advertising remained healthy. *The Reader's Digest* increased its circulation and advertising content, reflective of the go-go economy of the nation. Luce publications witnessed *Life* breathing its last gasps, but *Time* was, and remains, the healthiest of the American newsmagazines. Luce's *Fortune* was still the darling of the wealthy business community, and *Sports Illustrated,* a comparative newcomer, was rapidly assuming a position as the leading and most influencial magazine of its kind in the world.

In addition to the old-time companies, a few upstarts appeared in the periodical world. As the radio era of the 'fifties died, Walter Annenberg, a Philadelphia millionaire publisher (like Hearst, an heir to a fortune), subsumed into his Triangle Publications organization an old, so-so fan magazine called *Radio Guide* that had tried for years, during radio's golden era, to do for sound broadcasting what screen magazines had done for the movies. *Radio Guide* failed in this attempt but managed to limp along until it fell into Annenberg's hands.

Triangle Publications changed its name to *TV Guide*. The magazine was miniaturized to digest size. The old *Radio Guide*-style fan articles were slicked up a bit, and *TV Guide* continued its predecessor's practice of printing broadcasting program logs in a little more detail than most newspapers. This necessitated multiple editions of *TV Guide* around the nation in order that the magazine coordinate its listings with television coverage in the country's various regions.

TV Guide hit the jackpot in spite of much competition, mostly from special television sections in some Sunday newspapers that also listed video programs fully and correctly. But they did not give the reader *TV Guide*'s sense of peeking behind the tube right into the television industry. In addition to its inside dope and gossip, *TV Guide* also ran numerous excellent analytical articles about many aspects of video, and the magazine's television critics were, in general, harder to please than those of the nation's daily newspapers.

Whatever its alchemy, the magazine clicked. During the 'sixties, *TV Guide*'s circulation exceeded 17 million copies per week, and, by the 'seventies, was well on its way to the 20-million mark. National interest in television was, of course, mainly responsible for this success. *TV Guide* could offer its advertisers a weekly readership of involved, interested TV viewers, oriented to the commercialism of video, who would, they hoped, actually *read* and respond to their advertisements. While all television viewers did not read (or purchase) *TV Guide,* the cream of the crop from an advertiser's perspective, did. *TV Guide,* accordingly, not only became one of America's largest circulating magazines, it also became ironically one of the nation's best advertising mediums for the kind of products that were advertised on television.

The very same circumstances, therefore, that killed *Life* magazine made *TV Guide* fat and healthy. The latter's prosperity will probably continue until a substantial change occurs in the media habits of most Americans. When this occurs, as it must, Triangle Publications will doubtless shift gears to follow the change. For all its editorializing, crusading and influence in broadcasting circles, *TV Guide* remains a magazine that has (like *Radio Guide* before it) *followed* the parade of American popular culture and has influenced or changed the medium that it exploits very little, except to enhance its patronage.

The other remarkable magazine that reached puberty (I think that is the word!) in the 'sixties was also a close relative of an older publication, although the stepchild forced the parent radically to change its ways. The story of *Playboy* has been told many times: how Hugh Hefner, an alumnus of the old *Esquire,* "The Magazine for Men," in 1953 updated his former employer's format. *Esquire* was a mildly sexy, stuffy, oversized fashion and fiction periodical. Hefner turned his competing journal into a perky version of *Esquire*. He started *Playboy* on a shoestring and featured, in his first issue, a fold-out center-spread photograph of Marilyn Monroe wearing nothing more than a smile.

Voila: *Playboy,* the famous Hefner pseudo-philosophy, a lot of good fiction, racy cartoons, "naughty" sex just this side of pornography, air-brushed nude photographs of near identical nubile females, etc. By the 1960s, *Playboy* sold 7 million copies a month and eventually cost $1 a copy.

As interesting as *Playboy* itself, were the side effects it generated, most of them products of the 'sixties and as much a function of the general affluence of the country as of the magazine. Hefner possessed a sort of genius for self publicity and rose to celebrity status, as did some of his female "Playmates," real and pictorial. In his Chicago headquarters, he hosted modest orgies for the benefit of his photographers, published theories on society, religion, philosophy, and, of course, sex.

"Playboy Clubs" began springing up around the nation. All of them were pretty much the same: slick, expensive nightclubs that exuded an aura of sin but were, except for booze consumption, usually as innocent as Sunday school picnics—possibly more so. Hefner's book publishing arm, The Playboy Press, began issuing a wide range of erotic books, some serious, some trivial, and all slick. Then Hefner went into the resort business, losing money here, making it there. In a word, he was an "operator," whose base of command was a highly profitable Chicago based magazine that attracted advertisers selling their wares to millions of "Playboys" (or would-be "Playboys"). The ads usually exploited clothes, hi-fi sets, novelties, beverages and numerous other commodities that helped the reader to confirm an image of himself as a man-about-town.

Other Magazines: Sane and Mad

Playboy survived the 'sixties and continued into the 'seventies, but the fairy-tale world it had created had died somewhere in the transition. Changing sexual mores, the Supreme Court's consistent denial that the print and film media were anything less than absolutely free to print whatever they pleased, and changing life styles among many young people in the late 'sixties produced their effects on *Playboy*. Competitors with names like *Sage* and *Dude*—and later *Hustler* and *Club,* among many others—dealt lightly, if at all, in philosophy, religion and culture. Instead, they emphasized raw sex (many claimed it was pornography) in cartoons, articles and photographs.

Shortly after the end of the decade, Robert Guccione's *Penthouse,* born in England and eventually claiming a worldwide circulation of about 4.5 million, arrived at American newsstands. *Penthouse* was a magazine as slick and well produced, in its way, as *Playboy,* but it burst to the seams with kinky sex, and female nudes displaying copious amounts of pubic hair that *Playboy's* airbrushes had so meticulously shaved from its models for years.

Playboy tried to answer *Penthouse* back in kind, but Hefner could muster neither Guccione's nerve nor Al Goldstein's delight in non-suggestive, explicit raunchy words and pictures, no matter how artfully he presented them. *Playboy* ceased to be "naughty"; Hefner's "philosophy" now seemed plain silly. Even *Playboy's* good fiction and feature articles paled.

Another way of meeting his competition was Hefner's new publication, introduced in the early 'seventies, called *Oui. Oui* was a lower class, cruder, less subtle, version of *Playboy,* intended to lure the male reader away from *Penthouse* and other *Playboy* imitations. To a degree it succeeded. At least, it has survived to the present, claiming a readership of 2.5 million for its wide-ranging, perky coverage of everything from politics to porn.

Playboy probably experienced its greatest and most popular years in the 'sixties. As the decade ended, its publisher was aging none too gracefully, and neither, apparently, were its readers. They were "Playboys" less and less, and just dirty old men more and more. How *Playboy, Penthouse* and hosts of other magazines devoted to sex for sex's sake and illusions of hedonism will fare in the future is anybody's guess. Sex remains probably the most popular indoor, and possibly outdoor, activity in the world (next to sleeping, eating and working), so my guess is that *its* future is assured—but not necessarily that of the many expensive magazines that exploit it.

The 'fifties and 'sixties also saw the success of other types of periodicals as well that had, until this time, been considered by many to be mere flashes in the pan. Most of them are too familiar to list here, but new women's magazines, distributed now in supermarkets, achieved notable circulations and readerships without newsstand circulation or many prepaid subscriptions. One was pretty much like another: *Woman's Day, Family Circle* etc., but millions of American women read one or more, and, sold as they were in retail outlets, attracted many advertisers whose products were on sale in these stores.

For the adolescent market, William Gaines' *Mad,* a post-World War II phenomenon, at first looked like a trendy spoof of the 'fifties that would quickly pass into oblivion. It did not. By the time *Mad's* first young readers grew tired of it, a new generation of youngsters was ready to appreciate its satires, takeoffs and put-ons, along with many adults who appreciated *Mad's* clever ongoing comments on the mass media, particularly movies and television.

Mad reigned through the 'sixties as America's outstanding humor magazine, although many adults found its jokes jejune and its satire too obvious for their tastes. Kids, however, apparently loved it. *Mad* spawned a breed of imitators, none of which was notably successful, largely, I think, because of Gaines' (and editor Al Feldstein's) peculiar ability to see the world through the eyes of the young. *"Mad* isn't *for* anything,'' Gaines recently told me, ''It's against everything.'' I could not help noting how reflective of the behavior of many middle class youngsters during the past generation Gains' simple statement is. Gaines' personal irreverence finds its way into the work of his artists, editors and writers. The consistently high and relevant level of humor that *Mad* has been able to maintain for so long is one of its notable characteristics, in my opinion.

The New Yorker had also once been, largely, a humor magazine. But it emerged from World War II as a serious, quasi-literary journal, hard to characterize but far from consistently funny. Only its cartoons kept up the magazine's light-hearted façade. Its fiction, feature stories, articles and reviews were always well written and liberal (usually) in political orientation, but as funny, for the most part, as the editorials of the *Wall Street Journal.*

Editor Harold Ross had guided his celebrity writers (John O'Hara, James Thurber, E. B. White, Dorothy Parker, *et.al.*) through much of the 'fifties. At his death, new editor William Shawn changed the magazine little. Shawn merely replaced old writers and cartoonists with new ones as the oldtimers died off, each newcomer a bit more sober, pretentious and ''trendy'' than the one who had passed away. *The New Yorker's* circulation remained high in the 'sixties, the apogee of sophistication to many readers across the country who, in large part, neither knew nor cared much about New York City itself, possibly the *least* sophisticated metropolis of over one million in the world.

The city itself was better reflected in *New York* magazine, a product of the 'sixties. *New York* is a lively weekly, until recently edited by Clay Felker, that echoes certain characteristics of the success story of *Rolling Stone,* without the latter's interest in rock music. *New York* has, in recent years, encouraged and printed some of the nation's best so-called ''new journalism,'' subjective writing by people like Tom Wolfe and Gail Sheehy, among others. Less literary and meticulously edited than *The New Yorker*, *New York* seems to have syphoned off some of the former's readership by directing its attention to realistic means and methods of survival in the world's largest hick town. This means articles on politics, consumerism, sex and single men and women (and married ones too), raising house plants in apartments and just about anything and everything that catches Felker's eclectic eye. While *The New Yorker* is gentlemanly, usually decorous, literate and often fey, *New York* is a snappy upstart that often reminds me of the old irreverence *The New Yorker* itself had when I first met it in the 'thirties. But magazines change, victims of time and changes among their readers and the personalities of their writers and editors. They also come and go. *New York* is one of the more interesting to come our way in recent years.

Special Interest Periodicals

Any review of magazines in the 'sixties cannot, of course, neglect the numerous special interest journals that also burgeoned during this period. On my own desk at home, I notice a weekly newspaper-style magazine for collectors, *The Antique Trader*, that circulates hundreds of thousands of copies (containing mostly advertisements) to collectors of just about anything and everything, antique or not, from *The Trader*'s publication offices in Dubuque, Iowa. I also see *Coin World*, the world's largest circulating hobby publication, another weekly published in Sidney, Ohio. It contains hours of reading and multitudes of advertisements for the devout numismatist. Yearly subscriptions to both of these papers (or magazines) cost about $10, and they (and others like them) have been consistently gathering more and more new readers over the past decade.

But let us not overlook *Muscle* magazine, *Plates* magazine, *Baby Talk*, *Motor Trends*, *Industrial Photography*, *Popular Science*, *Field and Stream*, *Jack and Jill*, *Seventeen*, *Square Dancing*, *Nudist Monthly*, *Yachting*, *Dog World*, *Cats*, *Travel and Leisure*, *Glamour*, *Writer's Digest*, *The AMA Journal*, *The Columbia Journalism Review*, *Foreign Affairs*, etc., etc., etc., and a herd of comic "books" that are avidly read by youngsters and semi-literates as fast, it seems, as they can be printed.

The combined circulation of these publications is enormous. They say a good deal about the diversity of interests, professional, vocational, and leisure-time activities of the American public. That so many of them are able to survive is probably eloquent testimony to the fact that certain aspects of popular culture in the U.S.A. have not, and are not becoming, increasingly homogeneous, as many claim. In fact, quite the opposite seems true, considering the various interests reflected by these ever more diversified periodicals that, taken as a whole, grew in circulation during the 'sixties in proportion with the affluence of a public able to afford them and the special interests for which they speak.

Book Publishing in America

The apparently respectable authors of a recent edition of a mass communications "survey" text write, "As a mass medium, the book is a failure. Once they finish their schooling, most Americans have very little to do with books." The statement is true. The statement is also false. Like many other observations made in this and similar volumes about mass communications, the statement is also safe.

Examining the percentage of literate Americans who read (*and* read books) where alternate media did (and do) exist, it is true. Comparing publishing statistics to broadcasting statistics of any kind is like comparing a chipmunk to a pachyderm. So publishing statistics, particularly of books, do indeed seem minuscule when compared to television ratings translated into numbers of viewers. But, by the 1960s, the business of publishing books of every type in the U.S.A. had by far outgrown its own past and was *not,* by any sort of criteria, a phenomenon of any less than mass proportions.

Book clubs flourished. Some were aimed at the general reader, some for paperback enthusiasts, some for mystery story lovers, some for gourmets, gardeners, historians, psychologists, pornographers, film lovers, and even some for people who read books on mass communications. All in all, by about 1970, the book club industry alone did a yearly business of more than $250 million, most of its books hawked at artificial discounts that were somewhat less than first edition bookstore list prices, but still large enough to bring publishers and club operators healthy profits.

We have seen how the modern paperback industry started in the U.S.A. in the 1930s. By the 'sixties, two types of paperback books were generally available. First, there were *trade* paperbacks: simply soft cover editions of hardcover books, bound and printed simultaneously along with the latter and sold for somewhat less than their clothbound twins. The main reason that both can survive in a highly competitive market is that the paperbacks are usually used as texts and appeal to general readers, while libraries require hardcover books for their sort of circulation. If hardcover editions were not printed, librarians would then find it necessary to re-bind paperbacks, an expensive process. This book, for instance, will be available upon publication in both hardcover and paper editions for this reason.

Second, there are *mass market* paperbacks, which are either original editions of books that probably would not sell well in an expensive hardcover edition (a slick pornographic book or a special volume designed for fans of a television show, for instance) or an edition of a former highly successful hardcover volume like *Jaws* or *Looking For Mr. Goodbar,* an Eric Ambler thriller, an oddball story like *Jonathan Livingston Seagull,* or some other volume publishers hope will have wide appeal. Both types of book may be fiction or nonfiction. The only criterion for the success of a mass market paperback is to have a wide and/or long term appeal, so as to warrant the initial large printing required for a relatively low or competitive price.

Neither type of paperback remained inexpensive by standards of the 1930s, but both are less costly than hardcover books. Trade paperbacks find their way to thousands of outlets like college bookstores and cost between $3 and $10, depending upon size, topic and publisher. Mass market paperbacks are rarely printed in lots much smaller than a quarter of a million and usually cost from $1.50 to about $3.00. They are sold just about anywhere that a retailer of any sort thinks he can sell books.

The sales of many mass market paperbacks have crossed the million mark. Some are sold by the tens of millions, including the *Iliad* and the *Odyssey* of Homer which remain to this day one of the all-time paperback best sellers in the U.S.A. Trade paperbacks during the 'sixties constituted a modest market hovering around the $50 million per year figure, and their sale has been rising ever since. Mass market paperbacks, however, broke through the $250 million sales figure of the book clubs, and today they are approaching a $300 million per year gross.

Believe it or not, these markets constitute but a *fraction* of the publishing industry's dollar volume and of the number of books sold. The *big* money, and piles of books, are both found in the textbook market, in my opinion, one of the most remarkable phenomena of the entire communications revolution to date. During the 'sixties, stimulated somewhat by government funding of our overcrowded school systems at the time, about $1,400 million (one *billion* four hundred million dollars) worth of textbooks per year were shuffled into the hands of American students one way or another. These include first-grade readers, college texts, law books, business texts and others, not *all* of which were even used in school. But all were indeed involved, one way or another, with education. When one considers that one-quarter of the American population is, at any time, involved somehow in our institutions of education, the figure falls into proper perspective, but it is, nevertheless, both a substantial and lucrative one.

Trade hardbacks, religious books, juvenile books and other types of volumes that one expects to find on display at the book section of a large department store or bookstore account for a mere $500 million a year in sales. These books, however, make up a good share of the 40,000 book titles published in the U.S.A. each year, and include both fiction and non-fiction works, as well as reference books, encyclopedias and dictionaries.

All in all, the book publishing industry grew into a $3 billion enterprise during the 1960s. The industry was spread among about 6,500 publishing houses in the country, most of them relatively small companies. As in many mass communication businesses, a few giants dominate in the market, not all of them such familiar names as Doubleday, Harper and Row or McGraw-Hill. West Publishing Co., for instance, has grown fat and healthy printing and distributing law books. W. B. Saunders is a leader in the medical-dental field, etc. In the age of mass communications, specialization has paid off quite handsomely for many.

Considering that a single book, as opposed to a single showing of a film or television program, may, like a phonograph record or tape recording, be used any number of times by many people and be preserved indefinitely (except for some cheap paperbacks), the exact—or even approximate—number of readers exposed to a best seller, or any other kind of volume, is nearly impossible to determine. Many factors are involved: the edition, the price the buyer pays, his or her motivation for purchase, and the kinds of social environments through which the book will travel during its lifetime.

My strong feeling is that books, by and large, remain to this day by far the single most ubiquitous and influential of all of the modern mass media in the Western world, despite their all too cheerful detractors! Dr. McLuhan told us long ago that the age of print (meaning mostly books) is over. I think that common sense, simple statistics and daily experience tells us he was, as usual, dead wrong. What McLuhan overlooked was, 1) the ritual nature of reading in the Judeo-Christian world; 2) the prestige of print and the quiet superiority one *feels* when he reads the printed word; and 3) the magnificently protean and flexible nature of printed language that allows it to accomplish easily almost everything that any other modern means of communication can do—and achieve this miracle at the leisure of the reader, not once but over and over again as long as a printed page remains legible, which, in many instances, may be, in my opinion, *too* long.

15

The End of the Beginning

ONE OF THE MOST OVERUSED statements of our time—and possibly untrue—is one or another version of Santayana's chestnut claiming that those who do not understand history are doomed to relive it, or words to that effect.

No way!

Right now, we are perched at the end of the beginning of the history of the Communications Revolution. The journey through these pages constitutes a fascinating adventure, no matter how poorly or incompletely it has been told. Readers who have followed it (in part or completely) from the beginning will, I think, agree that they, like me, understand better than they once did certain relationships between the past and present and possibly even the future. But might we be condemned to relive this history if, for some reason, this knowledge were erased from our minds? I doubt it. We would merely be forced to turn the present moment into Year One of the Communications Revolution and start out writing a new history that followed its path into an unpredictable future.

That is precisely what the generation to follow will be forced to do anyway, even knowing, as it does, the ways in which the past has contributed to the present moment.

Why?

For many reasons. The most important is the irrefutable advance and novelty of communications technology that cannot be foretold or turned backwards. Simply illustrated, the printing press cannot be un-invented, nor can we responsibly predict the future of the printed word—in the long run. Despite some mystical thinking to the contrary, this volume, and others like it, indicate that the technology of print may well in the future (and barring atomic destruction) extend enormously its range and influence into and upon the lives of men and women, as new methods of transmission and so-called delivery systems are perfected. *Time, The Wall Street Journal* and the book industry (as well as the Xerox-type library of tomorrow, an issue we have not discussed) point in this direction. Culture may follow, or, for unpredictable reasons, may not.

My own guess is that the techniques, art and power of the printed word have just recently shed their infant clothes, as technology opens for them new worlds to infiltrate. Remember, one-half (or so) of our fellow men on earth today can neither read nor write *any* language. This portends an enormous new constituency for print. Nor do I believe that most of these people we like to call (incorrectly) ''underdeveloped'' will achieve societal maturity as so-called ''post-literate'' men—that is, as citizens of cultures beyond the *need* to read and write, fed by streams of electronic sounds and pictures. No, they are ''pre-literate'' at present, and chances are that their children will learn to read and write, and that technology will open for them their own (sometimes forgotten) literary traditions as well as the literature of other cultures *at the same time* as they are fed sounds and pictures by broadcasting media and motion pictures.

How they will respond to this new awareness of their own past and present, I cannot guess. They may possibly turn blind eyes towards these messages or be so repulsed and frightened by them that they rush indeed towards ''post-literacy.'' On the other hand, they may not. We may discover, as the world learns to read, that the global age of print is just beginning. Technology is entirely ready today for this eventuality.

Whatever the result, the past will probably not repeat itself. Nor, closer possibly to the concerns of my colleagues who teach courses in subjects like ''The Roles and Functions of Mass Media,'' will the history of broadcasting as we have seen it, on a limited number of frequencies by open circuit transmission, display much relevance to the uses man makes tomorrow of his wired cities, wired nations, CATV systems and satellite transmissions towards which today's technologies are leading us. True, certain communication instruments do, as we have seen, seem to show a peculiar proclivity for swallowing up one another, while others, apparently competing, somehow learn to live with one another. But predictions concerning exactly *how* these inevitable assimilations of old into new will occur in the future are best left to others in poorer health than I am, because they are more likely to die before I do, thus avoiding the consequences of playing fortune teller.

Why End Here?

Entering the end of a history that is just beginning is, for me, a discouraging undertaking. For this reason, I think it unnecessary to bring the story of the Communications Revolution exactly up to date.

First, this recent history is being told and forever retold redundantly in nearly countless books treating mass communications in the modern world, most of them designed for use in the simplistic and shallow courses in "media studies" offered today at junior colleges and colleges. Some of these volumes are anthologies, some original works, but it is surprisingly difficult to tell one from the other. No disciplinary literature of which I am aware quite as ineffectively covers its subject as the average "Mass Communications Reader" or "Introduction To. . . ." on the market today. None is as loaded with (intentional or unintentional) academic or industrial "propaganda," meaning persuasive discourse designed to influence opinions and attitudes towards this or that: usually the virtues (or inevitably the vices) of free enterprise broadcasting, the need for the "professionalization" of journalism, the ultimate role of the consumer as *the* significant decision-maker in the patronage of mass communications, and countless other legends and fabrications at which the reader of this history may well laugh, as he or she considers how easy it is to turn cultural complexities into simple sounding issues—*if* one disregards their histories.

Second, the main problem that much recent history presents to its students is that there is simply too much of it! I find this especially important for so ubiquitous a phenomenon as mass communications, particularly from the early 'sixties to the present. Events and issues involving the communications media that punctuate recent history run on and on, each seemingly as important and/or as earthshattering as the next. In this matter, one observes the pernicious fallacy of all studies (and courses) concerning "great issues" of the moment. No matter how they are selected, and whether they concern mass communications or politics or mental illness, we must remember that most of yesterday's "great issues"—like crosses of gold, bodily humors, methods of casting horoscopes, and whether or not the Social Security Act will destroy capitalism—turn in time to nonsense. Today's great issues will be, for the most part, tomorrow's great yawns. As we examine the past decade or so, how are we to know which of the plethora of events, crises, enigmas, changes and hysterias we see have recently survived will wash out into the future as trivia and which will be relevant to the progress of culture? In fact, we cannot.

Media, Images and Opinion

If *one* issue, however, rose during the 1960s, that pertains directly to our concerns, it is in my opinion, the invention of the idea (or terminology) of "media": that is, the recognition during these years by more than a few academics that the component parts of the institutions of print, broadcasting and film in any nation of the world add up somehow to more than just the sum total of their parts.

When we think of the word "media," many of us probably recall Marshall McLuhan and his slogans, quips and dense prose. But the Toronto professor, at best, merely exploited what was already in the air. Sociologist Daniel

Boorstin probably came nearer to the mark at which McLuhan was aiming in the early 'sixties than McLuhan himself. Boorstin, unlike McLuhan, defined in clear language the notion of "media" and told us precisely why a new word was needed to describe a new and contemporary phenomenon, although made up of old components.

Boorstin's ideas, despite their brilliance, were, however, neither original nor novel. Since the 1920s, journalist Walter Lippmann had described in countless articles and many books the "pictures in our heads" that mass communications during this century have projected for decades. In effect, Lippmann noted, most of us come about our ideas of the world in which we live as a result of assumptions provided for us, in large part, by *interpreters* of reality—journalists in Lippmann's time—who themselves are but superficially and in distorted ways related to that reality.

When we therefore support a political candidate, approve or disapprove of a piece of legislation, court decision or social program, we are not really reacting to *it* but to interpreted versions of both facts and issues seen through a glass darkly, as rendered by various interpreters who are themselves human beings and view life the way *they* have been taught to see it. Put these facts and issues into the matrix of a newspaper or news broadcast, edit them a bit and transmit them to the public. In the end, we discover that we are living in (and thinking about) a world that has *nothing* to do with our own living experiences but consists merely of what other people have imperfectly, and possibly incorrectly, told us about that world. We live, in fact, a great distance from reality, except as we follow the mundane rat tracks of our daily lives, lives which are expanded psychologically only to the degree that books, newspapers, broadcasters, movies and other people (who are all exposed to the same books, newspapers, broadcasters and movies as we are) permit them to move.

I was not even born when Lippmann first advanced this idea in his 1922 book, *Public Opinion,* a better volume on mass communications and its role in society than nine-tenths of the books and articles written since, including my own. I *was* very much around, however, at the time that Boorstin cleverly extended Lippmann's notion into the wider territory of all of the mass communication experiences in which we, by the 1960s, were then immersed. Calling this mental world of Lippmann a "pseudo-environment," Boorstin, in a book called *The Image,* reversed Lippmann's method of analysis. He first described and characterized the pseudo-environment in which you and I *think* we live and then traced its sources back, not to life experiences but to the magazines, newspapers, movie theatres, radio and television sets around us, and the way in which their output interacts with experience to provide for us a seamless "image" of the world "out there": that is, reality.

This world, of course, centers not only upon political matters and news events but extends to our personal ideas about morals, values, ethics and possibly to our opinions of what *is* real and meaningful about our own lives.

For example, you and I really *know* that most of the cities in the U.S.A. have, in recent years, turned into urban jungles: that it is unsafe as never before to walk urban streets and that our police departments are unable to cope with rising crime rates, particularly among the young and minority groups, and that all of this is caused, in part at least, by increasing drug addiction.

Now, *how* do we know this? On the basis of actual experience? If this were true, how important is this experience? With what can we compare it? Certainly, a girl *was* raped and murdered in my city (of millions) this week, and my neighbor was robbed of a television set two months ago. But what do these sad facts *mean,* unless I can legitimately compare them with murder and burglary statistics of the past and in other places today?

My late father, a native New Yorker, as long as I knew him bemoaned the fact that New York City was "going soft." According to him, it was not the "tough town" he had known during the first years of this century. Nearly everybody else proclaimed that it was going to the dogs for the opposite reason at the time, and my father died 30 years ago. I have a feeling that he was right and is still right. New York is today a *safer*—but *many times larger*—city today than it apparently was three generations ago. Certainly, people travel around more now and must guard their (now) more numerous possessions more avidly. Also, the gross amount of hard drug addiction in our cities— that is, the real number of urban addicts—has actually been *decreased* since the first ten years of this century, despite an enormous population growth. Here statistics, not my father's discontents, support truth.

We believe none of this, however, because we "know" that it cannot be true because of what newspapers tell us, what people say on television panel shows, what we read in books and what the movies portray—by and large. In other words, the pseudo-environment supports myths (in a nearly classical sense), because the myths are so easy to accept, having been fed to us by the pseudo-environment. So, in effect, says Boorstin. Like Lippmann, he is, I believe, self-evidently correct.

The Image was not a best seller. However, it started many entrepreneurs, critics and students of the pseudo-environment, some of them called "communications experts," thinking. The resulting questions some therefore asked were also good ones: Of what is this pseudo-environment compounded? What is its actual content? Certainly, it is drawn from newspapers, magazines, television shows, movies and the rest of modernity's grab-bag, but this potpourri is inconvenient to describe in common speech. The new term given it, "media," turned somehow from plural to singular. Instead of referring to communication devices, "media" now referred to "pseudo-environments" and "images" —good or bad, take your choice.

Then the "great issues" emerged. Are "media" able to create, package and sell political candidates to the American people, although they may be merely attractive idiots? Do the force of the "media" upon public opinion necessitate a reinterpretation of the rights of freedom as stated in the First Amendment of our Constitution? Is the "media" (note singular usage) an instrument of social control, propaganda or a new and powerful method of education? To what degree should the government control "media," and how much,

Color Television

305

and for whose economic gain? Is the "media" a governmental conspiracy, a spokesman for big-business-controlled Eastern academic intellectuals and liberals, or is it manipulated by phony, grass-roots Mid-Western fascists? How does one apply standards of honesty, ethics and responsibility to "media"? Should kiddies in a school be taught about "media" at the same time that they learn the truth about Santa Claus and the Easter Bunny? And so forth.

Pardon the irreverence, but any student of the history told in this volume should at least sympathize with my sarcasm. Boorstin's brilliance of yesterday became today's pedant's simplism, as well as the mystic's gospel. This, I believe, is the most important—and possibly lasting—effect of the growth and public preoccupation with "media" during the past decade or so. So let us conclude our history with further examination of some of the reasons why.

Contemporary "media" (in the new singular sense) is best exemplified by what television became in the 1960s: an American institution. By the end of the decade, it was also technologically stabilized, providing national services in both black-and-white and color.

Color Television

RCA had been the big winner in the color game. We noted that, as long ago as 1947, the FCC had accepted RCA's compatible color television transmission method and rejected CBS's "field sequential" system. But many believed that CBS's color unit, despite its drawbacks, was superior to RCA's. The RCA system featured two assets: The system was entirely electronic (meaning no mechanical moving parts), and the color broadcasts could also be transmitted in black and white. On the negative side, RCA's color fidelity was good but not entirely faithful to nature. The black-and-white compatible image was slightly fuzzier than the previous non-color image as well. CBS's system had one factor going for it: the excellence of the color pictures it was capable of transmitting and receiving. Its liabilities were, however, also formidable. CBS's field sequential pictures could not be easily and faithfully transmitted in black and white. The system was therefore not compatible with existing black-and-white receivers. The illusion of color was also achieved mechanically, by means of a spinning color wheel and not via an electronic system. All things considered, RCA's baby seemed, at the time, the better of the two.

Reversing itself in November of 1950, however, the FCC suddenly accepted CBS's standards on the basis of what the agency called its "long-range potential" and its general excellence chromatically. With its corporate nose out of joint, RCA, in 1951, sued the FCC, claiming that it had been, in effect, double-crossed. The Supreme Court subsequently upheld *both* the FCC and CBS.

An industry group representing the major manufacturers of television equipment in the country—called the National Television Systems Committee—petitioned the FCC to hold its fire and look more closely at the advantages of the RCA system. Motivated by the fact that the adoption of CBS's standards would render all existing black-and-white receivers immediately obsolete, because they could not receive color broadcasts or delay the arrival of color broadcasting until all present receivers were used out, the NTSC (quite correctly) claimed that the adoption of the CBS system spelled doom for the television industry. No matter how events worked out, accepting CBS's standards constituted an economic blow to the industry and was unfair to most viewers, certainly in the short run and probably in the long run, whether they owned black-and-white receivers or were about to purchase color sets.

In 1953, the FCC seesawed back to accepting RCA's system. The fact that it took nearly a dozen years for any appreciable number of American television stations to convert to color also worked out in RCA's favor. In 1965, only about 15 per cent of America's television stations were able to transmit color broadcasts. Most of them were NBC affiliates. But, within the next three years, color sets were sold by the millions.

With RCA's manufacturing arm in the lead, of course, the receivers became easier and easier to adjust and tune. Their prices soon fell to within the budget of most upper middle class families. By 1968, about 20 million of the 80 million receivers sold in the nation were able to receive color, and the proportion has been increasing steadily ever since, in spite of a sharp decline in the prices of black-and-white sets as color took over. It seemed that, with the introduction and general acceptance of color transmission, the basic electronic development of open-circuit television had gone about as far as it was likely to go for a decade or two, at any rate.

The Kennedy-Nixon Debates

What may turn out to be early television's single most influential broadcast (including its moon coverage and the Kennedy funerals) occurred just as the 'sixties were beginning. They were a series of programs remembered incorrectly as "The Great Debates." In fact, none of these programs was "Great" and none was a "Debate," in any meaning of either term. Books have indeed been written about these telecasts, but the case for their importance *as television programs* has yet to be made. (Unquestionably, they made political history!) They were dull and possibly irrelevant to all the portentous legends about them that have been told in the years since they occurred. It was, however, not what they actually were but what they stood for that made them notable occasions in the history of broadcasting.

First, what *were* they in fact? The major two presidential challengers in the 1960 elections were Republican Richard Nixon, Vice President under Eisenhower, and Democrat John F. Kennedy, a young, wealthy, good-looking Senator from Massachusetts. The notion that these two candidates might debate one another openly on television concerning the major issues facing the nation seemed to spring up spontaneously from a number of quarters. The American Civil Liberties Union's educational arm had recently published a monograph strongly favoring such an idea. It had apparently impressed a number of CBS executives and a number of people at CBS News. NBC was also willing to go along with the idea, if the candidates both agreed to it. But there was also a formidable legal hitch to the scheme.

Section 315 of the Communications Act guarantees *equal time* to all legitimate political candidates on radio and television in order to espouse their cases. If two major party candidates were permitted to use air time free of charge for a debate or series of debates, an endless string of minor candiates—socialists, prohibitionists, vegetarians, etc.—could legally demand their own shares of equal time and get it. All were legitimate candidates for public office. The networks could not refuse the minor candidates' pleas to be heard and to debate one another in any number of combinations. Section 315 had already caused no end of problems for broadcasters, and the idea of debates posed so many more that the notion seemed, on face, absurd, unless the FCC decided to do something about Section 315.

The networks took the bull by the horns. They invited both candidates to face one another on a series of debates to be broadcast both on the tube and on radio. What they probably had in mind was a legitimate series of confrontations, centering on certain subjects, held face to face between the two men with a minimum of interference or distraction. The model held up was the famous Lincoln-Douglas debates that centered largely upon the issue of slavery. It was agreed that these electronic confrontations would be more wide-ranging and less bound by rhetoric and therefore shorter than the Lincoln-Douglas contest.

Kennedy had, of course, nothing to lose in accepting this challenge. However the debates turned out, they would provide for him an excellent forum to introduce himself to a good part of the American public for whom he was an unfamiliar face. He accepted at once. Nixon was a bit more cautious. He was already as well known and popular national figure who, among other things, had traded quips with Nikita Khrushchev in Moscow concerning the relative virtues of capitalism and communism at a filmed and well publicized meeting. Nor, as a Vice-President, was he overly modest about self-serving publicity of any kind. Nixon, however, was also an attorney. Kennedy was not. And Nixon had won debating honors in college. The incumbent Vice President eventually decided that he was competent to take on the Massachusetts Senator.

With acceptances in hand, the broadcasters and the FCC then petitioned Congress for a suspension of the equal time provisions in the Communications Act—forever, they hoped. Congress agreed to such suspension during the summer of 1960. But this provision was to apply only to the presidential campaign then in progress. A bill to this effect was duly passed and signed by President Eisenhower.

Curious events followed. The first so-called "debate," live from Chicago, was, in effect little more than a two-way press conference. Each candidate was given eight minutes at the start to make what turned out to be his routine campaign pitch. In both instances, most viewers and listeners found it pretty unexciting. A selected group of journalists then began to shoot questions at both participants as rapidly as possible. Each candidate had a few minutes to answer them. Then Nixon and Kennedy were given a few more minutes to wrap up their ideas. The entire debate lasted one hour.

So it went. The first debate alone has, by now, spawned almost as many legends as the Loch Ness Monster. Both men were visibly nervous. Neither said much worth quoting in the newspaper the next day. Much has been made in the years since of Nixon's poor make-up, the way he was lit and televised, and a minor illness (an injured knee) from which he had recently recovered. There is little doubt that Nixon tried too hard. Kennedy looked cooler. Both men demonstrated that they were fluent and convincing talkers, but a nervous Nixon sweated too much. His clothes clashed with the background, making him appear somewhat grimy next to his poised, good-looking young Boston socialite adversary.

If any of the four debates produced any effects on viewers' political attitudes, it was probably the first one. It is now generally agreed that Kennedy "won" it, but I remain unconvinced, in the light of all the polls taken and evidence presented since, that his victory was of major political importance. Voters, it is held by many, are usually influenced little anyway by presidential campaigns. A good part of the audience may well have been predisposed towards Kennedy before the opening gun. Who knows? That a majority of those who merely *heard* the debates on radio (or where the television image was accidentally not transmitted) selected Nixon as the "winner" remains simply an unexplained curiosity. A study of the program's transcript—or audio portion—hardly reveals for Nixon any advantages or Brownie points he did not make in the flesh. He tried to be polite, gutsy and to look smart. Kennedy was also polite and crisp, but he may have succeeded better at sounding as if he knew what he was talking about. From the audience's viewpoint, the "winner" *must* have been the man who re-enforced each individual's preconceived idea of what a chief executive of the U.S.A. should be. This determination has nearly everything to do with the political preconceptions and biases of each individual listener and has little relationship to whether either man cut a swashbuckling figure as a television personality.

The remaining three debates were less sloppily produced than the first. One even switched from Nixon in California to Kennedy in New York. Audiences for them remained high, but they fell from about 75 million to 63 million, first to last. None of them was, or could be, anything like what we usually call "debates." Formats were changed along the way, and Nixon and Kennedy were given a few extra moments here and there to comment on the replies of one another. All in all, they remained glorified press conferences, remote, for the most part, from the genuine issues involved in the campaign. They may have succeeded as televised entertainments, but Lincoln and Douglas must have revolved in their graves.

If they accomplished anything, the Great Debates probably established a new principle that seems to have been accepted by many politicians, at least, those who run for major national offices. Kennedy could not help but profit from them, being comparatively unknown and appearing before a larger, more engaged audience than any other kind of campaign appearance could have provided for him. Nixon could not help but lose support from them, because, being an already familiar political figure at the national level, he probably had in his pocket as many total votes as he was likely to receive the moment before the first debate began. The people knew him—or they knew his image. All Nixon could accomplish was to maintain the support he had—or lose some of it. Apparently, he did lose some, although we cannot even be sure of this. Dual exposure of this kind can easily, by its nature, help a newcomer, but it cannot gain support for an *extremely* familiar figure. Smart politicians of strong reputations with considerable followings (like most incumbents) have, almost invariably since 1960, refused to follow in Nixon's footsteps, including Nixon himself in 1968 and 1972. Two presidential candidates who *think* they may improve their images have nothing to lose from confrontations of this type, especially if the images of both are ambiguous to start with. Witness the Ford-Carter confrontations in 1976.

Now, what were the Great Debates in fancy? Because of the publicity given them and the extensive chewing that they received from columnists, essayists, sociologists, political scientists and others—they have, over the years, spun a rich fabric of myth. This fancy centers upon the peculiar power of "media" to make or break any and all political candidates. Politicians had, for many years, been employing the talents of advertisers and their agencies in conducting their campaigns. But now, in the light of the debates, the facts that one large San Francisco agency was "handling" Kennedy and another in New York was "handling" Nixon took on diabolical and mysterious connotations. One began hearing talk about "image candidates," and the rumor circulated that politics was becoming more and more a matter of "media" manipulation: that people were no longer voting for issues or men but for packaged personalities presented to them by merchandisers of toothpaste and breakfast cereals.

These charges contain some measure of truth, but a small one. Television "spots," or short commercials featuring various candidates, did not originate in the 1960 campaign. Both Eisenhower and Stevenson had employed them— and advertising agencies—in the 'fifties in about equal portions between them. Nor were many selections made in the voting booths suddenly motivated by this sort of persuasion. America's outstanding "image candidate" of this century was, I'd say, Teddy Roosevelt, whose success (and later failures) occurred long before the broadcasting era. We have seen how Horace Greeley, it is said, was destroyed by "media," meaning Thomas Nast's vitriolic cartoons in *Harper's*. Define your terms as you wish, George Washington and Thomas Jefferson were certainly "image candidates," and Alexander Hamilton was almost certainly provided a poor hearing—and public *persona*—even by the "media" that supported him.

As a result of the Great Debates of 1960, however, and the legends that have clustered around them, it is indeed possible that greater scrutiny than ever before was given to *why* Americans vote for one political candidate rather than another. Do they vote for men and programs, or do they prefer "images?"

"Old Hickory," for instance, or "Honest Abe." And how concerned have they been about genuine political issues, except when they are simplified and boiled down to absurd phrases like "He kept us out of war!" or "Don't change horses in mid-stream!"

The Effects of "Media"

That the Great Debates turned into episodes of national importance, generating a set of illusions that have not yet died, however, tells us a good deal about the impact of television and the mystique of the "media" during the early part of the 'sixties. Neither movies nor radio were in those days indicted, except by an occasional hysteric, as instruments that might influence and/or possibly destroy virtually the political (and eventually the social) life of a nation. Television, on the other hand, seemed to many vastly more insidious than either motion pictures or sound broadcasting. One should therefore not be surprised that Boorstin's book, *The Image,* was published almost immediately in the wake of the 1960 elections, and that Marshall McLuhan's media mystics began their brief day in the sun in the wake of the "Great Debates" and the attention they had attracted.

One big question of the early 1960s was, therefore, "What are the effects of 'media' upon people, especially children?" To answer it, droves of psychologists, sociologists and others, looking for a new and fertile wilderness upon which to sprinkle their protean expertise, crept from the woodwork. True, an older bastion of social scientists, including Paul Lazarsfeld, Robert Merton, William Schramm, Harry Skornia, Charles Siepmann and others, had been asking and writing about similar questions since the early days of radio. But now these old timers were joined by a new echelon of media experts, led less by men like Boorstin (who retreated to former interests after *The Image*) than by new-style data collectors and sociologists like Joseph Klapper of CBS, Leo Bogart, an advertising man, Ithiel de Sola Pool and philosophically oriented George Gerbner, later Dean of the Annenberg School of Communications at the University of Pennsylvania, where, today, little *except* obtuse problems of media is considered the legitimate study of mass communications.

In the relatively short time since these newer academic investigators appeared, we have received neither new nor convincing answers to this question of how "media" affect us, nor much useful information about how the "images" by which we live influence our lives. Their answers, opinions and analyses have been so contradictory—and usually so confusing—that many of us are not even sure any longer that "media" or "images" (as they are used in academia) exist at *all*—or whether we believe that they do because we have been told they do, and therefore accept them without sufficient scientific skepticism.

If "media," as a psychological or social force, turns out to be a mere word, and if all men everywhere and at all times in all cultures have kept "images" in their head which are more mythic than real, *any* and *all* investigations into the effects of mass communications are likely to *seem* to hit pay dirt. But it will be fool's gold. Under these circumstances, Joseph Klapper may well be correct in his famous claim that television does not influence anybody to do anything much about anything, but merely re-enforces tendencies already present in one's behavior, attitudes and opinions. It may, also, be as entirely correct to say that children are corrupted by "media" violence as to say they are not, considering the "images" of violence the young carry about in their heads in most cultures, even and especially those that have not been industrialized and do not possess television services. If, in the end, these great minds have discovered that we learn what we learn from whatever we are exposed to, I doubt that their contributions to our intellectual heritage will turn out to be of major significance or pith.

We cannot yet be certain of this outcome, because the history of the very concept of "media" (and its attendant myths) is still a new phenomenon let loose in the intellectual environment. It was not born suddenly in 1960, but it entered our national discourse after the Great Debates of that year, which seemed to announce to the public that there was more to television than met the eye. Such insights, you may reply, were already self-evident, largely because of video's previous decade of enormous success in selling consumer goods.

It is also often simple, we know, to overlook the obvious. That there may have been (and be) *less* to the notion of "media" than meets the eye is a proposition not frequently advanced today in most up-to-date academic circles. But its day may come!

Television Audiences

If the 1960s saw American television operate in its most dramatic mode, this was the direct result of the dramatic events of the period, not because of anything written by video playwrights. Of course, the greatest part of the television audience spent most of its time during the years watching routine video fare, about which I have little of interest to say not covered in other volumes with kindliness and sympathy greater than mine. Its popularity, however, gave television new advantages of many sorts over other media in terms of raw audience numbers during the 'sixties and well into the 'seventies.

How big are these viewing audiences? In spite of their preoccupation with ratings and statistics, most broadcasters do not really know how many people actually watch their programs. They would rather talk about audience percentages, one show as opposed to another, or the proportion of sets in use tuned to this or that show. The reason is that video audience statistics must necessarily be based upon a miniscule "sample" of the total number of viewers in the nation, selected usually according to so-called "demographic criteria." This means that the sample (possibly a few hundred, or as many as a few thousand households) is supposed to represent the total number of viewers. It probably does, but it may not.

I shall not attempt to explain the various audience sampling devices used by Nielsen, Arbitron and the, roughly, 50 or so other polling and sampling organizations that provide viewing statistics to broadcasters and advertisers, national and local. These techniques have been harshly criticized both inside and outside the world of the mass communications. The reason is that these sampling instruments actually tell us little about *exactly* who has their television set turned to what program at what time, much less how many people are watching what—or if they are paying attention to it, or if what they view has any effect on them.

Before we join the throng and criticize video (and radio) ratings too harshly, let us remember that other media do not share broadcasting's special problems. Publishing statistics are pretty firm and unequivocal; a newspaper distributes a certain number of issues; any motion picture produces patronage numbers and profit-and-loss statements that cannot be refuted. Of course, we can never be sure of how much of any newspaper is actually perused by any reader, or how many people read from cover to cover any book sold. But, at least, we *can* obtain serviceable and reliable *circulation* figures. Motion pictures shown in theatres produce firm records of tickets sold and tell us how much business was done but little more than this. (Dollar revenues sometimes confuse the matter, because different theatres charge different prices.)

Patronage statistics of these sorts are not available to broadcasters. There are many indices that one *may* use to indicate a program's popularity, but all are, in the long run, to one degree or another unsatisfactory. When the *Laugh In* comedy show seemed to take the nation's mind from its troubles in the late 'sixties, for instance, enough people were talking about Tiny Tim, chicken jokes and repeated phrases like "Here come the judge!" to indicate that *Laugh In's* audience must have been enormous. How enormous was a different matter. The witticisms of Archie Bunker repeated in daily conversation indicate much the same degree of popularity for Norman Lear's *All in the Family* (an Americanization adapted from a British comedy series). These, however, are exceptional programs, and such informal data merely confirm the obvious.

On the other hand, if one regards television merely as a way of moving or selling consumer goods, an excellent indication of patronage—or the effectiveness of commercials—is how well products and services sell after extensive promotion on television. Unfortunately, this is frequently ambiguous information, depending in some measure upon the nature of a product, the quality of a commercial, how often it is repeated and at what times, current attitudes of viewers, their finances at the moment, and their psychological (or real) needs for certain kinds of goods and services.

The size and make-up of America's television audience also shifts according to the time of day or night. Kids, we know, watch largely on Saturday mornings, but they also watch much adult fare in the evening during the week. Daytime audiences seem to be made up largely of women. The average number of sets tuned to television during the so-called "prime time" hours in the evening hovers mysteriously around 40 million, although one cannot always be certain how many people are watching each set—or if nobody is watching except the household cat. When something *really* dramatic happens, like a man walking on the moon for the first time or when Frank Sinatra makes one of his periodic comebacks, the figure may shoot up to projected audiences of about 100 million. In fact, it is safe to say that the *potential* American audience for television broadcasting is about twice as large as for the readership of newspapers, and that the *potential* audience for radio is about three times that of the daily press.

During the 'sixties, however, it became quite clear that figures such as these meant little. Year after year, the Roper organization reported that the average American received more and more of his news, information and orientation to culture from television than from any other medium, a trend that continues apace to this day. Once again, depending upon certain demographic samples, Roper claims that about two-thirds of the American population say that they receive almost all of their "news" about what is going on in the world from television; about half also depend upon newspapers; about one fifth say "radio"; and a minuscule proportion mention magazines and other people as their primary source of news. The same sort of evidence also indicates that about twice as many people trust television reports when opposed to newspaper articles, and that an equal number value television *more* highly than newspapers. Also, whoever the average American is, he or she may be expected to watch television about three hours a day. These approximations vary slightly— but not dramatically—among the more educated and wealthier part of the population, who seem to rely in general upon television less than the poor.

The great audiences gather most fully and frequently at the great television dramas, as we have noted. And the great American dramas have been written, in recent years, by history. To say, for example, that ex-President Nixon addressed an entire nation when he resigned from office in 1974 is not hyperbolic. Nixon's television audience exceeded 100 million in all probability, including rebroadcasts. And if one could not get to a video set, radio brought his voice to many millions. He probably spoke to nearly 150 million Americans that August night in 1974, excluding only the mentally defective, the dead drunk, the totally indifferent and very small children.

Much the same sort of audience gathered for President Kennedy's "Bay of Pigs" speech in 1962. And, naturally, one of the largest video audiences ever assembled watched the events before, after and during the same President's funeral that occupied the weekend following his assassination on November 22, 1963. That audience fluctuated in number over the three days, but many were literally *forced* to watch the event, because little else was presented on the nation's television tubes during this period. Again, the event attracted as close to a total national audience as one can imagine.

The Impact of Television

Such occasions vivify the impact, real and potential, of video communications to provide instant and colorful communications to large audiences. Indeed, there seems to be something mystical (or amazing) about this notion, even though the difference in audience numbers between television and radio may not be great, and the impact of both is simultaneous. Given a nation of literate people, it is also possible for the printed page to reach all of our population in 24 hours, containing coverage of an event that may be richer—if not more emotionally fulfilling or startling—than that provided by television. Print journalists claim that they are able to explain things better and in greater detail than broadcasters.

I am not so certain that they *always* do, but the kind of semi-permanent, multi-faceted coverage that print is potentially competent to provide for news events is, in the short run, superior (and, I think, possibly *more* mystical) than the mere spontaneity of radio and television. The journalist may well ask the electronic news reporter, ''What is the big hurry to find out?'', just as I, an author of books and articles about events long past, have the right to ask the same question of the print journalist.

A professor of communications in an Iron Curtain country, where all news must pass rather slowly through a Ministry of Information for clearance, once asked me quite sincerely why Americans are always in such a hurry to find out so much about trivia. ''Wouldn't your people rather get correct news, important news and well investigated news a little *less* quickly than all of the inaccurate, thoughtless nonsense that comes to them so quickly?'' His was not a bad question, although this gentlemen knew, understood or cared little about the history and traditions of the American press.

The drama of a Kennedy funeral was, however, enormously heightened by its spontaneity, a fact that I think would even be understood and conceded in Communist East Europe. America's video coverage of that particular event was superb, indicating to us the heights of good taste and art to which television may rise when prompted by fate.

No video broadcast that I have ever seen, however, has had quite the impact upon me (and millions of others) as NBC-TV's more or less accidental coverage of the murder of Lee Harvey Oswald by Jack Ruby in Dallas, Texas on Sunday, November 24, 1963, shortly after noon. The audience watching at that time was, considering the hour, relatively small, but video tapes of this gruesome slice of history were repeated by all networks throughout the day. The event caused no end of controversy, even generating the claim that Ruby shot Oswald in a mad attempt simply to receive television publicity!

Whatever the reasons for the episode, it was both barbaric and fascinating, providing still another glimpse of television's near miraculous and frightening potential to record, or possibly make, history. Many people reacted in different ways to the broadcast. I was fortunate (or unfortunate) to be watching it as I was dressing to attend a wedding—not one of my own. The shooting hypnotized me. I simply stood for ten minutes in front of my receiver until it was replayed on tape, because I could not believe my eyes. I was late for the wedding, but so were the bride, groom and other guests. During the ceremony, I found myself asking, ''Would my shock have been as great if I heard it on radio? Read it in the newspapers? Learned of it from a friend?'' To this day, I am not quite certain what seeing the event really *meant* to me—if anything.

Nothing about that particular weekend seems quite real to me today, however. And in a day or two, video had reverted back to its endless game shows, soap operas, westerns, and panel shows.

The Video War

The next great drama of real life that was to find its way to the American video tube was to be far crueler than a mere assassination and murder. It was a slaughter, the first covered by television broadcasters, causing considerable conjecture about their roles and responsibilities as newscasters.

The American experience we call *in toto* "the Vietnam War" began, poorly covered by all the media (no better and no worse by television than by print journalists), in the summer of 1964, when the famous Gulf of Tonkin resolution was passed by Congress. In response to still disputed provocations by North Vietnam, whose torpedo boats were supposed to have fired upon a United States Navy ship, President Lyndon Johnson was given by Congress nearly unrestricted authorization for reprisals. How this resolution—and Johnson's power—eventually involved the U.S.A. in a full scale Far Eastern civil war a decade old between the Vietnam and Vietcong, communists and non-communists, and Buddhists versus Christians, remains one of the most complicated—and fascinating—histories of blunders in recent times.

Vietnam was an undeclared war. But it was also the longest war the U.S.A. has ever fought, the second one that the nation clearly lost, and the one for which America was least prepared in many ways. After two or three years of American casualties and military ineptitude, the conflict aroused enormous opposition among the general public. For all practical purposes, the U.S.A. might have ended its engagement in Vietnam at any time, but the tedious peace negotiations finally ended in 1973, when President Nixon, in effect, admitted defeat and called our troops home. The civil war itself ended in the subsequent conquest of South Vietnam by the Communist North Vietnamese, which had been the inevitable outcome from the start.

One reason—but merely one—that the Vietnam conflict remained such an open sore to the American public throughout its life was the extraordinary difficulty of providing reliable media coverage of it for the American people. In the early years of the war, press and broadcast correspondents depended largely upon military interpretations of current hostilities. These daily "briefings" were probably no more fanciful than similar events during World War II, but intentional and unintentional deceptions on the part of military public information officers made the complexities of the war more and more difficult to understand at home. Combat itself in Vietnam was disorganized, much of it consisting of guerrilla operations. Our own troops seemed to lack the same sense of purpose that American soldiers have known in other conflicts. Reporters, therefore, eventually centered their interests upon the barbarities of conflict, upon so-called "atrocities" (natural fallout from *all* wars) and the apparent senselessness of the hostilities as they saw it.

If the American public felt increasingly confused and enraged about Vietnam, this reaction resulted, probably in large part, from the coverage given it by television. Michael Arlen has appropriately entitled his book about television coverage of Vietnam, *The Living Room War,* and it is an excellent title. Vietnam was indeed the *first* war brought into American homes by means of television. Neither broadcasters, nor our military forces, nor Washington's politicians had, in any but minor ways, experience with this kind of coverage, involving, as it frequently did, the transposition of graphic film of warfare, in color and sent with great rapidity to a public unprepared to comprehend much about it or what it meant. Vietnam was also a particularly "visual" war, involving an endless number of daylight guerrilla actions that were eminently telegenic—often almost too picturesque. (Had the grime and gore of the battles of the Civil War been brought to the home front of either the North or South by means of color television, I wonder how the public would have reacted to it!)

As years passed, and thanks largely to some magnificent Vietnamese film photographers, Americans were treated to an amazing view of multiple tiny parts of the total conflict, an intimate view of our frequently demoralized fighting forces, and many glimpses of the raw terror of all warfare. One saw burned and ravaged villages, tearful civilians mourning their dead, and a now famous sequence, the execution of a suspected spy by a Saigon police chief, all in living color on the familiar television tube. Such experiences were not only unique. To many, they were shattering.

As public opinion crystallized against the war, the networks set their facile documentary programmers to create some kind of order out of this nightly news chaos. The effort was well intended. CBS and NBC and ABC produced some remarkable programs, not only about the war, but concerning issues allied to it.

For the most part, their efforts were fruitless, however. In the first place, it was questionable whether the simplistic format of the American television documentary program might conceivably do more than ask easy questions that were impossible to answer without complicating further an already complicated, and possibly somewhat insane, international tragedy. Second, Americans did not, in enormous numbers, desert their favorite westerns, detective stories, science fictions, spy stories, comedies and variety shows to grasp what information they could from these serious, often thoughtful, programs.

How I wish I might add some more constructive conclusions concerning the role of television during the Vietnam War than the superficial observations above! I cannot. The recent past is still with us today. Too many irresponsible charges concerning the current role of our new all-purpose hero-villian, the "media," are still flying around our heads. America's recent defeat in Southeast Asia can too easily, and incorrectly, be placed at the feet of the "media" (particularly television) for too many slick reasons, none of them convincing. On the other side of the coin, video may assume, for some, a hero's role as the potent force that finally tipped the scales of public opinion that forced President Nixon's disengagement from the Vietnam war.

The "Media" and Social Unrest

Let us not forget, also, that the late 'sixties were a period of urban riots, protests on college campuses, an infamous, riot-ridden Chicago Democratic convention in 1968, hippies, yippies, a supposed epidemic, spread across the nation, of heroin addiction, the discovery of that ancient drug marijuana by middle class "swingers," and Lyndon Johnson's ambitious and disastrous "Great Society" programs—all of which were somehow morally and psychologically related to the Vietnamese conflict but, once started, gained impetus on their own. Did the chaos at home, in the midst of an era of prosperity, result from our disasterous foreign policy; and what role did the mass media play in the societal theatre of the absurd through which we lived during these years? If somebody tells you that he or she knows the answer, listen carefully, because you are in the rare presence of a genuinely vain and stupid person.

Television stood out in the midst of it all, not only reporting blow by blow our national confusion, but apparently also creating some of it. Demonstrators, draft card burners, random attention seekers and others soon learned the art of attracting mobile televison crews to the scenes of their capers. Not only was video a mass medium now, it was also an instigator and publicist for anybody or any group able to command the attention of its cameras, newsmen or talk show moderators.

The decade ended with such well staged events as the New York State rock festival at Woodstock that provided grist for the mill, not only for copious video and newspaper coverage, but also a feature theatrical motion picture. A number of films in fact, managed to portray better than most critics and analysts the way in which history was interwoven with all of the mass media at this time. Haskell Wexler's movie, *Medium Cool,* portrayed a drama of human alienation and was actually shot against a background of the Chicago riots of 1968. Other films followed the travels of rock music heroes and exploited the caprices of young people, not all of them properly called "hippies," who demonstrated their variegated discontents with middle class homes, schools and American affluence in numerous colorful ways, just as they developed almost instinctively clever ways of exploiting the "media."

I would be deceiving my young readers, however, if I led them to believe that the majority of American television programs, movies or the behavior of the mass audiences were fundamentally different during the 1960s than they have been so far in the 'seventies. Far from it. Styles change. But, Vietnam or no Vietnam, urban riots or no urban riots, our video dream machine kept grinding out much the same sort of popular entertainments. The best were, by now, highly professional, slick and often enjoyable films or videotapes: *Star Trek* and *Mission Impossible* are two good examples of clever melodramas based on old ideas that often came up with new twists. *Bewitched, Laugh In, The Beverly Hillbillies* and their imitators continued along dispensing their supply of harmless nonsense. Game shows and soap operas held their ground during the day, and Johnny Carson ruled at night, telling many of the same jokes that his predecessor, Jack Paar, told for years on the *Tonight* program. Summer was filled with re-runs and occasional "pilot" programs of series that never got started.

By this time, the U.S.A. had also consolidated its position as number one purveyor of television programming to the rest of the non-communist world. Most nations were even forced to impose restrictions upon the number of American video film and tapes that might be telecast (often with foreign sound tracks) per week. These restrictions, of course, were designed to stimulate local broadcast production and to give programs from competing countries a chance. But the most popular fare around the world was American, except in such advanced nations (with considerable production resources of their own) as England, Japan, Germany, and the Scandanavian countries. A trip through much of Latin America, Africa and the Orient, however, allows one to look at a retrospective album of yesterday's American television programs and movies, some of the former 15 or 20 years old.

Cable and Public Television

Other types of video horizons have, however, expanded considerably since the early 1960s, less in commercial broadcasting on open circuits then in the development of Community Access Television and in what was once called "Educational Broadcasting."

CATV or "wired television" was born in the early 'fifties for the best of technological reasons: to bring to cable subscribers in nonpopulous areas programs not broadcast in their localities on the air but obtainable from a single receiver at a high, remote point. These broadcasts might then be distributed for a fee to subscribers by means of cable. A subscriber to a CATV system, therefore, in a community that was only served by one or two open-circuit networks might receive a second or third one as well. In areas where conventional reception was poor, CATV systems also sprang up one after the other. By the middle 'sixties, about 2000 such systems were operating around the country, some merely offering reception that was clearer and less bothered by static than those available on the air waves. Some were modest ventures with a few as 1500 subscribers. Some had as many as 20,000 or more.

By the early 'seventies, the FCC had opened up so-called "Class A" markets to exploitation by cable companies. This meant that a cable entrepreneur, if he wished to try, could now offer his services in an area where open-circuit reception already included clear pictures of all the networks—and even some independent stations. What advantages might CATV subscribers gain from this service not available to regular, open circuit television viewers? The CATV companies tried to answer this question by adding broadcast services of their own; special events, movies, sports contests not regularly telecast, and even, in some large cities "adults only" movies.

Some of these companies fared well; some did not. Others toyed with the notion of subscription or "pay as you go" video, featuring opera broadcasts, brand new theatrical films and other sorts of specialized programs. To this end, ingenious devices like coin boxes, computer cards and 'phone services, all involving the scrambling and unscrambling of video pictures, were attempted in order that viewers might fairly and voluntarily pay for any extra television services they wanted to watch. Strongest opposition to this form of CATV was heard from motion picture theatre operators who felt, quite correctly, that a national system of "pay as you go" television (combined with a gasoline shortage) might doom them shortly to oblivion.

The FCC has also insisted, as a condition of operating a cable company in Class A markets, that certain unused channels be turned over to the public for its own use. (Every cable operator has, at his technical command, a number of unused channels.)

Just what this "public access programming" is supposed to be has not yet been clearly defined. In most instances today, it simply means that, if a local organization of some kind owns a sufficient supply of video equipment to tape something that may be presented on a cable channel, it probably will be. Some cable companies have bravely attempted to originate their own public access programs. Their major problem, for the most part, is funding these programs, whether or not their channels are used for any of the FCC's three categories for such service: educational, governmental or general use. Audiences are small and costs tend to be high, although cable companies may charge a fee for the use of their facilities by local telecasters.

Today, there are more than 3000 CATV systems in the U.S.A., and their number is growing. What will become of them is anybody's guess. No shortage of wild conjecture exists in the pages of most mass communication readers (or anthologies) published today. Pay your money; take your choice.

The fate of what we once called "Educational Broadcasting" seems, at the moment, a bit more certain than that of CATV. "Educational Television" became "Public Television" with the passage by Congress of The Public Broadcasting Act of 1967. This Act, in fact a step-child of a Carnegie Commission study of the (then) miserable state of all non-commercial broadcasting in the U.S.A., created the Corporation for Public Broadcasting, an extra-governmental agency funded erratically by Congress, whose directors were appointed by the President of the U.S.A.

In effect, the CPB really is a funding agency for a Public Broadcasting Service that is supposed to represent most of the nation's non-commercial VHF and UHF stations. It subsidizes and distributes certain locally originated programs to other non-commercial affiliates—or members of what has been called America's "fourth network"—for a fee. A successful example is *Sesame Street,* the highly publicized and much-touted zippy children's program produced by the Children's Television Workshop. The Workshop is the beneficiary of monies from the CPB, various foundations, the U.S. Office of Education and other sources. The PBS distributes its programs to Public Broadcasting stations throughout the country. Individual stations may, in turn, have received the funds they have used to pay for the kiddie show from CPB in the first place—or may be aided in part by the state or local schools, local governments, foundations or by means of listener subscriptions and donations.

The complexities of Public Broadcasting in America, and its apparently psychotic fiscal schemes, are non-commercial broadcasting's least attractive aspect. After the organization of CPB and PBS, non-commercial programing improved markedly in the U.S.A., at least that part of it which was distributed nationally. Much of it continues to get better and better. Not only were well-produced serious programs like *The Advocates* funded by PBS, but also interesting shows were imported from Britain, most notably *The Forsyte Saga* and *Upstairs, Downstairs*. As more and more of the public tuned to non-commercial broadcasting, it became possible for PBS (and individual stations) to interest large corporations in underwriting some of the costs of their programs. Prohibited from selling commercial time to them, nothing prevented Public Television stations from merely announcing that such exemplary programs as Sir Kenneth Clark's *Civilisation* series or J. Bronowski's *The Ascent of Man* came to the viewer by courtesy of such-and-such a petroleum company or conglomerate.

For a good deal of their air time, however, many Public Broadcasting stations still concentrated on locally originated programs, mainly because of the expense of using PBS materials and the shortage of good ones. By the late 'sixties and early 'seventies, however, the old notion that noncommercial television was one day destined to become the great American school house and university had been discarded. The viewer was therefore no longer likely to run into too many televised ocarina lessons or lectures on Ming ceramics on Public Broadcasting stations. Much fare offered by these stations unfortunately remains today both jejune and dull when compared to commercial channels. But the possibility of operating a serious, non-commercial fourth network in America has, at least, been shown to be feasible.

Final Fade-out

At the outset of this chapter, I noted that the main problem in recording current history is that there is too much of it. So it seems. And remember that we have been concerned with one medium alone in these past several pages: television. Nor has mention been made of what was possibly the most spectacular television broadcast of all time, the Apollo 11 telecast from the surface of the moon on July 20, 1969. Nor have we launched into an extended discussion of the famous *Red Lion* decision of the Supreme Court of the United States, affirming the legality of the FCC's "fairness doctrine." This rule forces broadcasters to present on the air various views of controversial issues, because such coverage by broadcasters is now understood legally to be a right of listeners and viewers. (The court upheld the idea that broadcasters have accepted this responsibility as a condition of their licenses and that they have to make good on it.)

No, the story of the Communications Revolution should not, I think, be permitted to come to its climax in a plethora of "hot" issues that fill media journals, popular publications and textbooks on "media." To do so might certainly answer many student's supposed cries (not heard so much these days) for "relevance." Such a finale would, however, unfairly misrepresent the significance and impact of the present moment when held against all that has occurred in the past. We have been warned by many philosophers again and again not to spin the fancy that *our* time and place—and technology—is the ultimate summation of everything that has been passed on to us, and that all of history has had but one purpose: the creation of *our* culture, *our* values and *our* magnificent collective intellect.

The present is but a swiftly passing picture in the magic lantern show of history. It may be a more insignificant part of the whole than even our wildest fancies permit us to imagine.

The Communications Revolution itself is but a recent phenomenon. Most of the history told in this book is modern history, events that happened only moments ago as the story of the human race is told. The ultimate end of this revolution, indeed of all of our beloved technology as far as we can tell from the present moment, may turn out to be of no more consequence to future centuries than the technology of the Roman Empire is today, with its enormous arenas, viaducts, fire brigades, deluxe plumbing and superbly sophisticated system of commerce.

During a period that has seen both science and technology put to such unbelievably barbaric purposes as to make one shudder, I cannot now sing phony praises to the gods of modernity, or even discover much of a happy nature to say about our mass communications instruments as we know and use them today, or as *you* will know and use them tomorrow. Let me end this book, therefore, as I have ended others, noting that every technological revolution, including the one that involves communications, is a sword with two sharp edges. Good men and women use technologies wisely. Evil and greedy people use them for destructive, inhumane purposes. If the history we have examined in this book teaches us anything, this is it.

I cannot agree with high school valedictorians that these are "troubled times." All times past have been troubled one way or another by many things. Nor do I agree with the "media freaks" that a "global village" is just beyond the sunset, because a new gadget permits me to talk to a man in Tibet or to watch my fellow man in Moscow or Peking make a fool of himself. No, I am more concerned with the problem of communicating thoughts, sentiments, ideas and facts that encourage fools to act like sensible people, even if I am merely talking to someone down the street.

I promised the reader that this story of the Communications Revolution would turn out to be an interesting one, reflective of the many facets of life good and bad, in which man indulges. I think the facts of the matter, as many of them as I have been able to cover in these pages, have made good this promise. Or so I hope.

Selected
Bibliography

A WELL ANNOTATED BIBLIOGRAPHY of all of the events, inventions and figures treated in this volume would constitute a book larger than this one. The following reading list is therefore selective, divided according to subject and designed to help the serious student of most historical topics treated in the preceding pages to move on to other more detailed sources, including primary materials. Current availability of serious books on various phases of the history of mass communications has also been considered in this selection.

BROADCASTING

Abramson, Albert, *Electronic Motion Pictures: A History of the Television Camera.* Berkeley: University of California Press, 1955.

Archer, Gleason L., *Big Business and Radio.* New York: American Historical Society, 1939.

————, *History of Radio to 1926.* New York: American Historical Society, 1939.

Arlen, Michael J., *The Living-Room War.* New York: Viking Press, 1969.

Baker, W. J., *A History of the Marconi Co.* New York: St. Martin's Press, 1972.

Banning, William, *Commercial Broadcasting Pioneer: The WEAF Experiment. 1922–1926.* Cambridge, Mass.: Harvard University Press, 1946.

Barnouw, Erik, *The Golden Web: A History of Broadcasting in the United States. 1933–53.* New York: The Oxford University Press, 1968.

————, *The Image Empire: A History of Broadcasting in the United States from 1953.* New York: The Oxford University Press, 1970.

————, *A Tower in Babel, A History of Broadcasting in the United States to 1933.* New York: The Oxford University Press, 1966.

————, *Tube of Plenty*. New York: The Oxford University Press, 1975. (Contains materials from the same author's histories of television broadcasting.)

Bluem, A. William, *Documentary in American Television*. New York: Hastings House, 1965.

Brown, Les, *Television: The Business Behind the Box*. New York: Harcourt, Brace, Jovanovich, Inc., 1971.

Buxton, Frank and Bill Owen, *The Big Broadcast 1920–1950*. New York: Viking Press, 1972.

————, *Radio's Golden Age*. New York: Easton Valley Press, 1966.

Cantril, Hadley, *The Invasion from Mars*. Princeton, N.J.: Princeton University Press, 1940.

Chase, Francis, *Sound and Fury: An Informal History of Broadcasting*. New York: Harper's, 1942.

Cogeley, John, *Report on Blacklisting* (Volume II: Radio and Television.) New York: The Fund for the Republic, 1956.

de Forest, Lee, *Father of Radio*. Chicago: Wilcox and Follett, 1950.

Denisoff, R. Serge, *Solid Gold: The Popular Record Industry*. New Brunswick, N.J.: Transaction Books, 1975.

Dizard, Wilson P., *Television, A World View*. Syracuse, N.Y.: Syracuse University Press, 1966.

Dunlap, Orin, *The Story of Radio*. New York: The Dial Press, 1935.

Emery, Walter P., *Broadcasting and Government: Regulations and Reponsibilities*. East Lansing: Michigan State University Press, 1971.

Epstein, Edward Jay, *News from Nowhere: Television and the News*. New York: Random House, 1973.

Erickson, Don, *Armstrong's Fight for FM Broadcasting*. University of Alabama Press, 1974.

Everson, George, *The Story of Television: The Life of Philo T. Fransworth*. New York: W. W. Norton, 1949.

Faulk, John Henry, *Fear on Trial*. New York: Simon and Schuster, 1964.

Fessenden, Helen, *Fessenden, Builder of Tomorrow*. New York: Coward-McCann, 1940.

Friendly, Fred W., *Due to Circumstances Beyond Our Control . . .* New York: Random House, 1967.

Goldmark, Peter, *Maverick Inventor*. New York: E. P. Dutton Co., 1973.

Gross, Ben, *I Looked and I Listened*. New York: Arlington House, 1970.

Harmon, Jim, *The Great Radio Heroes*. New York: Doubleday and Co., 1967.

Head, Sydney, *Broadcasting in America* (Third Edition). Boston: Houghton-Mifflin Co., 1976.

Jolly, W. P., *Marconi*. Stein and Day, 1972.

Kahn, Frank J. (ed.), *Documents of American Broadcasting*. New York: Appleton-Century Crofts, 1973.

Kendrick, Alexander, *Prime Time*. Boston: Little Brown and Co., 1969.

Koenig, Allen E. (ed.), *Broadcasting and Bargaining: Labor Relations in Radio and Television*. Madison: University of Wisconsin Press, 1970.

Kraus, Sidney, *The Great Debates*. Bloomington: University of Indiana Press, 1962.

Lessing, Lawrence, *Man of High Fidelity: Edwin Howard Armstrong*. New York: Bantam Books, 1969.

Lichty, Lawrence and Malachi C. Topping, *American Broadcasting: A Source Book on the History of Radio and Television.* New York: Hastings House, 1975.

Lyons, Eugene, *David Sarnoff.* New York: Harper and Row, 1966.

Mayer, Martin, *About Televison.* New York: Harper and Row, 1972.

Mayo, John B. Jr., *The President is Dead.* New York: Exposition Press, 1967.

Metz, Robert, *CBS: Reflections in a Bloodshot Eye.* Chicago: The Playboy Press, 1975.

Murrow, Edward R., *In Search of Light.* New York: Alfred A. Knopf, 1967.

Opotowsky, Stan, *TV—The Big Picture.* New York: Collier Books, 1962.

Powell, John W., *Channels of Learning: the Story of Educational Television.* Washington: Public Affairs Press, 1962.

Ryan, Milo, *History in Sound.* Seattle: University of Washington Press, 1963.

Sanger, Elliott M., *Rebel in Radio: The Story of WQXR.* New York: Hastings House, 1973.

Sarnoff, David, *Looking Ahead.* New York: McGraw-Hill, 1968.

Schicke, C. A., *Revolution in Sound: A Biography of the Recording Industry.* Boston: Little Brown and Co., 1974.

Schulman, Arthur and Roger Youman, *How Sweet It Was—Television, A Pictorial Commentary.* New York: Chorecrest, 1966.

Schurick, E. P. J., *The First Quarter Century of American Broadcasting.* Kansas City: Midland Publishing Co., 1946.

Shanks, Bob, *The Cool Fire.* New York: W. W. Norton Co., 1976.

Slate, Sam J. and Joe Cook, *It Sounds Impossible.* New York: The Macmillan Co., 1963.

Stedman, Raymond, *The Serials.* Norman: University of Oklahoma Press, 1971.

Weinberg, Meyer, *TV and America.* New York: Ballantine Books, 1962.

MOTION PICTURES

Barnouw, Erik, *Documentary: A History of the Non-Fiction Film.* New York: The Oxford University Press, 1974.

Baxter, John, *Hollywood in the Sixties.* New York and London: A. S. Barnes, 1972.

Bogle, Donald, *Toms, Coons, Mulattoes, Mammies and Bucks.* New York: Bantam Books, 1974.

Bohn, Thomas W. and Richard L. Stromgren, *Light and Shadows.* Port Washington, N.Y.: Alfred Publishing Co., 1975.

Brownlow, Kevin, *The Parade's Gone By.* New York: Alfred A. Knoff, 1968.

Casty, Alan, *Development of the Film.* New York: Harcourt, Brace and Jovanovich, 1973.

Ceram, C. W., *Archeology of the Cinema.* New York: Harcourt, Brace and World, 1965. (C. W. Ceram is a pseudonym of Kurt W. Marek)

Chaplin, Charles, *My Autobiography.* New York: Simon and Schuster, 1964.

Clarens, Carlos, *An Illustrated History of the Horror Film.* New York: G. P. Putnam's Sons, 1967.

Conant, Michael, *Antitrust in the Motion Picture Industry.* Berkeley: University of California Press, 1960.

Crowther, Bosley, *The Lion's Share.* New York: E. P. Dutton Co., 1957.

Day, Beth, *This Was Hollywood.* Garden City, N.Y.: Doubleday and Co., 1960.

Farber, Stephen, *The Movie Rating Game.* Washington: Public Affairs Press, 1972.

Fielding, Raymond, *The American Newsreel, 1911–1967.* Norman: The University of Oklahoma Press, 1972.

French, Philip, *The Movie Moguls*. Chicago: Henry Regnery Co., 1969.

Fulton, A. R., *Motion Pitures: The Development of An Art from Silent Films to the Age of Television*. Norman: University of Oklahoma Press, 1960.

Geduld, Harry M. (ed.), *Focus on D. W. Griffith*. Englewood Cliffs, N.J.: Prentice-Hall Inc., 1971.

Goodman, Ezra, *The Fifty-Year Decline and Fall of Hollywood*. New York: Simon and Schuster, 1961.

Gow, Gordon, *Hollywood in the Fifties*. New York: A. S. Barnes, 1971.

Griffith, Richard and Arthur Mayer, *The Movies*. New York: Simon and Schuster, 1957.

Handel, Leo A., *Hollywood Looks at Its Audience*. Urbana: The University of Illinois Press, 1950.

Hampton, Benjamin, *History of the American Film Industry*. New York: Dover Publications, 1970.

Haskell, Molly, *From Reverence to Rape*. New York: Holt, Rinehart and Winston, 1974.

Hendricks, Gordon, *The Edison Motion Picture Myth*. Berkeley: University of California Press, 1961.

Higham, Charles and Joel Greenberg, *The Celluloid Muse*. Chicago: Henry Regnery Co., 1969.

————, and Joel Greenberg, *Hollywood in the Forties*. New York: A. S. Barnes, 1968.

Jacobs, Lewis, (ed.), *The Documentary Tradition*. New York: Hopkinson and Blake, 1971.

————, *The Rise of the American Film*. New York: Teachers College Press, 1967.

Kael, Pauline, *The Citizen Kane Book*. Boston: Little, Brown and Co., 1971.

Kahn, Gordon, *Hollywood on Trial*. New York: Boni and Gaer, 1948.

Knight, Arthur, *The Liveliest Art*. New York: The Macmillan Co., 1957.

Koszarski, Richard, *Hollywood Directors, 1914–1940*. New York: Oxford University Press, 1976.

MacCann, Richard Dyer, *The People's Films: A Political History of U.S. Government Motion Pictures*. New York: Hastings House, 1973.

MacGowan, Kenneth, *Behind the Screen*. New York: Delacorte Press, 1965.

Mapp, Edward, *Blacks in American Films: Today and Yesterday*. Metuchen, N.J.: The Scarecrow Press, 1972.

Mast, Gerald, *The Celluloid Muse*. New York: The Bobbs-Merrill Co., 1973.

————, *A Short History of the Movies*. New York: Pegasus Books, 1971.

Michael, Paul, *The Academy Awards*. New York: Crown Publishers, 1972.

Montagu, Ivor, *Film World*. Baltimore, Md.: Penguin Books, 1964.

Murray, James, *To Find An Image*. Indianapolis: The Bobbs-Merrill Co., 1973.

Randall, Richard S., *Censorship of the Movies*. Madison: University of Wisconsin Press, 1968.

Ramsaye, Terry, *A Million and One Nights*. New York: Simon and Schuster, 1926. (Also subsequent editions in London and New York.)

Robinson, David, *The History of World Cinema*. New York: Stein and Day, 1973.

Rosen, Marjorie, *Popcorn Venus*. New York: Coward, McCann and Geoghegan, 1973.

Rotha, Paul and Richard Griffith, *The Film Till Now*. New York: Funk and Wagnalls, 1950. (First published in 1930 as Rotha's work.)

Sarris, Andrew, *The American Cinema*. New York: E. P. Dutton and Co., 1968.

Schickel, Richard, *The Disney Version*. New York: Simon and Schuster, 1968.

————, *Movies: The History of an Art and an Institution*. New York: Basic Books, 1964.

Schumach, Murray, *The Face on the Cutting Room Floor*. New York: William Morrow and Co., 1964.

Solomon, Stanley J., *The Film Idea*. New York: Harcourt, Brace and Jovanovich, 1972.

Turan, Kenneth and Stephen F. Zito, *Sinema: American Pornographic Films and the People Who Make Them*. New York: Praeger Publishers, 1974.

Vardac, Nicholas, *Stage to Screen*. Cambridge: Harvard University Press, 1949.

Wagenknecht, Edward, *The Movies in the Age of Innocence*. Norman: University of Oklahoma Press, 1962.

White, David Manning and Richard Averson, *The Celluloid Weapon: Social Comment in the American Film*. Boston: Beacon Press, 1972.

Wright, Basil. *The Long View*. New York: Alfred A. Knopf, 1974.

Zierold, Norman, *The Moguls*. New York: Coward, McCann Inc., 1969.

THE PRESS

Anonymous, *The Wall Street Journal: The First Seventy-Five Years*. New York: Dow Jones and Co., 1964.

———, *The World In Focus, The Story of the Christian Science Monitor*. Boston: Christian Science Monitor Publ. Co., 1965.

Aronson, James, *The Press and the Cold War*. New York: Bobbs-Merrill Co., 1970.

Becker, Stephen, *Comic Art in America*. New York: Simon and Schuster, 1959.

———, *Marshall Field III: A Biography*. New York: Simon and Schuster, 1964.

Berger, Meyer, *The Story of the New York Times, 1851–1951*. New York: Simon and Schuster, 1951.

Bernays, Edward, *Biography of an Idea: Memoirs of a Public Relations Counsel*. New York: Simon and Schuster, 1965.

Bessie, Simon Michael, *Jazz Journalism: The Story of the Tabloid Newspapers*. New York: E. P. Dutton Co., 1938.

Carlson, Oliver, *The Man Who Made News: James Gordon Bennett*. New York: Duell, Sloan and Pearce, 1942.

Catledge, Turner, *My Life and the Times*. New York: Harper and Row, 1971.

Dennis, Everette E. and William L. Rivers, *Other Voices: The New Journalism in America*. San Francisco: Canfield Press, 1974.

Emery, Edwin and Henry Ladd Smith, *The Press and America*. Englewood Cliffs, N.J.: Prentice-Hall, Inc., 1954. (Later editions credited to Emery alone.)

Estren, Mark James, *A History of Underground Comics*. San Francisco: Straight Arrow Books, 1974.

Glessing, Robert J., *The Underground Press in America*. Bloomington: Indiana University Press, 1970.

Goldberg, Joe, *Big Bunny: The Inside Story of Playboy*. New York: Ballantine Books, 1967.

Hynds, Ernst C., *American Newspapers in the 1970s*. New York: Hastings House, 1975.

Johnson, Michael, *The New Journalism*. Lawrence: University of Kansas Press, 1971.

Kobre, Sidney, *Development of American Journalism*. Dubuque, Iowa: Wm. C. Brown Co., 1969.

———, *The Yellow Press and Gilded Age Journalism*. Tallahassee: Florida State University, 1964.

La Brie, Henry G., *The Black Press in America: A Guide*. Iowa City: Insitute for Communication Studies, University of Iowa, 1970.

Lee, Alfred McClung, *The Daily Newspaper in America*. New York: The Macmillan Co., 1937.

Lewis, Roger, *Outlaws in America*. Harmondsworth, England: Penguin Books, 1972.

Logue, Calvin M., *Ralph McGill, Editor and Publisher*. Durham, N.C.: Moore Publishing Co., 1969.

Madison, Charles, *Book Publishing in Amerca*. New York: McGraw-Hill, 1966.

McGivena, Leo E., *et al.*, *The News: The First Fifty Years Of New York's Picture Newspaper*. New York: News Syndicate Co., 1969.

Marbut, F. B., *News from the Capitol: The Story of Washington Reporting*. Carbondale: Southern Illinois University Press, 1971.

Martin, Harold H., *Ralph McGill, Reporter*. Boston: Little Brown and Co., 1973.

Mott, Frank Luther, *American Journalism*. New York: The Macmillan Co., 1962.

————, *A History of American Magazines* (Five Volumes). Cambridge, Mass.: Harvard University Press, 1930, 1938, 1957, 1968.

Nixon, Raymond S., *Henry W. Grady, Spokesman of the New South*. New York: Alfred A. Knopf, 1943.

Peterson, Theodore, *Magazines in the Twentieth Century* (Second Edition). Urbana: University of Illinois Press, 1964.

Rembar, Charles, *The End of Obscenity*. New York: Random House, 1968.

Reitberger, Reinhold and Wolfgang Fuchs, *Comics: Anatomy of a Mass Medium*. Boston: Little, Brown and Co., 1970.

Robinson, Jerry, *The Comics: An Illustrated History of the Comic Strip Art*. New York: G. P. Putnam's Son, 1974.

Steinberg, S. H., *Five Hundred Years of Printing*. Middlesex, England: Penguin Books, 1955.

St. Hill, Thomas Nast (ed.), *Thomas Nast: Cartoons and Illustrations*. New York: Dover Publications, 1974.

Swanberg, W. A. *Citizen Hearst*. New York: Charles Scribner's Sons, 1967.

————, *Pulitzer*. New York: Charles Scribner's Sons, 1967.

Talese, Gay, *The Kingdom and the Power*. New York: World Publishing Co., 1969.

Tebbel, John, *The American Magazine: A Compact History*. New York: Hawthorn Books, 1969.

————, *The Compact History of the American Newspaper*. New York: Hawthorn Books, Inc., 1969.

————, *The Life and Good Times of William Randolph Hearst*. New York: Dutton, 1952.

————, *The Media in America*. New York: New American Library, 1974.

Turner, E. S., *The Shocking History of Advertising*. New York: Ballantine Books, 1953.

Weber, Ronald, (ed.), *The Reporter As Artist. A Look at the New Journalism Controversy*. New York: Hastings House, 1974.

Wood, James Playstead, *Magazines in the United States* (Third Edition). New York: Ronald Press, 1971.

Wolseley, Ronald E., *The Black Press, U.S.A.* Ames: Iowa State University Press, 1971.

GENERAL

Boorstin, Daniel J., *The Image; or What Happened to the American Dream*. New York: Atheneum, 1962.

Chafee, Zechariah, *Government and Mass Communications* (Two Volumes). Chicago: University of Chicago Press, 1947.

Cherry, Colin, *World Communication: Threat or Promise?* New York: John Wiley and Sons, 1971.

Choukas, Michael, *Propaganda Comes of Age*. Washington, D.C.: Public Affairs Press, 1965.

Devol, Kenneth, *Mass Media and the Supreme Court* (Second Edition). New York: Hastings House, 1976.

Ernst, Morris L. and Alan U. Schwartz, *Censorship, the Search for the Obscene*. New York: The Macmillan Co., 1964.

Fabre, Maurice, *A History of Communication*. New York: Hawthorn Books, 1963.

Gowans, Alan, *The Unchanging Arts*. Philadelphia and New York: J. B. Lippincott Co., 1971.

Green, Abel and Joe Laurie, Jr., *Show Biz*. New York: Doubleday and Co., 1951.

Hogben, Lancelot, *From Cave Painting to Comic Strip*. New York: Chanticleer Press, 1949.

Innis, Harold, *The Bias of Communication*. Toronto: University of Toronto Press, 1951.

Kilpatrick, James Jackson, *The Smut Peddlers*. Garden City, N.Y.: Doubleday and Co., 1960.

Lasswell, Harold D., *Propaganda Technique in the World War*. London: Kegan Paul, 1927.

Maddox, Brenda, *Beyond Babel*. New York: Simon and Schuster, 1972.

Nye, Russel, *The Unembarrassed Muse*. New York: Dial Press, 1970.

Schiller, Herbert, *Mass Communications and American Empire*. Boston: Beacon Press, 1971.

Seldes, Gilbert, *The Great Audience*. New York: Viking Press, 1950.

————, *The Public Arts*. New York: Simon and Schuster, 1956.

——, *The Seven Lively Arts*. New York: Sagamore Press, 1957. (First published in 1924.)

Sorensen, Thomas C., *The World War: The Story of American Propaganda*. New York: Harper and Row, 1968.

Stanley, Robert H. and Charles S. Steinberg, *The Media Environment: Mass Communications in American Society*. New York: Hastings House, 1976.

Stein, M. L., *Blacks in Communication*. New York: Julian Messner, 1972.

Vaughn, Robert, *Only Victims, A Study of Show Business Blacklisting*. New York: G. P. Putnam's Sons, 1972.

Wells, Alan (ed.), *Mass Communications: A World View*. Palo Alto, Calif.: National Press Books, 1974.

Wood, James Playstead, *The Story of Advertising*. New York: Ronald Press, 1958.

Index